GONZO WALL STREET

Richard E. Farley

GONZO WALL STREET

Riots, Radicals, Racism, and Revolution: How The Go-Go Bankers Of The 1960s Crashed The Financial System and Bamboozled Washington

LEO | **Regan Arts.**

NEW YORK

First Regan Arts hardcover edition, Fall 2022

Library of Congress Control Number: 2021950014

ISBN 978-1-68245-198-4 (Hardcover)
ISBN 978-1-68245-199-1 (eBook)

Interior design by Aubrey Khan, Neuwirth & Associates, Inc.

Cover design by Richard Ljoenes

Printed in the United States of America

10   9   8   7   6   5   4   3   2   1

A man generally has two
reasons for doing a thing.
One that sounds good—
and the real one.

— J. P. MORGAN

CONTENTS

PART III ■ 1969
The Bear Market

PART IV ■ 1970
The Bailout

CAST OF CHARACTERS

(Positions Held at Times Relevant Herein)

In the Executive Branch

At the White House:

John F. Kennedy, thirty-fifth
President of the United States
Lyndon Baines Johnson, thirty-sixth
President of the United States
Richard M. Nixon, thirty-seventh
President of the United States
Peter M. Flanigan, Chief Economic
Advisor to President Nixon
H. R. Haldeman, Chief of Staff to
President Nixon
John B. Connally, unofficial advisor
to President Nixon

*At the Securities and
Exchange Commission:*

William L. Carey, Chairman
(1961–1964)
Manuel F. Cohen, Chairman
(1964–1969)
Hamer L. Budge, Chairman
(1969–1971)
Irving M. Pollack, Director of
Trading and Markets Division
Phillip A. Loomis Jr., General
Counsel
Eugene Rotberg, Chief Counsel,
Office of Policy Planning

At the Department of Justice:

John N. Mitchell, Attorney General
Richard W. McLaren, Assistant
Attorney General—Antitrust
Division

At the Treasury Department:

David M. Kennedy, Secretary of the
Treasury
Charles E. Walker, Under Secretary
of the Treasury
Bruce K. MacLaury, Deputy Under
Secretary for Monetary Affairs

*At the United States Attorney for
the Southern District of New York:*

Robert M. Morgenthau, United
States Attorney

In Congress

At the United States Senate:

Edmund S. Muskie, Senator from
Maine
Harrison A. Williams, Senator from
New Jersey; Chairman of
Subcommittee on Securities
A. Willis Robertson, Senator from
Arkansas; Chairman of the
Committee on Banking and
Currency (1959–1966)
John J. Sparkman, Senator from
Alabama; Chairman of the
Committee on Banking and
Currency (1966–1970)
Robert F. Kennedy, Senator from
New York
Eugene McCarthy, Senator from
Wisconsin
J. William Fulbright, Senator from
Arkansas
J. Allen Frear, Senator from Delaware

Edward W. Brooke, Senator from
Massachusetts

E. William Proxmire, Senator from
Wisconsin

At the House of Representatives:

John E. Moss, Representative from
California; Chairman of the
Subcommittee on Commerce
and Finance

Oren Harris, Representative from
Arkansas; Chairman of the
Committee on Foreign and
Interstate Commerce
(1957–1966)

Harley O. Staggers, Representative
from West Virginia; Chairman of
the Committee on Foreign and
Interstate Commerce
(1966–1981)

On Wall Street

At the New York Stock Exchange:

John A. Coleman, Former Chairman

Gustave L. Levy, Chairman
(1967–1969)

Bernard J. Lasker, Chairman
(1969–1971); member of Crisis
Committee

Ralph DeNunzio, Vice Chairman;
member of Crisis Committee

G. Keith Funston, President
(1951–1967)

Robert W. Haack, President
(1967–1972)

Joseph A. Meehan, member of
Board of Governors

Edward C. Gray, Executive Vice
President (1948–1968)

R. John Cunningham, Executive
Vice President (1968–1970)

Lee D. Arning, Senior Vice
President

Robert M. Bishop, Senior Vice
President

Felix G. Rohatyn, member of Crisis
Committee

Solomon Litt, member of Crisis
Committee

Stephen M. Peck, member of Crisis
Committee

At McDonnell & Co.:

T. Murray McDonnell, Chairman

Lawrence F. O'Brien, President

Paul K. McDonald, Acting President

Sean McDonnell, Executive Vice
President

Henry C. B. Lindh, Senior Vice
President and Treasurer

At Hayden, Stone, Inc.:

Alfred J. Coyle, Chairman

Ara A. Cambre, President

Donald R. Stroben, Executive Vice
President (as of May 1970,
Chairman and Chief Executive
Officer)

At Francis I. duPont & Co.:

Edmund duPont, Senior Partner

Charles Moran Jr., Managing
Partner (1963–1969)

Wallace C. Latour, Managing
Partner (1969–1970)

At Goodbody & Co.:

James E. Hogle, Chairman

Harold P. Goodbody, Senior Partner

Edward N. Bagley, Managing Partner

*At Cogan, Berlind, Weill &
Levitt, Inc.:*

Marshall S. Cogan, Partner

Roger S. Berlind, Partner

Sanford I. Weill, Partner
Arthur Levitt Jr., Partner
Frank Zarb, Executive Vice
   President

*At Merrill Lynch, Pierce, Fenner
& Smith Inc.:*

Donald T. Regan, Chairman and
   Chief Executive Officer

*At Donaldson, Lufkin & Jenrette
Inc.:*

Dan W. Lufkin, Partner
William H. Donaldson, Partner
Richard H. Jenrette, Partner

At Goldman, Sachs & Co.:

Gustave L. Levy, Senior Partner
Robert E. Mnuchin, Partner

At Salomon Brothers:

William Salomon, Managing Partner
Jay H. Perry, Partner
Michael J. Bloomberg, Vice President

At Lazard Freres & Co.:

Felix G. Rohatyn, Partner

At Adler, Coleman & Company:

John A. Coleman, Senior Partner

At M. J. Meehan & Co.:

Joseph A. Meehan, Senior Partner
Michael J. Meehan II, Partner

At Weeden & Co.:

Donald E. Weeden, Chairman

At Lasker, Stone & Stern:

Bernard J. Lasker, Chairman

At R. W. Pressprich & Co.:

Kenneth G. Langone, President

At Charles Plohn & Company:

Charles J. Plohn, Senior Partner

At Loeb, Rhoades & Co.:

John L. Loeb Sr., Senior Partner

At Bear, Stearns & Co.:

Salim L. Lewis, Senior Partner
Alan C. Greenberg, Partner

*At Fidelity Management and
Research Company:*

Edward C. Johnson II, President
Gerald Tsai Jr., Fund Manager

At First National City Bank:

Walter B. Wriston, Chief Executive
   Officer

*At Manufacturers Hanover Trust
Company:*

Horace C. Flanigan, Chairman

At Sullivan & Cromwell:

Hamilton F. Potter Jr., Partner
John R. Raben, Partner

*At Milbank, Tweed, Hadley &
McCloy:*

Samuel L. Rosenberry, Partner
A. Donald MacKinnon, Partner

At Casey, Dickler & Howley:

William J. Casey, Partner

The White Knights

- *At Electronic Data Systems, Inc.:*

  H. Ross Perot, Chief Executive
  Officer

- *At LSB Industries, Inc.:*

  Jack E. Golsen, Chief Executive
  Officer

- *At Utilities and Industries
  Corporation:*

  Arthur L. Carter, President

- *At Loews Theaters, Inc.:*

  Preston Robert Tisch, President and
  Co-Chief Executive Officer
  Laurence A. Tisch, Chairman and
  Co-Chief Executive Officer

The Real Characters

- *In Order of Appearance:*

  Anthony "Tino" DeAngelis,
  President of Allied Crude
  Vegetable Oil Refining
  Corporation
  Roy M. Cohn, Partner in Saxe,
  Bacon & Bolan
  Abbie Hoffman, radical left-wing
  activist
  Warren Hinckle III, Editor-in-Chief
  of *Ramparts* magazine;
  Co-founder of *Scanlan's* magazine
  Sidney Zion, reporter for the *New
  York Times*; Co-founder of
  Scanlan's magazine
  Francine Gottfried, computer
  operator at Chemical Bank
  Karla Jay, feminist activist and
  member of Media Women
  Peter J. Brennan, President of the
  Building and Construction
  Trades Council of Greater
  New York

PROLOGUE

"WE ALL HAVE OUR FATHERS, DON'T WE?"

∎

The Day the Market Didn't Crash

In 1963, the senior executives on Wall Street could recollect from personal experience the horrifying, historic events of the 1929 Crash and the Great Depression that followed. They could speak of where they were on October 24, 1929—Black Thursday—when stock prices collapsed and fortunes and firms were ruined. The old-timers at the New York Stock Exchange (N.Y.S.E.) would often speak of a Depression-era episode not mentioned in the history books, but as traumatic to the members of the N.Y.S.E.—the Club, as they called themselves—as the Crash itself. For the Club, the year 1938 was its *annus horribilis,* for that was the year when Richard Whitney & Co. collapsed in spectacular fashion.

Richard Whitney had been a revered figure at the N.Y.S.E. prior to his demise. His firm was J. P. Morgan's floor broker at the Exchange—and he had married the daughter of a J. P. Morgan & Co. partner. He was the hero of Black Thursday in 1929 when, at Morgan's behest, he placed an above-market bid for a block of U. S. Steel shares that reversed the collapse in stock prices that day. He parlayed that goodwill all the way to the presidency of the N.Y.S.E.

Whitney, however, kept hidden from the Wall Street community a secret they would consider most shameful: he was, in truth, a terrible investor. Throughout the 1930s, Whitney made enormous investments in a liquor company that failed. Notwithstanding the

Depression, he continued to live well beyond his means. After he had mortgaged and borrowed everything he legally could and exhausted those funds, he began embezzling from clients, family, and charities he oversaw. By 1938, it was over for Whitney and his firm; both were bankrupt.

The four-year-old Securities and Exchange Commission (S.E.C.) had been blindsided by the failure of Richard Whitney & Co., and it suspected—correctly—that the Club had closed ranks to protect one of its own. The S.E.C. used the Whitney debacle to bring the N.Y.S.E. to heel. The S.E.C. crackdown that followed—the investigation, the seething criticism of the N.Y.S.E. and its leadership in a formal report, the governance and rule changes the S.E.C. implemented—ushered in an era of heavy-handed regulation of Wall Street by Washington that lasted nearly two decades.

The thaw in the icy relations between Wall Street and its Washington regulators during the 1960s was largely due to the relentless lobbying of one of the twentieth century's greatest salesmen—Keith Funston, president of the N.Y.S.E. Funston's deft coddling and cajoling of politicians had loosened Washington's leash on Wall Street considerably. But if a scandal was outrageous enough or a failed firm large enough, Funston knew all bets would be off. Disgrace and ruin could come to the Club at any time with one swift tug of that leash.

On November 22, 1963, such a scandal emerged.

That the date is remembered solely for the terrible events in Dallas and not also for a financial calamity is perhaps the finest moment of the Club and likely the clearest manifestation of its fatal flaws. It began with, of all things, salad oil, but it involved the Mafia, a colorful con man named Anthony "Tino" DeAngelis, and many of the largest firms on Wall Street.

THE NEWSPAPER REPORTS, after the scandal broke, were not comforting. The whole mess was a comedy of errors with many zeros on the end.

If somebody thought it was a good idea to lend a million dollars to Tino DeAngelis for any reason, you could dismiss that somebody as an imbecile. But when many financial institutions thought it was a good idea to lend Tino DeAngelis hundreds of millions of dollars for speculative commodities bets, you had a crisis.

Tino DeAngelis, forty-eight years old at the time, was a Bronx-born child of immigrants with unlimited ambition and no discernable morals. His colorful resume included an indictment for perjury in an S.E.C. investigation. There were also charges by the U.S. Department of Agriculture that he supplied tainted beef to the federal school lunch program. Additional charges had been brought by the Department of Agriculture alleging that he shipped spoiled vegetable oil to Spain under the auspices of the Food for Peace program. F.B.I. files mentioned suspicion of bribery of a Department of Agriculture inspector. There was also a bankruptcy and millions of dollars in tax liens.[1] This was all before he got into real trouble.

Tino had somehow managed to scrape together enough capital to buy the Allied Crude Vegetable Oil Refining Corporation of Bayonne, New Jersey. Allied was a bit player in the enormous American business of exporting agricultural products. The company bought agricultural oils—soybean oil, cottonseed oil, and the like—from grain processors, then refined and stored the oils at its large tank farm near the docks in Bayonne. Most of the oils were sold overseas, either directly or through large agricultural export corporations like Cargill, Inc. and Continental Grain Company. Financing this capital-intensive business was a challenge for Tino, given his past and the ugly rumors of associations with figures well known in New Jersey and Chicago La Cosa Nostra circles. Tino had tried and failed to convince the large New York banks like First National City Bank (predecessor to Citibank) and Marine Midland Bank to lend to Allied.

But it turned out there was a way.

Companies with less-than-stellar credit could access asset-based loans secured by their inventory, certified by what is called a "warehouse receipt." To obtain a warehouse receipt, a borrower had to turn over control of its inventory to a reputable and creditworthy third-party operator. The American Express Company, with its gilt-edged credit rating, was perfectly positioned to be a major success in the warehouse operating business. Eager to grow that business line, American Express overlooked Tino's shady past and took him on as a client.

Tino quickly noticed that the American Express folks didn't like to get their hands dirty. It was always one of Tino's employees who would climb to the top of the tanks, drop in the measure, and call down the level numbers.[2] The American Express official would dutifully write them down, having no idea if the actual levels were as he called them. Tino soon had his men inflating the measurements. Tino would also move oil from one tank to another so that the same oil could be counted numerous times in different tanks. He would also fill a tank mostly with sea water and perhaps a foot or two of oil floating on top. Other tanks were fitted with false compartments with only a few hundred gallons of oil. Before too long, there were American Express warehouse receipts pledged to Allied's lenders certifying more vegetable oil than there were gallons of tank space at Bayonne. And when Tino was in a real pinch for cash, he just forged the signature of the American Express official on a warehouse receipt for whatever quantity of vegetable oil suited him. Tino had stolen a large stack of blank American Express warehouse receipts, and the theft had gone undetected.

Many of the fictitious warehouse receipts had been pledged as collateral to investment banks for Allied's commodity futures trading activities. Tino hoped to manipulate the futures market and drive up the prices for Allied's vegetable oil, which he would then sell at inflated prices. Allied's largest commodities broker was Ira Haupt & Co., an established N.Y.S.E. member firm. While Ira Haupt & Co. conducted a major securities brokerage and underwriting business, it did little commodities business. It was an area in which the firm hoped to expand, and Allied was its largest customer. As an accommodation to Allied, Ira Haupt & Co. accepted warehouse receipts in lieu of cash for Allied's margin payments.

It all began to unravel for Tino DeAngelis on Friday, November 15, 1963. Inspectors from the Commodity Exchange Authority of the U.S. Department of Agriculture became alarmed by Allied's suspicious trading activity. They raided the Bayonne office and seized Allied's financial records. Soybean oil and cottonseed oil prices declined that day as well. With the heat on, Tino had no ability to prepare fraudulent warehouse receipts to meet the day's margin calls. He promised the anxious partners at Ira Haupt & Co. that payment would be made Monday morning. Instead, Tino instructed his lawyers to prepare a bankruptcy filing. Rather than cashing out Allied's account, Ira Haupt & Co. borrowed $18.5 million (approximately $150 million in today's dollars) to meet Allied's margin calls.[3]

As a result of Allied's default on its margin obligations and Ira Haupt & Co.'s incurrence of the $18.5 million of debt to cover them, Ira Haupt & Co. was now in violation of the N.Y.S.E.'s minimum net capital requirements. If it were unable to obtain a capital infusion by Tuesday morning, it would need to report this violation to the N.Y.S.E., which could suspend its operations. News of this would panic its 20,000 retail customers, likely causing them to withdraw their cash and securities held at the firm—a run on the bank.

The Club took away one lesson from the humiliation of the Whitney debacle in 1938: the leadership of the N.Y.S.E. must fix problems at its member firms before the S.E.C. or, *God forbid*, Congress, did it for them.

Despite its frantic efforts that Monday night, Ira Haupt & Co. found no angel investor. Allied filed for bankruptcy on Tuesday morning. With this news, prices for soybean oil and cottonseed oil futures tumbled. The market discovered that it was Allied propping up the prices at artificially high levels. That same morning, Morton Kamerman, the managing partner of Ira Haupt & Co., showed up unexpectedly at the office of Robert Bishop, a senior executive at the N.Y.S.E.'s department of member firms, and told Bishop's team about his firm's exposure to Allied and its rapidly deteriorating capital position.[4] After the close of business on Tuesday, the N.Y.S.E.

informed Ira Haupt & Co. that it could not open for business on Wednesday. But the news got worse for Ira Haupt & Co. by day's end. Out at Bayonne, now crawling with F.B.I. agents, the pieces of the puzzle were coming together. Most of the vegetable oil that was supposed to be there didn't exist.

By Thursday morning, lawsuits against American Express were filed, which was particularly distressing to the company's management, as the company was formed not as a corporation, but as a seldom-used business entity known as an unincorporated association. No one seemed to know for sure whether the shareholders might be personally liable for the tab. (Ultimately, American Express settled the lawsuits for $60 million without liability to shareholders.)

As far as the public knew, the future of Ira Haupt & Co. was uncertain. At the N.Y.S.E. and in the boardrooms of the nation's largest banks, they knew the harsh reality that Ira Haupt & Co. would be liquidated, and the only thing uncertain was how much each of them would be ponying up to pay for its liquidation. Keith Funston knew that, within days, perhaps sooner, events could overtake them in a messy, angry, and public way. Haupt's retail customers were withdrawing the money and securities in their brokerage accounts at an alarming rate. This was precisely the sort of crisis that could undo his efforts of the past dozen years.[5]

Back in 1951 when Keith Funston had become president of the N.Y.S.E., the public equity markets were a financial backwater. By the closing months of 1963, however, the markets had been transformed and were poised for breathtaking growth. But Funston knew that the failure of Ira Haupt & Co. might very well shake the S.E.C. out of its benign, soft-touch regulatory oversight. It might attract the prying eyes of the press and might even attract the attention of congressional committees. Funston also knew better than anyone that Wall Street was not a thundering herd, but a herd in need of culling. Because of the combined effect of a number of well-intentioned laws designed to prevent investment banks from gambling with money from unsophisticated investors—laws approved of by the Club because they protected their firms from outside competition—the majority of Wall Street firms were relatively small, in many cases family owned. Most were undercapitalized. Many would be unable to make the looming large capital investments required to compete in an industry already in the computer age.

AS THE FLOOR traders and specialists arrived for work at the N.Y.S.E. on the morning of Friday, November 22, 1963, Keith Funston had not finalized a bailout plan for Ira Haupt & Co. For the time being, the S.E.C. was letting Funston manage the crisis. Llewellyn P. Young, director of the S.E.C.'s New York Regional Office, told the press: "Our position is one of watchful waiting. The N.Y.S.E. is taking the leading oar in this matter. At this time, we contemplate no action."[6]

The bad news was that Chase Manhattan Bank was no longer honoring checks drawn on Ira Haupt & Co.'s account, and word of this had leaked to the press. The S.E.C. in Washington sent a staff member, David Silver, up to New York the night before to camp in Ira Haupt & Co.'s offices to observe firsthand and intervene, if necessary, to protect investors. When Silver arrived, he was shocked to see a line of customers out the door trying to withdraw their cash and securities. Once in the offices, he was further shocked to see that representatives of a number of large New York banks had seized control of the Ira Haupt & Co. "cage" where its securities were stored and were seizing the collateral for their loans.

Trading began light that Friday morning. The Dow had fallen 1.3 percent the day before on news of the "Salad Oil Scandal," as the press was calling it. Without news regarding the condition of Ira Haupt & Co. and of J. R. Williston & Beane, Inc., another firm with large exposure to Allied, traders were jittery. Donald Stone, a thirty-nine-year-old trader for E. H. Stern & Co., was having lunch at the Stock Exchange Luncheon Club at 1:30 p.m. when he saw a clerk running between the tables in an agitated state. Stone stopped him and asked him what was going on: "Kennedy's been shot," he said. "Jack or Bobby?" asked Stone. "Jack," he replied. By the time the two of them raced down to the floor of the Exchange, an unforgettable horrifying sound overcame them: the roar of panic selling.[7] In a matter of minutes, the Dow had lost 3 percent of its value. Floor officials were trying to track down Funston to get him to halt trading. He was out of the building, dealing with the Ira Haupt & Co. creditors.

ON THE FLOOR of the N.Y.S.E., each stock was traded through a designated dealer for that stock, known as the "specialist." As the specialists were given a lucrative monopoly to effect trades in their designated stocks, they were required to make markets even in times of market dislocation. The relatively risk-free return they earned during stable markets was justified by the risks they were required to take in volatile ones. On the afternoon of November 22, 1963, a number of specialists slowed or stopped their market making, saving their own skins at the expense of their customers and the market.

In the minutes after news of the shooting broke, a very frightening scene on the floor of the N.Y.S.E. had developed at the RCA Corp. post. RCA shares were among the hardest hit by the panic selling. The specialist firm for RCA was M. J. Meehan & Co., which was owned and managed by Joseph A. Meehan and his brother, William M. Meehan. Joseph Meehan was a member of the Exchange's old guard, sitting on its board of governors and on many of its most powerful committees. His father, Michael J. Meehan, had founded the firm in 1918 and was the most successful stock pool operator of all time. Over four days in 1928, Michael Meehan made more than $200 million in today's dollars trading the same RCA stock that was threatening to crash the market after Kennedy's assassination. Joseph Meehan was also a prominent Irish Catholic and a friend of the president.

At the RCA post that Friday afternoon, Joseph Meehan had no time for grieving. If he didn't support the RCA stock price, it might well trigger a full-fledged market crash. Meehan would be remembered for turning tail at this dramatic moment in history—abandoning the very stock that made his family fortune. If he put out the massive amount of capital that would be required to support the stock and its price didn't recover, the firm would likely go bankrupt. For the Meehans, there was only one choice. Turning to the crush of frantic sellers at the post, they shouted, "I'll give you $85.00 for everything you've got," even though shares could have been bought at that time for dollars less. And like Richard Whitney's above-market bid for U.S. Steel that stopped the panic on Black Thursday, the Meehan bid of $85.00 for RCA saved the day. "If it's good enough for Meehan, it's good enough for me," one trader proclaimed, reversing his sell order to buy at $85.00. "Meehan had stopped the run," one trader remembered fifty years later. "Heroic" was how he simply described it.[8]

Moments after the tide had turned at the RCA post, the bell rang at 2:07 p.m., closing the Exchange. A quorum of the board of governors had been gathered and had authorized the early trading halt. An astounding 2.2 million shares were traded in the last seven minutes. At the same time, Father Oscar L. Huber, pastor of the Holy Trinity Church in Dallas, was giving the Last Rites of the Catholic Church to President Kennedy. Twenty-six minutes later, Walter Cronkite reported to the nation that Kennedy had died.

THE EXCHANGE WOULD be closed on Monday, the day of President Kennedy's funeral. The national day of mourning allowed for a long weekend to finalize a deal to liquidate Ira Haupt & Co. The deal Keith Funston had worked out was presented to the partners of Ira Haupt & Co. on Monday. The N.Y.S.E. would kick in $12 million, to be funded by a 50 percent dues increase for three years for all Exchange members. The banks would extend the maturity of their loans and be repaid from what remained after the assets were sold and the Ira Haupt & Co. customers made whole. The Ira Haupt & Co. partners would receive nothing, and they would be required to release the company from any claims against it they might have. Funston assured the partners that if any of them refused to go along they would be blacklisted, and no Exchange member would hire them. They all went along.

It was an agonizing long weekend for Joseph Meehan. He thought of the ironic intertwined fates of the Meehans and the Kennedys. His friendship with President Kennedy had been unlikely, as his father and the president's father, Joseph P. Kennedy, were bitter rivals on Wall Street in the 1920s and loathed each other. When Joe Kennedy became the first chairman of the S.E.C., the first Wall Street figure he went after was Michael Meehan, banning him from the industry. Joseph Meehan, still in college at Fordham, had to prematurely run the family firm and save it from disbanding. "We all have our fathers, don't we?" Jack Kennedy said to Joseph Meehan when they first met, and each took an immediate liking to the other.

Because of the assassination of President Kennedy, Joseph Meehan was very much at risk of losing the family firm he had struggled so hard to rebuild after the slain president's father had nearly ruined it. If the RCA stock price didn't recover when trading opened on Tuesday, there would be no way to settle Friday's trades and maintain compliance with the Exchange's net capital rule.

On Tuesday, November 26, 1963, RCA opened sharply higher at $89.75. The broader market rallied as well. Joseph Meehan ended up making a great deal of money on the RCA position.[9] By year-end, the Dow had recovered all of its losses.

But if RCA had been allowed to free-fall, it might well have led to a market crash that Friday. Given how thinly capitalized so many of the investment banks were, a crash would have shuttered many of them. If investment banks failed systemically, one or more of the large commercial banks might have needed bailing out. That might have brought on a full-fledged financial panic. Funston knew how close to reality all of this was on November 22, 1963. And he knew there would be a next time, and next time there might not be a Joseph Meehan.

■　■　■

THROUGHOUT THE WINTER of 1963–1964, Keith Funston regularly reminded the N.Y.S.E.'s lawyers that they needed to be very careful in reviewing all public statements regarding the Exchange's bailout of Ira Haupt & Co. He wanted it clear that the N.Y.S.E. had no legal obligation for the debts of member firms. "The board of governors took this unusual step on the basis of the exceptional facts surrounding this particular case," Funston announced to the press. Funston's lawyer, Sam Rosenberry of Milbank, Tweed, Hadley & McCloy, briefed everyone at the Exchange who had official contact with the press, government officials, or the general public to deny that the fund created for the bailout—named the Special Trust Fund—existed to protect investors against loss. On the contrary, Rosenberry insisted that all such constituencies be given the same official line: "The Exchange voluntarily, nobly, agreed to use its own funds to assist the Ira Haupt & Co. customers. In the unlikely event another firm was ever to fail, the trustees of the Special Trust Fund would decide, in their sole discretion, whether to provide assistance."[10]

Funston later undertook an investigation of the specialists' conduct on November 22, 1963. Those who refused to risk their capital and stopped trading were mildly disciplined. No distinction was made for those who were unable to perform because of insufficient capital as compared with those who were simply greedy or cowardly. This was because to acknowledge such a distinction would be to acknowledge that there were, in fact, firms with insufficient capital. Funston was well aware that he worked for the Club, which was controlled by the old guard, and well represented in the old guard were firms with woefully insufficient capital to be carrying on their businesses. So there would be no proposals for reform by Funston calling for stronger capitalization of N.Y.S.E. member firms.

With much juggling, Funston kept all the balls in the air until the end of his tenure, but just barely. There would indeed be a next time. It would not be a sudden market crash, however, that would cause more Wall Street firms to fail in the three years after Funston retired than during all of the Great Depression. Incredibly, the crisis would be born of a raging bull market and quite literally more business than anyone ever dreamed.

PART I

THE GO-GO YEARS

∎

Explosive Growth, Lax Regulation,
and Outdated Technology: What
Could Possibly Go Wrong?

CHAPTER ONE

"WIVES YOU'RE STUCK WITH,
BUT STOCKS YOU TRADE"

■

How Institutional Investors and the Return of Main Street to Wall Street Transformed Financial Markets in the 1960s

The fate of more than a hundred firms—more than one in six of all N.Y.S.E. member firms—was sealed at a meeting between two men in 1958, five years before the Kennedy assassination. That meeting took place on a Saturday afternoon on Cape Cod, about a fifteen-minute drive from the Kennedy compound in Hyannis Port. The older man, Edward C. Johnson II, age sixty, had founded Fidelity Management and Research Company twelve years earlier in 1946.[1]

Johnson had two revolutionary ideas about investing in stocks that made his company the leading mutual fund manager. The first was that mutual funds should not be managed by committee. This was thought to be a reckless heresy in the first years of recovery of the financial services industry following World War II. Johnson thought deciding by committee resulted not in the best investments but in the ones acceptable to the dumbest person constituting the majority of the committee. The individual who did the most research, was the smartest, and had the best "market feel" would outperform the decisions of a committee every time, Johnson concluded.

His second revolutionary idea was that portfolio composition should be questioned continuously. At the time, most institutional investors, if they were willing to hold any equity securities at all, bought only blue-chip, dividend-paying stocks and held them pending some disastrous event that compelled their sale. Investment committees would meet once a quarter, or at most once a month, to determine whether any stocks should be bought or sold. A turnover of even 10 percent annually raised eyebrows.[2] "If you picked them right the first time, you wouldn't ever need to sell them," went the conventional wisdom. Johnson thought this was madness. If a better buy appeared on Tuesday, why wouldn't you sell some of the stock you bought on Monday to buy it, so long as you ended up with more money come Wednesday? "Wives you're stuck with, but stocks you trade," Johnson would say.[3]

The second man at that meeting on Cape Cod was an employee of Johnson's, a twenty-nine-year-old Chinese immigrant named Gerald "Jerry" Tsai Jr. Tsai had a revolutionary idea of his own. He believed that the public would go for a mutual fund that invested in the best young, growing technology companies, just as much as a mutual fund that picked the best-established names. To get Johnson's undivided attention, Tsai drove out to Johnson's weekend house that Saturday to make his pitch. Johnson gave the new fund his blessing, and the Fidelity Capital Fund was born.

Jerry Tsai took Edward Johnson's ideas to another level. He thought not only should one individual—the portfolio manager—be empowered with making all the investment decisions for a fund, but the fund should be an extension of the personality of the portfolio manager. His Asian heritage alone gave Tsai an air of exotic mystery on Wall Street, which in the early 1960s thought diversity meant hiring an Italian American at an Irish American firm or an Eastern European Jew at a German-Jewish one. Tsai cultivated the belief that his outsider status gave him a unique insight, an ability to pick winners that more conventional fund managers would overlook. As he became prominent in financial circles, Tsai carefully rationed access by the business press, which was clamoring to find out just who was this secretive man in Boston racking up phenomenal returns. Jerry Tsai became the first celebrity fund manager. All who would follow—Buffett, Soros, Icahn, Paulson, and the rest—would be given their own rock-star media personas, but Tsai created the template.

Jerry Tsai also leveled up Johnson's principle of managing a mutual fund portfolio: he believed in "actively managing" the portfolio and would buy and sell 100,000-share blocks of stock a day. As soon as the Fidelity Capital Fund's profits proved out, others followed suit. Before long, the actively managed portfolio of technology stocks, the "high-fliers," became all the rage. They defined the Wall Street of the 1960s—the "Go-Go Years," as John Brooks of the *New Yorker* named the era.[4]

By 1963, even the more conservative money managers were piling back into equities. It took the Dow twenty-five years to recover from the 1929 Crash, but in the subsequent nine years, the Dow had doubled. Institutional investors like mutual funds, the trust departments of banks, insurance companies, private foundations, and especially public- and private-sector pension funds began buying large volumes of stocks. Pensions became a common benefit for the unionized workforce of the 1950s. By the mid-1960s, the assets under management of the pension fund industry were enormous, and the allocation of these enormous and growing pools of capital to equities was growing as well.

Tens of millions of middle-class Americans also began directly investing in the stock market. Keith Funston's patriotic public relations campaign to "Own a Share of American Business"[5] resonated with the readers of the N.Y.S.E.-sponsored ads in hometown newspapers. Merrill Lynch and dozens of investment banks with retail brokerage businesses ran their own advertising campaigns as well. Memories of the 1929 Crash had faded. By the end of 1963, greed had surpassed fear.

Keith Funston was indisputably a public relations genius. He believed that the one way to get ordinary Americans interested in stocks was to convince newspapers to cover the stock market the way they covered baseball. Baseball had its box scores and the N.Y.S.E. had its stock tables, and so Funston "convinced" papers by only advertising in those that agreed to carry the stock tables free of charge. Of all the major newspapers, only one, Dolly Schiff's *New York Post*, objected. Funston also sponsored investment seminars and economic conferences on university campuses, encouraging the study of stock markets as an academic discipline. He pushed for more business periodicals and encouraged the promotion of business columnists.

SINCE ITS FOUNDING in 1792, the N.Y.S.E. strictly regulated the commissions its members charged customers to execute trades in Exchange-listed stocks. This unabashed price-fixing was justified using a variety of arguments over the years. The argument in vogue in the 1960s was that an antitrust exemption was available to the Exchange because the rates were technically legally mandated by a regulator—the S.E.C.—which approved all N.Y.S.E. rules, including rate schedules. As the size of the blocks of stock traded by institutional investors grew larger—frequently tens of thousands of shares—the fixed per share rates resulted in an enormous windfall to member firms.

Despite the fact that N.Y.S.E. rules did not allow any sort of volume discount, the institutional investor community developed a number of techniques during the 1960s to recoup the non-competitive, overpriced commissions they paid. One method was to direct business to brokers that produced quality research reports that helped the fund managers pick stocks. Another method used by the large commercial banks whose trust departments actively traded in large volumes was to direct business to brokerage firms that kept their deposits at the bank or otherwise used the services of the bank. Mutual fund companies would direct brokerage business to firms that actively promoted and sold shares in the funds they managed. The N.Y.S.E. rules allowed commission sharing, however. This made sense, for example, where the brokerage firm that received the customer's order did not have a back-office operation to clear and settle trades, but relied on another N.Y.S.E. member firm with those capabilities.

Over time, the institutional investors' use of this commission-sharing technique, referred to as the "give-up," evolved into something completely unrelated to the actual division of labor in executing the relevant trade. The give-up became little more than an artifice to compensate other investment banks for unrelated services. For example, the firm that does the best job selling shares in a mutual fund may not be the best firm to execute trades on the Exchange. So why get less than optimal trade execution by rewarding the firm that sells your mutual fund shares with brokerage business when you can simply direct the executing broker to pay a portion of the commission over to that firm? Using the give-ups, many mutual fund companies paid over 90 percent of their commission dollars to firms that had nothing whatsoever to do with trade execution.

Another problem for institutional investors was "front running"—firms with knowledge of a customer's large trade buying or selling ahead of that customer's trade. If an institution was looking to off-load a large block of stock, more often than not the price of the stock would magically drop even before the trade was brought to the specialist. And equally magically, the price would return to its unaffected level shortly after the block was sold. Similar but opposite price movements would occur when an institution sought to buy a large block of shares. Those in the know, which often included the specialist, would pocket the discount incurred by the seller in addition to any share of the commission they might be entitled to. While front running was (and is) illegal, it was nonetheless rampant in the 1960s.

Ever the entrepreneurs, many of the investment banks that participated in and profited from front running saw a business opportunity. There were enormous commissions to be made on buying and selling large blocks so, unsurprisingly, the competition for that business was fierce. But for Wall Street firms with capital—and the nerve to put that capital at risk—enormous profits were possible. These firms offered the large institutional investors a superior solution: Rather than buying or selling at whatever price the market would dictate, these firms would guarantee the institutional investor a fixed price. They would buy the shares from the selling institution at a fixed discount to the then-current market price, so at least the institution would know how much it would be paid on the trade. The brokerage firm would then attempt to quietly sell the shares, preferably to another institution. If necessary, the shares would be sold in small blocks on the Exchange, hopefully not driving down the price significantly, but in any event selling as quickly as practicable to avoid market risk and free up the capital tied up in the trade.

Over the course of the 1960s, a number of firms became proficient in this business—known as "block trading"—including Salomon Brothers, Goldman, Sachs & Co. and a small research firm that entered the niche in a big way in technology stocks and would ultimately change the course of Wall Street, Donaldson, Lufkin & Jenrette (D.L.J.). Before long, it became nearly impossible to land institutional business on Wall Street unless you had a credible block trading capability. It was impossible to have a credible block trading capability, though, if you didn't have plentiful capital.

The block trading business would ultimately have a profound impact on how investment banks made money and on the culture of Wall Street itself. Before the block trading business, investment banks used their capital in relatively low-risk businesses like securities underwriting. In an underwriting, the investment bank didn't agree to purchase the securities from the issuer until it had fully sold the offering through numerous other broker-dealers, known as the underwriting syndicate, who shared the risk. Until the moment of the closing, the underwriter had the ability to cancel the offering if the issuer or the market deteriorated materially.

Block trading entailed monumentally more risk. To compete successfully for the trade, the investment bank had to make a split-second decision whether to bid for the business, with little more information than what was on the ticker tape. There was no undoing a trade if the market moved away from you. Millions of dollars of precious capital could be lost with a single bad trade. At the same time, millions could be made equally expeditiously on a spectacularly good trade. A new Wall Street species was born—the "trader."

Until the 1960s, trading was a low-margin, low-risk customer-driven execution function. But starting with block trading of equities, it became an enormous profit engine. With rising interest rates in the latter part of the 1960s, volatility in fixed income instruments soon meant enormous profits could be made in trading bonds as well. After the abandonment of the Bretton Woods system whereby the world's currencies were linked with the price of gold in 1971, the resulting continuous fluctuations in currency values created another enormously profitable trading business. With the trading of equity options and commodity futures—and later index options and futures—still more profitable trading opportunities presented themselves. Old-fashioned securities underwriting, brokerage, and merger advisory businesses were sleepy backwaters compared to the trading floors, where the real profits were made and the Masters of the Universe roamed.

Very quickly after the block trading desks were formed, the superstar traders emerged—the new celebrity gunslingers of Wall Street. At Salomon Brothers, head trader Jay H. Perry reigned over "The Room," as it was called, a 7,500-square-foot, two-story-high trading floor constructed in 1970 on the combined forty-first and forty-second floors of Salomon's new headquarters in Lower Manhattan, home to 200 traders at the time and 12,000 phone lines.[6] Billy Salomon, the firm's chairman, bet large on block trading to diversify Salomon Brothers' business beyond government bonds in the 1960s in a gamble that would pay off in the billions. Sitting at Jay Perry's side at the time was his protégé, a young junior trader named Michael J. Bloomberg.[7] Executing Perry's and Bloomberg's trades on the floor of the N.Y.S.E. was Michael Meehan II, Joseph Meehan's son, recruited by Salomon Brothers from his family firm to become head floor broker.[8] At Goldman, Sachs, the block trading business was headed by Robert E. Mnuchin, a tall, voluble man known as much for his bluntness as his incredible market feel.[9] His son Steven would follow him to Goldman, Sachs and later become U.S. Secretary of the Treasury.

EVEN WITH THE various give-ups and other commission-recapture strategies available to institutional investors, they were still overpaying to execute trades. In 1967, Donald E. Weeden, age thirty-seven, was working at his family's brokerage firm in San Francisco. Weeden held an economics degree from Stanford University and was one of those young men that saw the future and knew it was made of silicon. At age twenty-nine, he was a founder of the National Semiconductor Corporation, the pioneer microchip company.[10] Weeden, a continent away from the Club during the Summer of Love, welcomed the disruption block trading and new technologies were causing in the financial services industry. Weeden cared so little about the Club, he didn't even join the N.Y.S.E.

Weeden's proposition to institutional investors was simple: he would create an efficient, technology-driven trading platform for all stocks—including those listed on the N.Y.S.E.—and charge market-driven commission rates. What could the N.Y.S.E. do to him? He wasn't even a member. And the more institutional investors that joined his trading platform, the more robust it would become, meaning that execution could be as efficient, potentially even more efficient, than on the floor of the Exchange. Commission rates would decline as volume increased, because if they didn't, someone would simply duplicate Weeden's platform and take the business away from him. Weeden's platform, and those that competed with it, became known as the "Third Market," after the N.Y.S.E. and the over-the-counter (O.T.C.) market, which wasn't a formal market at all, but the name given to the trading in stocks not listed on a securities exchange.

Weeden didn't invent the Third Market: its origins went back to the beginning of World War I, when the N.Y.S.E. was closed for four months in 1914. During the hiatus, non-member brokerage firms began making a market in Exchange-listed stocks, to the fury of the Exchange members. But there was nothing the Exchange leadership could do. Nothing compelled investors to transact in listed stocks exclusively on the N.Y.S.E. What was true in 1914 remained true five decades later.

Weeden & Co. was started as a municipal bond dealer in San Francisco in 1922 by Don Weeden's father, Frank Weeden.[11] Weeden began making a market in equities as a service to its institutional customers. It discovered it could usually find buyers, and quickly, among its institutional clients for stock positions it bought from other institutional clients. Weeden discovered equally quickly that it made a healthy profit on trades in N.Y.S.E.-listed stocks at commission rates much lower than those the Exchange required its members to charge. By the early 1960s, Weeden had gotten so good at trading listed stocks "off-Exchange" that it was a cheaper option for many institutions even when taking all the give-ups into consideration.

The S.E.C. first got wind that there was substantial off-Exchange trading in N.Y.S.E.-listed stocks in 1963. Suspicious that it might be an unregulated dark corner where nefarious practices might be taking place, it called in Donald Weeden to explain his business. The S.E.C. staff quickly concluded that Donald Weeden had a thriving business because the N.Y.S.E. was taking advantage of its customers, rather than Third Market firms taking advantage of theirs. So began a long, friendly relationship between the reformers at the S.E.C. and Donald Weeden.

Over time, Weeden & Co. became more than simply an annoyance and a cause of marginal profit loss to the N.Y.S.E. It became an existential threat. Institutions accounted for more and more of the trading volume during the 1960s, nearly half of all trading by the end of the decade. Retail customers were becoming less and less profitable as N.Y.S.E. member firms choked on their certificates of low denominations. And after the give-ups were banned, Donald Weeden knew that price transparency would make his firm's market-making even more attractive. Because Weeden & Co. had the best computer systems money could buy, it had more profit margin to compete with than all but a handful of the most profitable N.Y.S.E. firms.

By the end of the 1960s, Weeden's platform would transact a volume of shares equal to about 10 percent of the Exchange's volume in those shares.[12]

WHILE 10 PERCENT is an impressive volume, the real question was why it wasn't even greater. Like any good monopolist, the Club did not take kindly to Donald Weeden's innovations, and it had a number of tools in the kit to stanch the bleeding of trading volume. The Club's first line of defense was enforcing discipline among its own members. The Exchange had a rule, formally known as N.Y.S.E Rule 394, which prohibited members from sending customer orders in listed stocks to the Third Market. Because of the logistics involved in securities trading, this rule made it difficult for all but the largest institutional investors to avail themselves of the Third Market. For example, if a N.Y.S.E. member firm was the custodian for a small mutual fund's securities, it could, by reference to Rule 394, decline to transfer a stock certificate to effectuate a trade on Weeden's platform. Very large institutional investors had enough trading volume to spread out over multiple custodians and clearing brokers—one of them not being a member of the N.Y.S.E.—but not so for most small mutual funds. Accordingly, they wouldn't trade with Weeden.

Holding securities outside an Exchange member firm might also make obtaining margin loans more expensive because another tool used by the Exchange was to threaten banks with boycotts if they financed Third Market firms. Given the considerable deposits and loans Exchange members had, the threat of concerted action was not to be taken lightly. Similarly, if a mutual fund company traded too much in the Third Market, it might notice a drop-off in assets under management. Exchange members would purchase and promote the shares of its competitors' funds instead. (Besides, many mutual fund managers were in on the game: their funds' investors paid the trading commissions while the managers themselves reaped the benefits of the give-ups by way of free research, promotion of their funds' shares, and other goodies.) All these things and more were threatened and done by the Exchange to tamp down on Weeden's volume. Most institutional investors concluded it was better to keep most trading with Exchange members rather than painting a big target on their backs.

"We didn't set out to destroy the New York Stock Exchange," Donald Weeden recalled years later, "we just wanted to conduct a quiet business and compete with them. The way we saw it, it was live and let live. We didn't feel any antagonism toward them. But when they came along and used slander and illegal boycotts and economic pressure on our customers to perpetuate their monopoly and to try and put us out of business, well it just pissed us off. So we said, Goddamn it, we're just not going to take it. We've got to do something about it."[13]

Some institutional investors came to the conclusion that if you couldn't beat them, join them. In 1965, Waddell & Reed, Inc., a large Kansas City–based mutual fund manager, filed an application to join the Pacific Coast Stock Exchange.[14] While the Pacific Coast Stock Exchange's volume was a fraction of the N.Y.S.E.'s, Waddell & Reed thought that if it could convince the Pacific Coast Stock Exchange to allow mutual fund companies and other institutional investors to become members, the Pacific Coast Stock Exchange might explode in trading volume and become a legitimate competitor to the N.Y.S.E. Waddell & Reed's convincing was also accompanied by the threat of an antitrust lawsuit against the Pacific Coast Stock Exchange if it was refused membership. The Pacific Coast Stock Exchange, calculating how much the value of seats on its exchange would increase with all the additional trading volume Waddell & Reed projected, approved the membership application.

The N.Y.S.E.—and most other regional stock exchanges—made it clear they would not be following suit. Instead of reacting to the rise of the Third Market and institutional membership on stock exchanges as a wake-up call, a timely reminder that competition would inevitably come, the Club doubled down on anticompetitive defensive maneuvers. It wasted time and effort that would have been better spent weaning itself off fixed commissions, upgrading technologies, and attracting permanent capital to become more cost-efficient. The institutional money driving the growth and profits of the Club in the 1960s was controlled by the same institutions that supported the Third Market and, in some cases, sought membership on regional exchanges to save on commissions. Being at odds with your most important customers is never a successful long-term business strategy. As these institutions became more important on Wall Street, they also grew more important in Washington. Their lobbyists would push and prod the S.E.C. and the Department of Justice throughout the decade to reform the fixed commission boondoggle.

In alliance with these institutions was Merrill Lynch, Pierce, Fenner & Smith Incorporated, Wall Street's largest firm and most efficient operator. Merrill Lynch pushed to eliminate fixed commissions as it would undoubtedly gain significant market share in a truly competitive market. Over the course of the 1960s, Merrill Lynch, buttressed by state-of-the-art computers and a fortress balance sheet, would transform itself from a broker to the small-account investor to a block trading and underwriting powerhouse and the most innovative investment bank on the Street.

WHILE SECURITIES TRADING was what occupied most employees of Wall Street firms in the 1960s, it was by no means the only profitable business. Raising capital for businesses by underwriting stocks and bonds was very profitable. After two decades of stagnant underwriting business, in the mid-1950s, American corporations were increasingly tapping the public securities markets to raise capital to finance growth. Until the 1960s, however, the public securities markets were available only to established corporations, usually in traditional brick-and-mortar industrial businesses. The business of underwriting securities at the start of the 1960s was dominated by a handful of Wall Street investment banks, referred to as the "bulge bracket" firms, so-called because more often than not they led the deals garnering the largest type in the *Wall Street Journal* "tombstone" ads that announced securities offerings. The lead underwriter for a deal would invite a group of other underwriters—sometimes dozens for very large deals—to assist in selling the issue, but equally important, to lay off risk and free up capital. The lead underwriter would retain more than its pro-rata share of the underwriting discount for originating and structuring the offering. At the beginning of the decade, these bulge bracket firms were Morgan Stanley & Company, The First Boston Corporation, Kuhn, Loeb & Company, Lehman Brothers, and Dillon, Read & Co. Over the course of the decade, Goldman, Sachs & Co., Salomon Brothers, and Merrill Lynch would join the bulge bracket fraternity, while Dillon, Read & Co., and Kuhn, Loeb would fall out of it, down to the next category of underwriter, a "major" bracket firm.[15]

Strength in underwriting at the start of the 1960s was surprisingly disconnected from strength of sales force. Merrill Lynch, which had more brokers and salesmen than any other Wall Street firm, was an underwriting laggard at that time. Success depended more on relationships with the senior management and directors of the large corporations that were voracious consumers of capital. To an extent unimaginable today, it was important not only to have gone to the right schools—Ivy League was practically a given—but also to have belonged to the right clubs at those schools. Breeding, polish, and social connections didn't hurt either. You didn't have to be a White Anglo-Saxon Protestant (W.A.S.P.), but you certainly needed to talk like one and dress like one.

While the old-boy network that presided over the bulge bracket of 1960 controlled an enormous amount of business, it did not by any means control all of it. As you moved farther away from Fortune 100 companies, other underwriters would likely be leading many deals as well. And certain industries, like retail chains, were

dominated by non–bulge bracket firms like Goldman and Salomon. The biggest initial public offering (IPO) of the 1960s, the
common stock offering of Ross Perot's Electronic Data Systems,
Inc. (E.D.S.), was led by R. W. Pressprich & Co., neither a bulge
bracket nor a major bracket firm. The IPO market for all but the
largest companies was a niche underwriting segment that the bulge
bracket left to others. Dealing in securities of small companies was
considered lowbrow. So, too, was the underwriting of securities for
new technology companies. The bulge bracket firms ceded this
underwriting business to less-established rivals—which turned out
to be an enormous strategic misjudgment. As the likes of Dillon,
Read and Kuhn, Loeb cast these pearls before the swine, firms like
D.L.J. and Merrill Lynch would gain invaluable experience and
"league table" credibility. (The league tables are the ranking of
underwriters based on either the number of underwritings or the
aggregate dollar value securities underwritten for each type of
security—common stock, convertible bonds, investment-grade
bonds, high yield bonds, etc.)

The bulge bracket held onto its prerogatives not simply on the
power of its white shoe gentility, but by the iron fist under the
velvet glove. First, there was a "gentlemen's agreement" among
the members of the bulge bracket that they would not poach each
other's clients. If a company wanted to move business from one
bulge bracket firm to another, that was one thing. But members
of the bulge bracket pitching each other's clients was quite another. It simply wasn't done. And woe unto any firm not in the
bulge bracket pitching the client of a bulge bracket firm. Not only
would that firm be blacklisted from all deals led by the aggrieved
firm, it would also be excluded from deals led by any other bulge
bracket firm.

During the 1950s, the bulge bracket led over 50 percent of all
underwritings.[16] The consequences of stepping out of line were not
trifling. Of course, bulge bracket firms could poach whatever clients of the non–bulge bracket firms suited them. But as the 1960s
progressed, the discipline of the bulge bracket collapsed. By 1969,

Merrill Lynch, with its enormous securities distribution capability and its large, stable capital base, decided it would go it alone and chase whatever business it wanted. Because its sales force was so valuable in selling deals, it simply wasn't feasible to blackball Merrill Lynch, at least not for very long.

BEFORE THE 1960S, merger and acquisition advice was not a very large business opportunity for Wall Street, as large corporations did not make very many acquisitions. Virtually all such transactions were friendly. And since companies back then almost always bought other companies in the same line of business, the antitrust laws limited how much market share could be acquired. The 1960s brought a new type of acquisition—the conglomerate merger. The theory of the conglomerate was that the application of scientific, modern management techniques transcended any particular industry. A good management team, it was believed, could run an oil company just as well as it could run a movie studio. This theory was sweet music to Go-Go Era Wall Street's ears. Unburdened by the need to stick to one's knitting, just about any company could be sold to a management team that thought itself superior—which was just about every management team. Conglomerates like Charles Bluhdorn's Gulf & Western, Harold Geneen's I.T.T., and James Ling's L.T.V. would buy and sell literally hundreds of companies a year. Since conglomerate acquisitions were by definition not limited to any particular industry, antitrust laws were generally not a limiting factor. By the end of the decade, the stigma of the hostile takeover had also diminished. Unsolicited tender offers by conglomerators wielding their high price-to-earnings stock valuations became so commonplace that an alarmed Congress held hearings and ultimately passed legislation—the Williams Act of 1968—regulating them.

The merger and acquisition wave of the 1960s also changed the status quo on Wall Street. Charlie Bluhdorn, Harold Geneen, and Jimmy Ling didn't much care about the bulge bracket firms or their prerogatives or what clubs their investment bankers belonged to. The next wave of raiders—Saul Steinberg, Meshulam Riklis, and Carl Lindner—cared even less. By decade's end, the fees available from these voracious acquirers rivaled those from the companies included in the Dow Jones Industrial Average. For those on Wall Street undeterred by the taboo of assisting on hostile takeovers, enormous merger and acquisition advisory fees and underwriting fees were available. Since money always beats taboos on Wall Street in the long run, even the whitest shoe firms started to get in on the hostile takeover action.

The sale of investment research was another business line that grew exponentially for many Wall Street firms in the 1960s. In addition, quality research facilitated winning business in other products. For example, research departments could be counted on to identify good merger and acquisition suggestions to pitch to corporate clients. Research analysts whose reports were often right acquired a following among both institutional investors and retail brokers pitching stocks. A research analyst with a following could also be counted on to sell securities the firm was underwriting if it wrote a positive research report about the offering. Here again, the upstarts like D.L.J. were beating the older firms of the Club in selling quality research.

Most firms in the 1960s, no matter what their other specialties, also traded for the account of the firm. Now called "proprietary trading," using the firm's superior access to information—euphemistically called "market intelligence"—to make favorable securities trades was very profitable for Wall Street. Conglomerate-driven merger and acquisition activity gave rise to new trading opportunities. Some of these proprietary trading strategies, like merger arbitrage, were becoming very elaborate and sophisticated as merger and acquisition activity boomed.

Some firms in the 1960s would even tie up precious capital for long-term speculative investments, referred to at the time as "merchant banking." Today it is better known as "private equity investing." Like block trading, in proprietary trading and merchant banking, capital was king. The firms with discretionary capital could harvest outsized returns; those without capital would languish. Bear, Stearns & Co. had the most active merchant banking operation on Wall Street in the 1960s, led by Jerome Kohlberg Jr. In 1965, he hired a young man out of college named George Roberts, and Roberts's roommate at the time, Henry Kravis, who landed a job at Goldman, Sachs, would join Bear, Stearns a few years later. Eventually the three men generated huge profits for Bear, Stearns. The three would leave the firm in 1976 to form what would become the premier private equity firm, Kohlberg Kravis Roberts & Co.

There was one financial business investment banks could not touch during the 1960s: commercial banking. With the passage of the Glass-Steagall Act of 1933, firms dealing in securities were prohibited from being affiliated with any deposit-taking institutions. Likewise, commercial banks could not own investment banks despite the obvious synergies of these combinations. Commercial banks could be a source of loans for investment banks, but not equity capital. With the nation's savings in their vaults, the commercial banks could make large loans that wouldn't mature for years. Not even the largest investment banks could compete with money-center commercial banks when it came to lending.

Because of the more fragmented commercial banking system of the 1960s, there were twice as many commercial banks then as now.[17] Interstate branch banking was prohibited, so the lending books of commercial banks were less diversified than today and reflected a regional bias. For example, six of the nation's largest commercial banks in 1967 were headquartered in New York City—Chase Manhattan Bank, First National City Bank, Chemical Bank, Morgan Guaranty Trust Company, Manufacturers Hanover Trust Company, and Bankers Trust Company—and lent heavily to investment banks.[18] This, in turn, put them at risk if there were to be a systemic crisis on Wall Street. But that was considered too remote to seriously consider in the 1960s, so those commercial banks loaned liberally to finance the stock market's explosive growth.

. . .

THE TRANSFORMATION OF Wall Street during the 1960s, driven by the huge flow of institutional money and the return of Main Street money into the equity markets, made it the best of times for the Club. The Dow kept rising, and trading volume rose even faster. The success of Keith Funston's Wall Street–to–Main Street campaign generated spectacular growth of retail brokerage commissions, a morphine drip that dulled the pain of competitive disadvantage being felt by undercapitalized members of the Club who could not compete for block trading and other capital-intensive businesses. Those undercapitalized firms convinced themselves that everything would be all right with a retail-heavy business model: they sought growth by rapidly expanding their retail operations by opening more and more branch offices and hiring additional brokers. Those brokers, if talented, would require a premium to switch firms, but very often they were inexperienced and not terribly talented. Even in a fixed-commission world, this was a high-cost way to grow revenues, and margins at most of these firms were thin.

With rich fixed commissions, even poorly run firms with antiquated systems were making money. Why invest in expensive computers for tomorrow when you could pay the partners more today? Why husband capital to develop a block trading capability, a proprietary trading operation, or a merchant banking division when you could pay the partners more today? Why hire a merger and acquisition specialist—and have to associate with the vulgar raiders—when you could pay the partners more today? Why invest in a research department to win IPO underwriting for pissant technology companies—and pay the partners less today—when you could live just fine off the scraps left over by the bulge bracket underwriters?

The continued prosperity of the Club in 1967, which was unquestioned by most, was dependent on two very foolish assumptions. The first assumption was that institutional investors—and the

S.E.C. and the Department of Justice—would forever tolerate the Club's anticompetitive practices. These practices were pervasive—fixed commission rates, the exclusion of mutual funds from Exchange membership, the prohibition on public ownership of N.Y.S.E. members, and the boycott of trading with non-member firms. The second assumption was that a prolonged bear market and sharp decline in trading volumes were unlikely, at least anytime soon.

The story told here would not have been possible if it were only a tale of the greed and shortsightedness of Wall Street. It takes a village to create a true catastrophe. Or at a minimum it takes bureaucrats and politicians in Washington, D.C.

The S.E.C. was tasked with regulating investment banks. Among the S.E.C.'s primary responsibilities since its creation was ensuring that they remain solvent. By outward appearances it seemed the S.E.C. had done this job well. Since the Great Depression, only one investment bank of any significance had failed—Ira Haupt & Co. (A second firm had also failed, a poorly run Boston company named duPont, Homsey & Co., but it was small and insignificant.) The N.Y.S.E. touted its successful handling of the Ira Haupt & Co. failure as a model of the effectiveness of self-regulation. Few outside the Club had any idea how close many other N.Y.S.E. members came to insolvency the weekend of President Kennedy's assassination. In addition, the fundamental financial soundness of the securities industry had been validated by a blue-ribbon S.E.C. report issued a few months before President Kennedy's death.

Washington in 1967 was willing to accept the foolish assumptions of the Club. So it is from Wall Street to Washington that we journey for the next chapter of our story.

CHAPTER TWO

"QUIET AND EASY"

◾

Congress and the S.E.C.
Asleep at the Switch

B y the 1960s, the S.E.C. had settled into a passive accommodative regulatory mode. The dean of Wall Street lawyers, Sullivan and Cromwell's Arthur Dean, who along with his partner John Foster Dulles had spent much of 1933 trying to prevent passage of the Securities Act, was lavishing praise on the S.E.C., calling it "the very model of what an administrative agency should be."[1] The diminished enforcement and rule-making activity of the S.E.C. during the last years of the Eisenhower administration wasn't entirely driven by Ike's country club economic policies. The fact was that Wall Street was a pretty unexciting place for most of the 1950s.

In fact, it had been pretty unexciting for most of the 1940s too. After the passage of the last of the New Deal securities legislation in 1940, the legislative and regulatory impulses of the federal government were directed elsewhere. World War II brought government control over the financial system and consumption of nearly all available capital for the war effort. The post-war years of the 1940s witnessed an enormous growth in private-sector industrial activity as well as Cold War military spending and related industrial production. Much of this economic growth was experienced by large, well-established companies—General Motors, Mobil, U.S. Steel, General Electric, and duPont. Their corporate finance needs were uncomplicated. These companies were profitable, and as a result, much of their capital needs were financed with cash from operations. Inventory financing and other short-term borrowing needs were provided by friendly local commercial banks, on whose boards of directors senior executives of the large industrial corporations sat, and vice-versa. If there was a large capital project—a new factory, for example—bulge bracket firms such as Morgan Stanley, Dillon Read, First Boston, or Kuhn, Loeb could underwrite and float an investment-grade bond offering. With the strict anti-trust enforcement of the era, few large mergers or acquisitions took place. And despite the prosperity of that time, there was in hindsight a surprising dearth of new companies with breakthrough technological innovations. By comparison to later decades, there were relatively few new ventures seeking capital. There were precious few notable IPOs (the Ford Motor Company in 1956 and Hewlett Packard in 1957 being the exceptions). Those would not come until the next decade: 1969 alone had more IPOs (683) than in the 1940s and 1950s combined.[2]

In December 1960, President-elect Kennedy had chosen one of his father's New Deal cronies, James Landis, to review all federal regulatory agencies and recommend changes to shake things up. Landis had served as a member of the original S.E.C. under its first chairman, Joseph Kennedy, and was the S.E.C.'s second chairman. Landis reported back to President-elect Kennedy that the first order of business at the S.E.C. had to be appointing better-qualified members to the Commission.[3] Kennedy's first choice for S.E.C. chairman was Harvard Law School professor Louis Loss, author of the leading treatise on securities regulation. Loss, however, turned him down. His next choice was Professor William L. Carey of Columbia Law School, who accepted the appointment.[4]

Carey, the son of a Columbus, Ohio, utilities lawyer, graduated from Yale in 1937 and Yale Law School three years later. He came to the job with the belief that the S.E.C. had lost touch with what was happening in the securities industry. It had been twenty years since any significant securities legislation had been passed, over twenty-five years since the S.E.C. was formed, and perhaps most

importantly, nearly thirty years since the last wide-ranging congressional investigation of Wall Street.

After the 1929 Crash and subsequent economic depression, the
American people blamed Wall Street for the catastrophe and Congress responded with lengthy hearings, summoning to Washington
the titans of finance and putting them under oath. The most spectacular hearings were held in 1933 and 1934 by a Senate subcommittee under the direction of its special counsel, Ferdinand Pecora,
and they exposed all of the dirty dealings and greedy excesses of
Jazz Age Wall Street. The public outrage generated by the sensa-
tional media coverage of bombshell testimony at the hearings provided the political fuel that enabled the Roosevelt administration
to pass the foundational federal securities legislation that regulated
Wall Street for the first time. Carey believed it was time for a 1960s
version of the Pecora hearings.

DURING HIS FIRST months at the S.E.C., Carey spent much of
his time up on the Hill, explaining to lawmakers how the securities
markets were due for dramatic change as a result of the influence
of institutional money and how little the S.E.C. (and Congress)
knew about the consequences to investors of those changes.
Speaker Sam Rayburn was convinced by Carey's lobbying, and in
September 1961, he pushed through a bill appropriating $750,000
to the S.E.C. "to make a study and investigation into the adequacy,
for the protection of investors, of the rules of national securities
exchanges and national securities associations."[5] It became known
as the Special Study of the Securities Markets. It was undertaken by
a crackerjack staff of forty attorneys, economists, and investigators
under the direction of Milton Cohen, a former S.E.C. division
chief. Cohen was given remarkable independence to conduct the
investigation, establishing what was, in effect, an agency within the
agency.[6] To avoid interference by the S.E.C. commissioners, he insisted on a process whereby he would present his study to the full
Commission—and to Congress—prior to any review by the regular

S.E.C. staff or any of the individual commissioners. Carey was perfectly happy to let Cohen take the heat from Wall Street and Congress if his recommendations brought disfavor. Carey, in truth, believed that Congress itself was better equipped to conduct such an investigation, but he was happy to have an S.E.C. loyalist conduct the study, likely assuring that any criticism of the S.E.C.'s job performance would be muted.

For two years, Milton Cohen conducted the investigation, most of it behind closed doors. Keith Funston, president of the N.Y.S.E., like a Mafia don trying to figure out what a grand jury was up to, would send trusted lieutenants to comprehensively debrief every Wall Street executive who was called to testify by Cohen. Funston also tried killing Cohen with kindness. Throughout the process, Funston would send memos to Cohen educating him on various aspects of the operation of the Exchange, always making the case that no more regulation was needed.[7]

When the first segment of the long-awaited Special Study of Securities Markets Report was released on April 3, 1963 (all chapters would be released by August 8, 1963), Funston breathed easier. He would not, unlike Richard Whitney before him, be required to lead a crusade in Washington against new legislation that might threaten the privileges of the Club. Of course there were recommendations in Cohen's report that the Exchange would resist, but they were of the sort he had hoped for and was prepared for. Most importantly for Wall Street, the Special Study Report proclaimed no outrages of greed or excess. There were no compelling villains identified. Unlike the Pecora hearings, there would be no tax-cheating, insider-trading figures like National City Bank's "Sunshine" Charlie Mitchell to march before the cameras. The Pecora hearings were operatic. The Special Study was bureaucratic. The theme of it was "all is well, but we can do better." It affirmatively declared that its two-year investigation discovered "no pattern of fraudulent activity" in the securities markets. Furthermore, it reaffirmed the principle of self-regulation on Wall Street and praised the "strong performance" of the N.Y.S.E. in that effort.[8]

It's not that the Special Study Report was a whitewash. It pointed out a great number of things that needed fixing. For example, the report addressed head-on the nonsensical disparate regulatory treatment of publicly traded companies that chose not to list their securities on an exchange but rather have them trade in the O.T.C. market. Listed companies were required to file with the S.E.C. annual and quarterly financial reports, as well as reports on changes in insider stock ownership and proxy statements. O.T.C.-traded companies were not required to make any of these filings. In addition, purchases of O.T.C. stocks were not subject to the margin requirements that applied to listed stocks. The Special Study Report brought an end to this regulatory arbitrage.[9]

It wasn't as if Milton Cohen was unwilling to rattle the N.Y.S.E.'s cage. There were plenty of questionable practices near and dear to the Club that the Special Study Report targeted. It reopened the debate, unresolved since even before the Pecora hearings, of whether floor traders should be allowed to exist at all. Floor traders had the right to operate on the floor of the Exchange, but did not make markets in stocks or execute trades on behalf of customers. They only traded for their own accounts, taking advantage of being close to the action. It rightfully shone a light on the dark corners of the Exchange's operations. The conduct of odd-lot dealers, for example, where old, questionable practices took advantage of customers. The long-neglected issue of insider trading, addressed in the first draft of the Exchange Act in 1934, but dropped under pressure from corporate lobbyists, was finally given prominence on the S.E.C.'s rule-making agenda.

While floor traders, odd-lot dealers, and insider traders had long been easy targets for reformers—and had been served up by the Club in order to take the heat off more important constituencies— the Special Study Report didn't stop with them. It criticized the most powerful constituencies, the specialists and the governing committees of the Exchange on which the specialists had always exercised power disproportionate to their numbers and economic importance. The perennial problem of the Exchange willfully turning a blind eye to specialist self-dealing and shirking of market-making in volatile trading was called out, and the Exchange pressured to do better. The report called for structural change in Exchange governance to give more power to members who dealt with the public and executed their trades—the "public utility" function that the Club always trumpeted when arguing for the maintenance of special treatment from lawmakers and regulators. It called for less power for the specialists and floor traders who dealt predominately or exclusively for their own accounts. The glacial pace of this power shift, which the S.E.C. had been prodding the Exchange to expedite since Joe Kennedy's very first days at the new Commission, was specifically called out for correction in the recommendations relating to N.Y.S.E. governance.[10]

The most significant contribution of the Special Study Report was that it identified the challenges raised by the changes in the financial markets since World War II. It proposed new legislative and regulatory solutions to the risks presented by the growth of American middle-class stock ownership since the war and the transformational impact on the markets of the rise of the institutional investor. In 1963, there were significant gaps in the oversight of the business of bringing stocks from Wall Street to Main Street. Unless a broker was employed by a firm that was a member of a stock exchange—and a large proportion of Middle America's brokers were not—the S.E.C. had little authority to discipline that broker. The Special Study Report recommended empowering the National Association of Securities Dealers, Inc. (N.A.S.D.), a trade organization under the oversight of the S.E.C., to regulate all brokers and dealers, setting uniform standards for licensing and establishing rules of conduct.

Unscrupulous brokers would excessively trade customer accounts and recommend stocks that were too risky for customers of modest means. The Special Study Report required the newly empowered N.A.S.D. to establish rules governing what securities brokers could recommend to clients based on the concept of "suitability," which takes into account the customer's investment objectives. Once adopted, these rules provided a mechanism to punish brokers who sold speculative stocks to those who could not afford a loss.

In 1963, there were no rules governing what an investment bank could say in a research report, save the rather low bar of illegal market manipulation. The line between promotion of stock ownership and company research was often nonexistent. Less reputable investment banks would publish puff pieces masquerading as research to promote the stocks they underwrote. The Exchange itself was one of the worst offenders in this regard. Funston loved the slick, statistic-dense handouts his publicity department produced to encourage stock ownership. Unsophisticated investors loved to think their investment decisions were scientific rather than dart throwing. The Special Study Report charged the exchanges and the N.A.S.D. with the task of adopting rules to separate advertisements from securities analysis.

In 1963, the price quotes for O.T.C.-traded stocks were tracked and published by private companies, completely unregulated by the S.E.C. or any other agency. While the Special Study Report noted that the companies that operated these stock quote services—known on Wall Street as the "pink sheets," for the color of the paper many of the daily subscription reports were printed on—did so with a high degree of professionalism and found no fraud or abuse, it believed the function to be one inherently requiring oversight. Thereafter, the N.A.S.D. would oversee the publication of stock quotes in the O.T.C. market.[11]

The portions of the Special Study Report dealing with the emerging importance of the institutional investor foreshadowed the battle lines on Wall Street for the next decade and beyond. Two sacred cows were called into question by the Special Study Report, age-old practices at the very center of monopoly power: fixed rate commissions and the ban on N.Y.S.E. members trading Exchange-listed stocks off the Exchange. These were enshrined in N.Y.S.E. rules backed with harsh penalties, religiously enforced, and long upheld by the S.E.C. and protected by friends in Congress. Milton Cohen made no recommendations, however, for immediate regulatory changes with respect to findings in the report. But he did question the viability of a business model that charged ten times as much for a thousand-share block as a hundred-share order when the work involved reflected nowhere near a ten-times multiple. And he questioned why the keeper of the cathedral of free market capitalism engaged in ruthless protectionism in the making of markets in stocks. Why wouldn't competition—in the form of the Third Market or institutional membership on the Exchange—be as good for the N.Y.S.E. as it was for the companies whose stocks it traded? These questions, the report asserted, were worthy of additional attention.[12]

DESPITE ALL OF what the Special Study Report got right, it nonetheless must be judged harshly for what it missed—for out of what it missed a financial crisis emerged. There was very little mention in the report about the capital condition of the investment banks, or the structure of that capital, or what additional capital needs rapidly evolving technology might require of them. Only in the context of new entrants into the securities business was the sufficiency of capital discussed, and even those levels of capital discussed were absurdly low, even for 1963 dollars. It required $5,000 of capital for a firm to be registered as a broker-dealer, plus an additional $2,500 for each branch office and $500 for each broker.[13] No consideration was given to allowing non-securities firms to own investment banks, thereby becoming a source of capital. No study was recommended as to whether public ownership of investment banks might be beneficial for enhancing the stability of their capital. And certainly no questions were raised as to whether or under what circumstances commercial banks might be allowed to own investment banks, as they were allowed to do in virtually every other industrialized country. No limitations were proposed on the use of customer cash by investment banks, only that a reserve of 15 percent be maintained in cash to satisfy withdrawals. And nothing was proposed, other than more study, to address the inefficiencies of the physical movement of stock certificates in securities transactions, despite the fact that Milton Cohen and his team were well aware that existing technology was capable of eliminating paper nearly entirely from the process.

EVEN AS MILD as the Special Study Report reforms were, and despite their support by most securities and banking industry interests, they ran into opposition in Congress. Representative Oren Harris of Arkansas, chairman of the Committee on Interstate and Foreign Commerce, was a conservative states' rights Southerner suspicious of any expansion of federal authority. He was also vigilant in protecting the South's regional insurance and securities firms, which would be disproportionately affected by the new broker-dealer registration requirements.[14] He held up the bill that came out of the report's findings for fourteen months, unrelenting despite a *New York Times* editorial criticizing his obstruction.[15] Harris finally agreed to report the bill under pressure from President Johnson when an amendment preserving the intrastate registration exemption for brokers and dealers was added and a few insurance industry exemptions were included as well.

On August 2, 1964, President Johnson signed into law the amendments to the Securities Act of 1933 and the Securities Exchange Act of 1934 designed to make current the laws that President Franklin Roosevelt imposed on a crooked Wall Street a generation earlier. There was hope that the amendments would leave the financial markets soundly regulated for another generation. Now O.T.C-traded stocks would play by the same rules as those listed on exchanges, all brokers and dealers would be subject to N.A.S.D. oversight, and the N.Y.S.E. would be required to tidy up some of its messier affairs. There was a sense of relief mixed with self-congratulations for all involved. The intrusive investigation by the bureaucrats in Washington was over, and it had been less painful than they had feared. And then, in the summer of 1964, LBJ and the men and women in Congress who decided what the laws would be and what the wars would be turned their attention away from Wall Street, a remnant of a central drama of the Washington of their youth, back to the central dramas of the present—civil rights, the Great Society, and Vietnam.

ON THE DAY President Johnson signed the Special Study Report amendments into law, William Carey resigned as chairman of the S.E.C., returning to Columbia University to teach law. With the passage of the 1964 Securities Acts Amendments, he felt he had accomplished what he set out to do at the S.E.C. They were commonsense reforms, modest and moderate. Yet, they had taken over a year to enact. It wasn't Representative Harris's opposition over special interests that Carey found most frustrating; it was the indifference and lack of interest of the bill's supporters, who included LBJ, House Speaker Sam Rayburn, the entire Senate leadership, and the N.Y.S.E. The S.E.C., he concluded, had been placed on the bureaucratic back burner. In part, he thought, this was because of its prior success in eliminating fraud and undue risk in the financial markets and in part because other issues of historic import were dominating the national political agenda.[16]

For Carey's replacement, President Johnson selected someone who appeared perfect to head an agency in which a supportive but mostly indifferent president had little interest. Manuel "Manny" Cohen was a twenty-two-year veteran of the S.E.C. legal staff who had been named a commissioner by President Kennedy in 1961. He was not thought to be in possession of a great legal mind in the academic sense, like William Carey or Bill Douglas before him, and there were never any comparisons of him to a force of nature like Joe Kennedy. Manny Cohen, however, was a smart and talented practical lawyer who was savvy in the ways of Washington and perfectly suited to a president who wanted no fuss from the Commission.

What Manny Cohen learned best after a quarter-century of regulatory turf fights and budget battles at the S.E.C. was that the only way to live to fight another day was to give the president of the

United States what he wanted. What LBJ wanted out of Manny Cohen was peace and quiet, and that's exactly what he got:

COHEN: Good morning, Mr. President. How are you?

LBJ: I'm well, and I hope you are too.

COHEN: I'm doin' pretty good.

LBJ: Thank you, that's good. You got the S.E.C. running right?

COHEN: I think so, sir.

LBJ: Is it quiet and easy?

COHEN: Yes, sir. We've got a lot of things under the table, a few things might come out in the next few months, but, uh, I think we're doing it in a way that keeps things as you suggest, quiet and peaceable but moving.

LBJ: That's good.[17]

Manny Cohen spent much of his first four years as S.E.C. chairman dealing with the perennial issues of reforming the fixed commission structure and related abuses, off-Exchange trading by N.Y.S.E members, and lowering mutual fund management fees. Cohen also pursued a vigorous enforcement program, combating insider-trading abuses and initiating one of the most high-profile lawsuits in the Commission's history—against the notorious lawyer Roy Cohn. A serious heart attack early in his tenure as chairman probably played a role in curbing a more aggressive agenda. His major legislative initiative during this time was support for Senator Harrison Williams's 1965 bill regulating tender offers, which had proliferated during the conglomerate acquisition wave, including many hostile tender offers that were spooking corporate America.[18] It would take three years to enact Williams's bill, despite the public unpopularity of corporate raiders and support for the bill from LBJ, congressional leadership, and the N.Y.S.E.

Manny Cohen would propose no laws or regulations to strengthen capital requirements at Wall Street firms. In fact, the responsibility of assuring the solvency of Wall Street firms of great systemic importance continued to be delegated by the S.E.C. to the N.Y.S.E.

WHEN IT CAME to the financial condition of the grand firms on Wall Street, looks were deceiving. McDonnell & Co. was a well-regarded, socially prominent investment bank with a large retail brokerage business. Its main brokerage office in 1967 was located at 400 Park Avenue, on the northwest corner of Fifty-Fourth Street. Then, as now, this was among the most desirable and expensive commercial real estate on the planet. The interior of that office space was elegantly carpeted, and on that carpet, brokers sat at fine antique desks with Tiffany lamps.[19] There was not a single functional reason why a business engaged in the buying and selling of securities and commodities for customers would incur the rental and furnishing expenses for such an office. There were many psychological reasons, however, that made choosing that location and decor a very good business decision.

In the days before federal deposit insurance, the main public rooms of most banks had high, ornate ceilings, marble columns, and rich furnishings. Behind the tellers' windows there was often a safe with a very heavy door, always open, with a very large and complex looking lock. Through the open safe door there were typically visible bars of gold and piles of currency. Almost always, the safe where nearly all the cash and gold was actually stored was located in the basement, far from the public. What could be seen by the eyes of depositors was carefully designed to instill a sense of confidence, of stolidity, of solvency—for the lack thereof might lead to panic. In a panic, depositors want their money back immediately. Even the best-managed bank does not have sufficient liquid assets to satisfy the withdrawals of all (or even a substantial portion) of its deposits. Banking, at its very essence, is and always will be a confidence game.

The investment banking business in the 1960s was even more of a confidence game than commercial banking. Unlike commercial banks, investment banks had no federal insurance agency like the F.D.I.C. protecting customer accounts. There was no Federal Reserve window to which an investment bank could turn to pledge assets for emergency loans if liquidity got tight. Many brokerage customers did not know that the securities and cash reflected on their monthly statements were not held separately and segregated from the accounts of other customers or from the trading and investment accounts of the investment bank itself. Even fewer knew that investment banks could use their cash—interest free—as they saw fit. The assets in the customer accounts were available to satisfy the claims of all of the investment bank's creditors in the event of its insolvency.

What all but the most sophisticated customers did not know was how leveraged investment banks were. For the industry as a whole in the late 1960s, there was only about $2 billion of equity capital supporting nearly $20 billion in liabilities.[20] Equally surprising was how little equity even the largest firms had. Merrill Lynch, far and away the largest investment bank, had about $300 million of equity capital at the time, less than that of over 150 companies on the Fortune 500 list.[21] And only a very few outside the Club knew how illusory, how impermanent, even that thin slice of equity capital was.

Nearly all of the equity capital in investment banks at the time was provided by the upper tier of management of the investment banks—the partners. Until the failure of Ira Haupt & Co., virtually all investment banks were partnerships. After that failure, where partners faced the real prospect of personal liability, many firms changed to a corporate form to shield the partners from potential liability. Nonetheless, the charters of these private corporations mirrored the partnership agreement provisions. When partners retired—and the oldest partners typically had the largest amounts in their capital accounts—their capital was typically paid out either immediately or over a relatively short period of time (unless the retiring partner, at his option, chose to leave some investment capital in the business as a limited partner if the firm was doing well). It was estimated in the late 1960s that over 60 percent of the industry's equity was owned by partners over sixty years old and that 95 percent of all equity capital could be withdrawn within a year.[22] Active partners could also withdraw from the firm (when defecting to a competitor, for example) and similarly request a return of their capital. Typically, a retiring or withdrawing partner had to give the firm only ninety days' notice to require a return of a substantial portion, if not all, of his capital. And with that capital went the ability to survive trading losses, bear markets, and all the rest of the inevitable hazards of finance.

High leverage, of course, maximizes returns for equity owners. However, it is an indisputable tenet of responsible corporate finance that the more volatile the value of an asset, the less it should be leveraged. Investment banks owned few assets, with a stable value. Certainly they owned exchange memberships, office leases, furniture, equipment, and the like, but these items represented a small fraction of their asset base (and were illiquid). Most of what they owned were stocks, bonds, and commodities, whose values are subject to significant market volatility. The post-war period had brought two decades of ever-increasing equity valuations and a period of interest rate stability, which made bond investments subject mostly to credit risk. There had not been a sharp bear market or a period of rapidly rising interest rates in recent memory (and securities markets have notoriously short memories). There was a sense that a 10 percent equity cushion was reasonable, and that when a 10 percent bear market occurred, there would be time and tools to deal with it.

Who was providing this leverage? As one might expect, the commercial banks lent heavily to the investment banks, but nearly always on a fully secured basis with margin requirements. Who was providing the unsecured debt? Some was owed to partners and to other investment banks, but to a large extent, it was the brokerage customers of the investment banks, by way of the cash balances in their accounts.

The interconnectedness of the firms in the securities industry wasn't just limited to the not insubstantial amounts they owed one another. If one failed, the commercial bank that provided secured loans would sell the securities serving as collateral for those loans as quickly as possible, at fire-sale prices if necessary. This would lower securities prices and depress the values of other investment banks. But the most serious risk of a firm failure was the loss of confidence of customers and other counterparties generally. One investment banking firm failing could start a run on all of them. Accordingly, a standard of financial solvency capable of enforcement was in the self-interest of all responsible firms.

IN 1922, THE N.Y.S.E. first enacted a financial solvency rule. It required each Exchange member to maintain salable assets with a value at least equal to its liabilities to its customers. In 1934, with the passage of the Exchange Act, the S.E.C. was empowered to regulate ratio of indebtedness to net capital of Exchange members, with the ratio being no more than 20-to-1. But it wasn't until November 9, 1944, that the S.E.C. finally put into effect a net capital rule, setting the ratio at the statutory maximum 20-to-1. In the meantime, in 1939, the N.Y.S.E. adopted its own Rule 325, which set the maximum ratio at 15-to-1. This preemptive action proved to be genius, for when the S.E.C. adopted its rule, it exempted all brokers and dealers so long as they were members in good standing of a major securities exchange that had a comprehensive net capital rule. The S.E.C. noted that at the time the ratios set by those exchanges (all were then set at 15-to-1, following the N.Y.S.E.) were more restrictive than the S.E.C. rule. Most critically, the S.E.C. exemption did not state that the exemption was effective only so long as a firm met the ratio set by the exchange. The exemption lasted for so long as the firm wasn't ruled "no longer in good standing" by the governing body of the relevant exchange. Therefore, technically, an investment bank could legally operate even if its net capital ratio was higher than the maximum set by the exchanges so long as the exchanges did not deem it no longer in good standing. And critically, Rule 325 permitted the board of governors of the N.Y.S.E. to grant exemptions from compliance with its net capital rule. Accordingly, the N.Y.S.E., and it alone, would decide whether one of its members was no longer financially strong enough to continue operating.[23]

This loophole would be used regularly during the crisis that lay ahead. If one change could have prevented the coming crisis, it would have been the elimination of this loophole. No one asked—not Bill Carey, nor Manny Cohen, nor Milton Cohen, nor anyone else at the S.E.C.

This regulatory loophole was the brainchild of a governor of the N.Y.S.E. who would later serve as chairman and perhaps its most powerful member in the twentieth century: John A. Coleman.

JOHN A. COLEMAN was a founding partner, along with Paul Adler, of Adler, Coleman Co., a specialist firm on the N.Y.S.E. While successful and well respected among its peers on the floor of the Exchange, it was neither the largest nor the most profitable specialist firm. John Coleman's power was not derivative of Adler, Coleman's. John Coleman's special genius was not making money, though he made an enormous amount of it. His extraordinary gift was a thorough understanding of power: how to attain it, how to exercise it, when and how not to exercise it, how to help some attain it and prevent others from attaining it.

John Coleman was born on Christmas Eve, 1901, on West Sixty-Second Street in Manhattan, at the time a working-class Irish neighborhood. His father's New York City policeman's salary was not enough to support John and his five siblings, so at age fourteen, John dropped out of the prestigious Regis High School and went to work as a runner on the floor of the New York Curb Exchange, a predecessor of the American Stock Exchange (AMEX). His annual salary that year was $192. Like all clerks, he was given an I.D. badge. As the new kid, according to the custom, he was assigned I.D. number 13, as no one with seniority was required to keep the unlucky number. For Coleman, it brought only luck.[24]

After six years as a clerk, the very Catholic twenty-year-old Coleman was sponsored for membership on the Curb Exchange by Edwin H. Stern, founder of E. H. Stern & Co. (the predecessor of Lasker, Stone & Stern), a successful Jewish American specialist with an eye for talent, who lent Coleman the money required to purchase the seat. Trading floors rightly earned their reputations as cruel and vulgar places where profanity and all manner of the worst ethnic and religious insults were hurled with abandon, but they were also places of remarkable tolerance in their own way, nearly always ahead of the other major business institutions of the country in terms of admission of religious, ethnic, and other minorities. A woman had a seat on the N.Y.S.E. in 1960, long before the refined investment bankers at the white shoe firms let in any female partners. An African American had a seat on the Exchange by 1970. The only thing never tolerated was losing money.

By 1924, Coleman made enough money in two years trading with Stern to be able to pay back the loan and accumulate the capital needed to purchase a seat on the N.Y.S.E. At age twenty-two, he was at the time the youngest member in the history of the N.Y.S.E. He went into partnership with Paul Adler in 1928. Adler, Coleman & Co. chose to occupy Post No. 13 on the floor—for good luck.[25] He brought his brother William into the firm in 1929, the year everything changed at the Exchange.

In the aftermath of the Crash came the Pecora hearings and the Exchange Act of 1934, and with it, the S.E.C. Joe Kennedy, who they all knew, turned out to be better for the Club than they thought he would be, notwithstanding Kennedy's personal enmity toward Exchange legend Michael J. Meehan. Kennedy pretty much let the Exchange run its own affairs, focusing instead on building the credibility of the S.E.C. in the business community and building the S.E.C.'s regulatory infrastructure.

When future Supreme Court Justice William O. Douglas became the S.E.C.'s third chairman in 1937, he had a much more antagonistic relationship with the Exchange and made governance reform there his top priority. The Exchange had been able to resist most interference by the S.E.C. with its internal affairs for nearly four years, until the Richard Whitney scandal destroyed any claim to effective self-governance. John Coleman was right in the middle of the S.E.C. investigation of Whitney and its aftermath, having loaned hundreds of thousands of dollars to Whitney and his affiliated companies. Unlike many, Coleman was smart enough to get repaid before the bottom fell out.

Douglas mandated that the board of governors of the N.Y.S.E. have three public members to keep an eye on things and required that the president of the Exchange be a full-time, professional position. Douglas forced the board of governors to elect his own handpicked candidate as the first full-time president of the Exchange, thirty-one-year-old William McChesney Martin Jr., who would later go on to be the longest-serving chairman of the board of governors of the Federal Reserve. Douglas also insisted that the Exchange clean house at the board of governors and bring in fresh, younger, more reform-minded governors. One of those young thought-to-be-reformers elected to the board of governors in 1938 was thirty-six-year-old John A. Coleman.[26]

Bill Martin was as stiff as a fireplace poker, but without the occasional warmth. While he diligently focused on expanding the authority and influence of the S.E.C. over the Exchange, John A. Coleman was focused on expanding the authority and influence of John A. Coleman, and the members of the Exchange preferred the latter. Coleman was perfectly willing to allow the do-gooder Martin to try and make a blushing bride out of a fine old whore. Coleman let the ambitious Martin monopolize all the face-time with the S.E.C., the committees in Congress, and the press and never challenged his decisions. But Martin never noticed that fewer and fewer decisions affecting the nuts-and-bolts operation of the Exchange were reaching his desk. While it would not be accurate to say that the presidency of the Exchange had been reduced to a ceremonial function, it was, nonetheless, reduced in fundamental ways.

The way John Coleman accomplished this was through control of the committees of the board of governors of the Exchange. Patiently and quietly, through tinkering with by-laws and resolutions and retirements and appointments, those committees would control more and more of what mattered at the Exchange, well out of view of the public members of the board of governors and its president. By the 1960s, Coleman had arranged the by-laws so that the public members of the board of governors were only invited to one meeting of the board of governors per month, even though the other members of the board met weekly. He was elected vice-chairman of the Exchange in 1941 and chairman in 1943. In total, he was elected chairman in four straight elections, unprecedented at the time. And all that time, he studiously kept his name out of the papers, never making himself a target for the S.E.C. or Congress, letting whomever might be president of the Exchange get all the attention.

By 1967, John Coleman had been a member of the Exchange for forty-three years and had served on its board of governors at various times for half of them. Adler, Coleman by this time had acquired nine seats on the Exchange and employed not only Coleman's brother, but two of his sons and a son-in-law, Harry C. Hagerty Jr., the son of the vice-chairman and chief investment officer of the Metropolitan Life Insurance Company. Adler, Coleman was the specialist for blue-chip stocks like W. R. Grace, Motorola, J. C. Penney, Squibb Corporation, Avon, and Coca-Cola Bottling Co. When the closing bell rang and John Coleman went home, his dealings for the day were far from over. Waiting for him in the spacious study of his co-op apartment at 812 Park Avenue were the princes of the Church and of Tammany.

In 1920, while still an eighteen-year-old clerk at the Curb Exchange, Coleman managed somehow to get appointed by the new archbishop Patrick Hayes to the Cardinal's Committee of the Laity, a prominent fundraising committee for wealthy Catholic businessmen in New York. He would become its chairman in 1934. He raised so many millions for the Church and its charities during the

Depression that Pope Pius XI appointed him a Knight of St. Gregory the Great in 1937. In 1940, Pope Pius XII made him a Knight of the Order of Malta. In 1957, he was appointed a Papal Chamberlain by Pius XII, the highest honor that could be bestowed on a layman. Francis Cardinal Spellman named a high school after him in 1967. He raised millions more for the Federation of Jewish Philanthropies and was a major patron of the Wall Street Synagogue. "I was ecumenical before it was fashionable," he once quipped to the *New York Times* in one of the few interviews he ever gave.[27]

John Coleman also raised millions for Democratic Party politicians. Starting when his friend Alfred E. Smith ran for governor of New York in 1922, John Coleman would be a major fundraiser for over half a century. He donated generously to Smith's doomed presidential run in 1928 and, along with Joe Kennedy and only a handful of others, raised Wall Street money for Franklin Roosevelt in 1932. Unlike Kennedy and many of the Irish who parted with FDR in 1940 and supported James Farley for president that year, Coleman was an FDR delegate at the convention in Chicago, supporting him for a third term. Most assumed his loyalty to the president would not be forgotten by FDR if Coleman ever had the need to ask a favor. Armed with this knowledge, most at the S.E.C. preferred to avoid the consequences of Coleman making that call. Accordingly, Coleman never had any trouble with the S.E.C. In 1942, when the S.E.C. adopted the net capital rule, John Coleman politely requested his exemption. The staff and commissioners of the S.E.C. kindly obliged.

With every check written for a politician, every charity fundraising dinner attended, and every job dispensed at the Exchange or a hundred other companies he could call, John Coleman would accumulate a marker. Over the years, the value of those markers would be many times more than the many millions in his bank accounts. And while he ran the Exchange like an old-fashioned Irish ward boss, he was, like the trading floor, oddly democratic and progressive in his own way. In 1960, when Muriel Siebert sought to become the first woman to own a seat on the Exchange, many, perhaps most, members were dead-set against it. Prospective members had to pass an oral "floor exam" given by a senior official of the Exchange on the floor during trading hours to test the applicant's knowledge of the rules and customs. In truth, it was also a mechanism to blackball undesirables. John Coleman arranged to personally give Muriel Siebert her floor exam. It was conducted for a half hour, in the middle of the trading floor for all to see, and when he gave her a smile and hearty handshake, all knew the Exchange had its first female member.[28]

It was said during the 1960s that three men ran New York: Mayor Robert Wagner, Francis Cardinal Spellman, and John A. Coleman—not necessarily in that order.[29] By 1967, long after he had become a legend at the Exchange, there were innumerable "John Coleman stories." One involved a particularly officious member of the board of governors, a scion of one of New York's oldest, most socially prominent W.A.S.P. families, who threatened to resign from the board during a meeting if it took a certain action. Without hesitating, Coleman moved that his resignation be accepted immediately, without debate, and instructed him to take his leave from the meeting. The motion was approved unanimously. Another involved his son-in-law, Harry Hagerty Jr. John Coleman was a stickler about certain rules of the Exchange, one of which was that no food or drink was allowed on the floor. Many on the floor skirted this rule, discreetly hiding a soda can or a half-eaten sandwich beneath a pile of papers at a trading post. Coleman, however, would tolerate no deviation by his employees. Soon after his son-in-law started working on the floor, Adler, Coleman had accumulated a large proprietary position in Coca-Cola Bottling, believing (correctly, it would turn out) the company would soon be a takeover target. This tied up a large portion of the firm's capital, so the daily price movements of that stock were a constant focus and topic of conversation among the Adler, Coleman traders. Young Harry Hagerty, looking to impress his father-in-law, took it all in, mesmerized by the high-stakes drama of it all and hoping to play a bigger part in it. In the midst of it one morning, Harry looked up and saw the agitated face of John Coleman, who sputtered "Dump the Coke!" and stormed off. Harry then sprang into action and successfully sold the entire Adler, Coleman position in a matter of minutes without tanking the stock price. As he headed back to Post 13 expecting a hero's welcome, he noticed the blood-drained faces of the other Adler, Coleman traders, one of whom was holding the half-empty Coke can Harry thought he had hidden at the post.[30]

IN 1953, WITH LITTLE public notice and without any objection from the S.E.C., the N.Y.S.E. amended Rule 325 to increase the permitted net capital ratio to 20-to-1. Soon thereafter, most other exchanges followed suit. And in the years to come, in many other ways less obvious, the Exchange, often at the direction of John Coleman, would take action, formally and informally, to further dilute the protections of its net capital rule. The S.E.C. never contemplated the creative and brazen exemptions, exclusions, and interpretations that would arise when it granted the exchange membership exemption in Rule 15c3-1. In most instances, the S.E.C. never even knew, for the Exchange never informed the S.E.C. of these exemptions, exclusions, and interpretations.[31]

To understand how the Club could legally permit so many clearly insolvent Exchange members to continue to remain open for business with the investing public—in some cases for years—without the S.E.C. becoming aware of their dire condition, it is necessary to understand with some granularity exactly how the net capital rule worked. It is also necessary to get a bit technical.

To start with, the name of the rule was doubly a misnomer. First, it was a ratio, not a minimum net capital requirement. Second, the denominator was not the net capital of the relevant investment bank. Net capital—the difference between the book value under generally accepted accounting principles (GAAP) of the total assets and the total liabilities of a company—was just the starting point for calculating compliance with the rule. Deducted from GAAP net capital were all non–readily marketable assets, including all fixed assets—office leases, furnishings, computer equipment—as well as exchange memberships, intellectual property, and goodwill. Also deducted was the value of securities that were not immediately salable, as a result of either legal restrictions (because public sale of the securities would require registration under the Securities Act) or contractual restrictions on sale. Freely tradable securities were also reduced in value—the "haircut"—to take into account the risk of reduction in market value. For most equity securities, the haircut was 30 percent. The numerator in the rule's calculation was also a misnomer. While Section 8(b) of the Exchange Act refers to "aggregate indebtedness," in fact all liabilities, and not simply those for money borrowed, were included in the calculation.[32]

What the ratio was trying to get at was a reserve requirement—a reasonable level of liquidity to satisfy repayment of liabilities that might come due at times of market stress. The liquidity reserve level of 5 percent of total liabilities (20-to-1) was, of course, arbitrary and would only be a reasonable test if the holders of 95 percent of the liabilities couldn't or wouldn't demand repayment during the time of stress.[33]

Predictably, the investment banks soon found creative ways to manipulate the net capital rule in order to increase leverage. The first method was to convert a liability into an asset. This should be impossible, you might be thinking, but it was simple in practice. If a customer agreed that in exchange for an interest payment on the nominal value of its brokerage account it would not withdraw the cash and securities in the account for a period of time (typically one year) and that those amounts would not be returned to him until all liabilities owing to others were repaid, the value of that customer's account was no longer treated as a liability, but rather as an asset for purposes of the rule. The effect of this maneuver, referred to as a "subordinated account," was profound. For every dollar of customer account value (less the applicable haircuts) subordinated, twenty dollars of additional debt could be taken on. However, the subordination agreements typically allowed the customer to withdraw the cash and securities in the account after the expiration of the one-year period so long as three months' prior notice of withdrawal was given. The Exchange allowed up to 25 percent of an investment bank's net capital to be in the form of subordinated accounts.[34]

Another gimmick used to increase leverage involved turning an excluded asset into one included in the calculation of net capital. As mentioned above, unregistered stock held by an investment bank was given no value in calculating net capital. However, if the investment bank sold that unregistered stock to a financially solvent third party in exchange for an immediately payable-on-demand promissory note secured only by the unregistered stock (referred to as a "secured demand note"), that secured demand note could be included as an asset in calculating net capital—even if the third party had no personal liability for the secured demand note. Magically, more debt in an amount equal to twenty times the value of the illiquid unregistered stock could be taken on by the investment bank. Of course, if the value of the stock subsequently decreased, there was no ability to recover the deficit.[35]

Another way investment banks turned excluded assets into includable ones was by way of the sale and lease-back transaction. A sale and lease-back transaction is essentially a loan secured by assets that are "sold" to the lender. The borrower has a right to take back ownership of the pledged assets once the loan is repaid. Since fixed assets like computers were excluded from the calculation of net capital, the sale of those assets didn't decrease net capital, but the cash received from the sale would increase net capital. And the investment bank would not be required to include all future lease payments as a liability, only one year's lease payments, as the lease was permitted to be accounted for as an operating lease.[36]

The N.Y.S.E., free to interpret Rule 325 as it pleased thanks to John Coleman and the S.E.C. exemption, had by 1967 accumulated a number of additional leverage-increasing permitted practices. One involved subordinated customer accounts. The S.E.C. required that the subordination agreement prohibit the withdrawal by the customer of any cash or securities in its account if the investment bank would fall out of compliance with the net capital rule as a result. The Exchange had no such requirement.

If the books of an investment bank revealed that it owed securities to a customer or other third party, but it did not have in its inventory the securities that it owed (referred to as a "short stock difference"), the S.E.C. required that investment bank to include the value of the securities it owed as a liability. The Exchange in 1967 did not require its members to include short stock differences as a liability unless they had established a reserve for short stock differences. This created the perverse incentive for investment banks to not reserve for these liabilities on their books. During the crisis that followed, when the S.E.C. finally expressed concern that the enormous amount of unaccounted-for customer securities was not being reflected on the books of investment banks, the Exchange decided to allow its members to net "long stock differences," which represent securities in inventory that the investment bank's books indicate it does not rightfully own, against short stock differences. This also created a perverse incentive for investment banks to delay delivering wrongfully held securities to their rightful owners.[37]

Another area of disagreement between the S.E.C. and the N.Y.S.E. involved the treatment of receivables—money owed to the investment bank. The S.E.C. would not allow receivables to be treated as assets in calculating net capital except to the extent the receivable was secured by valuable collateral. The Exchange had no such requirement. To say the Exchange was liberal in allowing the inclusion of receivables with less than certain collectability and value would be an understatement. Tax refunds claimed on tax returns, even if subject to audit, were allowed in full. Insurance claims, even before the insurance company acknowledged coverage, were also allowed in full.[38]

By far the most important differences between the S.E.C.'s and the Exchange's net capital rules arose through the Exchange's granting of exemptions from compliance, usually informally and always confidentially. During the crisis to come, not even a pretense of rationale was maintained. Restricted securities were allowed to be included as assets. Haircuts were reduced or eliminated. Subordinated accounts were allowed to account for more than 25 percent of net capital—in some cases accounting for 100 percent of net capital. And in many instances, when despite all the loopholes and sleight-of-hand, firms could no longer remain in compliance with the net capital rule, the Exchange simply allowed them to continue to operate, hoping their financial condition would improve, because to shut them down would only make matters worse for the Club. Many of the firms in violation were large: given the interconnectedness on Wall Street, their failures would have had systemic consequences for Wall Street and beyond. But the Exchange closing even a small firm was bad for the Wall Street brand and would result in scrutiny of the financial condition of all firms by many prying eyes—of institutional investors, commercial banks that lent them money, the S.E.C., and Congress.

THE AIRING OF dirty laundry was to be avoided. Keith Funston personified this prime directive with his successful handling of the Ira Haupt & Co. collapse. Joseph Meehan's halting the Kennedy assassination market break by going long on RCA stock, despite putting his firm in violation of the net capital rule, reinforced the notion on Wall Street in the 1960s that secrecy and rule-bending weren't necessarily self-serving, but could be in the public interest. The Special Study Report found nothing fundamentally wrong with this status quo. The boom years on Wall Street of 1964 through 1968, unprecedented since the Roaring Twenties, only furthered the absurd overconfidence of the industry. In the unlikely event another firm failed, surely the Exchange's Special Trust Fund could cover any customer losses. So went the complacent thinking at the S.E.C. and in Congress that rationalized the degradation of Rule 325.

Washington, distracted by rioting in the cities and the war in Vietnam, essentially ignored Wall Street after the Special Study Report during the Kennedy and Johnson years. The dominant thinking in Congress was that the Special Study Report had exposed any ills in the securities industry, and the 1964 Securities Act amendments addressed all required legislative actions. The S.E.C. could certainly handle all other issues or concerns. Besides, Wall Street was booming with a raging bull market and exploding trading volume.

As for the capital of Wall Street firms in 1967, there was too little of it, and what little there was could be withdrawn by partners and subordinated lenders in relatively short order if really at risk; and the value of that capital, since so much of it was invested in equity securities, was illusory, for when it was needed most—in a bear market—it would evaporate.

CHAPTER THREE

"THEY DON'T KNOW WHAT MONEY IS; THEY DEAL IN STOCK CERTIFICATES"

■

The Technology Gap on Wall Street in the 1960s

A t the 1933 World's Fair in Chicago, the International Business Machines Corporation (I.B.M.) sponsored a pavilion that displayed the company's wide array of sorting, filing, tabulating, and typing machines, as well as the latest hardware it was developing. One summer day during the fair, a curious young partner from E. A. Pierce & Co., a leading retail brokerage firm, wandered into that pavilion. That partner, Winthrop H. Smith, could take time away from the office that summer as the business of buying and selling securities was practically nonexistent during that worst year of the Great Depression. Applying the latest technology to his business was an obsession of Smith's. E. A. Pierce & Co. was already using I.B.M. tabulating machines, but Smith's eye was caught by the most technologically advanced product on display—an early punchcard computer. Inquiring about the machine's capabilities, Smith was told by the amiable I.B.M. technician that there was no conceivable task for which the computer could be applied to the brokerage business.[1] Smith politely nodded and walked away from the man, knowing he was in the company of a featherbrain. He knew instantly his business would be transformed by the power of that punchcard computer.

Seven years later, E. A. Pierce merged with Merrill Lynch & Co., and Win Smith, by then the right-hand man of Mr. Pierce, would soon become the right-hand man of Charles Merrill in building the world's largest investment bank. All the while, throughout the 1930s and 1940s, Smith kept abreast of the advancements in computer technology. By the early 1950s, mainframe computers were in use, mostly for the Pentagon and Cold War defense industries. These early computers were unreliable, and they were enormous by today's standards. Not only was the hardware itself huge, but the hundreds of thousands of thin cardboard punchcards on which all the data it processed was stored took up a vast amount of square footage. With space in Lower Manhattan office buildings limited and expensive, most operations executives at investment banks balked at integrating mainframe computers into their businesses. They thought the business imperative for such a large investment was many years away. Smith was completely convinced there wasn't a moment to spare.

In 1955, Win Smith established an Electronics Feasibility Committee at Merrill Lynch to figure out how the company's operations throughout its far-flung, multi-office empire could be computerized and centrally controlled.[2] The space problem had by then been solved for those firms with foresight and capital to buy the state-of-art computers, as I.B.M. had developed a replacement for the punchcards. One twelve-inch reel of magnetic tape could store data that previously required 50,000 punchcards. And once built, a well-designed mainframe computer system with magnetic tape could process a million trades a day nearly as easily as a thousand and at practically no incremental expense. The implications of this math, which should have sent shivers up the spines of executives at firms with outdated technology, were ignored by most members of the Club—but not by Win Smith and, therefore, not by Merrill Lynch.

Merrill Lynch had long been the Wall Street firm most attuned to Main Street and least concerned about its popularity at the Exchange. Mr. E. A. Pierce, while a member of the Club, never much cared for its way of thinking. He was among the few Wall Street executives, even among his fellow Democrats, who had supported FDR's securities legislation and governance reforms at the Exchange. Pierce was what was referred to at the Exchange, with a bit of derision, as a "customer's man"—one who made more money from a commission business than proprietary trading or underwriting. Pierce didn't care that his business was thought to be less glamorous and less courageous than those of the risk-taking traders and specialists who dominated the Exchange. Neither he nor Charlie Merrill nor Win Smith cared that their firm's executives were underrepresented on the Exchange's committees. They knew if they had the customers, they would be indispensable in distributing and trading securities. The customer buying power at the other end of the phones of its army of brokers would ultimately bring it the power and status on Wall Street that the old guard had tried so long to deny Merrill Lynch.

The development of magnetic tape meant it was only a matter of time and money. Social connections would be no match for computerized speed and efficiency. The old guard would need to either adapt or die. The mainframe computers would surely continue to get smaller and more powerful. The customization of computer systems for the securities industry and each particular firm would also no doubt improve. When the day of reckoning arrived, those firms that could afford to make the investment in the technology might survive; those that couldn't, wouldn't survive. A star producer can be paid much more at a firm where the variable cost of processing his trades is more cheap rolls of magnetic tape, a rounding error, as opposed to more punchcard operators and clerks to file, and often misfile, cardboard cards. It was a dozen years away, but Win Smith realized consolidation was inevitable for the securities industry.

In 1958, the year Win Smith retired and his name was added to the letterhead, Merrill Lynch, Pierce, Fenner & Smith installed an I.B.M. 705 mainframe computer. The bright-red, L-shaped computer, along with its twenty attendant machines, took up nearly the entire third floor of Merrill Lynch's headquarters at 70 Pine Street in Lower Manhattan. The machine was so heavy that engineers had to retrofit the building's structural supports to handle the additional weight. But tasks that took an hour using the prior system now took seven minutes. Before the I.B.M. 705 was fully operational, Merrill Lynch had already ordered an I.B.M. mainframe in development to replace it, the I.B.M. 7080, to be ready for delivery in 1960. Beginning in the late 1950s, Merrill Lynch became known for the fastest and most accurate trade executions on Wall Street.[3]

MOST OF THE millions of stock trading transactions in the 1960s found their way to the floor of the N.Y.S.E., to the specialist for that particular stock. In the 1960s, the process of effectuating those trades was almost unbelievably labor-intensive when viewed with hindsight from the Internet Age. The foundational technology of corporate ownership—the share certificate—had changed little since the thirteenth century. (The world's oldest known stock certificate, still in existence, is a Swedish document, dated June 16, 1288, written in Latin and representing a one-eighth of a share in a copper mine owned by Bishop Peter Elofsson.)

An individual who wished to buy stock had to open up a brokerage account in person, at the office of a retail brokerage firm. Such a firm was not difficult to find in the 1960s: there were dozens of investment banks with retail brokerage operations in thousands of offices. A salesman—and almost all in those days were male—would ask the questions and fill out the paperwork to open the account. The salesman would likely be young and even more likely inexperienced as turnover among salesmen was high, with the average tenure less than two years. There would be no ability to negotiate the commission paid to effectuate your trade, and no need to comparison shop among brokers, for commissions were set by N.Y.S.E. rule in accordance with a pricing schedule approved by the S.E.C.

Although about a hundred of the larger securities firms had computerized order-taking technology in the mid-1960s, most did not. Accordingly, the salesman typically would make a manual notation of your order and more-or-less simultaneously call in the order to the purchasing department located at the firm's main office. There, the order would be called down to the firm's floor operations manager on the Exchange floor where its telephone operator would manually take down the order and hand it to a floor broker who would execute the trade with the designated specialist.[4]

This is actually a simplified version of how most trades were executed. Often the firm that took the order did not have a floor broker at all and had to fill the trade with another firm that did. As one might expect, errors at one of the many manual or verbal steps along the chain of execution were not uncommon. And the order execution stage of a stock trade was practically foolproof when compared to the transaction settlement process.

After the purchase was made, the Exchange would prepare a written confirmation of the trade—the number of shares, the price, and the settlement date, which was four trading days thereafter (extended to five days in 1967). This confirmation would work its way back in the reverse order of the steps used to execute the trade. Absent an identified error, the broker was obligated to pay for the stock on the settlement date. Ideally, the purchasing broker would also receive a stock certificate representing the shares purchased. But this was often not the case. Instead, the purchasing broker would often receive a promise of delivery of the stock certificate, for the journey of the stock certificate from its seller to its new rightful owner was nearly always circuitous and often plagued by dead ends.

If the seller of shares held them in a margin account, the certificates for the shares would likely be held at the commercial bank in New York that provided credit to the seller's brokerage firm. Instructions would be sent to that commercial bank by the seller's broker to deliver a certificate representing the shares to be sold. A messenger from the seller's broker would pick up the certificate and bring it back to the operations department of the firm. In the secure, gated room where stock certificates were kept—called the cage—stock powers were attached to the certificate along with instructions for the transfer agent appointed by the company whose stock was being sold. Those instructions would ordinarily be to cancel the certificate and issue two new ones: one in the name of the purchaser for the amount of shares it had purchased; the other in the name of the seller's broker for the number of unsold shares represented by the certificate. Another messenger then ran across Lower Manhattan, where nearly all cages and transfer agents were located, delivering the certificates, stock powers, and instructions.

When the new certificates were ready, the transfer agent would call the cage and another messenger would pick them up and bring them back to the cage where they would be checked for accuracy. Assuming all went well on the settlement date, the right certificate would be delivered to the cage of the buyer's broker and the other certificate would be delivered to the cage of the commercial bank that financed the seller's broker.

If the buyer purchased the shares via a margin account, the certificate would be delivered by messenger from the cage of the buyer's broker to the cage of the commercial bank that financed the buyer's broker. If not bought on margin and the buyer chose to have its stock held in "street name," the certificate might remain in the buyer's broker's cage. It might also be delivered by messenger to the cage of a bank or trust company where the broker kept certificates for safekeeping. If the buyer elected to have the certificate in its own name, it would be sent by insured mail to the branch office where the buyer's broker resided. Thereafter, it would either be kept in a vault there for safekeeping or picked up by the buyer and kept in his personal safety deposit box or some other safe place.

In 1967, Keith Funston's last year at the N.Y.S.E., stock certificates took this journey—or likely one more complicated—over 5 million times. On hundreds of thousands of occasions, somewhere along the journey, a certificate made a wrong turn.

Today, nothing about the execution and settlement of a stock trade in the 1960s is recognizable. An account is opened online and funded with an electronic transfer of funds. Trades, too, are executed electronically online, with no human involvement. On settlement, funds likewise flow electronically and there is no movement of any stock certificates. Transfers are recorded by electronic book-entry through the facilities of Depository Trust Company, which directly or through its agents holds virtually all certificates for publicly traded and institutional privately traded securities in the United States in its vaults in Lower Manhattan. The last time the movement of stock certificates was even remotely newsworthy was in 2012 when Hurricane Sandy flooded those vaults, floating many of the 1.3 million certificates stored there.[5]

MERRILL LYNCH'S 1958 mainframe computer was state-of-the-art for months, not years. The frustrating reality of business computing even in the 1960s was that something better—be it a new mainframe or a component or a piece of software—was released monthly by the likes of I.B.M., Honeywell, Remington Rand, Control Data, Burroughs, General Electric, R.C.A. and N.C.R. And most new improvements only worked on the mainframes they were designed for. You could never have the best of everything.

Tom Watson Jr., the chairman and chief executive officer of I.B.M., was as frustrated by this reality as his customers were. In 1962, he made a breathtakingly bold decision that would guarantee the continued dominance of his company in business computing for a generation. At the time, I.B.M. sold a product line of eight computers and was the clear market leader in mainframes. "Fortress I.B.M." was how *Fortune* magazine described its seemingly impregnable dominance that year. Surveying his much-envied empire, Watson decided to trash it all. Scrap it and start over. Watson concluded that key to future success in business computing was compatibility. If the customer upgraded to a new mainframe, the existing peripherals—the monitors, printers, and storage devices—must work on that new mainframe, and upgraded peripherals must work on an old mainframe with modest software revisions.

Watson's answer was the I.B.M. System/360, launched on April 7, 1964. I.B.M. had spent $5 billion (over $30 billion in today's dollars), about as much as was spent on the Manhattan Project, in slightly over two years to develop the product. Compatibility was what was demanded before every one of those dollars could be spent. The System/360 mainframe was faster and more powerful than its predecessors, and real leaps were made in memory and other technologies of computing. The revolution it wrought, however, was in the "open" nature of its software operating system and the forethought of the design of its hardware. Every peripheral I.B.M. developed would thereafter work with every new upgraded mainframe, and vice-versa. The additional code needed for any upgrade of a mainframe or a peripheral, or the addition of an office or new accounting system, would be a fraction of what was required previously. Before the System/360, a company might have one mainframe that handled orders, inventory, and shipping, another that handled billing and receivables, and a third that handled payroll, each from a different manufacturer and none of which "spoke" to each other. That diversity might be duplicated at separate facilities of the same company, particularly in an acquisitive company whose acquired businesses had different systems. With the System/360, systems integration was no longer a years-long capital project.[6]

Wall Street has always highly valued (many say overvalued) the contribution of the individual. Any trader or banker who's lived through one bonus season can tell you how much revenue he or she produced for the firm, what compensation should be paid for that revenue, and what the bank down the street would pay for that production. Most haven't a clue as to the breakdown of expenses that reduce that revenue to profit. That is the realm of lesser species. The names on the letterhead or in the C-suite belong to those who were bold enough to make a bet-the-firm trade and win, those who convinced the corporate titans to let them lead the IPOs, those who invented the junk bond or the syndicated loan or the credit default swap. But over time, what has always differentiated the survivors from the failures has been managing costs and mitigating risks. Systems have always mattered more than superstars.

■ ■ ■

IN TRUTH, TECHNOLOGY existed long before the 1960s to eliminate much of the human labor involved in securities transactions. With the exception of the salesmen taking the orders, there was no technological need for the other steps to be done by human labor—even execution of trades on the floor of an exchange. A few years later, on February 8, 1971, a switch would be turned on a computer in the Trumbull Industrial Park outside Bridgeport, Connecticut, and members of the N.A.S.D. could turn on a desktop computer monitor on their desks and see price quotes for all O.T.C.-traded securities.[7] Executives of the Bunker Ramo Corporation, which built and operated the National Association of Securities Dealers, Inc. Automated Quotations system, or N.A.S.D.A.Q., told the executives of the N.A.S.D. before the system became operational that it would not take much investment to modify the computer's functionality to have it execute trades. The system could easily allow for certificate-less securities, which it would hold and track in electronic form and arrange for the flow of funds on settlement. And settlement could be effectively instantaneous upon the order being placed. The technology for all this existed in 1967. Yet it was not adopted by the securities industry until well into the 1980s.

All of the basic data processes of Wall Street firms of the 1960s—order taking, trade execution, control of cash and credit, movement of securities, and customer control—were widely mismanaged. At most firms, many of these functions were handled by separate computer systems that didn't communicate with each other. Some remained on punchcard systems with others on magnetic tape, and in the more poorly managed, still on a manual input system.[8] Add to the confusion that many branch offices had their own different systems. Contrast this chaos with an I.B.M. System/360 mainframe system where all those functions were fully integrated and coordinated, capable of spitting out reports and analyses of every operational and financial aspect of an investment bank's business. The efficiencies, the lack of errors, the better-informed management decisions would turn revenue into profit faster than the best bankers, salesmen, or traders could get you more revenue. By Memorial Day 1964, more than 2,000 I.B.M. System/360 mainframes had been sold. Most investment banks were not among those customers. Merrill Lynch was.

While a star banker, broker, or trader could not overcome the efficiencies of the new technology, a raging bull market could, at least temporarily. Between 1964 and 1967, trading volume on the N.Y.S.E. would more than double. That enormous increase in commission revenue masked the pain of the technologically obsolete operations systems of most Wall Street firms. But those thinly capitalized firms were unable or unwilling to use their capital to make the investment in technology even during one of the most sustained bull markets in history.

ON SEPTEMBER 12, 1966, Keith Funston summoned the reporters who covered the N.Y.S.E. to a press conference where he announced that he would be stepping down as president of the Exchange upon expiration of his contract the following year.[9] The rumored list of the possible candidates under consideration by the Exchange's board of governors to replace him was long and included former Treasury Secretary Douglas Dillon, Federal Reserve Chairman William McChesney Martin, S.E.C. chairman Manny Cohen, Defense Secretary Robert McNamara, and former vice president Richard Nixon. A search committee of ten influential members of the board of governors was established to choose a replacement by year-end. The search committee included Exchange chairman Walter Frank, vice chairman and Goldman, Sachs managing partner Gus Levy, and Joseph Meehan of M. J. Meehan & Co.[10] On April 25, 1967, the Exchange announced that Robert W. Haack, president of the N.A.S.D., would succeed Funston.[11]

KEITH FUNSTON HAD no illusions regarding the challenges Wall Street would soon face. His responsibility to keep the juggled balls in the air would end in September 1967, but he knew they might drop any day. As the trading volume continued to soar, so did the customer complaints, the employee grievances, and the outlandish stories he knew to be true. They told of stacks of undelivered stock certificates piled to the ceiling in the cages, customer statements with glaring errors month after month, hundreds of proxy cards mistakenly fed into shredders in the rush to create order out of the chaos of the back office. Senior executives of Wall Street firms had lost control of their harried, low-paid, mostly uneducated back-office employees, many of whom had essentially given up on doing their jobs effectively. The runaway trading volume in the Go-Go market of 1967 was overwhelming the long neglected back offices. Failure to invest in technology left them captive to an antiquated system of physical stock certificate deliveries.

The year 1966 had witnessed record trading volume at the N.Y.S.E., an average of 7.5 million shares a day, up from 6.2 million in 1965. Yet industry profit margins had declined, and one of every five member firms actually lost money. This doesn't happen in healthy industries. The break-even N.Y.S.E. daily trading volume for the industry was 5.9 million shares, up from 4.8 million in 1965.[12] Funston knew why. Firms with technologically outdated systems were hiring more salesmen and paying producers more to capture market share so higher volume and revenue would mask increasing costs. By August 1967, N.Y.S.E. volume was averaging 10 million shares a day—but the break-even volume had also risen, to 6.5 million shares per day.

During the first week of August 1967, N.Y.S.E. volume exceeded 12 million shares a day and there was simply no way many firms could dig out of the paper backlog. The lost share certificates and failures to close trades were not only customer relations nightmares. The magnitude of the problem was now a serious financial concern. Unwinding those failed trades and purchasing the securities lost for customers would be so costly that many firms would be in violation of the net capital rule if they were required to accurately account for them. After the close of trading on Monday,

August 7, Funston called an emergency meeting of the board of governors of the Exchange where it was decided that trading sessions would be shortened by ninety minutes for the next four trading days, opening at 10:00 a.m. and closing at 2:00 p.m. to allow the back offices to catch up with the paperwork.[13]

On Wednesday, August 9, Funston convened a meeting of two hundred partners and other top officials of the Exchange membership to brief them on the decision. As for longer-term solutions, Funston proposed recruiting housewives and schoolteachers to work part-time in the back offices and reassigning sales and trading personnel to the back offices until the logjam was broken. During the question-and-answer period, every questioner, after prefacing his question with the assertion that his firm was in very good shape, pointed the finger of blame elsewhere. The small firms blamed the large firms, the large firms blamed the transfer agents, and all firms blamed the non-member O.T.C. dealers.[14] The following day, the Exchange extended the shortened trading days through Friday, August 18.[15] It also mandated that firms keep their cages open until 7:00 p.m. on business days and from 10:00 a.m. to 3:00 p.m. on Saturdays to catch up with the paperwork.

The stark reality that the cathedral of capitalism had fallen into such disrepair that it had to close for business was not enough to awaken Washington to the fact that something was fundamentally broken on Wall Street. The denial was strengthened when it seemed the absurd fix of turning away business was actually working. The trading volume eased during the two weeks of shortened trading days, and normal trading hours resumed on August 21. The last two weeks of August traditionally have substantially lower-than-average trading volume.

ON THE FOURTH day of renewed full trading hours, a dozen young people queued up at the N.Y.S.E.'s entrance at 20 Broad Street waiting to gain access to the Exchange's visitors' gallery on the third floor. The group was eclectically dressed, some in coats and ties, others in the fashionable shabbier dress code of the young in 1967. They were led by a man who identified himself as George Metesky. (This was an alias. The real George Metesky, better known as the "Mad Bomber," terrorized New York City during the 1940s and 1950s by planting thirty-five bombs in busy public places such as Grand Central Station, Port Authority Bus Terminal, and Radio City Music Hall.) Once in the visitors' gallery, the group began throwing handfuls of dollar bills over the railing, raining cash down on the trading floor. The traders, clerks, and runners on the floor looked up, mostly in amusement, but some in annoyance. A few smiled and blew kisses, while others shook their fists or flipped the middle finger. Most in range grabbed at the fluttering currency. It lasted less than a minute before John Whighton, captain of the N.Y.S.E. security force, ejected the motley crew back to the Broad Street sidewalk. Waiting for them outside was a large contingent of reporters.

The press had been alerted cryptically the night before that a demonstration of some sort would be occurring at the Exchange that day. The *New York Times,* the *Daily News,* the *New York Post,* and the local television news divisions had all sent reporters to the Exchange to see what might unfold. They were expecting another of the increasingly frequent protests against the war in Vietnam.

"We just want to make a loving gesture to these people," one of the ejected young men declared. "They don't know what money is; they deal in stock certificates." James Fourrat, the real name of the "George Metesky" ringleader, explained to the press the purpose of the episode: "It's the death of money. This is a paradise, earth. There's enough for all." A middle-aged woman visiting from Warren, Ohio, curious as to what the fuss was about, walked away after hearing Fourrat's explanation, telling the *New York Times* reporter, "I think they're nuts."

Nearby, another group of young people joined hands and skipped in a circle chanting "Free, free, free." One of those holding hands and skipping was a particularly attractive young blonde woman, twenty-one-year-old Candice Bergen, dabbling in radical left politics whenever her modeling and acting career allowed her the time. In the middle of that circle was Fourrat's right-hand man in the mischief, a long-haired thirty-year-old named Abbot Howard Hoffman. Hoffman was holding high in the air a $5 bill he had set ablaze. This was too much for one runner from the Exchange, who barged into the circle, slugged Abbie Hoffman, grabbed the blazing bill from his hand, and stomped out the fire.[16] The Summer of Love had found its way to the N.Y.S.E.

BY THE EARLY 1960S, the N.Y.S.E. knew that continued reliance on the physical delivery of stock certificates was irresponsible. Before 1967, no one knew exactly what the breaking point of the securities settlement infrastructure was. It became clear that year that a sustained N.Y.S.E. daily volume of 9 million shares, together with the associated volume on the AMEX and the O.T.C. market, would exceed its capacity. As recently as 1964, volume had averaged less than 5 million shares a day. In 1967, it was double that. That wasn't predicted to happen until the mid-1970s.[17]

The N.Y.S.E. began planning for immobilization of the stock certificate in 1962. What was clear from the start was that a massive investment in computer technology by the N.Y.S.E. and its members would be required to accomplish this. There would also be a time-consuming and expensive legal process to change laws to recognize ownership of stock, not only through possession of a certificate, but by means of a computer "book-entry" that said one owned the stock. Corporations are creatures of state, not federal, law, so changing how ownership of them is legally recognized required a fifty-state lobbying effort. Not only would states need to amend their corporate statutes, but also each state's Uniform Commercial Code in order to permit the pledging of securities owned in book-entry form to lenders, so critical to the functioning of markets where securities were purchased with borrowed money. Because it was not a simple and inexpensive matter, it was not prioritized by the Exchange.

Once the legal impediments were removed, the next obvious issue was who in the new book-entry world would control the "books." Under the physical certificate regime, this function was dispersed: each company's transfer agent kept the records of share ownership for that company. Because most stock transactions took place on the N.Y.S.E., most transfer agents were banks and trust companies with offices in Lower Manhattan (in fact, the listing requirements of the N.Y.S.E required listed companies to have a transfer agent located in Manhattan). The N.Y.S.E. had an answer as to who would serve the "transfer agent" function for book-entry transfers: it would. The problem was that no other affected constituency trusted the Exchange to do the job effectively.

WITH BACK OFFICES in disarray, Robert Haack made the elimination of the physical stock certificate his top priority as the new president of the N.Y.S.E.[18] At the time of Haack's arrival, the official in charge of this effort was Edward C. Gray, the executive vice president of the Exchange. Gray, then sixty-five years old, had been with the Exchange since 1918 and had planned to retire with Funston's exit. Haack begged him to stay until the Exchange's book-entry facilities were ready to open for business. What Gray had to say to Haack, Haack did not want to hear. Despite the lip service the Club paid to the effort—named the Central Certificate Service or "C.C.S."—it was a long way from being operational, and it was, without participation by the other exchanges, the O.T.C. market makers, and the commercial banks, at best a half-measure.

The C.C.S. contemplated the formation of a new company, owned by the Exchange, to which all Exchange members would transfer each of their share certificates. In exchange they would receive computer book-entry interests in a single stock certificate for each listed security (a "global certificate") registered in the name of and held by C.C.S. All transactions by members in N.Y.S.E.-listed stocks would be settled by a debit/credit on their accounts as reflected in the computer records of C.C.S. As planned, C.C.S.

would eliminate the physical transfer of stock certificates, and the system could easily handle daily volumes in the hundreds of millions (and possibly billions) of shares.

Gray told Haack of the enormous cost of implementing C.C.S.—at least $1 billion. Gray had the foresight to invest the Exchange's money in I.B.M. System/360 mainframes for C.C.S., so at least its computers would be able to communicate with other I.B.M. System/360 mainframes.[19] But Exchange members used a hodgepodge of computer systems. Developing the software to allow all these computer systems to "talk" with the C.C.S. I.B.M. System/360 mainframes would cost a fortune, more than the entire computer systems budgets of many Exchange members, and more than the net capital of some of them. And unlike opening a branch office or hiring a star broker or investment banker, there was no immediate payoff to the bottom lines of the members by implementing C.C.S. Why spend in 1964 for infrastructure that likely wouldn't be needed until 1974?

It wasn't just the cost that put off the Club. The transfer agents were most often New York commercial banks and trust companies with a lot of commission dollars to throw around. They were the same folks who executed billions of dollars of stock and bond transactions every year on behalf of their clients—pension funds, college endowments, trust funds of wealthy families. These banks and trust companies were not at all happy at the thought of all those transfer agent fees migrating from them to the Exchange. They could threaten to move business from any investment bank pushing hard for C.C.S. But in reality, they didn't really need to be heavy-handed. All the commercial banks and trust companies needed to do was to insist on holding their stocks and bonds in physical form, which is what they did. And not just the securities they or their customers owned. Since these institutions provided credit and cash management services to most of the large mutual funds and hedge funds, they had the power to require those securities, ordinarily pledged as collateral to them, to be held in physical form by them. These were also the same institutions that provided credit to the Exchange members themselves. There were plenty of reasons to convince the Club to leave well enough alone. So it was left alone.

Even if all these impediments were surmounted, the Exchange had no jurisdiction over securities listed on the AMEX or regional exchanges or traded in the O.T.C. market. Only Congress or the S.E.C. could have compelled the financial industry as a whole to move to C.C.S. or something similar. But the Special Study Report didn't recommend that, and the Johnson administration had enough on its plate with civil rights, urban unrest, and Vietnam. It had no appetite to alienate Wall Street, with the rising stock market one of the few bright spots during a troubled time.

C.C.S.'s computer operations were located at 44 Broad Street, one block away from the Exchange. After taking stock of things there, Haack held a press conference his first week on the job announcing his commitment to make it a reality: "I'm reluctant to pinpoint a starting date for C.C.S. because of the problems involved. But we hope we'll be able to do something constructive in early 1968."[20]

Edward Gray had never worked anywhere but the N.Y.S.E. As a high school dropout, he started as a stenographer, and rose to the number two job at the Exchange. At first blush, he was an odd choice to the lead the technology modernization effort. But in truth he was the perfect man for the job. As a symbol of the old school—he had known most of the key members of the Exchange like John Coleman and Joseph Meehan since they were practically boys and also knew many of their fathers—he aroused little suspicion of radical change. The decisions he made in the early days of C.C.S. were sound, and none was sounder than his choice of a successor. Most expected Gray to recommend an Exchange oldtimer to Haack to succeed him as executive vice president. With Haack himself an outsider, it was thought that an insider, a pleasant, amiable, familiar face, would smooth the transition. Gray took the completely opposite tack. He recommended not only an outsider, but one never described as pleasant or amiable.

R. John Cunningham was a forty-one-year-old Irish Catholic from Detroit who put himself through the University of Notre Dame working a punch press at the local Studebaker plant. Before joining the Midwest Stock Exchange as its operations chief in 1962, Cunningham had been a management consultant with Arthur Young & Co. and had held executive positions in the electronics, automotive, brass, and public utilities industries. When he arrived at the Exchange as the new executive vice president in January 1968, the six-foot tall, two-hundred-pound bear of a man spent little time ingratiating himself to the old-timers. Chain-smoking three packs of Lucky Strikes a day, the gruff Cunningham drove himself and all around him relentlessly to implement C.C.S. before the next spike in trading volume overwhelmed the already-clogged plumbing on Wall Street.[21]

In addition to pushing ahead aggressively with C.C.S. in the fall of 1967, Haack extended the securities settlement period from four trading days to five, thereby allowing for a weekend over which all trades could be processed. At first, N.Y.S.E. trading volume stabilized at around 10 million shares a day in September and October, already too many for the back offices to handle. But it rose during November and even more sharply in December, to an average of 11.5 million shares per day. During the holiday season, back-office workers were more reluctant to work overtime. Absenteeism in the back offices ran higher than 20 percent. The number of failed trades in December rose an astonishing 40 percent.

The breaking point had been reached. The paperwork backlog had moved past crisis proportions into the catastrophic. The expansion of sales forces and rich marketing budgets of the prior four years had gunned the engine to full throttle. The S.E.C. and Congress had kept all the lights green. Now, the car was about to hit a brick wall. In his newly renovated office, Robert Haack had a palpable sense of foreboding about 1968.

PART II

1968

The Year It All Fell Apart

CHAPTER FOUR

"TROUBLE COMES ALONG THE LINE"

◼

Tet, Assassinations, and Riots— Nothing Stops the Paper

I t was the year everything came apart in America. Wall Street was no exception. Its unraveling took place alongside the death and tragedy and lost promise of Martin Luther King, Robert F. Kennedy, and the 16,899 young Americans who would die that year in Vietnam. The financial world's havoc was an exhibition of a preposterous irony. The failure of some of its largest firms, and many times that number of smaller firms—more in total than the number that failed during the Great Depression—was not precipitated by collapsing stock prices and evaporating business. The carnage was caused by the greatest bull market since the Roaring Twenties— record stock prices, soaring volume, a hot IPO market, and a swashbuckling mergers and acquisition wave. It should have been the best of times. It was all obliterated by the paper.

In cages of the investment banks all over Lower Manhattan, the backlog of unprocessed stock transfers grew to dangerous and comical proportions. Stacks of stock certificates—literally from the floor to the ceiling—were piled on every available square foot of floor space. In many instances, the shares represented by those unprocessed stacks of certificates would be traded again—sometimes multiple times—before the new owner could even obtain the certificate.

Obsolete computer systems at many of those investment banks lost control of the inventory of the firm's and its customers' securities. Shares would be entered as sold in the system before a customer's purchase of those shares was reflected. The computer system would treat it as a short sale—improperly charging the customer a stock borrowing fee. Physical order slips were lost. Shares were credited— and debited—to the wrong customers. Customers who never bought the shares credited to them were charged margin loans, as cash was never deposited for the erroneous purchase. The customer who actually bought the shares fumed that his account didn't reflect the purchase. Quite often the missing shares couldn't be located. All these mistakes cost the investment bank money: improper interest and fees had to be refunded; the proper customer couldn't be charged those loans or fees until the error was corrected; and when missing shares couldn't be located, they had to be purchased again with the firm's money. Millions of these and other errors occurred in 1968. Thousands of customers complained to the N.Y.S.E. and the S.E.C.

As the mountains of unprocessed and misplaced paper in the back offices of Wall Street grew during 1968, the demands for intervention from Washington grew. The era of light-touch regulation ended. The S.E.C. brought a slew of enforcement actions against the investment banks and demanded the N.Y.S.E. and the other self-regulatory bodies discipline members who failed to maintain control of their operations. The U.S. Department of Justice pressured both the S.E.C. and the N.Y.S.E. to end the most anticompetitive practice in the securities industry—the fixed commission. To stave off a worse outcome, the Exchange reduced rates just as a bear market was taking hold. The result was plummeting revenues at the worst possible time.

THE PRESSURE ON the N.Y.S.E. to reform its fixed commission structure had been growing for nearly five years. As the volume of institutional block trading increased over the 1960s, the windfall profits accruing to N.Y.S.E. members on block trades became absurdly out of balance with the actual cost of executing these trades. Institutional investors, well aware of this, were not going to simply shrug their shoulders and watch the Club fleece them. Mutual fund managers developed the mechanism of the give-up to recapture a portion of the windfall. Fund managers directed their brokers to pay a portion of the excessive fixed commission on a trade to other N.Y.S.E. members who provided unrelated services such as research or, more often, who aggressively sold shares of their funds. These give-ups, which typically involved over 50 percent of the commission on each trade, raised two troubling issues for the S.E.C. First, they indicated that the commission rates approved by the S.E.C. were excessive (how else could firms afford to be kicking back a majority of the commission?). Second, the benefit of the give-up was going to the fund managers, not the investors in their funds.

Federal antitrust law was also evolving during the 1960s, with private litigants trying to get the courts to pare back the N.Y.S.E.'s antitrust exemption. In 1963, the N.Y.S.E. lost a U.S. Supreme Court decision that paved the way for direct legal challenges to fixed commissions. The case cost the N.Y.S.E. and its members millions to defend and settle. (Ironically, the N.Y.S.E. could have settled the seminal 1963 case prior to its appeal to the Supreme Court for $75,000. Its refusal of that offer—an epic blunder—wasn't openly discussed, for it was John Coleman who dictated that lamentable decision.)

The seemingly petty bullying by the N.Y.S.E. of Harold Silver of Municipal Securities Co. in Dallas, Texas, a bit player in municipal bonds and bank stocks, would prove to be the proximate cause of the end of fixed commissions. It all began in February 1959, when for reasons still not known, the N.Y.S.E. decided to ban its members from dealing with Municipal Securities Co. and remove its access to the N.Y.S.E. ticker.[1] No reason was given, either to Harold Silver or to the members of the N.Y.S.E. that dealt with him. Silver decided to sue. He claimed that the N.Y.S.E. had no right to engage in concerted action—a boycott—to prevent its members from doing business with him. It was, Silver claimed, an illegal restraint of trade and therefore a violation of the antitrust laws. For two years, the case dragged on in the U.S. District Court for the Southern District of New York. In June 1961, Judge Frederick van Pelt Bryan handed down his decision: the N.Y.S.E. had violated the Sherman Antitrust Act.[2]

The Exchange appealed, arguing that as a regulatory body its actions were exempt from the antitrust laws. In April 1962, the Court of Appeals for the Second Circuit reversed the District Court ruling by a two-to-one vote, granting the Exchange a broad antitrust exemption. The Second Circuit Court of Appeals held that as a self-regulatory body under the aegis of the S.E.C. and authorized by the Securities Exchange Act of 1934, the rules of the N.Y.S.E. were given the force of law and could not be stricken down by private plaintiffs under a restraint of trade antitrust claim.[3]

It was at this point that John Coleman made his grave error. Shortly after the Second Circuit decision, Harold Silver died and Municipal Securities Co. went out of business, leaving behind enormous legal bills. Silver's widow, Evelyn Silver, initially had no desire to continue the fight. Silver's lawyer, David Shapiro of Dickstein, Shapiro and Galligan, approached A. Donald MacKinnon of Milbank, Tweed, Hadley & McCloy, the Exchange's law firm, offering to settle the case if the Exchange would pick up Silver's legal expenses of $75,000. MacKinnon thought it was a great deal—locking in a favorable Court of Appeals ruling and avoiding the risk of losing an appeal at the liberal Warren Supreme Court, not to mention forgoing the expenses of that appeal, which would cost the Exchange at least $75,000. MacKinnon recommended the settlement to the board of governors. John Coleman exploded. He declared that the N.Y.S.E. would never pay Harold Silver, his widow, or David Shapiro a cent. They were stick-up artists, scoundrels, as far as John Coleman was concerned.[4] Evelyn Silver, herself a lawyer, emboldened by the Exchange's arrogance and a faith in the Warren Court, filed an appeal on May 31, 1962.

On May 20, 1963, the Supreme Court reversed the Second Circuit Court of Appeals by a lopsided vote of seven to two. It held that the Exchange's antitrust exemption was very limited, extending only to formal regulations that are clearly in furtherance of the policies manifest in the Securities Exchange Act of 1934 and that are adopted with due process. Yanking Harold Silver's ticker with no explanation fell far short of the mark, in the Court's opinion.[5]

The Silver decision meant that a wide swath of N.Y.S.E. practices and prohibitions were open for attack in the courts on antitrust grounds. These included the fixing of commission rates, the rules against dealing in listed securities off the Exchange floor, denying membership to mutual funds, and prohibiting public ownership of members. The S.E.C. and the Justice Department could no longer ignore the monopolistic behavior of the Club. They would slowly but consistently chip away at these practices for the next dozen years, and the Exchange would fight a rearguard battle, unsuccessfully trying to hold on to the prerogatives of the Club.

Robert Haack, in his position as president of the N.Y.S.E., paid a courtesy call to the S.E.C. in Washington on December 4, 1967. During that meeting, Haack acknowledged that the Exchange needed to present a proposal reforming the fixed commission regime, which hadn't been changed since 1958.[6] It had been three years since the last serious discussions between the S.E.C. and the Exchange regarding rate reform. (Those discussions had gone nowhere as the Club would not entertain a meaningful volume discount.)

On January 2, 1968, Haack, together with Exchange chairman Gus Levy, the Goldman, Sachs & Co. senior partner, traveled to Washington to submit the Exchange's new commission rate plan.[7] It contemplated a volume discount on large trades and a percentage cap on the portion of commissions allowed to be subject to a give-up. It also allowed for non-member brokers to share a third of the commission on N.Y.S.E. trades.[8] Eugene Rotberg, chief counsel for the S.E.C.'s Office of Policy Planning, who had authored much of the Special Study Report's sections dealing with fixed commissions, was the S.E.C.'s point person on those issues.

Unimpressed with the Exchange's plan, Rotberg and Manny Cohen decided to turn up the heat on the Exchange in order to expedite a satisfactory outcome on a new commission rate regime. That heat came in the form of a proposed Rule 10b-10, drafted by Rotberg and publicly proposed two weeks later. The rule would make it illegal for a mutual fund manager or other institutional investor acting in a fiduciary capacity to direct a give-up unless the benefit of that give-up directly accrued to the investors in the fund making the relevant trade. This, of course, would outlaw directing give-up dollars to reward firms for selling mutual fund shares, the largest recipients of give-ups. Rotberg knew that institutional investors would never stand for the current high fixed commissions absent the give-up. As a result, the N.Y.S.E. would need to lower its rates or the institutional business would go to the Third Market or the regional exchanges. Proposed Rule 10b-10 was a blunt instrument—the end of give-ups would hurt many small firms for whom mutual fund sales and issuing research in exchange for give-up dollars generated a large portion of their revenues. Those small firms generally were not members of the N.Y.S.E.[9]

As the battle lines over fixed commissions were being drawn that January, the bull market on Wall Street continued and the back-office situation grew worse.

DURING THE FIRST eight trading sessions of 1968, volume on the N.Y.S.E. skyrocketed to over 12,750,000 shares per day, with the number of undelivered stock certificates growing at an alarming rate. The immediate response of many firms was to hire more employees for their back offices as inexpensively as possible, often entry-level, inexperienced workers to staff second shifts, and in some cases third shifts. Some kept their back offices operating twenty-four hours a day to try and keep up with the paperwork. As usual, Merrill Lynch was ahead of the curve. It had already implemented a plan to hire retired Merrill Lynch employees with years of experience and good work records to bolster its back office.[10]

At other firms, the new employees for the back offices were hired with less forethought. Hayden, Stone hired a hundred U.S. Coast-Guardsmen for weekend shifts. Shields & Company hired almost the entire senior class of a local parochial school. Many of the newcomers were young people with no intention of making the back office their life's work. The tension between the newcomers and the old-timers was palpable and open: "All they talk about is sports and gossip," one newcomer told the *New York Times*, "like inmates of an old-age home. . . . Actually, they think we're here for a visit and goof off, leaving us to do the work. They sure are experts in goofing off. They know every trick."

There were no criminal background checks before hiring. There were no drug tests.[11] Both likely would have prevented some very bad hires that contributed to the misery to come. But so desperate had the paperwork crisis become, avoiding delay in adding bodies to the back-office workforce trumped discernment in hiring practices.

By mid-January, with trading volume rising to nearly 14 million shares a day, the board of governors of the Exchange voted to implement a four-hour trading day, 10:00 a.m. to 2:00 p.m., effective January 22.[12] The AMEX and the regional exchanges immediately followed suit.[13] Again, the best minds on Wall Street had no better answer than to close up shop early.

The shortened trading days gave time off to most of the front-office employees of the investment banks, but not the beleaguered back-office employees. They continued to labor overtime and on weekend shifts. Merrill Lynch again was an exception. It required even high-ranking executives to pitch in after-hours to assist the back-office staff in keeping ahead of the crush of paper—and Merrill Lynch's back office was the best run on Wall Street.

The shortened trading sessions seemed to have the intended effect. By January 31, volume on the Exchange was down to 9.4 million shares, the lowest of the year. That night, events half a world away would shock the markets and continue to dampen the volume of trading—at least for a time.

DURING THE NIGHT of January 31, 1968, tens of thousands of Viet Cong communist guerrillas assisted by their comrades from North Vietnam began a coordinated attack on the major cities of South Vietnam in violation of a truce negotiated for the Lunar New Year, Tet in Vietnamese. That the communists were able to attack every major city in South Vietnam during the Tet offensive— not that they had been repulsed and suffered extremely heavy casualties—dominated the headlines in American newspapers. Most Americans concluded that their leaders in Washington had not leveled with them, and they were not happy about that.

On the morning after the Tet offensive began, Richard Nixon and a young aide, Patrick Buchanan, quietly took a flight to Boston's Logan Airport, where they were met by another Nixon aide, Nick Rowe, who drove the men to a motel in Nashua, New Hampshire. Nixon had preregistered under a pseudonym, "Benjamin Chapman." In the motel room, Nixon signed the papers that would be filed in Concord the next morning, the deadline to enter the state's Republican presidential primary. Nixon formally announced his candidacy that day. A smiling photo of Nixon appeared on the front page of the February 2 edition of the *New York Times* next to Associated Press photographer Eddie Adams's iconic photo of South Vietnamese Brigadier General Nguyen Ngoc Loan putting a slug from his .38-caliber revolver into the head of Viet Cong captain Nguyen Van Lem.[14] The contrast—Nixon, the throwback to the simpler days of Ike's America, versus the murder, mayhem, and chaos of the LBJ administration—would define Nixon's 1968 campaign.

MANNY COHEN AT the S.E.C. at first believed the paperwork issues were a temporary glitch that the N.Y.S.E. would soon rectify. Robert Haack did nothing to dissuade Cohen of this belief.

Cohen's primary concern was that the S.E.C. was a trick behind when it came to the games mutual fund managers were playing with their investors' money. Cohen wanted to fire a shot across the bow of the investment management industry. In a blockbuster announcement on February 9, the S.E.C. told the press that it was bringing charges for violations of the Investment Company Act against Roy M. Cohn, the controversial prosecutor of Julius and Ethel Rosenberg and former chief counsel to the disgraced senator Joseph McCarthy.[15] As perhaps the most controversial lawyer in the world, anything involving Roy Cohn was sure to attract headlines, which was exactly what Manny Cohen wanted. Nothing would better announce the S.E.C.'s new "get tough" enforcement policy regarding investment manager abuses than going after a household name, especially a person as known for guts and guile as Roy Cohn.

The suit involved the use of funds of Fifth Avenue Coach Lines, Inc., formerly the operator of a number of bus lines in New York, but at the time in possession of a large pile of cash and securities since the City of New York took its assets by condemnation years earlier in midst of a labor dispute. The S.E.C. declared the company to be an "investment company" under the federal securities laws, essentially a mutual fund owned by its shareholders. As an investment company, transactions with company insiders required prior S.E.C. approval. The S.E.C. in its complaint alleged that Fifth Avenue Coach Lines entered into many such transactions without S.E.C. approval. It was seeking to have a receiver appointed to protect shareholders from the defendants' illegal self-dealing and to enjoin them from future violations of the securities laws.

The S.E.C. suing Roy Cohn was a surprise, particularly since Cohn was neither an officer nor a director of Fifth Avenue Coach Lines. He was the company's outside counsel, but the S.E.C. alleged in the suit that he in fact controlled the company. It was a rather extraordinary assertion by the S.E.C. since Cohn owned a very small interest in the company. But Roy Cohn was no ordinary outside counsel.

Commenting on the S.E.C. suit, Cohn told the press: "Today, twenty-four hours after I had the temerity to criticize this government agency, they cited me for the first time in their four-month-old lawsuit. This is a thinly veiled message to every attorney in the United States: Keep your mouth shut about the S.E.C. or you will get in trouble."[16] So began a three-year-long odyssey in U.S. Federal Court for Roy Cohn. Against all odds, Cohn would emerge from the ordeal even more formidable than before it began.

THROUGHOUT FEBRUARY, continuing pessimism over the war in Vietnam restrained trading volume. In addition, the shortened trading days, the new T+5 settlement period, the hiring binge, and lengthened back-office shifts had slowed the rate of failed trades. Unresolved failed trades had fallen from over 3 million immediately prior to the implementation of shortened trading days to less than 2 million total. For many firms, however, too much damage had already been done.

The February reprieve came too late for Pickard & Co. Inc., a retail brokerage house owned and run by two brothers, John and Peter Pickard. The firm had racked up a troublingly long list of regulatory infractions given its relatively small size—only five branch offices and 3,500 accounts. Throughout 1967, Pickard's back office fell more and more behind in its paperwork. When its auditors arrived to begin work on its 1967 annual financial statements in early February, the back office was so out of control that the auditors came to the conclusion that they would be unable to express an opinion on the accuracy of the firm's financial statements.

The N.Y.S.E. was notified of this and sent twenty staff members to Pickard to evaluate the situation and help clean up the mess. The Exchange quickly saw all it needed to.[17] On February 19, 1968, Pickard was ordered by the Exchange to cease business immediately and liquidate, making the firm the first casualty of the back-office crisis. This brought the S.E.C. onto the scene. Their staff uncovered that the Pickard brothers had unlawfully withdrawn $600,000 of the firm's capital. This earned them a lifetime ban from the securities industry. The firm's creditors would lose over

$2 million, and the N.Y.S.E. Special Trust Fund was tapped to make whole Pickard's customers, the first use of the Special Trust Fund since the Salad Oil Scandal took down Ira Haupt & Co.[18]

The lesson those outside the Club took from the Pickard debacle was exactly the one Robert Haack had hoped they would: the N.Y.S.E. had zero tolerance for operating unsafely. Insolvent member firms would be promptly shut down, liquidated, and their customers unharmed. The actual practices of the Exchange in such matters were far more complicated. There was one set of rules for systemically unimportant firms—and those unpopular with the old guard—and another for those too big or too favored to fail. Because Pickard had always been poorly run and insignificant, the Exchange acted quickly and unemotionally to shut it down. There were other firms with profound operational problems that were not shut down. The S.E.C., once informed that the Exchange's Special Trust Fund would make Pickard's customers whole, had no interest in digging into the situation any deeper. Congress was preoccupied with developments in Vietnam and expressed no interest at all in Pickard's failure.

By the end of February, Robert Haack was convinced it was safe to resume normal trading hours. The board of governors of the Exchange approved the resumption of normal trading hours beginning March 4.[19] At the end of March, that decision appeared to have been a sound one. The last nine trading days of the month saw not a single day with more than 10 million shares traded, and three days with fewer than 8 million shares traded. Many at the Exchange thought the worst of the back-office crisis had passed.

But again, the outside events of 1968 would intervene to upend Wall Street.

RICHARD NIXON WON the New Hampshire primary on March 12 with 77.6 percent of the vote, trouncing Nelson Rockefeller who polled at 10.8 percent. President Johnson won the New Hampshire primary on the Democratic side with 50 percent of the vote. Johnson's challenger, Minnesota senator Eugene McCarthy, running on a peace platform, garnered a surprising 42 percent of the vote. Four days after the New Hampshire primary, New York senator Robert Kennedy entered the presidential race. On the evening of Sunday, March 31, President Johnson gave the rambling forty-minute televised speech announcing that he would stop the bombing of North Vietnam if Hanoi would agree to immediate substantive peace talks. At the end of the speech, he announced he would not seek reelection.

THE DAY AFTER LBJ threw in the towel, markets roared with approval on the hope of peace. The trading volume on the N.Y.S.E. exceeded 17.7 million shares, surpassing a record that had stood for over thirty-eight years, set on Black Tuesday. At 3:13 p.m., when the record was broken, it was announced over the Exchange's public address system, and the brokers and traders on the floor let out an enormous roar. When trading ended, confetti was thrown in the air like a ticker-tape parade. The scene was captured by television cameras and photographers, leading the evening news and the headlines in the next morning's papers.[20]

Two days later, another record was set: over 19 million shares were traded. There would not be a day with fewer than 10 million shares traded until August. Any hope that the back offices might have breathing room to work their way out of the paperwork backlog evaporated. For the press and the public, it was all smiles and cheers. In the boardrooms and the back offices, there was abject panic. There was simply no way to manage this volume of paper. If 10 million share volume days blew up Pickard & Co., 19 million share volume days would soon fell more substantial firms.

In addition to the market euphoria over the possibility of an end to the war in Vietnam, a phenomenon of excess from earlier in the decade had reemerged: the new issue craze, this time fueled by the easy money, guns-and-butter fiscal policies of the LBJ administration. The number of IPOs for the first three months of 1968 was more than double those in the same period in 1967. There were

236 IPOs during the first three months of 1968, nearly four each trading day, and over half of that total came out during the relative quiet of March. Many of the new issues doubled in price on their first day of trading. Advanced Computer Techniques Corporation went public at $7.50 per share and closed that day at $29.00. This phenomenon brought publicity and the dream of quick riches to undisciplined retail investors. Accordingly, the IPO stocks changed hands frequently, adding disproportionately to the increase in trading volume in April. The churning of these hot issues—many of them O.T.C. stocks whose market makers were in possession of the most dilapidated back offices—during the spring and summer added to the already crushing volume and operational chaos. Asked about the record number of new issues at a press conference, S.E.C. chairman Manny Cohen commented that "when turbulent activity is unrelated to the fundamentals, trouble comes along the line."[21] He would be proven right.

In response to the explosion in trading volume, Robert Haack joined with the chief executives of the ten largest commercial banks of the New York Clearing House Association to develop an industrywide effort to address the crisis. John Cunningham and Henry J. Rolf, senior vice president of the Morgan Guaranty Trust Company of New York, were appointed co-chairs of a committee that included representatives of fifty-six commercial banks and investment banks. They divided the group into five joint committees: securities deliveries, transfer procedures, securities collateral, credit, and uniform securities identification. In all, the committees were tasked to address seventeen defined topic areas.[22]

There would be little disagreement between Cunningham and Rolf in identifying the problems or the actions necessary to address them. The most desperately needed action was getting C.C.S. operational, but that would require time. At the then-current trading volume, they had no time. The most pressing concerns the commercial bankers had was whether Cunningham, whom they all respected and trusted, could deliver the support of the board of governors of the Exchange and its members for an agreed plan of action for the rapid rollout of C.C.S.—and whether the hundreds of investment banks had management competent enough to execute on such plan. Cunningham quietly shared those same concerns.

THE DAY AFTER the Exchange's first 19 million share day, four days after President Johnson quit the race, civil rights leader Reverend Martin Luther King was in Memphis, Tennessee, to support a sanitation workers strike. Just after 6:00 p.m., he stepped outside on to the balcony outside his room, No. 306, on the second floor of the Lorraine Motel to head to a dinner with colleagues. Moments later, a bullet ripped through his jaw and severed his spinal cord and jugular vein. King never regained consciousness, and was pronounced dead at 7:05 p.m.

Soon after news of King's assassination was made public, the rioting began. Washington, D.C., was first. There, rioting and looting would continue for five days, with an estimated 20,000 people taking part. Nearly 14,000 federal troops were sent in to restore order. In Chicago, the rioting and burning started the day after the assassination on April 5 and continued for three days. New York City saw rioting and looting in Harlem and sections of Brooklyn. Dozens of other cities saw violence as well.

DURING THAT FIRST week in April that began with the record-breaking day of euphoria on the Exchange floor and ended with violent protests over King's assassination, the Antitrust Division of the U.S. Department of Justice filed with the S.E.C. in Washington, D.C., a sixty-seven-page comment letter, in the form of a legal brief, ostensibly providing comments on the S.E.C.'s proposed Rule 10b-10 restricting give-ups. It did not discuss the advisability of the S.E.C.'s rule proposal in any direct, substantive manner. Instead, it made a clear and cogent argument that the setting of fixed commission rates, a core economic term of the securities industry since the Buttonwood Tree Agreement established the N.Y.S.E. in

1792, was an illegal price-fixing scheme.[23] In its comment letter, the Justice Department urged the S.E.C. to hold public hearings on the legality of fixed commissions, the reasonableness of the current rate structure, and the interconnection of fixed commissions with other anticompetitive practices of the N.Y.S.E. It assumed that those hearings would also look into N.Y.S.E. Rule 394, which prohibited Exchange members from trading in Exchange-listed securities with brokers who were not Exchange members, as well as the N.Y.S.E.'s prohibition on institutional investors becoming members of the Exchange.[24]

The Department of Justice was not satisfied with the pace of change the S.E.C. had in mind regarding fixed commissions, notwithstanding proposed Rule 10b-10. While Manny Cohen was certainly in favor of changes at the N.Y.S.E., the Department of Justice was not so sure about the other four S.E.C. commissioners. The N.Y.S.E. had submitted its own comment letter in opposition to proposed Rule 10b-10, claiming the rule would splinter primary markets and impair trade execution to the disadvantage of investors, result in "destructive price competition," limit the flexibility of fund managers, and disadvantage small, regional investment banks. The Department of Justice was concerned that those other four S.E.C. commissioners might find these arguments persuasive, kill the proposed rule, and leave everyone back at square one.[25]

The Exchange, with the acquiescence of the S.E.C., had long taken the legal position that fixed commissions were a necessary feature of self-regulation, and that self-regulation by the Exchange was embedded in and integral to the Securities Exchange Act of 1934. Accordingly, the N.Y.S.E. will still asserting, notwithstanding the *Silver* decision, it had an antitrust exemption when it came to the fixing of commission rates. This assertion had never before been formally challenged by any official government action. But with that comment letter, while not binding on anyone, the Department of Justice was announcing it wasn't buying it anymore. Choosing an S.E.C. rule-making approval process as the forum in which to raise its objection was as unusual as it was brilliant.

The Justice Department was making sure the political hot potato stayed in the lap of the S.E.C. Those S.E.C. commissioners who had no stomach for taking on the N.Y.S.E. over the issue had a compelling argument: if the Department of Justice thought that fixed commissions were an antitrust violation, it ought to file a lawsuit asserting so. In truth, the Justice Department did not relish the idea of suing the N.Y.S.E., and it was doubtful President Johnson would have approved of such a lawsuit being filed. But forcing the S.E.C. to address the issue might prompt regulatory action to weaken and ultimately eliminate the fixed commission regime, a victory as far as the Justice Department was concerned. For years the S.E.C. had been uncomfortable with industry practices on give-ups. There were other widespread seedy practices as well. The S.E.C. had caught wind of one investment bank that held a party for its large institutional trading clients and auctioned off call girls to the highest bidders in give-up dollars. The Justice Department had just given the S.E.C. enormous leverage to convince the Club that voluntary reform of fixed commission practices was the wisest path.

Competitive commission rates would mean the end of the small private partnership model of investment banks, already under stress by the capital requirements of technological modernization in the computer era. The larger firms, particularly the efficient and well-run ones, would be able to lower their commissions and make up lost revenue per trade with market share taken from the less efficient firms that would be forced to exit the brokerage business. Not surprisingly, Merrill Lynch applauded the Department of Justice's new position. Few others agreed, and none publicly.

To the regulators in Washington, the spring of 1968 seemed an ideal time to end fixed commissions and the corruption and economic distortions that went along with them. Business had never looked better on Wall Street to outsiders. Trading volume records were being smashed and record commissions were being collected. So effective had the Club been in masking the true operating conditions of most Wall Street firms that no one questioned whether the financial impact of dramatically lowering commission rates might risk the solvency of the industry.

Manny Cohen liked the idea of public hearings proposed by the Justice Department. He announced that the S.E.C. would hold them beginning on July 1 on the broad menu of interrelated issues identified in the Justice Department's comment letter.[26]

The looming public hearings sent waves of fear over the Club. Memories of the Pecora hearings and the Whitney scandal had informed the thinking of the Club since the 1930s: airing dirty laundry publicly was to be avoided at all costs—and there was plenty of dirty laundry involving give-ups. Since the Department of Justice had inextricably linked the issue of give-ups with the legality of fixed commissions, off-Exchange trading, and institutional membership—prerogatives dear to the Club—Robert Haack had a minefield to navigate in advance of the July 1 hearings. He had to show some movement to get the regulators off his back, but any concession risked alienating some important constituency at the Exchange.

THE LAST THING Robert Haack needed with the prying eyes of the S.E.C. and the Department of Justice was more customer complaints over failed trades. With trading volumes at historic highs, Robert Haack urged the board of governors to take a number of remedial actions that spring to resolve failed trades. On April 18, the board of governors approved a mandatory buy-in for fails fifty days old effective August 1. This rule required the buyer's broker to purchase undelivered shares in the open market and charge the selling broker for the net excess cost.[27] While the mandatory buy-in would create financial consequences for the failure to deliver certificates at settlement, it would not reduce the likelihood of fails. It would just make it much more expensive for firms with poor back-office operations to keep doing business.

Haack was also putting more pressure on the N.Y.S.E. staff and members to get C.C.S. up and running. With that accomplished, the fails would plummet, the customer complaints to the S.E.C. would subside, and the growing voices of concern in Washington over the efficacy of self-regulation would be muted. If it could happen quickly, it might come in time to save many firms with inefficient back offices and insufficient capital to upgrade their computer systems.

On May 16, John Cunningham held a press conference at the Exchange announcing that "limited activation" of C.C.S. would begin the following day. In that phase, 320 stocks whose corporate names started with the letters A through C would be included. Full activation—actual settlement via book entry—would start in late June. All N.Y.S.E.-listed stocks would be eligible for inclusion by year-end, and it was hoped that all AMEX-listed stocks would be included, along with the more actively traded O.T.C. stocks, by the end of 1969. Cunningham predicted that this would eliminate 75 percent of all stock certificate handling by 1970, ending the crisis. It was a very ambitious timetable.[28]

Manny Cohen at the S.E.C. did not believe that the Exchange's timetable was even remotely achievable. Customer complaints to the S.E.C. were at record levels that May, and the financial filings by the investment banks were showing that fails were rising. While Cohen had initially believed that the reluctance on the part of the commercial banks to cooperate with the Exchange's C.C.S. initiative had been principally motivated by turf battles and fee squabbling, he began to consider the merits of the concerns raised by the large commercial banks. The evidence was mounting that the N.Y.S.E. and its members lacked the controls and management expertise to be trusted with possession of the bulk of the nation's stock certificates.

On May 22, the S.E.C. instituted an official inquiry into the back-office operations. First, Manny Cohen sent out information requests to all of the investment banks. Then, armed with their responses, Cohen sent S.E.C. staff to Wall Street to physically inspect the cages.[29]

* * *

SHORTLY AFTER DAWN on June 4, in Greenwich, Connecticut, Sean McDonnell, the thirty-four-year-old executive vice president of the white-shoe investment bank McDonnell & Co., went out for his morning jog. He never returned. He was found unconscious on the side of Round Hill Road by a passing motorist. An ambulance was called and McDonnell was brought to Greenwich Hospital, but he was already dead of a massive heart attack.[30]

McDonnell & Co., founded in 1906 by James McDonnell, Sean's father, benefited greatly by family connections. James McDonnell married a daughter of Thomas Murray, Thomas Edison's partner, and the wealthiest Irish American at the turn of the century. James's children also married well. Sean's brother, Murray, the chief executive officer of McDonnell & Co., had married Marjorie Flanigan, the daughter of Horace Flanigan, the president and chairman of Manufacturers Hanover Trust Company, one of the largest commercial banks in the country. Marjorie Flanigan was also the sister of Peter Flanigan, a partner at Dillon Read & Co., the bulge bracket investment bank, and later President Nixon's chief economic advisor. Sean's sister Sheila married Richard P. Cooley, president of Wells Fargo Bank. Another sister, Anne, had by far made the most famous marriage in 1940, to Henry Ford II, the grandson of Henry Ford and the heir to the Ford Motor Company fortune.[31]

During the 1960s, McDonnell & Co. was among the elite investment banks. While not bulge bracket in underwriting like Morgan Stanley or First Boston, and smaller in retail brokerage than Merrill Lynch and Bache & Co., it was nonetheless a respected competitor in each of its businesses. It also had enormous social cachet, particularly among wealthy Catholic business executives and investors. Its large client base included the Archdiocese of New York, as Murray McDonnell, like John Coleman, had cultivated a close friendship with Francis Cardinal Spellman. By 1968, McDonnell & Co. had 26 branch offices in the United States and France, 350 brokers, 1,500 employees, and over 100,000 customers.[32]

Sean McDonnell joined the bank in 1962 as an executive in its operations department with responsibility over the back office. With his Harvard MBA training, he quickly saw that the technology used by McDonnell & Co. was inadequate and implemented a modernization plan.[33] He began the installation and transition to a state-of-the-art N.C.R. computer system that year. However, right after that system became fully operational, the I.B.M. System/360 came out, rendering the N.C.R. system obsolete. McDonnell & Co., thinly capitalized to begin with and stretched by Murray's aggressive expansion plan, could not invest the money to scrap the inferior N.C.R. system and purchase an I.B.M. System/360.

Between 1963 and 1967, McDonnell's trading volume quadrupled and its profits tripled. By 1968, its computer system, anchored by the outdated N.C.R. mainframe, was overwhelmed and needed to be replaced. Sean's marching orders from Murray were to find the least expensive fix. Sean hired Dr. Norman Zachary, the director of the Harvard University computer center and founder of a firm called Data Architects, Inc. Zachary promised the most sophisticated and efficient system on Wall Street, a fully automated, online, real-time management information system. Best of all, Zachary promised all this for only $2 million. But Data Architects had only been formed a few months earlier and had never embarked on a project of this scale—or any project on Wall Street for that matter.[34]

In early April 1968, fifty senior executives of McDonnell gathered at an offsite meeting at the Tryall Club in Montego Bay, Jamaica, to hear the final plan to implement the Data Architects computer system that was to solve all of McDonnell's back-office woes. Data Architects would be installing an I.B.M. System/360 mainframe-based system to replace the N.C.R. computers and customizing software tailored to McDonnell's unique operations.[35] Data Architects named the proprietary system SECURE—System to Eliminate and Correct Recurring Errors. It would, the McDonnell executives were told, reduce their cost per trade from $30.00 to $2.50.[36] Because the McDonnell back office on lower Broadway in downtown Manhattan was so small, it could not accommodate duplicate mainframes during a transition period, so the existing N.C.R. system was being dismantled at the same time the I.B.M. System/360 was being installed. This was highly unusual. In every other back-office conversion in memory, the firm would run parallel systems until the kinks in the new system were worked out. These kinks were not simply computer glitches. Personnel had to be taught how to properly use often radically different procedures and technology. Old habits had to be replaced with new ones. It was not dissimilar, say, from teaching someone used to using a rotary phone and handwritten letters to communicate exclusively on an iPhone.

While the executives were being assured by Zachary in sunny Jamaica that this would not expose the firm to serious risk, the N.C.R. mainframe computer caught fire while it was being removed, making it impossible to install the new I.B.M. System/360 and leaving the firm with no trade processing capabilities. Sean McDonnell hurriedly returned to New York, now suspicious of all Zachary had promised. He questioned all aspects of the implementation of the new system, and the gravity of the crisis was quickly apparent. McDonnell & Co. had recently negotiated the acquisition of F. P. Ristine & Company, a Philadelphia brokerage with six branches. Completely unintegrated into McDonnell & Co.'s systems, it was nonetheless adding an enormous amount of new trading volume into the malfunctioning back office. Worse, Ristine's operations utilized some of the most archaic systems in the industry— literally a pen-and-ink bookkeeping system.[37]

Under the best of circumstances, with the best of back-office employees, digging out of this mess would have been a herculean task, but McDonnell & Co. had a reputation for having among the worst back-office employees. It was ranked thirty-fifth out of thirty-eight large Wall Street firms in efficiency in 1968. It had perhaps the highest turnover. At one point during the conversion, of the forty-two clerks in the margin department, thirty-five had less than a year's experience.[38]

The Harvard boys from Data Architects did not know what to make of the ruffians in the McDonnell cage. Open liquor bottles were passed around from the early morning to quitting time. Drunkenness and, more frequently during 1968, other forms of intoxication were considered normal occupational hazards. The typical McDonnell & Co. back-office employee was a high school dropout. The Data Architects technicians attempting to train the McDonnell back-office staff barely contained their contempt for the cage savages, whom they thought unworthy of pawing their precious I.B.M. equipment. And the back-office unwashed took glee in torturing the elitist snobs with the pocket-protectors, intentionally making mistakes to see who among them could cause the I.B.M. System/360 to go haywire. For those who even cared about keeping their jobs, they were in no hurry to see the system operational, as it would eliminate many of their positions. Perhaps the biggest obstacle to a non-disastrous conversion was the fact that neither Data Architects, the startup, nor McDonnell & Co., the overextended family business/piggybank, had the dough to invest in an effective training program.

In the midst of all this, Sean McDonnell keeled over on his morning jog. Despite his poor decision to engage Data Architects, he was thought of then, and still today, as an able executive who may very well, had he lived, have pulled McDonnell & Co. through what was to follow. His mother, Anna McDonnell, still a force in family business matters, had let it be known that Sean was her choice to lead the company, when he was ready. "One of the most popular and admired young executives on Wall Street," remembers Michael Meehan II, Joseph Meehan's son and a partner at Meehan & Co. at the time. "Just a terrific guy."[39] The plan was always to have Sean run the company, family insiders recall; the only question was how to diplomatically get Murray out of the way.

Murray was a superb salesman, but not known for his grasp of the numbers or his management style. He surrounded himself with men like himself or, more accurately, an idealized version of himself. Nearly all the senior executives he hired were Irish Catholics or W.A.S.P.s from wealthy families, credentialed from elite boarding schools and Ivy League colleges: tall, handsome, and polished.

Gentility and pedigree mattered to Murray, who preferred those with memberships in private clubs that might not have him to those who might solve securities valuation issues he couldn't.[40] Murray also tried too hard, adopting the persona of an English country squire, riding the hounds in full regalia at his weekend estate in Peapack, New Jersey.[41] It got to be too much, particularly for the cynical Irish of Wall Street, when, in the summer of 1967, Murray rented Woodstown House, in County Wexford, Ireland, the former family seat of Baron Robert Shapland Carew of the hated nineteenth-century Anglo-Irish nobility. Murray invited Jackie Kennedy and her children to visit Woodstown House and made sure their presence there with him was leaked to the New York tabloids.[42]

After Sean McDonnell died in the glory of his dawn, like it or not, the fate of McDonnell & Co. was in the hands of Murray. Given the high profile of the McDonnell family, this meant that the fate of the Club and possibly of self-regulation at the N.Y.S.E. were also in Murray's shaky hands.

SEAN MCDONNELL DIED on the day the presidential primary election was being held in California. The week before, in the Oregon primary, Senator Eugene McCarthy had upset Robert Kennedy by a vote of 44 percent to 38 percent. (President Johnson, still on the ballot, received 11 percent.) Kennedy's campaign for the nomination would only survive if he won in California. The party bosses (who mostly supported Hubert Humphrey) were cheering on McCarthy, for with Bobby bloodied in the primaries and arguably not a clear cut above Humphrey against Nixon in November, there would be little risk of delegates jumping on a Kennedy bandwagon at the Chicago convention. It did not go the way the bosses wanted. Bobby won the California primary with 46 percent to McCarthy's 42 percent.

Those gathered in the ballroom of the Ambassador Hotel in Los Angeles to hear his victory speech just after midnight on June 5 included writers George Plimpton and Pete Hamill; athletes

Rafer Johnson and Rosey Greer; his brother-in-law and campaign manager, Steven Smith; and his wife, Ethel, pregnant with his eleventh child, Rory. In a narrow corridor connecting the stage from which he would speak to the ballroom's kitchen, waited a misfit, insignificant in all ways save his malevolence. After the speech, Sirhan Sirhan fatally shot Robert Kennedy with three bullets, one in the back of his head, and also wounded five other people, Paul Schrade, William Weisel, Elizabeth Evans, Ira Goldstein, and Irwin Stroll. The following day, Kennedy would succumb to his wounds.

On June 6, a presidential plane sent by President Johnson flew the body of Robert Kennedy back to New York. An hour after it landed, the hearse carrying Kennedy's body, accompanied by a fifty-car motorcade, arrived at St. Patrick's Cathedral in Midtown Manhattan, where the body would lie in state the following day. More than 150,000 mourners passed through St. Patrick's to pay their respects. The funeral Mass was held there at 10:00 a.m. Saturday with Archbishop Terrence Cooke and Richard Cardinal Cushing officiating. Five minutes after the Mass had ended, radio and television broadcasts of the day's ceremonies were interrupted by a bulletin out of London, England: James Earl Ray, the assassin of Martin Luther King, had been arrested there. This news further added to the surreal feeling of the day.

The RFK funeral train from New York City to Washington, D.C., was scheduled to arrive at 4:30 p.m., but due to a late start and the slow pace given the unexpected crowds of trackside mourners, it did not arrive until 9:08 p.m. William D. Eckert, the commissioner of Major League Baseball, had rescheduled the games that were to be held in New York and Washington, D.C., that day and further ordered that the starting times of all other games were to be delayed until Robert Kennedy was buried. The nearly five-hour delay wreaked havoc on the scheduling. In Cincinnati, the Reds were scheduled to play the Cardinals and, given the delay, were going to start the game before the body of Robert Kennedy had been buried. Reds player representative Milt Pappas vehemently objected and threatened a sit-down strike. Reds manager Dave Bristol threatened to take nine kids out of the stands to field a team, if necessary. Pappas relented, but filed a grievance with the commissioner. Not long thereafter, the Reds traded Pappas to the Atlanta Braves. In Houston, the Astros were scheduled to play the Pittsburgh Pirates, at a later start time than usual. At first, the Astros players voted to boycott the game out of respect for RFK, but after the team's general manager, Spec Richardson, promised to fine any player who did not show up in uniform, the game was played. One player who would not play despite Richardson's threat was the Astros' leading hitter, Rusty Staub. Staub, too, would be traded, following the season, to the Montreal Expos.

There was dissension, too, at the N.Y.S.E. Robert Kennedy's death was formally observed with only a two-minute moment of silence and delay to the start of trading. This upset most employees of the Exchange, who thought it should have closed to honor RFK's memory as it had after the assassinations of President Kennedy and Martin Luther King. Exchange officials tried to explain that those closings marked national days of mourning declared by President Johnson, but since the national day of mourning declared for Robert Kennedy was June 9, a Sunday, the Exchange would already be closed. The bad feelings over the perceived slight were remembered by old-timers at the Exchange over half a century later.

The dislocation of feelings for many at the N.Y.S.E. was heightened by the torrid pace of trading during the three days after Robert Kennedy was shot. On Wednesday, volume on the Exchange was 15,590,000 shares. The next day, 16,130,000 shares were traded, and on Friday, more than 17,000,000 shares. The trading volume on the Exchange during the week of RFK's assassination and funeral was 82,040,000, averaging over 16 million per day, by far the busiest trading week ever. It is hard to explain why. Prior to 1968, there had only been one trading day in the history of the Exchange that exceeded 16 million—October 29, 1929, Black Tuesday.

CHAPTER FIVE

"THE WHOLE WORLD
IS WATCHING"

■

Private Threats and Public Hearings

During the tragic, record-breaking week of Robert Kennedy's assassination, Robert Haack and his team at the N.Y.S.E. put in motion a multifaceted plan to prevent an operational and financial catastrophe. Most obviously, the volume of paper needed to be dramatically reduced. Pending full activation of C.C.S., this was to be accomplished by curtailing trading and requiring member firms with significant operational issues—and even those without such issues—to turn away business. The expeditious rollout of C.C.S. remained the only long-term solution to permanently reduce paperwork. But with C.C.S. months away from being fully operational, the toolkit was limited. The best approach at the time was to slow down the trading volume and direct business to the firms with the best functioning back offices. This meant punishing the weakest firms with fines and sanctions as well as making failed trades more costly. This, of course, would make the weak firms financially weaker—just in time for an industrywide revenue hit by means of the first-ever reduction in commission rates.

On May 28, Manny Cohen sent a letter to Robert Haack demanding that the Exchange approve a plan that either abolished fixed commissions on transactions involving more than $50,000 or volume discounts acceptable to the S.E.C. on transactions involving 400 or more shares. If the Exchange didn't voluntarily come up with a plan satisfactory to the S.E.C., the Commission would implement its own rate schedule effective September 15, 1968.[1]

Robert Haack knew what the S.E.C. and Justice Department did not: the financial condition of the securities industry was far shakier than the bull market and record trading volume might lead outsiders to believe. Haack needed to beat a strategic retreat by way of a volume discount on commission rates without spooking the regulators with frank disclosure about the insufficient capital of most investment banks. Haack also needed to crack down on the member firms with the worst operational issues in order to fend off the increasingly aggressive S.E.C. enforcement activity. Haack feared that soon the focus of the S.E.C. would shift from operational problems in the back offices of O.T.C. firms to more nettlesome issues closer to home—like net capital rule compliance by Exchange members.

On June 7, Robert Haack issued a special bulletin announcing the unprecedented action of a series of three consecutive Wednesday closings, beginning on June 12. The Exchange and the other securities markets, including the O.T.C. market, would use those days to catch up on paperwork and reduce the number of open transactions.[2] These one-day-a-week closings—on Wednesdays, unless a scheduled holiday occurred on another day of a week—would continue through the end of 1968.

Haack also urged that member firms cease soliciting O.T.C. transactions.[3] Fails in the O.T.C. market ran at a much higher rate than on the Exchange, in part because transfer agents for O.T.C.-listed companies were not required to be in New York City. Many of those out-of-town transfer agents were not equipped to handle the skyrocketing volume. In many cases, it took more than a month to receive return delivery of share certificates from those transfer agents.

In addition, Haack requested that member firms reduce trading for their own accounts, disallow commissions to salesmen on stocks selling for less than $10 per share, reduce advertising and promotion efforts, and penalize brokers who made bookkeeping errors or who failed to obtain timely securities deliveries. New brokers would not be registered to do business by the Exchange if the Exchange believed the hiring firm's back-office operations were severely impaired.[4] "A business—as usual—attitude," Haack declared, "is a luxury that the industry can no longer afford."

On the same day, the Federal Reserve Board in Washington, D.C., in an effort to discourage the use of credit in the booming stock market, ordered an increase in margin requirements to a down payment of 80 percent from 70 percent. This was the first increase since December 1963 when they were raised from 50 percent to 70 percent. The amount of credit in customer brokerage accounts had ballooned by $200 million in April to a record $6.4 billion. Margin accounts with brokers had increased by 20,000 that April to 885,000, 165,000 more than a year earlier.[5]

ROBERT HAACK KNEW he had to prepare a counterproposal in advance of the S.E.C. hearings on fixed commissions that would be palatable to the Exchange's board of governors and, ultimately, a majority of its members. The member firms hit hardest by the back-office crisis were generally those with a large retail brokerage business. Reducing their commission revenue at a time when they desperately needed capital to modernize and clean up their failed trades could be the death of many of them.

Haack needed to find the minimum size trade that he could offer to meaningfully reduce commissions that would not bankrupt the retail brokerage industry. The problem he faced was that the larger the size-of-transaction minimum was, the greater the commission discount would need to be in order to show the S.E.C. meaningful aggregate reduction in commissions. This would also pit those firms that did a disproportionately large institutional business against those that did a disproportionately large retail business. The Exchange sent out questionnaires to members seeking trading data to figure out the right mix of transaction sizes and rate reductions to appease both the regulators and its members.

On June 10, Haack sent out a special bulletin to all Exchange members indicating that a volume discount in some form would be proposed by the Exchange prior to the July 1 S.E.C. hearings. Haack stated that: "Our staff has developed three alternative schedules which are being tested out with representatives of member firms and are under discussion with the Cost and Revenue Committee and the Advisory Committee representing the viewpoint of the regional firms."[6]

On June 27, four days before the S.E.C. was to begin the rate hearings, the boards of governors of the N.Y.S.E. and AMEX approved a counterproposal to the S.E.C. Both exchanges agreed to propose to the S.E.C. substantial volume discounts on trades involving 1,000 shares or more and agreed to eliminate give-ups entirely. No details were disclosed regarding the amount of the discounts. In a letter to members announcing the decision, Robert Haack said: "An intricate maze of give-ups, giveaways, reciprocal practices, manufactured participations in trades, transported trades form one exchange to the other, and the like, have resulted in considerable leakage of the commission dollar. At a time when the principle of minimum commissions is being questioned, it may be more difficult to defend the economic basis of the minimum commission under the law if members are able to give up, or give away, a substantial part of the minimum commission. In any case, a commission schedule that includes a volume discount would reduce the wherewithal for give-ups."[7]

The strategic decision to agree to outlaw give-ups in advance of the hearings was motivated by the hope that, with give-ups eliminated, any discussion of the shady practices involving give-ups would be irrelevant. Gene Rotberg, the S.E.C. lawyer who would be leading the questioning of most witnesses, had something very different in mind.

WEDNESDAY, JUNE 12 marked the first of the midweek trading holidays. That day also brought the second notable casualty of the crisis. The S.E.C. announced that it would hold a hearing to suspend the operations of L. D. Sherman & Co., an O.T.C. broker that made a market in over three hundred stocks, for inadequate record keeping. The firm would ultimately voluntarily agree to suspend all operations. Since L. D. Sherman was not a member of the N.Y.S.E., its failure was technically not the Exchange's problem, at least as far as tapping the Special Trust Fund was concerned.[8] But two firms had now failed in four months. Among the idle brokers, the talk was monopolized by speculation as to which firm would be the next to fall. Most bet on another O.T.C. firm, as over 80 percent of fails involved O.T.C. stocks, and book-entry transfers for these securities in the Exchange's C.C.S. system wasn't expected for more than a year.

The Wednesday holiday did little to reduce overall weekly volumes, but did result in very heavy volume on Thursday when trading resumed, particularly in the troubled O.T.C. market. "The volume's going through the roof," one dealer remarked to the *New York Times* that first Thursday. "We can't write tickets fast enough." Another trader commented, "We've got fifty phones and twenty people handling them. A lot of the calls are going unanswered. It's virtually impossible to reach other dealers."[9] O.T.C. brokers decided to stop transacting business at 3:30 p.m., rather than the usual 4:00 p.m., in addition to the Wednesday holidays.

Chairman Cohen, concerned that the industry self-regulatory organizations did not have the back offices under control, had the S.E.C. put out an unusual release on June 17, best described as a warning notice, informing brokers that the Commission considered a dysfunctional back office to be a violation of the Securities Exchange Act of 1934. He declared it illegal for brokers to transact business for customers "when books and records are not current or when firms cannot meet their obligations to deliver securities or promptly settle transactions." The release further stated that: "We caution all brokers and dealers of their individual responsibilities to comply with all applicable provisions of the Federal securities laws and particularly those relating to the maintenance of current books and records, financial responsibility, and prompt delivery of securities and settlement of transactions." The Commission noted that while some firms were taking appropriate action to address back-office challenges, "there are other firms that are not adequately dealing with such problems. Firms that do not meet their responsibilities are not only potential sources of financial problems but also are subjecting themselves to the possibility of disciplinary action by the commission."[10]

In connection with the warning release, Cohen summoned the heads of all of the major exchanges and Richard Walbert, head of the N.A.S.D., to a "summit meeting" at the S.E.C. in Washington on Thursday, June 20.[11] In addition to Cohen, two other commissioners were present, Hamer H. Budge and Richard Smith. During the two-and-a-half-hour session, Cohen presented a seven-point plan that he wanted the industry to implement as soon as possible. First, he wanted rules providing for a specific time period in which deliveries of securities must take place. Second, he wanted a change in the exchanges' net capital rules to provide for the booking of a liability for fails to deliver over thirty days old. Third, he wanted rules requiring periodic confirmation of fails in order to eliminate record-keeping problems that complicated resolving fails. Fourth, he pressed for the creation of more robust clearing facilities for the O.T.C. market. Fifth, the S.E.C. would be proposing a regulation applicable to transfer agents to ensure they were competent and well resourced for the increased volume of transactions. Sixth, he demanded more stringent mandatory buy-ins for undelivered shares. Seventh, he demanded they establish better standards for their members regarding accounting and bookkeeping systems and the number of back-office personnel.[12]

Cohen also informed the executives that the S.E.C. would be increasing its enforcement activity and would soon be announcing proceedings against three small firms active in the O.T.C. market— Allied Securities Company, for bookkeeping and net capital violations; Kroeze, McLarty & Buddleson, for net capital violations; and Ferris & Co., also for net capital violations.[13] All present at the meeting agreed that the only long-term solution to the industry's problems was the roll-out of C.C.S. Robert Haack had some good news to report to the assembled group on that front: C.C.S. would begin processing actual trades that Friday.

On June 28, the first book-entry transfer trades were executed. The stocks included in C.C.S. were phased in alphabetically, with the first trades being 5,000 share trades in each of four stocks: Abbot Laboratories, Abex Corporation, Acme Markets, and Adams Express.[14] A total of 535 stocks, 43 percent of the total listed issues, were to be included by the end of 1968, with 40 being included by mid-July. All 277 clearing members of the N.Y.S.E. were obligated to participate, but only to the extent they were the custodians of the share certificates being transferred. This left out most institutional investors, who either kept custody of their own shares or had them held by banks or trust companies, who were not obligated to participate. Given their concerns about the solvency and competency of the Exchange and its members, these institutions were not about to hand over control of securities held by them in a fiduciary capacity or the legal record keeping for transfers and ownership thereof to either the firms who disastrously lost control of their own securities and record keeping or the Exchange, which allowed, and perhaps enabled, the whole debacle and wasn't exactly coming clean as to the extent of the mess.

Another additional major limitation of C.C.S. was that securities listed on other exchanges or trading in the O.T.C. market were not obligated to allow inclusion, and the regional exchanges and the major O.T.C. market makers were not onboard with handing their clearing functions over to a competitor exchange. Five business days after those first trades were executed, Robert Cunningham's I.B.M. System/360 computers recorded the transfers by book entry. The Exchange had finally accomplished what William Douglas had recommended thirty years earlier.

THE S.E.C. RATE hearings began as scheduled on Monday, July 1 at the Commission's headquarters in Washington. The first witness called was Robert Bishop, the Senior Vice President of the N.Y.S.E. in charge of its department of member firms. Gene Rotberg led off the questioning by asking Bishop about the Exchange's current rate schedule. In particular, Rotberg asked why the commissions on two trades involving the same number of shares were vastly different where one involved a higher share price (and received a much higher commission). For example, a trade involving 100 shares of an $80 stock received a commission equal to 250 percent of the commission for a trade involving 100 shares of a $10 stock. Bishop sounded like a patient trying to talk his way out of rehab. He explained that the schedule had been approved in 1958, when he had only been at the Exchange for three years. After floundering about, he finally admitted that he "could not rationalize or defend" the Exchange's current fixed commission rate schedule. In a strategy he would continue throughout the first phase of the hearings, Rotberg let Bishop off the hook by changing the line of questioning whenever such an uncomfortable answer arose, avoiding confrontation and embarrassment.[15] But the S.E.C. stenographer recorded every word, as did the Justice Department observer attending each session of the hearings.

After Bishop's day of testimony, Rotberg called several executives of investment banks to testify. The first was Michael J. Heaney of Michael J. Heaney & Co., an AMEX member firm, who appeared on July 2. Rotberg asked Heaney what the typical give-up was for a large trade by a mutual fund. Heaney responded that it could be as high as 90 percent of the commission, if he wasn't acting as the clearing broker. The clearing broker actually handles the settlement of the trade by arranging the transfer of money or share certificates, as the case may be. In the case where he was acting as a clearing broker, the give-up typically ranged between 30 percent and 50 percent of the fixed commission.[16] Having established that executing brokers would work for 10 percent of the aggregate commission and clearing brokers at 20 percent to 40 percent, Rotberg demonstrated that 50 percent to 70 percent of the commissions on large trades was "gravy," monopoly profits that showed that current fixed commission rates were unreasonable. If they were unreasonable, they were illegal even if the Exchange's asserted antitrust exemption was valid because the antitrust laws required that "public utility" rates had to be reasonable in terms of a rate of return on investment and costs of operation. "Reasonableness" had to be demonstrated under the antitrust laws with hard economic data prepared by experts. Rates couldn't be set on the basis of what least offended influential monopolists.

On July 3, Boyd L. Jeffries of Jeffries & Co. was called to testify. Jeffries & Co. was not a member of the N.Y.S.E., but was a member of the Pacific Coast Stock Exchange. Jeffries was asked to explain how give-ups could be directed to non-N.Y.S.E. members on trades executed on the N.Y.S.E., given the N.Y.S.E.'s prohibition on sharing give-ups on those trades with firms that were not N.Y.S.E. members. Jeffries explained that this was accomplished with the "four-way ticket." N.Y.S.E. firms, many of whom were also members of the Pacific Coast Stock Exchange, would simply add the names of the non-N.Y.S.E. member firms to completely unrelated trade tickets as additional buying and selling brokers entitled to 50 percent of the commissions on the various unrelated trades until they "trued-up" with the amount of the give-up on the N.Y.S.E. trade.[17]

On July 8, Henry A. Jacobs Jr., president of Bache & Co., Inc., the second largest investment bank, was next to testify. He revealed that most of the give-ups Bache received came from mutual funds that Bache sold shares in. When pressed by Rotberg for a more precise percentage than "most," Jacobs answered that mutual fund give-ups and share sales had an "almost perfect correlation." Jacobs also disclosed that there were mutual fund managers who gave Bache give-ups from trades by one fund they managed as compensation for share sales of a different fund. Additionally, Jacobs described how Bache would structure give-ups to avoid the N.Y.S.E. prohibition on paying them to non-N.Y.S.E. firms: Bache would give the non-member firm an allocation for a portion of the underwriting fee from an unrelated securities offering—but with no requirement to put capital at risk by actually underwriting the securities and no requirement to sell any shares.[18]

Two days later, William Donaldson of D.L.J. was called. Donaldson stated that the end of fixed commissions would cause "the complete deterioration of the present industry system." Donaldson predicted a drastic reduction in the amount of research Wall Street firms would produce for investors if commission rates were negotiated. Much of the research prepared was paid for by give-ups, by institutional investors paying rich fees on large trades. The institutions effectively subsidized research for all investors, Donaldson claimed. Donaldson expressed the belief that mutual fund performance would deteriorate as a result of the reduction in quality research.[19] Gene Rotberg again refrained from pushing the issue with the obvious question as to why, with lower, reasonable commission rates, a mutual fund couldn't use the savings to separately purchase the research it wants.

On July 17, Richard B. Walbert, president of the N.A.S.D., the primary regulator of small brokerage firms that were not members of a major stock exchange, announced that the board of governors of the N.A.S.D. had approved the elimination of the give-up, so long as it was phased out gradually and replaced with some form of commission sharing with N.Y.S.E. members. Walbert stated that the proposal made by the N.Y.S.E.—a two-thirds/one-third split on trades non-members bring to the floor of the Exchange—was not something he was prepared to agree to, noting that give-ups accounted for approximately 60 percent of the revenue of the typical firm that was not a member of the N.Y.S.E. Walbert said he was without data to indicate if a one-third split would offset such lost revenue.[20] But with no power to compel the N.Y.S.E. to agree to a higher split, there was little the small firms could do to recoup lost give-up revenue when the Exchange outlawed the practice. This would have a profound financial impact on the O.T.C. firms in the years to come.

The following day, the hearings continued with testimony of even more elaborate schemes to distribute give-ups. Bernard R. Dishy, partner in the AMEX firm of Dishy, Easton & Co., described how his firm would receive give-ups on N.Y.S.E. trades by way of unrelated AMEX trades in a manner similar in effect to the "four-way ticket" used on the Pacific Coast Stock Exchange—but with an added twist. Dishy, Easton & Co. was often simply a conduit through which the give-up dollars passed to their intended beneficiaries. The partners of Dishy, Easton & Co. would write personal checks in the amounts directed by the mutual fund manager, Investors Overseas Services, which was owned by renegade financier Bernard Cornfeld. (Cornfeld would later become the partner of fugitive financier Robert Vesco.) Those checks included payments to a judge in the Bahamas. Dishy testified that he never asked Cornfeld's people what the purpose of any of the payments was.[21] (The following May, Bernard Dishy would be suspended from the AMEX for five months and fined $40,000, the maximum amount then permitted for an individual, as a result of these disclosures.)

On July 19, more give-up schemes were discussed. Maxwell Ohlman, managing partner of Maxwell Ohlman & Co., a member of the Philadelphia-Baltimore-Washington Stock Exchange, described yet another way around the N.Y.S.E. rule against commission sharing with non-members. Ohlman's gambit was to contract with N.Y.S.E. members and provide them services ranging from investment research to psychological testing and simply inflate the invoices to reflect the give-up amounts due to his firm. In fact, Maxwell Ohlman & Co. provided none of these services itself. It simply subcontracted all services out to the actual providers and sent bills, inflated as agreed, to the N.Y.S.E. member firms.[22] Again, Gene Rotberg took notes, never pressing with questions as to how all these phony payments were accounted for and reported to auditors, exchanges, the S.E.C., the I.R.S., and others expecting financial statements to be accurately prepared.

The following week the hearings continued with testimony from the mutual fund managers. On July 22, John R. Haire, chairman of the Investment Company Institute, the leading mutual fund industry trade organization, appeared. Haire acknowledged that he never attempted to recover for his shareholders the give-ups paid by his managed funds. He further acknowledged that he directed give-up dollars to investment banks that sold his mutual funds shares—frequently directing give-up dollars attributable to one fund's trading to an investment bank that sold a different fund's shares.[23]

George McEwan, the chairman of Fidelity Group's brokerage subsidiary, testified the following day. McEwan first insisted that all give-ups Fidelity paid were for bona fide services, like research, inuring to the benefit of the fund paying the give-ups. When Gene Rotberg produced a schedule of give-ups paid to firms that did not produce research, McEwan responded that those firms were "listening posts" for Fidelity to source deal flow. When asked to detail what deal flow those firms actually produced, McEwan finally acknowledged that the give-ups paid to those particular firms were paid solely for selling shares of Fidelity funds.[24]

The first phase of the rate hearings ended on July 31 with testimony from Robert M. Loeffler, vice president of Investors Diversified Services, the nation's largest mutual fund complex. Investors Diversified Services had its own captive mutual fund sales force, so it did not rely on third-party investment banks to sell its funds' shares. Loeffler testified that he agreed with the Justice Department that fixed commission rates were an antitrust violation and should be eliminated. Because Investors Diversified Services didn't need to compensate the investment banks for fund share sales, it literally could not buy enough research or other services from the investment banks executing its trades to use all the give-up dollars available to it. Loeffler estimated that 25 percent of the brokerage commissions Investors Diversified Services paid were "leaks," as he called them, or wasted give-up dollars.[25]

Gene Rotberg was pleased with the first phase of the hearings. He was convinced he had demonstrated the unreasonableness of the current N.Y.S.E. rate schedule as applied to large block institutional trades. He thought he had effectively shown the corruption and irrationality of the give-ups, which proved conclusively in his mind—and the mind of the Department of Justice—that, at a minimum, rates needed to be substantially reduced on large trades. There would be no doubt that the give-up would be eliminated. Ultimately, if fixed rates were allowed to continue, a rational, methodical, economically sound basis for setting rates would need to be implemented going forward. Whether that last requirement was capable of being satisfied would be the subject of phase two of the hearings, which would resume in mid-August. In the meantime, over seventy class action lawsuits had been filed against mutual fund managers for breaches of duty involving the use of give-ups, with the transcripts of sworn testimony from the first phase of the S.E.C. hearings figuring prominently in many of the complaints.

THE S.E.C.'S MORE aggressive enforcement policy against investment advisors, its companion initiative along with the hearings on fixed commissions to end abuses, yielded mixed results. In the S.E.C.'s case against Roy Cohn, Judge McLean ruled on July 26 that the general antifraud provisions of the federal securities laws applicable to all public companies were not violated by the questionable insider transactions. He did find, however, that Fifth Avenue Coach Lines qualified as an investment company, so many of those same transactions did violate the Investment Company Act. Accordingly, he granted the request that a receiver be appointed for the company. He also enjoined Cohn and co-defendants Victor Muscat and Edward Crock from further violations of the securities laws.[26]

More troubling for Cohn was the grand jury U.S. Attorney Robert Morgenthau had empaneled shortly after the S.E.C. had filed its case back in October. When the S.E.C. case went to trial on March 25, one of Morgenthau's lawyers was in the courtroom. He monitored the testimony through the end of the trial on May 6. On June 12, the Morgenthau grand jury handed down its first indictment in the Fifth Avenue Coach Lines matter. Victor Muscat was charged with lying to the grand jury. It was an open-and-shut case against Muscat, as the findings of fact in Judge McLean's opinion directly contradicted his grand jury testimony. The only question in Cohn's mind was when Muscat would flip on him.

THROUGHOUT JULY, Manny Cohen made good on his threats during the June 20 summit meeting with the securities industry leaders. He brought enforcement proceedings against three more firms—Eastbrook & Co., Inc., Schwabacher & Co., Inc., and B. J. Securities, Inc.[27] In addition, to expedite the improvement of clearing facilities in the O.T.C. market, the S.E.C. insisted that the N.A.S.D. hire management consultant Arthur D. Little, Inc. to study the causes of the high percentage of O.T.C. fails.[28] On July 29, in another unusually threatening release, Cohen announced that the S.E.C. would be targeting additional firms with high fails, particularly aged fails, unless they curtailed operations: "Broker-dealers who are unable to consummate all their securities transactions in accordance with traditional customs and usage of trade, or who are encountering any delays because of back-office problems of any kind, are compounding their difficulties and increasing the likelihood of disciplinary action being taken against them if during any such period they advertise, employ additional salesmen, or take any other action designed to expand the volume of their businesses."[29]

Two days later, Cohen sent a letter to Robert Haack and the other exchange chairmen urging that they take action against their members with serious back-office problems before the S.E.C. stepped in to discipline them as threatened in the release. Cohen urged the exchanges to implement disciplinary measures limiting advertising and promotional activities, prohibiting the opening of new offices or the hiring of new salesmen, limiting the publication of stock research, and prohibiting firms and their executives from trading for their own accounts.[30] Confidentially, so as not to spook the public, Haack and the N.Y.S.E. staff increased the number of firms subject to Exchange-mandated operational restrictions. Those restrictions forced those firms to turn away business, which reduced cash flow and weakened their financial position.

On August 1, the N.Y.S.E. put into effect the mandatory buy-in rule its board of governors had approved in April, as promised to Cohen during the June 20 summit meeting. The rule required members to purchase for their customers any securities that had not been delivered within fifty days of the settlement date and bill the selling broker for the cost. These purchases added over 100,000 shares to the trading volume that day.[31] As predicted, the new rule further added to the liquidity woes of firms with the worst back offices, which were generally also the firms with the weakest capital positions.

Two weeks later, again under pressure from Cohen, the board of governors of the N.Y.S.E. approved a tightening of the mandatory buy-in rule by reducing to thirty days (from fifty) the time when buy-ins must be executed by purchasers' brokers. In addition, the board of governors required sellers' brokers to impose a charge to net capital ranging from 10 percent to 30 percent of contract value for fails that were forty days old or longer. These changes would become effective on December 1. The AMEX adopted similar rules that day as well.[32]

Until August, all of the S.E.C.'s enforcement actions were directed at smaller firms typically operating primarily in the O.T.C. market. That changed on August 5 when the S.E.C. instituted proceedings against Lehman Brothers, a bulge bracket underwriter and one of the most powerful and storied firms on Wall Street.[33] The charges related to its back-office and record-keeping issues arising out of a botched computer system upgrade conversion similar to the one that had gone wrong at McDonnell & Co. This shook the Club deeply, for if Lehman Brothers could be hauled into the dock by the S.E.C. over honest mistakes, no firm—no matter how large or prominent or politically connected—would be immune from Manny Cohen's crackdown. That same day, the S.E.C. brought actions against four other N.Y.S.E. member firms for back-office-related issues: D. H. Blair & Co., J. R. Timmons & Co., Kelley & Morey, Inc., and Auchincloss, Parker & Redpath.[34]

■   ■   ■

IN MIAMI BEACH, Florida, the Republican National Convention was held during the first week of August to nominate its presidential candidate, Richard Nixon, who outlasted George Romney, the early favorite; New York governor Nelson Rockefeller; and California governor Ronald Reagan. Nixon's nomination was considered very good news for Wall Street. Despite Rockefeller being a native New Yorker and inextricably linked in the mind of the public to moneyed interests, the truth was that Nelson never carried much water for the securities industry. With his family money and commercial banking relationships—his brother David was the president of Chase Manhattan Bank—Nelson had no real need to raise money from the Club. Harvesting dollars from investment banking interests was a great opportunity for Nixon, and he took full advantage of it. With Maurice Stans of Glore Forgan, Wm. R. Staats, Inc. spearheading Nixon's fundraising efforts, millions poured in, and the candidate discreetly gave every assurance to his donors that they would not regret their generous contributions.

The nomination of Richard Nixon was also very good news for Roy Cohn. Cohn had been in Miami that week at the convention, lobbying conservative delegates on Nixon's behalf. Cohn also spent a good deal of time there with Maurice Stans discussing fundraising strategy. Cohn was convinced that with the Democrats out of the White House, his legal problems might go away with them.

THE BOARD OF governors of the N.Y.S.E. had no illusions regarding the damage caused by the first phase of the S.E.C. rate hearings. To mitigate the potential fallout, the board of governors met on August 8 and formally approved the first reduction in commission rates in the Exchange's 177-year history. After parsing through the member questionnaires and taking the pulse of the S.E.C., Robert Haack was ready to put forth a proposal that he hoped would stave off the Justice Department's efforts to do away with fixed commissions entirely.

The discount off the regular rate schedule would apply only to trades of 1,000 shares or more. It was referred to as the "volume discount," and its calculation was complex. The more expensive the stock, the lower the commission rate. For stocks $30 or less, the commission rate was 0.5 percent of the dollar value per 100 shares (above the first 1,000), plus $4 for stocks $28 per share or less. For stocks greater than $30 but less than $90 per share, 0.5 percent of the dollar value per 100 shares (above the first 1,000), plus $3. For stocks greater than $90 per share, 0.1 percent of the dollar value per 100 shares (above the first 1,000), plus $39.

The aggregate revenue loss for Exchange members was projected to be $150 million, or 7 percent of total revenue. This was nearly as large as the dollar reduction under the S.E.C. plan and an amount essentially equal to the entire profit margin of the industry as a whole in 1967. The pain would be disproportionately inflicted on the firms that did an institutional business, most particularly the block trading houses. Their commission revenues were projected to decline 19.5 percent. There would be less pain for the retail firms, which would not survive if the loss of revenue were evenly distributed.

As the N.Y.S.E. had done very little actual economic analysis to support the reasonableness of these rates, it called its proposal an "interim rate schedule." It would do the economic analysis later and modify the schedule as appropriate—putting the cart before the horse.

In selling the plan as a positive for retail investors, Haack highlighted that the average mutual fund investor would recognize a 2 percent additional annual return based on the cost savings to the mutual fund industry. Gus Levy—Goldman, Sachs was the largest block trading house—was tasked with selling the plan to members with large institutional businesses: "You're looking at the fellow whom it hurts the most, and who is most strongly for this," Levy told reporters.[35] The block traders were not convinced and took to referring to the volume discount plan as the "V.D.," slang at the time for "venereal disease." The stronger firms, those with the lower cost structures and not averse to the exit of inefficient competitors, fully supported the plan. Merrill Lynch called it "a move in the right direction when prices are generally moving upward."[36] The biggest impediment to quickly implementing the plan was the time required to reprogram antiquated computers with the new rates at many of the weaker member firms.

On August 19, Robert Haack, Gus Levy, and Frederick Barton of Dillon, Union Securities & Co. appeared before the S.E.C. to present the interim rate schedule and advocate for its approval. Again, the Exchange made the case for fixed commissions, this time after having banned the give-ups that Chairman Cohen had so stridently criticized and having reduced commission rates significantly more than the S.E.C. had expected it would. "The time for expounding theory is past," Haack said. "One does not remove the keystone to an industry which is responsible for billions of dollars of public money, which operates the largest securities markets in the world, and which facilitates the raising of capital for this country without presenting irrefutable evidence. . . . This is not an area where one experiments, tries a new system, and returns to the old if the results are unsatisfactory."[37] Without fixed commission revenue, the Exchange would lack the resources to effectively police its members, Haack warned.

Gus Levy went so far as to say that Goldman, Sachs would resign from N.Y.S.E. membership if fixed commissions were eliminated, as they were the principal reason the firm subjected itself to the additional regulatory burden of Exchange membership. The Exchange itself might shut down, he cautioned, and with it the efficient centralized auction market that provided "best execution" for the individual investor. All 2,300 Exchange employees would be at risk of losing their jobs, he told the S.E.C.[38]

After Haack, Levy, and Barton made the initial presentation, Dr. William C. Freund, the Exchange's chief economist, testified as to the economic rationale behind the interim fee schedule.[39] This opened phase two of the S.E.C. rate hearings, which focused on determining the proper methodology for setting rates. In truth, it was to demonstrate that fixed pricing had no proper place in securities trading as the industry did not resemble the classic "public utility" in the least. Historically, rate setting at the N.Y.S.E. was essentially a political exercise. With much less institutional trading back in 1958, the "gravy" was much thinner and, therefore, the give-up abuses fewer and less egregious. Back then, the S.E.C. was more concerned about protecting the small investor than it was in ensuring the Exchange had a logical basis for its rates. In fact, prior to 1968, the S.E.C. requested very little substantive economic analysis from the Exchange prior to approving its commission rates. Those days were over.

Freund's presentation focused on the evils of unfixing rates much more than on the economic underpinnings of the interim rates being proposed. He had little choice. The rates were set according to what was palatable to a majority of Exchange members, rather than a cost-basis analysis typically prepared at utility rate hearings. Freund's first example of the evils that would result from competitive rates was that research would diminish, as investors wouldn't separately pay for it, resulting in less informed investment decisions. He also predicted that commissions on small orders would increase, hurting returns for small investors. He further predicted that small firms that relied heavily on mutual fund sales would go out of business, also hurting the small investor.[40]

On the issue of the economic underpinnings of the new rate proposal, the Exchange essentially punted—for twelve to eighteen months. The Exchange hired the economic consulting firm of National Economic Research Associates, Inc. (N.E.R.A.) to conduct a comprehensive study of member firms and their cost structures and to produce a report upon which a traditional cost-basis rate structure could be based so that a longer-term rate schedule could be approved. On August 20, Irwin M. Stelzer, president of N.E.R.A., appeared at the S.E.C. hearings to explain the methodology he expected to utilize in his study and report.[41]

After Stelzer's appearance, the Department of Justice publicly commented on the N.Y.S.E. proposal. It called the proposal "a first step, long overdue, toward an economical, realistic N.Y.S.E. rate structure." It emphasized that it should only be an interim measure, however.[42] The Department of Justice would insist on proof that a reasonable fixed-price system could, in fact, be devised. It also stated that the problem of access to the Exchange by non-member firms remained an issue of immediate concern. Exchange access would be taken up in the fall, during the third phase of the S.E.C. hearings.

On August 26, Ralph Saul appeared before the S.E.C. on behalf of AMEX. Saul echoed the concerns raised a week earlier by the N.Y.S.E. Saul focused his testimony on the risk of loss of members at AMEX and the weakening of self-regulation. "Why submit to exchange surveillance, to disciplinary procedures, to capital requirements, to restrictions on trading, and to a book of rules and regulations covering virtually every phase of the business?" Saul asked.[43]

On August 30, Manny Cohen sent a letter to Robert Haack approving the N.Y.S.E.'s interim commission fee schedule. It would take effect on December 5, rather than the previously imposed S.E.C. deadline of September 15. Time did not permit the required member approval process by that deadline. In his letter, Manny Cohen stated that the S.E.C. and its staff "wish to emphasize that these changes are interim steps" and that the Commission had reached no conclusion on whether the new rates "reflect the optimum form of rate structure for your exchange." Cohen left open the possibility that the Commission might ultimately decide to eliminate fixed commissions entirely.[44]

THE DEMOCRATS MET in Chicago during the last week in August for their nominating convention. With Bobby Kennedy dead and Gene McCarthy unable to expand his base beyond the anti-war movement, the nomination of Hubert Humphrey was a foregone conclusion. The delegates feared disruptive protests from the anti-war Left but were not expecting what would await them. Chicago mayor Richard J. Daley declared a curfew for 11:00 p.m. When protestors violated it the night before the convention opened, Daley's police, swinging billy clubs, enthusiastically cleared the park. On Monday morning, in his welcoming address to the delegates, Mayor Daley beamed: "As long as I am mayor of this city, there's going to be law and order in Chicago."

The protests and police clashes continued throughout the convention, but reached their apex on Wednesday night after the "peace plank," which would have made immediate military withdrawal from Vietnam the official policy of the Democratic Party, was overwhelmingly rejected by the convention. When word of this reached the 15,000 protestors in Grant Park, they erupted in fury. They attacked the police with rocks, bottles, and clubs, many spitting on the officers and verbally attacking them. The National Guard had sealed off the park at the corner of Michigan Avenue and Balbo Drive with machine guns and grenade launchers, trapping the protestors. The police were ordered to clear the streets, right in front of the television cameras set up outside the Conrad Hilton, where many of the delegates were staying. As the police clubbed protestors into submission and loaded them into paddy wagons, a chant was heard from the scattering crowd: "The whole world is watching!"

Overjoyed by the Democrats' convention debacle, on the day delegates left town stunned and ashamed, Richard Nixon began the general election campaign—with a well-organized, peaceful motorcade parade through downtown Chicago.

CHAPTER SIX

"TOO MUCH HAS GONE TO THE MEMBERS AND NOT ENOUGH TO AUTOMATION"

Commission Revenues Reduced at the Worst Possible Time

The Club was betting on Richard Nixon more than ever after the Democrats' disaster in Chicago—and not simply because his chances had improved dramatically as a result of the debacle. LBJ was not exactly a friend to Wall Street, and Wall Street concluded that Humphrey would be worse. On the second day of the convention, LBJ's S.E.C. charged Merrill Lynch and fourteen of its executives with insider trading violations—for conduct that every investment bank thought was not only legal, but ethically proper.

The insider trading charges arose out of a bond offering Merrill Lynch had managed for Douglas Aircraft Co., Inc. in 1966. During the course of Merrill Lynch's financial due diligence, its investment banking team learned that Douglas would report lower than expected earnings for the first half of 1966 and would lower earnings guidance for the full year as well. Prior to Douglas publicly announcing this days later, the Merrill Lynch investment banking team informed its institutional sales desk of the disappointing earnings news. The brokers on the desk informed their clients who held Douglas stock. Those clients, as one might expect, dumped the stock ahead of public announcement of the disappointing news, thereby avoiding losses of more than $4.5 million when the stock naturally tanked.

Today, everyone working in investment banking is well tutored in the legalities of internal information walls and the consequences of breaching them. They are frequently reminded in formal training sessions of the draconian consequences of trading while in possession of material non-public information. In 1968, however, the law of insider trading was new and undeveloped. Investment banks and their employees knew they were prohibited from trading on inside information for their own accounts or accounts over which they had discretionary authority to trade on behalf of. That was established after the Cady Roberts & Co. firm had been charged with insider trading by the S.E.C. in 1961. (Cady Roberts had sold stock for accounts it managed after one partner leaked information to another partner about an imminent dividend reduction by a client.) Few thought it was illegal to pass on to customers inside information acquired during investment banking activities. Indeed, many executives thought it would be failing the firm's customers to refrain from doing so. Donald Regan, the president of Merrill Lynch, said: "We are convinced that none of our people acted wrongfully, and you can be sure we will defend our position vigorously."[1]

Regan, then forty-nine years old, had joined Merrill Lynch right out of the Marines in 1946. He was the son of a Boston policeman and made his way to Harvard, class of 1940, where he had a casual friendship with another Irish Catholic classmate, John F. Kennedy. Regan gained admission to Harvard Law School, but dropped out in 1942 to go fight in the South Pacific. He rose fast at Merrill Lynch: he started as a broker in the Washington, D.C., office, then managed the Philadelphia office, then was brought to the corporate headquarters in New York to run marketing. He became Merrill Lynch's youngest president in 1968.

The S.E.C. thought differently than Regan. Manny Cohen claimed Merrill Lynch wasn't acting out of any humanitarian impulse: it was paid commissions and give-ups in connection with the sales of the Douglas shares. Worse, while it warned its large institutional customers, it continued to take buy orders—and collect buy-side commissions—from its small retail investors who purchased Douglas stock despite Merrill Lynch knowing the stock would soon tank. Three months later, Merrill Lynch would settle, without admitting wrongdoing. It agreed to suspend for a time certain underwriting and institutional sales activities estimated to cost the firm approximately $2,000,000.[2] While this would be considered, even after inflation, laughably lenient for a similar insider trading violation today, it was considered by Wall Street to be unduly harsh at the time.

ON SEPTEMBER 1, the board of governors of the N.Y.S.E. adopted two new rules it hoped would address another concern Manny Cohen raised at the June 20 summit meeting—the prompt delivery of securities at settlement. The first, Rule 430, required purchasers' brokers to accept delivery of certificates representing some, but not all, of the shares their customers had purchased. Before Rule 430, purchasing brokers could require that all shares owed pursuant to a trade be delivered or none be accepted. The second, Rule 433, prohibited Exchange members from executing trades on behalf of customers unless the customer could assure the selling broker that the customer would be able to produce certificates for the shares to be sold on the settlement date.[3]

With fails declining and the N.Y.S.E. able to point to the implementation of at least part of Cohen's program, Robert Haack was hoping to get S.E.C. approval for a return to a five-day trading week. Cohen was not so sure the back offices could handle it, and trading volumes were creeping up again in September. The S.E.C. insisted Haack wait.

There was one constituency that Cohen felt had not been enlisted in the battle against the paperwork backlog: the companies that issued stock. While most of the bottlenecks were with the back offices of the investment banks, the transfer agents were hardly models of efficiency. Cohen thought they also could do better and wanted companies with publicly traded stock to do their part in the crisis by holding their transfer agents accountable. The only part of Cohen's seven-point plan that required the S.E.C. to enact new regulations was oversight of transfer agents, which had theretofore been unregulated. Accordingly, on September 25, the S.E.C. proposed a new rule, Rule 10b-14, which would have made it illegal for a company to fail to have a transfer agent reasonably capable of promptly processing transfers of its stock.[4]

Cohen's rule, read literally and broadly, would have made every public company responsible for Wall Street's back-office mess. Since it would have at the time been next to impossible for a company to find a transfer agent reasonably capable of promptly transferring stock certificates, nearly every public company would have been a violator of the federal securities laws. Corporate America has always been resentful of both Washington and Wall Street for the regulations placed on it as a result of the excesses and misdeeds of Wall Street. Many of the harsher provisions of the New Deal securities laws as originally proposed were dropped because of the burdens they would have imposed on regular corporations and their executives, who had power and influence that reached deep into every state and congressional district. Cohen's proposed rule 10b-14 was opposed by the commercial banking industry, the investment banking industry, and public companies of every industry. The rule was never adopted by the S.E.C.

DURING THE THIRD week of September 1968, a phenomenon had captivated the imagination of Wall Street. At precisely 1:28 p.m. every weekday, Francine Gottfried of Williamsburg, Brooklyn, a twenty-one-year-old operator of an I.B.M. System/360 computer at Chemical Bank's downtown data processing center, would emerge from the BMT Subway's Wall Street station. She would then walk for two minutes to her office and punch in for the 1:30 p.m. to 9:30 p.m. shift. Soon after she started the job at Chemical Bank in late May, she noticed many of the same smiling faces each day among a group of men loitering around the subway entrance on their lunch breaks when she'd walk out. By September, the group had grown to over a dozen, and it continued to grow exponentially. By the third week of September, over 15,000 men clogged the entire intersection—and each of the four corners—of Broad and Wall Streets. Even on Wednesdays, when the exchanges were closed, more than 2,000 men would turn out. Men climbed light poles for better vantage. Heads poked out of windows. A lecherous old gray-haired Morgan partner peered anxiously from the oversized windows of the Corner, the stately House of Morgan office. They even started throwing ticker-tape at her.

"It even happened at her brother's wedding," a friend of Francine's told a reporter. This phenomenon got the attention of the press, which covered it as a whimsical diversion from the horrors of the daily news that year. "When she walked down the aisle, nobody looked at the bride," the friend remembered. Francine, who stood 5'3" with measurements of 43-25-37, was used to the attention and tried to take it in stride. "When I was sixteen," she told *New York* magazine, "the teachers in Eastern District High School, which I attended, started to look at me and so did the construction workers in the area. After I saw this happening, I'd just ignore it because otherwise I would smile and it could lead them on. You know, about two years ago, my doctor said that I would not grow in height anymore, but my bustline was still growing."[5]

The press called her the "Sweater Girl of Wall Street," with cheeky headlines like "Boom and Bust on Wall Street" and "A Bust Panics Wall Street as the Tape Says 43." With the press attention, Francine Gottfried was bombarded with offers for modeling gigs, television appearances, and a movie deal. A Times Square strip bar offered her a $100,000 contract. She turned them all down. Mostly, Francine thought about the sanity of those charged with running the nation's financial system. "I think they're all mental cases. I'm just an ordinary girl. There are thousands of girls on Wall Street and they act as though I'm the only one. . . . These people in Wall

Street have the responsibility of handling millions of dollars and they act like they're out of their minds. I think they're all crazy." By October, Francine, fearful of losing her job, took a different route to work. The disappointed gawkers looked elsewhere and the hysteria died.[6]

Not everyone thought it was lighthearted fun.

Karla Jay was a recent graduate of Barnard College who was working in a low-level job at a publishing house while she pursued her master's degree at New York University. Karla had participated in the protests against the Vietnam War at Columbia during the previous spring but was put off by how the male-dominated leadership of that movement had treated female members and supporters. She became increasingly drawn to organizations forming the burgeoning feminist movement in New York City. The Francine Gottfried craze was an epiphany for Karla Jay. Whether they were buttoned-down conservative men of Wall Street or long-haired radical Weathermen, men thought they were entitled to sexually objectify women, on the street, on campus, or in the workplace, even to the point of humiliation or worse.

Back then, there wasn't a label to describe it and the concept lacked any legal recognition. Karla Jay began referring to this male bad behavior as sexual harassment. By means of her creative activism and brilliant public relations skills, Karla Jay would, eighteen months later, force the men of Wall Street to confront their sexual harassment of women—at the same subway station Francine Gottfried ran the gauntlet.

WITH A VOTE of N.Y.S.E. members to approve his volume discount plan pending, Robert Haack was eager to appease the investment banks that did a large block trading business. What these firms wanted most was a return to a five-day trading week, as they generally had the least back-office issues. And Haack gave them what they wanted, stating in a special bulletin to members on September 30: "It seems apparent that the exchange cannot continue to rely on shortened trading weeks for the entire membership. This broad-gauged measure penalizes those member organizations who are able to carry a full operational load. With a return to normal trading weeks, those firms under restriction will remain limited to present levels of volume input (as represented by daily tickets) until greater operational capability is established."[7]

Haack's problem was that while the condition of the back offices as a whole had improved, there were still underperforming firms whose back offices were still dysfunctional. Out of the approximately four hundred firms that dealt with the public, forty-four were under some form of Exchange-mandated operational restriction. Ten of those firms were limited in the amount of additional volume they were allowed to handle. Five were instructed to cut back on volume. The Exchange refused to identify any of the forty-four firms under restriction, fearing doing so might cause customers and other firms to cease transacting with them, causing a run on the bank. On October 2, the *New York Times* published for the first time what was theretofore only spoken of privately: "The private fear of some brokers is that a major firm might be forced to suspend operations because of bookkeeping difficulties and thus trigger a possible lack of confidence on the part of the investing public."[8] The S.E.C. was not yet ready to take that risk. Manny Cohen told Haack that, notwithstanding his political problem with the block trading houses, he would not allow a return to normal trading. Volume was again picking up again, exceeding 15 million shares per day on the N.Y.S.E. during the first trading week in October.

Much of the market optimism that week was attributed to friendly comments coming out of the Nixon campaign. On October 2, a fundraising letter sent by Nixon to potential donors on Wall Street entitled "The Role of the Securities Industry in the National Economy" was leaked to the press—motivated apparently by displeasure at Nixon's blatant pandering to special interests. Speaking to how the growth of institutional investing has "overburdened our nation's stock exchanges" and the need to protect the investing public, Nixon criticized the Johnson–Humphrey administration:

"The response of this Administration to these new challenges, however, has been to simply to trot out all the same tired old 'cure-alls' of the Democratic party, that is, more heavy-handed bureaucratic regulatory schemes." This was interpreted by Wall Street as a thinly veiled promise to roll back the aggressive insider trading enforcement by the S.E.C. and rein in the Justice Department on antitrust challenges to fixed commission rates.[9]

Roy Cohn received his own thinly veiled promise of assistance from the Nixon campaign. On October 8, Cohn held a fundraising lunch for Nixon at the exclusive Lotos Club in Manhattan, which Maurice Stans attended on behalf of the Nixon campaign. In front of a dozen moguls that Cohn had invited, Cohn bluntly asked what a Nixon administration would do to rein in Manny Cohen and Robert Morgenthau. Without hesitating, Stans promised those assembled that Cohen and Morgenthau would be replaced forthwith if Nixon were elected. With that out of the way, Cohn handed to Stans the $40,000 he had raised from his well-heeled clients and friends.[10]

ON OCTOBER 11, the board of governors of the N.Y.S.E. formally presented its S.E.C.-approved volume discount plan to the Exchange's 1,336 members. The approval vote would take place over a two-week period.[11] A week later, concerned about the grumbling over the proposal, Haack sent a memorandum to the membership warning them that if the volume discount plan was not approved, the S.E.C. likely would impose its own plan on the Exchange members. The S.E.C.'s plan would undoubtedly be much less acceptable than what was on the table for their approval. "While the interim schedule is not perfect," Haack wrote, "we believe it is a definite improvement over the S.E.C.'s original proposal. It represents a balanced and responsive answer—formulated within our industry—to the immediate commission problems facing us."[12] On October 24, the balloting was completed. The plan was approved by a vote of 925 to 266 (with 175 members abstaining or not voting). Haack hailed the victory, declaring that members "have strengthened the principle of the minimum commission."[13]

THE PRESERVATION OF the existing fixed commission schedule for transactions under 1,000 shares was a reprieve for many firms with a large retail brokerage business. No firm needed a reprieve in the fall of 1968 more than McDonnell & Co. The computer systems consulting firm McDonnell & Co. had hired, Data Architects, still had not been able to get the SECURE computer system fully operational for the McDonnell & Co. back-office operations in mid-October. Nevertheless, during the first six months of 1968, the firm netted a profit of $750,000. It also received a clean bill of health from the S.E.C. in early July. It made another $1 million in profit for the month of August. On paper, all appeared to be going swimmingly for McDonnell & Co. Sales were up 50 percent from 1967. It had hired a hundred new salesmen.[14]

Many would later ask why Murray McDonnell hadn't simply scrapped SECURE, dumped Data Architects, and started over, or at least outsourced back-office operations until the system was functional. The likely answer is that Murray was too invested, financially and psychologically, with Data Architects' success. By the end of October, McDonnell & Co. spent $2 million internally preparing for SECURE and had paid Data Architects nearly $500,000. When Data Architects ran short of working capital that fall, McDonnell & Co. purchased a 24.5 percent stake in the firm and lent it $35,000, interest-free. McDonnell & Co. was providing 86 percent of Data Architects' revenues. Perhaps most importantly, Data Architects had on August 16 filed a registration statement with the S.E.C. for a public offering of 125,000 shares, underwritten by D. H. Blair. A third of the proceeds of the offering were to establish a New York office and staff it for six months, which would alleviate the burden on McDonnell & Co. to provide it with working capital. The offering closed in December at $11 per share.[15]

Finally, in desperation, McDonnell & Co. outsourced its back-office function to Shields & Co., which ran one of the most efficient back-office operations and had excess computing capacity.[16] Given the overtime fees—and Shields's profit on the deal (very healthy, as it knew it had McDonnell & Co. over a barrel)—the arrangement cost McDonnell & Co. an additional $500,000 during the fourth quarter of 1968.

Data Architects finally declared SECURE operational in early November. It shut down three days later. "It just stopped working," one McDonnell & Co. executive later recalled. "It aborted. Trades got lost. There were no confirmations. It was as simple as that. What we had was our old N.C.R.-based system operating at an inadequate rate on top of a new system with hardware that wasn't functioning. As a result, when heavy trading volume aborted the computer programming, there were fantastic breaks in our stock record account, which controls the inventory of stock certificates. This is a basic record. Once it goes, you have a real problem."

All during the summer and fall of 1968, McDonnell & Co.'s fails rose and its aged fails grew at an even faster rate. With mandatory buy-ins required for shares remaining undelivered for long periods under the recently adopted Exchange rule, firms were required to book a liability for the cost. This would have profound implications for McDonnell's net capital rule compliance, already weakened by the capital drain from the Data Architects debacle.

McDonnell & Co.'s outside auditing firm, Lybrand, Ross Bros. & Montgomery, discovered that McDonnell & Co. had nearly $10 million worth of stock certificates on hand it could not determine the ownership of. It owed another $1.5 million worth of stock that it did not have in inventory or could not find. Most ominously, its audit showed that McDonnell & Co. had less than $4 million of net capital. As a result of the irreconcilable differences in securities ownership and dividend accounts, McDonnell & Co.'s net capital ratio was over 30-to-1, substantially in excess of the maximum allowable ratio of 20-to-1. Lybrand, Ross Bros. & Montgomery, a major independent accounting firm and a leading auditor of Wall Street firms, was duty-bound to report the net capital rule violation to the N.Y.S.E.[17]

This left Murray McDonnell with two new problems in addition to the continuing horror of the Data Architects incompetence and the resulting ballooning of fails and aged fails. First, McDonnell & Co. needed to secure additional capital to quickly erase the deficiency revealed by the Lybrand audit, as the Exchange would require at least a colorable claim of compliance with the net capital rule to allow McDonnell & Co. to operate. Second, it needed to somehow convince the Exchange not to inform the S.E.C. of its net capital rule violation. With the zero-tolerance environment of late 1968, this would have led to McDonnell & Co. being placed on operational restriction at the very least. It may have led to enforcement action against it. And if the S.E.C. knew the extent of the disaster in its back office, it may well have shut McDonnell & Co. down, like Pickard & Co. and L. D. Sherman & Co.

Raising capital from an outside third party would have been impossible. Any rudimentary due diligence investigation of McDonnell & Co. would have unveiled the Lybrand audit and the Data Architects catastrophe, which would have made a capital raise dead on arrival. In addition, teams of lawyers and accountants kicking the tires also would increase the likelihood of a leak to the Street of the true extent of McDonnell & Co.'s financial and operational problems.

Friends and family were Murray's only hope. It is said that Murray reached out to his former brother-in-law, Henry Ford II, who passed on the opportunity to invest. It was also rumored that he reached out to Jackie Kennedy, recently remarried to Aristotle Onassis, to seek her intervention in arranging an investment from the Greek shipping billionaire. In any event, no investment from Onassis materialized either.

Murray put the arm on potential investors over whom he had leverage, and who were unlikely to ask too many due diligence questions—McDonnell & Co. employees. Despite previously hoarding the firm's equity for himself and his family, Murray was now extolling the virtues of employee ownership. During November and December 1968, Murray sold approximately $3 million worth of McDonnell & Co. stock and subordinated notes to over eighty employees, fifty-nine of whom were neither officers nor in supervisory positions. Instead of offering the securities by way of an offering circular with disclosure similar to an S.E.C.-filed prospectus, Murray used a fourteen-page puff-piece promoting an investment in McDonnell & Co.[17] No mention was made of the Lybrand audit. No mention was made of the Data Architects disaster. No mention was made of the net capital rule violation. The capital raised from McDonnell & Co. employees was enough to satisfy the Exchange, at least for the time being. McDonnell & Co. was allowed to operate without any formal restriction or heightened supervision by the Exchange. This solved the first of Murray's two new problems. (It would turn out that all of the $3 million would be eaten up by operating losses by the end of 1968.)[18]

The solution to the second problem—convincing the Exchange to keep the S.E.C. in the dark about McDonnell's woes—required calling in many markers and calling upon many old tribal loyalties.

With the Department of Justice and the S.E.C. unconvinced as to the legality of fixed commissions, Robert Haack was by no means permanently out of the woods on that issue. Chairman Cohen had made it explicitly clear that he held the Exchange responsible for the back-office crisis. He considered it a failure of self-regulation. Simply put, too much heat was on the Exchange for any formal grant of relief to McDonnell & Co. If Exchange officials were found to be intentionally hiding violations from the S.E.C., those complicit would have been driven from office by Manny Cohen.

What is known is that the Exchange never informed the S.E.C. of McDonnell & Co.'s violation of the net capital rule in 1968.[19] Nor did the Exchange inform the S.E.C. of the dysfunction in McDonnell's back office. All of this was laid out in plain language in the Lybrand report, which the Exchange had in its possession. What is also known is that there were very few men who could have arranged for such an omission under those circumstances in the fall of 1968. Certainly Haack would never have acceded to it. Even more certainly, John Cunningham would not have done so without Haack acceding to it.

There was one man who could arrange it: John Coleman.

A scandal involving McDonnell & Co. would have caused Coleman no small amount of grief. McDonnell & Co. was unquestionably the "Irish" investment banking firm in the eyes of the public. And it employed a great many sons of wealthy Irish Catholics, the same families from whom Coleman solicited money for the Church and the politicians. While Murray McDonnell was nowhere near as important a fundraiser or advisor to Cardinal Spellman and the archdiocese as Coleman, he was a generous donor and he was the broker through whom the archdiocese and its many foundations and trusts executed their securities transactions. And because the McDonnells had been staples of the society and gossip pages for two generations, widespread press coverage of any of the family firm's troubles was guaranteed.

The truth was that Coleman was not particularly close with Murray McDonnell. He thought him rather a lightweight. In particular, Coleman was not a fan of Murray's compulsive socializing and publicity-seeking. In Coleman's inner circle were mostly other Irish specialists, discreet men like his brother and Joseph Meehan. In the pecking order of Wall Street, especially at N.Y.S.E, retail brokers like Murray, "customer's men" as they were referred to, not entirely without derision, were near the bottom. Specialists like Coleman, who risked their own capital daily in the jungle warfare of raw capitalism on the floor of an exchange, were at the very top of the testosterone and bravado food chain. Near to the top were block traders. Somewhere between the customer's men and the block traders were the investment bankers. They hobnobbed in boardrooms with Fortune 500 executives, arranging IPOs and billion-dollar conglomerate mergers, but were considered a bit too fastidious by the traders and specialists. Investment bankers were more likely to prefer taking a client sailing in Newport than wild boar hunting in Tennessee.

When Murray turned to his former brother-in-law, Henry Ford II, for a bailout, he knew that Ford would consult his best friend and closest financial advisor, who happened to be Joseph Meehan, the specialist for Ford Motor Company's stock at the Exchange.[20] Upon hearing of Murray's predicament, Joe Meehan's first call was to Coleman. While Coleman would neither provide capital to McDonnell & Co. nor try to persuade others to, he did pull the strings to keep word of the net capital rule violation and back-office debacle from the ears of S.E.C. to give Murray time to work things out.

DESPITE THE DISASTROUS convention in Chicago, the continuing war in Vietnam, and the dissolution of the southern Democrats over civil rights and George Wallace's third-party campaign, Hubert Humphrey was climbing in the polls against Richard Nixon throughout October. On October 31, five days before the election, President Johnson announced that North Vietnam had agreed to meet with South Vietnam to negotiate peace terms and, accordingly, Johnson was halting the bombing of North Vietnam. Wall Street, along with the rest of America, cheered. Humphrey surged in the polls, to a dead heat with Nixon. It was the October surprise Nixon had feared. But Nixon, too, had a trick up his sleeve. He had back-channeled with the government in South Vietnam in anticipation of this development and advised them to hang tough and reject the overtures from the communists for peace talks. He promised them that after the election, a President Nixon would get South Vietnam better terms than a President Humphrey would. Saigon bet on Nixon and rejected the peace offer.

On election night, the television pundits warned viewers they might be in for a long evening. The popular vote margin turned out to be razor-thin, but Nixon's "Southern Strategy" worked. The outcome wasn't certain until the following morning, when Humphrey finally conceded.

Wall Street cheered the Nixon victory and the expected general direction of his economic program: controlling inflation, strengthening the dollar, reducing federal spending, and tamping down on regulation. The Dow was up only slightly, 3.24 points, the day after the election, as the market had already priced in a Nixon victory. Stock prices had run up 11.5 percent from August through mid-October. It was speculated that Manny Cohen would not be long for the S.E.C. with the change of administration. It was rumored that Robert H. Volk, Commissioner of the Division of Corporations in California, would replace him. The former rumor would prove to be true; not so the latter.

THE THIRD PHASE of the S.E.C. rate hearings focused on the Department of Justice presenting evidence challenging the N.Y.S.E.'s economic testimony in support of fixed commissions and on determining whether the S.E.C. should set the terms upon which non-members would be given access to execute trades on the Exchange.

The first witness called by the Department of Justice was Dr. Paul Samuelson, the eminent economics professor at the Massachusetts Institute of Technology. Samuelson testified that the securities business was no more a public utility than the grocery business. "No one has suggested that the 1,000 most important grocers be allowed to form a club to regulate mark-ups and charges," Samuelson asserted. "No one has suggested that competition in the grocery industry would be ruinous and should be supplanted by monopoly." Samuelson also stated that Wall Street had made poor use of its monopoly profits: "Too much has been going to the members and not enough to automation."[21]

After Samuelson, Dr. William J. Baumol, professor of economics at Princeton University, testified. Baumol rebutted point by point the arguments made by the N.Y.S.E. for the preservation of fixed commissions. For example, regarding the argument that investment research would cease, Baumol replied: "Surely there is no better evidence of the viability of a competitive market for research services than the continued existence of a number of investment advisory services which are able to sell their information despite the availability of brokers' research services at zero cost." With regard to the criteria used to set N.Y.S.E. commissions rates, Baumol testified that no criteria of reasonableness have ever been articulated by either the Exchange or the S.E.C.: "The basic point is that this is no accident. It should really be obvious that there can be no accounting procedure, no cost calculation capable of defining justice and equity when competitive pricing is abandoned in such a market."[22]

Henry C. Wallich, a former member of the Council of Economic Advisors under President Eisenhower and a professor of economics at Yale University, appeared next at the S.E.C. hearings. Wallich reasoned that the fixed commission rate system had the effect of taxing institutional investors in order to subsidize small, inefficient securities firms that would fail in a competitive marketplace. He further noted that there existed plenty of capacity among the healthy firms that would survive in a competitive commission rate environment to service both institutional and retail investors. Accordingly, he found little public policy justification for fixed commissions. That day's other witness was Michael Mann, a staff economist at the Antitrust Division of the Department of Justice who methodically discredited the economic data the N.Y.S.E. had presented earlier. It had aggregated data from all operations of all investment banks, Mann pointed out, rather than narrowing its cost and revenue data to the brokerage operations and breaking out the data by institutional and retail brokerage operations.[23]

On November 7, the hearings turned to focus on non-member access to the N.Y.S.E. The first witness was Morris A. Schapiro, the managing partner of M. A. Schapiro & Company, a leading investment bank focused on the commercial banking industry. Historically, most commercial banks prior to the 1960s did not list their shares on an exchange. Accordingly, M. A. Schapiro & Company did not become a member of the N.Y.S.E. and was the leading

O.T.C. dealer in bank stocks. Schapiro's testimony focused on N.Y.S.E. Rule 394, which prohibited a member firm from buying or selling listed stocks to or from a non-member unless it had under-taken "a diligent effort to explore the feasibility of obtaining a sat-isfactory execution of the order on the floor" and concluded that such an execution would not be feasible. Schapiro testified that Rule 394 was a ruse in that it served no purpose other than preserv-ing the Exchange's monopoly. He also criticized the S.E.C. for not having completed its promised review of how Rule 394 was actually operating in practice. In truth, few trades were actually made off the Exchange by its members even when better execution in the Third Market was demonstrably available.

The following day, Donald Weeden of Weeden & Co., the largest Third Market firm, appeared. Weeden testified that compliance with Rule 394 "is too complicated and too time-consuming to make it workable" and, accordingly, resulted in few trades leaving the floor. Weeden shared his trading records with Gene Rotberg. They showed that Weeden & Co. had been approached by Exchange members 131 times during the prior two years for Rule 394 trades. In 114 of those cases, Weeden & Co. offered a price that was more advantageous than the price available on the floor. In only 65 cases was Weeden & Co. permitted to make the trade. Weeden said the rule allowed the Exchange to "claim complete fulfillment by its members of their responsibilities as brokers to get the best possible price for their customers" without actually doing so.

Representative Emmanuel Celler, the Brooklyn Democrat who chaired the House Antitrust Subcommittee, followed closely the S.E.C. hearings relating to Rule 394. What Celler heard sounded like an antitrust violation to him. In December, he sent a letter to Edwin M. Zimmerman, head of the Antitrust Division of the De-partment of Justice, recommending that the Antitrust Division file a lawsuit against the N.Y.S.E. to strike down Rule 394 as an illegal restraint of trade. Zimmerman demurred, replying that the S.E.C. rate inquiry, for the time being, "appears to be an expeditious way of resolving critical issues." He did not rule out a suit at a later date, however. With Celler, one of the most powerful members of Congress, now focused on the N.Y.S.E.'s anticompetitive conduct, Robert Haack had another major problem in Washington.

ROY COHN WAS finally indicted by Robert Morgenthau on November 22, 1968. It was clear to Cohn that Muscat, who was listed as an unindicted co-conspirator, would testify against him. He was charged with bribing a state court official in connection with a shareholder suit against Fifth Avenue Coach Lines and with filing a false proxy statement with the S.E.C. Cohn immediately proclaimed his innocence and accused Morgenthau of persecuting him as a result of a personal vendetta. "For over six years now Mr. Morgenthau has carried on an almost unbelievably vicious campaign of harassment against me, apparently to seek redress through criminal proceedings for a personal grievance he developed against me due to my work with the United States Senate committee many years ago."[24]

IN LATE NOVEMBER, the board of governors of the N.Y.S.E. approved the return to a five-day trading week starting on January 2, 1969, with shortened hours from 10:00 a.m. to 2:00 p.m., rather than the usual 3:30 p.m. closing bell.[25] The S.E.C. was not enthusiastic about the decision, convinced that too many firms had not yet stabilized, but it did not intervene to prohibit it.

On December 1, when the N.Y.S.E.'s mandatory buy-in rule took effect, visibility into the financial damage that back-office problems had inflicted on the firms would emerge. As that picture became clearer in 1969, it would not be pretty. The nature of the crisis would evolve from one principally operational in nature—managing the mountain of paper—to reckoning with the cost of the lost certificates, the failed trades, and the enormous investment undertaken, begrudgingly by many firms, in computer systems and personnel to modernize the back offices and implement

C.C.S. And this reckoning would occur during the worst possible environment—a bear market.

A harbinger of events to come occurred that December with the forced sale of Schwabacher & Co., a large San Francisco–based brokerage with fifteen branch offices in western states that was struggling with profound back-office issues. The N.Y.S.E. arranged for it to be acquired by Blair & Co., a larger, healthier firm with thirty-two branch offices, all in the East.

Despite having 12 percent fewer trading days as a result of the Wednesday closings, volume for 1968 increased 16 percent. On twenty-five trading days, N.Y.S.E. volume exceeded 16.4 million shares, the record from Black Tuesday that had stood for over thirty-eight years. Notwithstanding the record volume in 1968, the actions taken by the N.Y.S.E. and the S.E.C. in 1968—the shortened trading hours, the Wednesday closings, the punitive restrictions on firms with deficient back offices, the enforcement actions and new rules—had improved operations, reducing fails and prodding the industry to upgrade its technology and human resources. Industry-wide, aged fails at year-end totaled $652,860,000, down from the mid-July peak of approximately $837 million.

Despite record trading volume and a 29 percent increase in revenues, profit margins for the industry had declined dramatically, from 7.2 percent of revenues in 1967 to 4.7 percent in 1968. The daily N.Y.S.E. volume "break-even" level had risen to 10.1 million shares a day in 1968 from 7.2 million shares in 1967. Despite the record revenue, 17 percent of all N.Y.S.E. firms lost money. Quite obviously, costs were out of control.

The disastrous year of 1968 ended with the worst flu outbreak New York had suffered since the 1918 Spanish Flu Pandemic. The 1968 flu, named the Hong Kong flu for the place of its believed origin, hit New York City hard in December. By Christmas, nearly a million New York City residents had been infected, and new cases were running 150,000 per week. Vice President Hubert Humphrey came down with an early case and spent much of December recovering in Phoenix, Arizona. In Chicago, Mayor Daley caught it early as well and missed his first City Council meeting since 1955. On December 18, President Johnson fell ill with a bad case and was sent to Bethesda Naval Hospital, where he was kept for five days. Former C.I.A. Director Allen W. Dulles caught the Hong Kong flu around Christmas and never recovered, passing away in Washington on January 29, 1969.

Whatever 1969 held in store, the widely held belief on Wall Street at year-end was that it could not be any worse than the year just passed, and with Nixon taking office, most were cautiously optimistic. 1969 would shatter the optimism.

PART III

1969

The Bear Market

CHAPTER SEVEN

"ARE WE PAYING FOR ALL OF THIS?"

■

The Bill Comes Due

The annual prognosticators predicted that 1969 would see mostly stable trading volume, solid economic growth, and a tempering of nascent inflation, with the supposed inflation-hawkish Nixon in the White House. They were wrong on all counts. The decline into the deepest bear market since the Great Depression had already begun when the Dow topped out at 990 in December 1968, as had an economic slowdown that would drag the economy into recession by the end of 1969. These brought a decline in trading volume and an even steeper decline in commission revenue fueled by the volume discount and increasing competition. The competition came from the Third Market and new computerized trading platforms directly linking institutional buyers and sellers, taking the broker and commission costs completely out of the transaction—what were referred to as the "Fourth Market." Trading volumes in the O. T. C. market would decline even more than on the N.Y.S.E. The seemingly insatiable appetite for stocks during most of 1968 had already been sated by New Year's Day 1969. The hot technology stocks had cooled. So, too, had those of the conglomerates with their high-flying price-to-earnings ratios goosed by creative accounting that fueled the hottest of the Go-Go stocks. Also gone were the rich merger and acquisition advisory fees from the stock-for-stock conglomerate mergers.

Any drop in stock prices was a direct hit to the net capital of firms that owned those stocks. The 1969 bear market's sharpest bite would not be the loss of commission and fee revenue, but rather the decrease in asset values on the balance sheets of the investment banks. The S.E.C.'s aggressive enforcement actions against firms with deficient back-office operations were costing money as well. So, too, was the N.Y.S.E. imposing operating restrictions on those firms. The industry had finally gotten religion, but at a steep price, deploying scarce capital to invest in computer systems to modernize back offices and incurring the expenses to aggressively hire new back-office personnel and raise the salaries of good back-office employees to stem defections. Because much of that investment and expense was financed with borrowed money and did not produce additional revenue, it had a negative impact on the net capital of many firms—many of which were struggling to remain in compliance with the N.Y.S.E.'s net capital rule.

ALFRED J. COYLE, the chairman and president of Hayden, Stone, Inc., one of the largest brokerage firms in the nation, sent a memo to the firm's employees on January 14, 1969, disclosing that the firm had established a $16 million reserve for possible losses due to operational problems and that it had recently added $11 million to its capital to strengthen its financial position. The memo—and its leaking to the press—was intended to quell growing rumors that Hayden, Stone was in financial distress. Several weeks earlier, the firm had dismissed two hundred salesmen and gutted its research staff. It had also removed its former president, Ara A. Cambre, in classic Wall Street style, giving him the lofty-sounding title of vice-chairman while substantially reducing his responsibilities. "Our financial position is sound," Coyle stressed in the memo, noting that the firm maintained $43 million of equity capital. "We continue to enhance our capital position, both by resolving operational difficulties and by additions to capital funds. These additions will not only strengthen our capital base, but also allow the exploitation of business opportunities which will open up as sufficient capital funds can be contributed to their development. We do not envisage a need for additional business restraints and the need to continue currently effective restraints will be reviewed continuously in the light of our operations progress. As we and the investment industry emerge from the current abnormal situation, this firm will not duplicate the same business pattern which existed early last year."[1]

The memo did not stop the rumors. This was primarily the result of the rumors being true: Hayden, Stone's net worth was dropping fast. It was whispered that the capital raise was mandated by the S.E.C. and that Hayden, Stone would have been subjected to severe regulatory restrictions on its operations if it hadn't complied. The whisperers also noted that Hayden, Stone's numbers did not reflect the effects of the mandated reductions to capital to take into account the mandatory buy-ins that had gone into effect on December 1, 1968, and that the true extent of its financial problems were being understated. At the N.Y.S.E., Robert Haack was deeply concerned that a collapse of Hayden, Stone would be the trigger for the kind of systemic event that Keith Funston feared might be underway during the weekend of President Kennedy's assassination. "If one member firm went out of business with a huge backlog of fails, every firm that had done business with that firm would find that its own fails problem had become far more severe," wrote financial columnist Robert Metz in the *New York Times* that week.[2]

The rumors that Hayden, Stone was in the crosshairs of the S.E.C. were also true.

HAYDEN, STONE & CO. was originally a Boston firm, founded in 1892 by Charles Hayden (the patron of the Hayden Planetarium at the American Museum of Natural History in New York) and his partner, Galen Stone. The firm opened a New York City office in 1906. In 1919, Galen Stone hired thirty-year-old Joseph Kennedy away from the Bethlehem Shipbuilding Corporation's Fore River

Shipyard in Quincy, Massachusetts, having been impressed by Kennedy's work there during World War I. With Galen Stone as his mentor, Kennedy would emerge a decade later as one of the wealthiest men on Wall Street. With Kennedy sourcing deal after lucrative deal, Hayden, Stone would emerge from the 1920s as a premier investment bank. Over the following decades, Hayden, Stone grew modestly and maintained its reputation as a major white-shoe underwriter with a retail business catering mostly to older, wealthy families.

This all changed in the 1960s as Hayden, Stone, much like every investment bank during the decade, drank the Kool-Aid of the Go-Go Era. It went on a broker hiring binge, eliminating its traditional requirement that all of its salesmen have MBAs (preferably from an Ivy League school) and instead requiring no specified level of education. As one observer noted, Hayden, Stone "hired the butcher, the banker, and just about anyone who could write an order in legible English." What it did not invest in was state-of-the-art computers, or much else, for the back office. In 1969, with the New York Regional Office of the S.E.C. breathing down its neck, the consequences of its breakneck expansion and shaky capital structure would be devastating.

HAYDEN, STONE'S FINANCES would be damaged further by regulatory developments in Washington. Three days before Richard Nixon's inauguration, the Antitrust Division of the Johnson Justice Department escalated its war on fixed commissions by formally declaring to the S.E.C. that fixed-rate commissions were illegal. Having heard enough of the S.E.C. rate hearings testimony to conclude that deferral on the question of legality of fixed commissions was no longer the preferable course, the Justice Department urged that the S.E.C. initially order an end to fixed commission rates on all transactions involving $50,000 or more, then reducing the floor by $10,000 annually to eliminate fixed commissions entirely in five years.[3]

The initial reaction from the N.Y.S.E. was to buy time—perhaps an S.E.C. and a Justice Department dominated by Nixon appointees would be more sympathetic to the securities industry. On January 22, Robert Haack, speaking at the Institutional Investor Conference at the New York Hilton, reminded the audience that the Exchange had engaged N.E.R.A. to undertake one of the most comprehensive studies of commissions ever undertaken.[4] The study, Haack assured them, would lead to a permanent rate proposal that would be acceptable to the S.E.C. Haack estimated that the study would take another twelve to eighteen months (and would cost more than $400,000) and hoped that the Exchange would get a reprieve during that period—long enough for the Nixon appointees to be confirmed and for the industry lobbyists to remind the Wall Streeters in Nixon's cabinet—Maurice Stans, the new Secretary of Commerce, and John Mitchell, the new attorney general—of their generosity during the 1968 campaign.

ON THE DAY the Justice Department sent the inflammatory memo to the S.E.C. on fixed commissions, the D.O.J. made news in New York as well. U.S. Attorney Robert Morgenthau announced that he had brought an additional ten-count indictment against Roy Cohn relating to the Fifth Avenue Coach Lines affair. The indictment alleged that Cohn had conspired to bribe the expert appraiser retained by the City of New York in the company's eminent domain valuation litigation. Morgenthau alleged that Cohn paid the appraiser, Bernard Reicher, $25,000 if he would leak confidential appraisal documents to Cohn. The indictment further alleged that Cohn had blackmailed Lawrence Weisman, the former president of Fifth Avenue Coach Lines and a co-conspirator in the alleged blackmail scheme, into selling his stock in Fifth Avenue Coach Lines to a new owner preferred by Cohn, the Victor Muscat group.[5]

Cohn told the press that the new indictment was simply a desperate attempt by Morgenthau to bolster the flimsy November 1968 charges.[6]

■ ■ ■

AFTER EIGHT YEARS of Democratic administrations in Washington, the leaders of the New Frontier and the Great Society were leaving government and looking for work in the private sector. More than a few would find themselves with jobs on Wall Street. Henry Fowler, Johnson's Secretary of the Treasury, accepted a partnership at Goldman, Sachs & Co. C. R. Smith, Secretary of Commerce, became a partner at Lazard Freres & Co. George Ball, former Under Secretary of State and later ambassador to the United Nations, returned to Lehman Brothers. Surprising to many was the selection of Larry O'Brien, postmaster general under President Kennedy and chairman of the Democratic Party under President Johnson, to be the president of McDonnell & Co. O'Brien, a lifelong pol, had no business experience at all, not to mention no finance experience.[7]

Larry O'Brien had been introduced to Murray McDonnell by a mutual friend, George Bissell, in December 1968.[8] Still grieving from the assassination of his friend Robert Kennedy and dispirited by Humphrey's loss to Nixon, O'Brien was eager to leave politics and was considering forming his own consulting business when Murray offered him the top job at McDonnell & Co. Over the Christmas holiday, O'Brien decided to accept Murray's offer and came to McDonnell & Co.'s office, literally for the first time, as president of the firm on January 20, 1969, Nixon's inauguration day.[9]

Beginning work that day in the White House was Murray McDonnell's brother-in-law, Peter Flanigan, the Dillon, Read & Co. partner who was selected by Nixon as his chief White House advisor for economic affairs. Flanigan would become so powerful in the Nixon White House that Ralph Nader would call him a "mini-president." Peter Flanigan was also the son of Horace Flanigan, the chairman of Manufacturers Hanover Trust Company, and Aimee Magnus, the granddaughter of the founder of the Anheuser-Busch brewing dynasty.

With Nixon in the White House, but the Democrats in control of Congress, Larry O'Brien was an insurance policy to Murray Mc-Donnell, who didn't care what O'Brien knew about finance, only about whom he knew in Congress. If matters continued as they were for McDonnell & Co., the necessity of a government bailout was not out of the question. As losses continued in January 1969, Murray attempted to shore up the firm's capital with nearly $2 mil-lion contributed by family members and $1.6 million contributed by him with the proceeds of a personal loan to him from First Na-tional City Bank. Of course, none of the firm's problems were dis-closed to Larry O'Brien. At his first official event for McDonnell & Co., the opening of a new San Francisco office, amid the clinking of crystal champagne glasses, O'Brien eyed the opulent office with its grand chandeliers and expensive furniture and asked a junior salesman: "Are we paying for all of this?"[10]

OUTRAGEOUS SPENDING HAD also brought about the de-mise of the most prominent New Left magazine of the 1960s—*Ramparts*. What no one knew in January 1969 was that the bankruptcy of *Ramparts* was the proximate cause of the last hot is-sue IPO of the Go-Go Era and quite possibly the most unlikely stock offering of them all. The tales of largesse of *Ramparts*'s editor-in-chief, Warren Hinckle III, became literary legend. At the 1968 Democratic convention in Chicago, *Ramparts* had a larger cov-erage team than the *New York Times* and the *Washington Post* com-bined. Hinckle rented suites of rooms on multiple floors costing tens of thousands of dollars a night at the Ambassador East and invited scores of pals to eat, drink, and be tear-gassed on the *Ram-parts* dime. Every night after the convention program ended, Hinckle and his pals Hunter S. Thompson and Sidney Zion, the legal affairs writer for the *New York Times*, held court in the Pump Room at the Ambassador East with an open tab for all until the wee hours of the morning. Roy Cohn, in town for the convention and friendly with Zion, who covered his trials for the *Times*, made an appearance every night. During daylight hours, the *Ramparts* gang put out a daily paper in the form of a wall poster that cost $50,000 a day to produce.[11] Two years earlier, when the domestic airlines were hit by a labor strike, Hinckle was stranded in Chicago on his way to New York. Rather than take the train, Hinckle booked a first-class ticket on the next international flight to London and another from London to JFK: British Airways was not on strike. He always paid his writers well above going rate, thinking correctly that they would write nice things about him, even if he sometimes didn't have ready cash to pay them when promised. When *Ramparts* investors blanched at his latest excess, Hinckle would laugh at them, then charm them, usually walking away with another check.[12]

But by January 1969, *Ramparts* was over $2 million in debt, an astounding feat in the sense that Hinckle was able to convince vendors to extend a radical left-wing magazine that much credit. On January 29, 1969, it was over. With the board of directors preparing a bankruptcy filing, Hinckle resigned. "I tried until 4:00 a.m. to raise new money but I've found nobody willing to cover our deficits," Hinckle told the *New York Times*. "I'm convinced no more rabbits can come out of the hats."[13] Hinckle said he would start a new magazine, but declined to identify the new backers. (He couldn't identify them because they didn't exist.) But Wall Street would soon solve Warren's financial problems.

THE S.E.C. CONTINUED its strategy of whipping the back offices into shape by making it financially costly for firms to tolerate errors. On January 30, the S.E.C. announced it was tightening its net capital rule—which applied to O.T.C. firms that were not members of a major securities exchange—by requiring a reduction in capital to account for the cost of settling aged fails. The new rule, which would become effective March 6, 1969, required a 10 percent haircut for fails to deliver up to forty-nine days outstanding, 20 percent for fails fifty to fifty-nine days outstanding, and 30 percent for fails sixty days or more outstanding.[14]

Manny Cohen also continued enforcement actions against firms and executives for back-office violations. The week after the S.E.C. adopted the new aged fails rule, Cohen shocked Wall Street again by announcing the S.E.C. was censuring Lehman Brothers and thirty-nine of the firm's general partners, including Lucius Clay, the former commander of U.S. military forces in Europe, and George Ball, the former Under Secretary of State and United Nations ambassador, for failure to keep proper books and records.[15] At one point during the worst of the back-office crisis in 1968, Lehman was unable to account for the ownership of over $500 million of securities. The Lehman action would be the last brought by Manny Cohen.

ROY COHN GOT his money's worth from the Nixon administration. While there was some speculation that Nixon might keep Manny Cohen at the S.E.C.—and Cohen had indicated through the press that he would gladly continue to serve under Nixon—he simply had ruffled too many feathers. President Nixon announced his choice for the new chairman of the S.E.C. on February 22. It was Hamer Budge, a Republican member of the S.E.C. since 1964, a safe but somewhat surprising choice. Simultaneously with that announcement, the White House also announced that Cohen, the incumbent chairman, had submitted his resignation from the Commission, effective immediately, citing personal reasons.[16]

Hamer Budge was fifty-eight years old at the time of the appointment. He had been born in Pocatello, Idaho, and served in the state legislature there before being elected to the U.S. House of Representatives in 1960 and serving four terms. Since his appointment to the Commission by President Johnson, he had been a moderate, generally on the side of lighter regulation. Budge was sympathetic to the interests of small-town securities brokerage firms, but those firms generally were not members of the N.Y.S.E. He was less accommodating to Wall Street, and it was uncertain whether he would be an ally on preserving fixed commissions or other issues near and dear to the Club. It was equally uncertain whether Budge would be successful in rallying the staff of the S.E.C. to meet its greatest challenge since its founding, as Budge had the charisma of a modestly successful undertaker.

TO DEMONSTRATE THEIR commitment to cleaning house, on February 12 the N.Y.S.E. and AMEX announced that they had jointly retained Rand Corporation to develop a long-range plan to improve the operations of the securities industry.[17] The Rand Corporation study was hardly the first, however. In 1955, Ebasco Services had turned out a major study for the N.Y.S.E. that recommended numerous implementations of computer technology. Nearly all were ignored. The N.Y.S.E. didn't install a major computer system until 1959. In the mid-1960s, another study on the same topics by Price Waterhouse & Co. was commissioned. Then another by Haskins & Sells. Then one by Peat, Marwick, Mitchell & Co. Another by Arthur Young & Co. I.B.M. undertook the next such study. Followed by the Arthur D. Little, Inc. study. In all, seven major studies on the uses of technology for operational improvements in fourteen years. This doesn't include several other, lesser studies commissioned during that period that also touched upon technological deficiencies. There was certainly no lack of thought on the subject. But studies cannot implement; they can only suggest. The obvious long-term solution remained getting C.C.S. operational and fully adopted by all exchanges, O.T.C. market makers, and the commercial banks.

During the last week in February, the corporation that would become the world's largest securities owner, Cede & Co., came into existence. It acquired 500 million shares worth over $25 billion that week. Cede & Co., which had no employees, was the nominee for all shares participating in C.C.S. "Cede" is an acronym for **ce**ntral **de**pository, and Cede & Co. is the name printed on all "global" certificates for shares held in "street name." The computer records of C.C.S. indicated which N.Y.S.E. member firm, or "participant," owned the securities (with the ultimate beneficial ownership reflected in the records of the N.Y.S.E. member firms).[18]

In conjunction with the formation of Cede & Co., Robert Haack made the blockbuster announcement that the major commercial banks had agreed to cooperate with the Exchange and participate in C.C.S., a critical step toward full implementation. In February 1970, First National City Bank would begin a pilot program tying certain of the bank's securities transactions into C.C.S. First National City Bank would later deem the plan feasible and expand its participation to include all of its securities transactions, which paved the way for all commercial banks to participate in C.C.S.[19]

After the success of the First National City Bank pilot program, the buy-in by the commercial banks was essentially complete. A pilot loan collateral operation commenced in March 1970 involving ten brokerage firms and First National City Bank, Manufacturers Hanover Trust Company, Marine Midland Bank, and Morgan Guaranty Trust Company. On March 11, 1970, the Banking and Securities Industry Committee, referred to by its acronym, B.A.S.I.C., was formed to make physical transfers of securities a thing of the past. B.A.S.I.C. retained Hamilton F. Potter Jr., a partner of Sullivan & Cromwell, as its counsel to navigate the thicket of legal issues in rolling out C.C.S. By the end of 1970, the corporate laws and uniform commercial codes in all fifty states would be amended to recognize ownership of and security interests in global securities.

B.A.S.I.C.'s plan was that C.C.S. would be spun out of the N.Y.S.E. and established as an independent, self-supporting interindustry company with a bank charter, and therefore regulated and inspected by bank regulators, not the N.Y.S.E. or the S.E.C., which the large commercial banks simply didn't trust to safeguard their and their customers' billions of dollars of securities. Most importantly, the new entity, which would be named The Depository Trust Company, would have a board of directors controlled by the commercial banks. The formal transfer of securities custody and operations of C.C.S. to The Depository Trust Company would take place in May 1973.

. . .

OFFSETTING THE GOOD news on the back-office operations front was the unhappy reality that the market was not cooperating.

On February 25, 1969, the Dow fell below 900 for the first time since August 1968. The culprit was inflation and the expectation that the Federal Reserve would tighten credit. Interest rates had been rising since 1965, when high-grade corporate bonds yielded around 4.50 percent. Similar bonds in February 1969 were yielding over 7.00 percent. With the war still raging in Vietnam, investors expected higher budget deficits and higher taxes and were losing confidence in the Nixon administration's ability to curb inflation.

The last week in February also brought the third notable casualty of the back-office crisis. James Anthony & Co. consented to the appointment of a receiver to liquidate its business on February 27 at the request of the S.E.C.[20] From late 1967 on, James Anthony & Co.'s back office was out of control, principally because of an insufficient number of back-office employees and accounting professionals. By 1969, it was also in violation of the S.E.C.'s net capital rule. Like L. D. Sherman, James Anthony & Co. was an O.T.C. dealer and not a member of the N.Y.S.E. Accordingly, the Special Trust Fund was not available. While a small firm, customers and other third parties would lose nearly $1 million in the liquidation.

AS THE NEW Congress settled in, Representative John E. Moss, Democrat of California, announced that the Commerce and Finance Subcommittee of the House Interstate and Foreign Commerce Committee, which he chaired, would immediately hold hearings on the back-office crisis on Wall Street. The rash of S.E.C. enforcement actions and increasing press attention on the problems on Wall Street had finally roused Congress. On February 26, Robert Haack was called to testify. Haack stated that the back-office crisis had been mostly contained: "In our opinion, the actions taken by individual firms and by the industry have managed to contain and reduce the paperwork backlog and overall operational problems—except in the area of aged fails in the over-the-counter market." Haack made news in his testimony mostly for his assertion that the crisis may have been exacerbated by the infiltration of Wall Street by the Mafia. Haack testified that he had been told that "organized crime had moved in with all these new employees that had been taken on."[21] For Haack, hoping to lull Congress back to sleep with reassuring testimony, raising the specter of gangsterism was a colossal error.

Haack's assertion that there was a Mafia presence on Wall Street was promptly contradicted by Ralph Saul, president of AMEX, who testified the following week that "we have no evidence of organized crime in the securities business."[22] Haack, pressed to further explain the basis of his accusation, walked back his testimony in a letter to the House subcommittee asserting that while he had no firsthand knowledge of gangsters in the back offices, "we have reason to believe that thefts of securities have been increasing in recent years. This can be viewed as evidence of organized crime, but cannot be presumed as conclusive," he wrote. Haack also pointed out that New York State law prohibited most private-sector employers, including the securities industry, from requiring employees to be fingerprinted, so background checks using the F.B.I. fingerprint database were not possible. In any event, Haack relayed that he had asked the F.B.I. a year earlier if it would assist in making available its fingerprint resources, and it refused, citing cost and resource constraints.[23] Congressman John Murphy of Staten Island introduced legislation (which became law in 1975) to preempt state law to allow the N.A.S.D. to require fingerprinting of employees of investment banks and to allow the F.B.I. to share fingerprint data with the stock exchanges.[24]

Robert Morgenthau also took note of Robert Haack's testimony and began sniffing around Wall Street for mobsters in need of indictment. It didn't take him long. Within weeks, Morgenthau announced that his office had brought charges against several Mafia figures who had infiltrated the back offices of Wall Street brokerage houses and stolen more than $4 million in securities certificates over the prior year, taking advantage of the back-office chaos. The leader of the ring was Norman "Roughhouse" Rothman, a Florida gangster and close associate of Miami Mafia boss Santos Trafficante.[25] Prior to Fidel Castro's revolution, Rothman operated the San Souci, a casino in Havana owned by Trafficante and other La Cosa Nostra figures. Thereafter, Rothman remained at the mysterious center of the diabolical C.I.A.-Mafia plots to assassinate Fidel Castro, when he was not otherwise committing felonies or serving time therefor. The apprehension of Rothman's ring vindicated Haack's allegation of organized crime involvement in the back-office crisis and laid bare the great need for better security procedures on Wall Street. It also guaranteed more congressional scrutiny.

ON MARCH 10, Francis I. duPont & Co., the third largest investment bank behind Merrill Lynch and Bache & Co., announced that while its revenue for 1968 had risen 32 percent from 1967, its net income had fallen 26.8 percent.[26] Costs had skyrocketed as a result of a doubling of back-office personnel and overtime costs in the back-office operations. An appurtenance of the duPont family, the firm, which had 500,000 customer accounts in 1969, was presided over by its chairman, Edmund duPont. Edmund was the grandson of the firm's founder, Francis I. duPont, who was himself a great-grandson of Eleuthere Irenee duPont de Nemours, who immigrated to America from France in 1802 and founded the chemical colossus. Edmund was more a figurehead than an active day-to-day manager, however, and had delegated most decision-making authority to the firm's general manager, Charles Moran. This structure did not produce optimal decision-making. Charlie Moran's principal qualifications were having been a college buddy of Edmund duPont at Princeton and, like Edmund, a child of wealth and an automobile racing enthusiast.

When Charlie Moran wasn't racing at Le Mans or presiding over the Sports Car Club of America, he could usually be found at the bar of one of the world's exclusive gentlemen's clubs. In 1968, the firm operated ninety offices, only ten of which were profitable. Its marquee Park Avenue office in New York was losing $50,000 a month in 1969. In addition to its high overhead, it suffered from having a terrible research department, which severely limited its ability to attract lucrative institutional customers and block traders. With mostly individual investors often executing small-dollar trades, back-office efficiency was critical to profitability; but duPont had one of the least efficient back-office operations. At one point in 1968, duPont could not identify the owners of more than $35 million worth of securities that it held. This made it nearly impossible to get an accurate read as to the firm's regulatory net capital ratio. At the end of 1968, the firm calculated it to be 17.56-to-1; the N.Y.S.E. examiners calculated it at 24.75-to-1.[27]

Francis I. duPont & Co. was unquestionably a Wall Street leader in customer complaints. In 1968, it acknowledged receiving over 40,000 of them.[28] The total number was probably much higher, but the firm had no system to track complaints, and it took the firm between two and six months to even acknowledge a complaint and investigate the cause.

On March 11, 1969, in response to the flood of complaints against Francis I. duPont & Co., the S.E.C. instituted private administrative proceedings against the firm to ensure that it would take steps to amend procedures and hire additional personnel as necessary to improve its dismal customer service.[29] Francis I. duPont & Co. made the decision to convert from a partnership to a corporation as a result of concerns about partner liability arising out of these S.E.C. proceedings and the firm's worsening financial condition. This conversion would not take place until the following year, and its implementation, which required a unanimous vote of all partners, would take center stage in a deal upon which the fate of the firm—and possibly the entire financial system—would hang in the balance.

BY THE END of March, industrywide fails had been reduced significantly, from a December 1968 high of $4.13 billion to less than

$2.5 billion. This was principally the result of trading volume being down, to an average of 11.3 million per day on the N.Y.S.E. during the first quarter of 1969, from 14.3 million in the first quarter of 1968. Aged fails, too, had declined sharply, to $433 million on March 31, 1969, off a high of $837 million on July 31, 1968.[30] Also contributing to the improvement was the reduction in paper flow by reason of the commencement of operations by C.C.S., although its ramp-up continued to be plagued by computer glitches and an inability to cope with the mountain of stock certificates to be on-boarded into the system.

Slowly, expensively, the industry was finally making the necessary investments in technology. One computer consultant with more than thirty years experience at the time said in March 1969: "The operating procedures of most brokerage houses on Wall Street are in the green eye-shade era where Bob Cratchit would have no trouble fitting in. We can put people on the moon, but we can't match stock orders. How's that for an indictment?" Another computer expert on Wall Street commented at the time: "Keith Funston and Bob Haack were well aware of the need for drastic operational improvements. They both tried desperately to sell the ideas to the old guard. But the old guard wouldn't buy and they couldn't or wouldn't take the stick to them. Things have improved in the last year or year and a half, though."[31]

In contrast to the Exchange's struggles with C.C.S., innovation was flourishing in what was thought to be a technological backwater of the securities markets—the O.T.C. market. Events developing rapidly in 1969 would leapfrog the O.T.C. market over the exchanges, including the N.Y.S.E., in terms of automation and computerization.

George Levine joined a little-known stock market data compiling firm called Scantlin Electronics in 1963. At the time, Scantlin mostly prepared stock price data in bespoke formats for research departments of investment banks. Levine, thirty-five years old at the time, had a different business model in mind. Rather than simply collecting stock price data and manipulating and selling it, why couldn't Scantlin Electronics gather stock price bid and ask data from dealers in its network and communicate it in real time to all other dealers in its network? Levine imagined a computerized ticker tape for unlisted stocks traded in the O.T.C. market by way of a computer terminal on every broker's desk. And why not the same for bonds and commodities? The N.A.S.D., the broker self-regulatory body, imagined the same future as George Levine and selected Scantlin as one of the firms to develop N.A.S.D.A.Q.[32] By May 1969, Levine was rolling out his desktop computer terminals, named Counterquote Service. He would rename it Quotron the following year. The Quotron became the dominant trading terminal on Wall Street until Michael Bloomberg left Salomon Brothers and formed his own financial data and media company, whose terminal overtook the Quotron in market share in the late 1980s.

Also in 1969, AutEx Corporation launched a computerized communication system to assist Third Market dealers in providing block trade price quotes to institutional investors, competing with the N.Y.S.E. ticker. Another company, Institutional Networks Corporation, launched its Instinet service, which allowed institutional investors to provide bid and ask quotes directly with each other, bypassing a broker—whether a N.Y.S.E. member or a Third Market broker—entirely. The Instinet service was designed to ultimately go beyond a mere price quotation service to provide for actual computerized execution of trades—the Fourth Market. All of these technologically superior trading services took commission revenue away from N.Y.S.E. member firms in 1969 when they were desperately in need of more revenue.

Notwithstanding the N.Y.S.E.'s rollout of C.C.S., alternative proposals to improve upon the outdated technology of physical share certificate transfers were still being advanced. A leading technology upgrade proposal was the punchcard share certificate—a standard-sized 3 ¼ inch by 7 ½ inch computer-readable cardboard card that would contain all relevant ownership information. The machine-readable punchcard certificate would have expedited transactions by reducing human error and counterfeiting. But there was a powerful interest group lobbying the Club that was opposed to the punchcard replacement, namely the bank note printing companies.[33]

N.Y.S.E. rules mandated that listed companies have share certificates measuring 8 inches by 11 inches, specified the amount of engraving on the certificates, regulated the type of allowed artwork, and even regulated the materials used in manufacturing the certificates. The Exchange's listing committee had an "approved list" of bank note companies, and companies seeking to list on the Exchange rarely went off-list. Accordingly, these favored bank note companies had a monopoly on the production of share certificates. If punchcards had been adopted, they would have ended that. But they never were. At the Exchange, the Club argued that a punchcard certificate would not immobilize the share certificate as the C.C.S. book-entry system did, and movement of punchcard certificates would have an inherent risk of fails. This argument, of course, was nonsense, as the punchcard certificate and a book-entry delivery system were not mutually exclusive. C.C.S. could hold immobilized, modern computer punchcard certificates just as easily as it could seventeenth-century technology share certificates. Many investors would continue to want to hold physical certificates notwithstanding a paperless option, and punchcard certificates were unquestionably functionally superior.

In June 1969, the American Bankers Association, the Association of Stock Exchange Firms, and other industry groups publicly advocated for the punchcard.[34] The Club, accustomed to the golf outings and ball games sponsored by their pals at the banknote companies, did not. Naturally, the punchcard alternative went nowhere at the Exchange (and to this day old-school share certificates are required by the Exchange).

The N.A.S.D. pursued another low-tech reform. Rather than a computer-readable certificate, the N.A.S.D. established a committee, the Committee on Uniform Securities Identification Procedures, that ultimately recommended that each traded security be assigned a universally accepted eight-character number that would appear on certificates as well as trade confirmations and accounting records. The aim was to provide the entire securities industry with a common language for brokers, transfer agents, banks, and exchanges in clearing and settling transactions. This reform would be adopted, and to this day each traded security is issued a "C.U.S.I.P." number.

ON MAY 1, 1969, the N.Y.S.E. submitted its formal reply to the Department of Justice's January 17 memorandum to the staff of the S.E.C. declaring fixed commissions illegal. In its reply brief, the Exchange argued that the S.E.C. did not have the authority to end fixed commissions. The S.E.C. couldn't overturn fifty years of practice and outlaw fixed rates, the argument went. "The Division's position misconceives the nature of this proceeding as involving application of the antitrust laws, rather than a regulatory statute and ignores the statutory duty of the S.E.C. to act in the area of commission rates by applying its own expertise in determining the reasonableness of rates."[35] The S.E.C.'s statutory duty, the Exchange argued, was to set reasonable rates, not second-guess the wisdom of fixed rates, which had been endorsed by Congress in passing the Securities Exchange Act of 1934. The Department of Justice would need to take the issue up with Congress if it wanted to eliminate fixed commissions, the Exchange argued. "Since, of course, the S.E.C. lacks the power to amend the 1934 act, the Division's contentions are addressed to the wrong forum."[36]

The Exchange's brief was placed into evidence in connection with the testimony before the S.E.C. that day of William C. Freund, the Exchange's chief economist. "The characteristics of the brokerage business are such that elimination of any form of commission-rate regulation would seriously reduce the efficiency of the world's leading stock exchange, undermine the stability of the securities industry and weaken the established safeguards for the protection of investors."[37] Freund predicted that the end of fixed commissions would result in the death of many firms, a diminution in services to investors, and a lack of brokers in rural areas of the country.

The Exchange's legal position, however, suffered from the absence of any legislative history indicating that Congress intended to exempt the securities industry from the antitrust laws in passing the Exchange Act. The purpose of the Exchange Act was to rid the securities markets of fraud and manipulation and improving disclosure by listed companies, none of which necessitated fixed trading commissions.

Robert Haack and Gus Levy, the outgoing chairman of the N.Y.S.E., appeared again before the S.E.C. in the rate hearings the day after Freund. Haack spent much of the day criticizing the "reciprocal arrangements" between N.Y.S.E. firms and the regional exchanges. Reciprocal arrangements involved an N.Y.S.E.-member firm executing transactions on a regional exchange and paying a portion of the commission to the regional firm, as directed by a mutual fund. While not technically give-ups, these arrangements had the same purpose and effect. Haack indicated that in the new era of the volume discount and no give-ups, these reciprocal arrangements would need to end. To replace them, Haack again touted his proposal that non-member broker-dealers be allowed to keep one-third of the applicable commission. "If reciprocal arrangements are used principally for access to the New York Stock Exchange," Haack stated, "the question arises whether such access might not be more constructively granted by means of a direct discount to non-member brokers."[38]

The obvious problem with Haack's proposal was that many of the regional exchange members, who aggressively sold mutual fund shares, were not equipped to execute trades on behalf of the mutual funds. In addition, the S.E.C.'s pending study on institutional investors was likely to end the practice of indirect compensation for mutual fund share sales. The direction all this was leading to was the end of the mutual fund gravy train for many regional exchange members reliant on reciprocal agreements. The viability of the regional exchanges was at risk because those reciprocal trades constituted meaningful volume for them. The Club would not grieve the demise of the regional exchanges, of course.

Thomas P. Phelan, president of the Pacific Coast Stock Exchange, alleged that Haack's proposals "undoubtedly were designed with the express intent of completely eliminating any and all competition" from regional exchanges. The regional exchanges held one trump card: institutional membership. One way to keep those trades on the regional exchanges was to offer a form of membership on the regional exchanges to mutual fund managers to allow them to execute trades for their managed funds at substantially reduced commission rates. This, of course, would take business from the N.Y.S.E., perhaps even more business than was being lost to the Third Market firms. Phelan threatened that if Haack went ahead with his proposal, the Pacific Coast Stock Exchange "would have to reconsider its prior position on a number of subjects, including institutional membership."

Gus Levy tried to preempt this in his testimony on May 2 before the S.E.C., calling for the S.E.C. to declare a moratorium on any institutional membership on all exchanges pending conclusion of the Exchange's study of commission rates and the S.E.C.'s study of institutional investors' impact on the markets. "There is the possibility that widespread institutional membership might radically alter stock trading as we know it today, to the detriment of the small investor," Levy said. "Business is being taken away from the primary marketplace and we think this weakens the primary marketplace."[39]

Again, Gene Rotberg questioned Haack and Levy thoroughly and respectfully on their proposals. Rotberg gave no indication of support for any of them and gave no timetable on when a formal S.E.C. response should be expected. All he would say was that further testimony was needed.

CHAPTER EIGHT

"WE'RE BLEEDING TO DEATH"

■

Public Ownership, Institutional
Membership, and Declining Stock Prices

On May 21, 1969, Dan Lufkin, the thirty-nine-year-old co-founder of the high-flying investment bank D.L.J., attended his first meeting as a member of the board of governors of the N.Y.S.E. That, however, was simply a footnote, and an inconvenient and embarrassing one, compared to the historic event that Lufkin took part in that day. D.L.J. defied the N.Y.S.E. and infuriated the Club by filing with the S.E.C. a registration statement for a public offering of 800,000 shares of its common stock for $30 per share, an act prohibited by the constitution of the Exchange.[1]

While Dan Lufkin had been a Marine, and a good one, he didn't put much stock in being a good "company man" on Wall Street. Growing up in Rye, New York, he watched his father work loyally for Texaco, only to be fired during the Depression. He saw how this nearly broke his father's spirit. But his father got back on his feet and started a small family company, putting Dan though Rye Country Day, Hotchkiss, Yale, and Harvard Business School. The lesson young Dan Lufkin took away from all this was that all big businessmen were sons-of-bitches and you needed to look after yourself, ideally working for yourself.[2]

At Yale, Dan Lufkin met Bill Donaldson, who went to work for the G. H. Walker investment bank. At Harvard Business School, he met Dick Jenrette, who went to work for Brown Brothers Harriman.

Dan went to work for a private investor, Jeremiah Milbank. The three friends often talked of starting their own firm together, focusing on providing research on smaller, rapidly growing technology companies neglected by the research departments of the major firms.[3] Dan Lufkin floated the idea by a number of Wall Street luminaries. None encouraged him.[4] Sydney Weinberg, chairman of Goldman, Sachs at the time, was the kindest, saying: "I won't say it's a stupid idea, but I don't see how you can compete on the issues and in the areas you're describing compared with the strength Goldman, Sachs has, which shares your objectives on a worldwide scale. And how will you compete with Lehman Brothers, who has a hundred-odd years of experience and a history of relationships?" Bobby Lehman told Lufkin it wasn't such a good idea. A fellow Lehman Brothers colleague, later a close friend of Lufkin's, was even blunter: "We're going to squash you like a fly on the wall."[5]

Undeterred, the three friends opened D.L.J. in 1959, setting up shop with used furniture in an old shipping company building in Lower Manhattan, just in time for the Go-Go years of 1960s Wall Street.[6] Because D.L.J. produced the best research on technology stocks, the ascendant mutual fund and pension fund managers soon became D.L.J. customers. With these customers giving the firm distribution credibility, D.L.J. was soon invited to participate in technology stock underwritings, which led to market-making and, by the mid-1960s, a top-tier block trading operation.[7] By 1969, D.L.J. had arrived, with Dan Lufkin welcomed into the Club. He had not forgotten what Texaco had done to his father, however.

Despite the official embargo on the news that D.L.J. was planning to go public, Dan Lufkin felt compelled to tip off the incoming chairman of the N.Y.S.E., Bunny Lasker, chairman of the specialist firm Lasker, Stone & Stern.[8] Lasker was a close friend of Lufkin's and a proponent of the upstart's candidacy for the board of governors despite resistance from some of the old guard. Lasker had started out as a runner at the Exchange when he was seventeen years old, forty-two years earlier. He had worked his way up to become a specialist and was himself elected to the board of governors before he turned forty. Like many nicknames on the floor of the Exchange, Bunny's was an obvious joke: he was a giant of a man, standing six feet four inches, usually weighing well over 230 pounds, and with a personality just as large. Stunned by Lufkin's betrayal by brazenly challenging the N.Y.S.E. rules immediately after Lasker supported his candidacy to the board, Lasker initially responded with profanity, but quickly regained his composure and said the Exchange would react to D.L.J.'s filing in due course and taking into account the best interests of the Exchange membership as a whole and the public interest.

Going public was viewed as a betrayal by Lasker and many other members of the Club not simply because it was against the rules of the Exchange. Public ownership threatened the hierarchy on Wall Street because it guaranteed that change need not be incremental. Without public equity, explosive growth was only possible by one of three means: self-generated capital (such as undistributed profits), combining with another investment bank, or attracting capital from a wealthy individual or family that wished to enter the investment banking business—family money was always welcome on Wall Street. But public equity would be a great equalizer. Practically any firm could enter the business or expand nearly overnight if it could access the virtually limitless supply of public equity capital. Capital meant freedom to hire the best producers and buy the best technology. You could become Merrill Lynch before too long, and one Merrill Lynch was one too many as far as many members of the Club were concerned. With access to public equity, the game would become a fair fight. The D.L.J. public offering would double the firm's equity capital.

If it wasn't D.L.J., however, it would have been one of any number of other firms, very possibly Merrill Lynch itself. The demands of block trading, exploding trading volume, larger underwritings, and rapidly changing computer technology all required an enormous amount of capital. Given the restrictions in Glass-Steagall, obvious synergistic partners—the commercial banks—were legally prohibited from owning investment banks. N.Y.S.E. rules prohibited another likely source of capital from owning investment banks: mutual funds and other institutional investors that would benefit from vertical integration. With public ownership likewise prohibited, that left the old and slow means of raising capital. Successful, growing young firms like D.L.J. were too impatient to rely only on those.

Michael McCarthy, then chairman of the board of directors of Merrill Lynch, had first proposed to the N.Y.S.E. that member firms be allowed to go public in 1961. The Exchange took no formal action for three years. In 1964, Keith Funston decided to establish a committee, headed by Avery Patrick Rockefeller, to study the possibility of allowing member firms to go public. The committee members included Joseph Meehan of M. J. Meehan & Co., Alfred Coyle of Hayden Stone, Inc., Charles Moran of Francis I. duPont & Co., and Donald Regan of Merrill Lynch.[9] There was no appetite for public ownership among the family-controlled firms that dominated the Club. So Pat Rockefeller's committee droned on and on and decided nothing.[10] Finally, in November 1967, the committee issued a report recommending that members be permitted to publicly issue debt securities, but not equity. The Exchange submitted the proposal to the S.E.C. for approval, but the Exchange never responded to S.E.C. comments on the proposal and effectively tabled the matter.

Lufkin and his partners gambled that the N.Y.S.E. would blink. If the choice was to allow public ownership or risk firms like D.L.J. surrendering their N.Y.S.E. memberships and taking their enormous volume of block trading business and associated commissions to the regional exchanges or to Weeden & Co. and the other Third Market firms, the N.Y.S.E. would begrudgingly allow public ownership. Not that leaving the N.Y.S.E. would be painless to D.L.J. Doing so would result in blue-chip client defections, particularly among commercial banks and trust companies eager for the deposits, custody business, and financings from Exchange-member firms who would no doubt retaliate against those doing business with a prodigal D.L.J. The wrath of John Coleman still sent shock waves of fear throughout the boardrooms of Lower Manhattan and beyond. D.L.J. estimated that as much as 70 percent of its revenue would be at risk if it gave up its N.Y.S.E. membership.[11]

The board of governors meeting began at noon on May 22. As if scripted by Hollywood, just as the assembled governors sat down at the conference table, Robert Haack rushed in, agitated, carrying a broad tape from the *Dow Jones Newswire* and handed it to Bunny Lasker. Lasker read the news he already knew to the governors: D.L.J. had filed a registration statement with the S.E.C. for a public offering of 800,000 shares at $30 per share. Adding insult to injury, the offering was being underwritten by the First Boston Corporation, the most prominent investment bank not a member of the N.Y.S.E. (and itself publicly owned). Lasker then asked sarcastically whether the newest governor would like to make a statement to the board. Lufkin distributed to each of the governors a copy of the preliminary prospectus that had been filed with the S.E.C. To the governors, it read like a ransom note. Lufkin took to the podium to explain what everyone in the room already knew: like it or not, the days of the Club just got shorter.[12] Public ownership would democratize Wall Street. Lufkin delineated the rule changes that would be needed to effect public ownership and proposed suggestions for policies to safeguard the public and the Exchange with the onset of public ownership. The board of governors referred the matter to Pat Rockefeller's public membership committee with instructions to report back to the board of governors at its July 17 meeting.[13]

At the board dinner that evening, the other governors didn't speak to Lufkin; they just glowered at him. Lufkin overheard Felix G. Rohatyn, the star merger and acquisition specialist and partner at Lazard Freres, compare him to Judas Iscariot.[14] Finally, at the end of the evening, Gus Levy of Goldman, Sachs, the outgoing chairman of the Exchange, took Lufkin aside. He told Dan that while he didn't agree with what D.L.J. was doing and certainly didn't agree with how Dan had done it, he "admired the guts it took to come to the dinner."[15] Both men laughed and shook hands as the others looked on. The ice had cracked, ever so slightly. It would be nearly a year before the Exchange would finally resolve the matter of public ownership in D.L.J.'s favor, opening the door for Merrill Lynch and others to go public. Gus Levy's Goldman, Sachs would be one of the last holdouts, not going public until 1999.

After the registration statement was filed, Dick Jenrette, D.L.J.'s chairman, released a statement: "For nearly 200 years, the New York Stock Exchange has been a cornerstone of the American free-enterprise system. Yet the lack of access by exchange members to permanent public capital has begun to erode the exchange's historic role as the nation's central auction market." In its preliminary prospectus, D.L.J. stated "[w]e believe in the public interests served by this central market and are fearful that, without permanent public capital, this erosion will repeat the decline path of bond trading on the exchange. In view of the substantial portion of the company's total revenues attributable to exchange commissions, it is hoped that means may be found whereby such membership may be retained. However, D.L.J.'s ability to avail itself of opportunities for continued growth is a more important consideration. Capital additions can be effectively utilized immediately and are essential to the maintenance and improvement of its competitive position."[16]

Robert Haack issued a measured statement in response: "The issue is extremely complex by reason of its being closely woven into the matter of institutional memberships on stock exchanges and surveillance of its members."[17]

Less than a month after D.L.J.'s bombshell IPO registration statement filing, Weeden & Co. followed suit. The Third Market leader filed its IPO registration statement with the S.E.C. on June 16, 1969, for 300,000 shares in an offering led by Equitable Securities, Morton & Co., hoping to raise up to $10 million. Given the furor over the D.L.J. filing, Weeden could not find a bulge bracket N.Y.S.E.-member firm to lead its IPO.[18] (When it finally went public in October 1970, after D.L.J., tempers at the Exchange had cooled, Bache & Co. was brought in to lead the offering.)

The Exchange begrudgingly accepted the inevitability of public ownership. On June 25, 1969, it moved a step closer when the board of governors approved the public issuance by member firms of debt securities with a minimum tenor of four years. Richard Jenrette, chairman of D.L.J., called the decision a "step in the right direction," but added: "Most investors today want equity, not debt." Noting the rising interest rate environment, Jenrette said, "I don't think member firms would be comfortable raising $25 million through debentures at 10 percent or 12 percent, considering the long-term nature of such debt."[19]

On July 17, 1969, the board of governors of the N.Y.S.E. approved in principle allowing member firms to go public. D.L.J. had called the Exchange's bluff, and the Exchange folded. Robert Haack announced that the Exchange would take formal action to implement public ownership at a policy committee meeting on September 18, 1969.[20]

ON JUNE 9, 1969, Congress commenced a legislative response to the back-office crisis with the introduction of S. 2348 by Senator Edmund S. Muskie of Maine.[21] (Muskie had been Hubert Humphrey's running mate in 1968 and was the leading Democrat to challenge President Nixon in 1972.) The bill would establish an F.D.I.C. for the securities industry, to be called the Securities Investor Protection Corporation, or S.I.P.C. He proposed insuring brokerage accounts up to $50,000. The bill would also give S.I.P.C. resolution powers to wind up the affairs of insolvent investment banks. In addition, it was proposed that S.I.P.C. would be governed by a board of directors comprised of S.E.C. commissioners. S.I.P.C. was to be funded by an assessment each year of 0.5 percent of the net capital of all investment banks. Most troubling for the Club, S.I.P.C. would be a new regulatory agency that, like the F.D.I.C., would be empowered to issue prudential regulations—taking away from the N.Y.S.E. oversight of the financial solvency of investment banks.

Muskie never imagined at the time that the N.Y.S.E.'s Special Trust Fund might become insolvent. He was concerned that there was a gap in protection of customers of O.T.C. firms that were not members of the N.Y.S.E. The O.T.C. firms were often smaller, undercapitalized, and poorly run firms with the worst back-office operations and the highest risk of failing. These firms had no access to the Special Trust Fund so their customers would be out of luck if they were to fail. Muskie's bill would require the industry as a whole to pay for the protection of those customers, with the firms with the most capital paying the lion's share. However, the firms with the most capital were nearly all members of the N.Y.S.E., and they had no interest in subsidizing their smaller, weaker competitors.

Mandatory insurance of brokerage accounts had been considered by Congress before. In 1957, Congresswoman Edna F. Kelly of New York had introduced a bill that would have required all brokers to obtain private insurance of customer account balances.[22] The leadership of the N.Y.S.E. killed Kelly's bill, and they hoped to do the same to Senator Muskie's, calling it an unnecessary intrusion on self-regulation. Besides losing control over enforcement of the net capital rule, the Exchange was concerned about the cash drain to support non-members and the likelihood of additional regulation from S.I.P.C.

The board of governors of the Exchange, like Muskie, did not believe that the Special Trust Fund was likely to experience substantial depletion. Unlike Muskie, the governors knew that the possibility was not completely remote, given the condition of many Exchange members in the spring of 1969. Nonetheless, the Exchange assured all that its Special Trust Fund would be sufficient to make customers of any insolvent member firms whole, in the unlikely event another firm were to become insolvent.

As the bear market extended into the summer of 1969, the paperwork burden continued to recede, but was overtaken by concerns of revenue loss and loss of capital as a result of plummeting stock prices. On June 27, 1969, the N.Y.S.E. and AMEX announced that trading hours would be extended a half hour, to 2:30 p.m., commencing July 7, 1969. "The securities industry has made substantial progress in dealing with its paperwork problems, warranting the extension of trading hours for the public," Robert Haack said in announcing the decision.[23] Haack noted a 60 percent reduction in aged fails and a 40 percent decrease in all fails since the end of 1968. He also highlighted a 38 percent increase in back-office personnel and an estimated $100 million spent on automation by member firms. What he didn't highlight was the significant reduction in trading volume and revenue loss compared to 1968.[24]

THE OTHER TREND disturbing Robert Haack and the Club in July was that of institutional investors implementing strategies to reduce commission costs now that the give-up was gone and reciprocal arrangements were also on the way out. The volume discounts that had been in effect since December 1968 were not nearly enough to reflect true free market commission rates. Mutual fund managers obtaining regional exchange membership was one way to recoup commissions. Another was acquiring an investment bank and effectively transforming it into a Third Market firm. This is precisely what happened on July 9 when Investors Diversified Services, Inc., the nation's largest mutual fund manager, announced that it had agreed to acquire Jefferies & Co.[25] In connection with the deal, Jefferies announced to a surprised Wall Street that it had resigned all of its stock exchange memberships in order to permit it to be owned by an institutional investor. It would henceforth transact only as a Third Market firm in listed stocks and in O.T.C. stocks.[26]

The following week, the Nuveen Corporation, which had 450 employees in 15 branch offices, announced that it had resigned its memberships on the N.Y.S.E. and AMEX in order to permit an investment in it by the Paul Revere Insurance Company, another institutional investor. Nuveen, which had suffered substantial losses in its bond portfolio, needed the investment to remain in net capital rule compliance. Like Jefferies, it would thereafter operate as a Third Market firm.[27]

In response to these developments, the board of governors of the N.Y.S.E. announced on July 17 that it was "studying the possibility" of granting some form of institutional membership to qualified financial institutions such as mutual funds, pension funds, and insurance companies. "Such a form of access might have the advantage of bringing the eligible non-members at least partially into the exchange community, with possible beneficial results in terms of more effective self-regulation, improved industry standards, and cohesiveness," Robert Haack stated.[28]

Haack further disclosed that the Exchange was accelerating the rate study being undertaken for it by N.E.R.A. with a view toward enabling a permanent rate structure to be proposed by the Exchange to the S.E.C. by year-end. Haack indicated that there would likely be a "reallocation" of commission income by increasing volume discounts and raising rates on small orders.[29]

ON JULY 18, 1969, a registration statement, File No. 2-34010, was filed with the S.E.C. in Washington, D.C., for an initial public offering of 250,000 shares of common stock of a newly-formed company named Scanlan's Literary House, Inc., with its office at 36 Gramercy Park East, New York, N.Y.[30] The founders of the soon-to-be public company, which planned to publish a magazine named *Scanlan's Monthly*, were Warren Hinckle III and Sidney Zion.

After his denouement at *Ramparts* in January, Warren Hinckle had spent his many free evenings at Elaine's saloon in New York with Zion, who had been bored with his legal affairs beat at the *New York Times*. The two hatched a scheme to start their own magazine.

At first, the fundraising for *Scanlan's* proved difficult. After tapping out all their friends and family, Hinckle and Zion raised barely $50,000, a sum Hinckle could spend in a weekend. But one night in

May 1969, Zion was having a drink with the lawyer and fight promoter Bob Arum at Sardi's bar in New York discussing his fundraising struggles when Arum told him: "Why don't you go public?"
Sidney looked at him cross-eyed. *Scanlan's* hadn't published a single
issue; how on earth could it go public? "It's the best time to do it,"
Arum continued. "Before they know what you've got. While they can
dream. I'll get Charley to do it—don't worry about it, you're in."[31]

The "Charley" Bob Arum was speaking of was Charles J. Plohn
Sr., a client of Arum's law firm—and a good client, for Charles
Plohn was very often in trouble with the S.E.C. "Two-a-week Charley," as he was known on Wall Street, was the foul-mouthed senior
partner of Charles Plohn & Co., the prolific underwriter of new
issues of dubious quality. He achieved some renown in 1969 when,
despite the bear market, his firm underwrote forty new issues in the
first half of the year.[32]

Plohn, sixty-seven years old at the time, had been on Wall Street
since 1927, but had an unremarkable career until the mid-1960s,
when he began underwriting small IPOs. In 1963, his company had
only four employees. By 1969, it had grown to 350 employees.
Plohn made many millions in those half-dozen years, accumulating
an impressive art collection of over 650 important pieces. His great
run was untainted by any obsession with legality. Plohn had also
been suspended from doing business for thirty days by the S.E.C.
in 1968 for selling unregistered shares in a public offering. And
during the time of the *Scanlan's* public offering, he was being investigated by the N.Y.S.E. for failing to properly supervise his employees, which ultimately led to his receiving the largest fine levied by
the Exchange at the time.[33]

Scanlan's initial public offering was ultimately successful, closing
November 25, 1969, making it the last "hot issue" IPO of the 1960s,
and Plohn's last IPO ever. Hinckle and Zion printed the check for
the $675,000 from the offering on the front cover of the first issue
of *Scanlan's Monthly* in March 1970, promoting the magazine with
newsstand signs that said "Plohn's Folly."[34]

As John Kennedy's father had been the first chairman of the S.E.C., reinvigorating the agency was high on his son's domestic agenda. His administration's Special Study of Securities Markets ushered in many sensible reforms—but failed to identify the growing financial instability of many large investment banks.

Bill Cary (left) was President Kennedy's second choice to lead the S.E.C. After the Special Study of the Securities Markets was completed and its legislative recommendations adopted by the Securities Acts Amendments of 1964, Cary resigned in order to return to teaching law. Wall Street reform was no longer a priority in Washington, despite the dangerous conditions at the investment banks having been left unremedied.

Keith Funston, the evangelist of stock ownership in America during the 1950s and 1960s, oversaw the N.Y.S.E. during a dramatic rise in trading volume and profits for Wall Street. He stepped down just as paperwork problems were reaching crisis proportions.

Tino DeAngelis, the swindler behind the Salad Oil Scandal, whose fraudulent schemes took down a major investment bank and nearly triggered a market collapse

On the day of President Kennedy's assassination, Wall Street was in the throes of a crisis as a number of firms suffered staggering losses due to their exposure to commodities trades by swindler Tino DeAngelis. The closing of the financial markets the following Monday gave the N.Y.S.E. time to arrange rescue financing from large New York City commercial banks, narrowly averting a market crash.

John A. Coleman (right), a former chairman and longtime governor of the N.Y.S.E., used his political influence with FDR to obtain an exemption from the S.E.C.'s solvency rule that allowed the N.Y.S.E.—and not the S.E.C.—to determine which firms could operate when under extreme financial stress. Coleman's power at the N.Y.S.E. was unparalleled, and it extended far beyond the exchange, to the political, religious, and philanthropic realms, making him one of the most powerful men in New York over three decades.

President Johnson (with Larry O'Brien) was preoccupied with Great Society and civil rights legislation, as well as the growing debacle in Vietnam, and had little time to focus on the brewing problems of Wall Street.

Just as a paper crisis began to overwhelm Wall Street, the cultural and political upheavals taking place throughout America arrived at the N.Y.S.E. In one of his first capers, the yet-to-be-world-famous Abbie Hoffman led a protest at the Exchange in August 1967.

Manny Cohen, center, with David Rockefeller, right. Cohen was an effective, practical lawyer at the helm of the S.E.C. during the Johnson years who made reform of investment company abuses, ending fixed commissions, and combating insider trading his priorities. His high-profile lawsuit against Roy Cohn doomed his chance of staying at the S.E.C. after Nixon's election.

Robert Haack's presidency of the N.Y.S.E. was consumed by the back-office crisis. He lost whatever goodwill remained with the old guard that controlled the Exchange when he publicly advocated for the end of fixed commissions in the middle of a bear market.

Like a diabolical Zelig, Roy Cohn's political influence in the 1960s extended to both political parties, and his feuds and vendettas—with Robert Kennedy, Robert Morgenthau, and Manny Cohen—dominated headlines. His financial backing of Nixon came with a price: Morgenthau's and Cohen's jobs.

Gus Levy (left, with Robert Haack), the senior partner of Goldman, Sachs & Co., made his firm a bulge-bracket powerhouse during the 1960s with aggressive expansion into block trading and a dominant commercial paper franchise. The firm nearly went under as a result of the Penn Central bankruptcy in the middle of the bear market crippling Wall Street in 1970.

Before he was New York City's mayor and before he founded his eponymous media empire, Mike Bloomberg was a stock trader at Salomon Brothers and the right-hand man of the legendary block trader Jay Perry.

Murray McDonnell, scion of the Murray-McDonnell clan, the first family of Irish society, was the chairman of the McDonnell & Co. investment bank. Despite financial ruin and disgrace in the wake of the family firm's bankruptcy, Murray would rebound, becoming a beloved figure on Wall Street.

The week of Senator Robert F. Kennedy's assassination after his victory in the California presidential primary in 1968 coincided with the highest weekly trading volume ever. The decision by the N.Y.S.E. not to close in remembrance of RFK angered many at the Exchange.

Gene Rotberg was one of the first officials at the S.E.C. to conclude that the N.Y.S.E.'s fixed-rate commission structure was illegal price fixing. His skillful interrogation of Wall Street executives at the S.E.C. rate hearings exposed the industry's abuses.

Donald Weeden, chairman of Weeden & Co., the largest market maker in stocks that was not an N.Y.S.E. member, wanted to be left alone to run a modest and successful business—but the N.Y.S.E. wanted to run him out of the business. The more monopolistic the N.Y.S.E. became, the better business got for Weeden.

Francine Gottfried, a computer operator at Chemical Bank, became the unwilling object of unwanted attention, creating a hysteria in September 1968 as the "Sweater Girl of Wall Street." The mistreatment of Francine inspired Karla Jay, a young feminist leader, to begin the movement to make workplace sexual harassment illegal.

Sean McDonnell (right), with Michael J. Meehan II, was being groomed to lead McDonnell & Co. into the 1970s and beyond. His sudden premature death—on the same day Robert Kennedy was assassinated—left the firm without a steady hand to guide it through the crisis that lay ahead.

Senator Edmund Muskie was the front-runner for the Democratic presidential nomination in 1972. His bill to create the Securities Investor Protection Corporation— an F.D.I.C. for investment banks—started off as a way to protect customers of small firms not members of the N.Y.S.E. It would morph into Wall Street's first government bailout, saving many of its largest firms.

Congressman John Moss of California chaired the hearings of Senator Muskie's S.I.P.C. legislation in the House. As the financial condition of investment banks grew worse during 1970, the more suspicious his committee became of the Wall Street witnesses.

President Nixon was elected with the financial support of Wall Street and his appointment of John Mitchell, a prominent bond lawyer, as attorney general cheered the slumping financial markets.

Peter Flanigan, a Dillon, Read & Co. partner, was President Nixon's chief White House economic advisor. He was also Murray McDonnell's brother-in-law. Flanigan would use his influence to assist financially troubled investment banks, and the potential conflicts of interest in this regard never came to light during his time at the White House.

Larry O'Brien was a career politician with no business experience when Murray McDonnell tapped him to become president of McDonnell & Co. With his brother-in-law as President Nixon's chief economic advisor, Murray had a wire into the Republicans in Washington. O'Brien would give the firm a call into the Democrats.

John Connally was tasked by President Nixon to convince Ross Perot to rescue F.I. duPont & Co, Glore Forgan. Despite their Texas ties, Connally could not prevail upon Perot. Ultimately a sweetheart tax deal did the trick.

John Mitchell was Richard Nixon's law partner and his entrée to the big-money men on Wall Street. He was rewarded with the cabinet post of attorney general. It was Mitchell who arranged for the tax ruling that Perot demanded to rescue F.I duPont, Glore Forgan & Co.

Hamer Budge was President Nixon's choice to head the S.E.C. He found himself at odds with his New York Regional Office over inaction in the face of the mounting crisis.

Bunny Lasker (right) with Ross Perot (center). Lasker became chairman of the N.Y.S.E. during its darkest days since the Great Depression. His natural political talents—and his fundraising for President Nixon—were instrumental in cajoling assistance from the White House for failing investment banks.

Ross Perot thought he would do for Wall Street what he did for the Medicare program and become the back-office operator for all N.Y.S.E.-member firms. It would be a costly misadventure.

Donald Regan, chairman and chief executive officer of Merrill Lynch, the largest and best-managed investment bank, championed reform and the interests of the small investor while shrewdly taking advantage of the crisis on Wall Street to further increase Merrill Lynch's dominance.

Even insiders on Wall Street thought that the seemingly limitless wealth of the duPont family would insulate the Francis I. duPont & Co. investment bank from financial catastrophe. It was a misimpression that Edmond duPont, the senior partner at the firm, did nothing to dispel.

Marshall Cogan of the upstart investment bank Cogan, Berlind, Weill & Levitt, Inc. succeeded where Bunny Lasker, Felix Rohatyn, H.R. Haldeman, and President Nixon failed. Cogan convinced Jack Golsen to accept the C.B.W.L. takeover offer for Hayden, Stone, Inc.

Felix Rohatyn, Lazard Freres & Co.'s star mergers and acquisitions banker, was tapped to be the public face of the N.Y.S.E.'s Crisis Committee. Never one to hide from the limelight, Felix masterfully managed the press to have himself portrayed as the savior of Wall Street.

William Casey's long and varied career put him at the pinnacle of power both on Wall Street and in Washington. He was a trusted advisor to major investment bankers like Maurice Stans of Glore Forgan, as well as a chairman of the S.E.C. and, later, Director of the C.I.A.

Sid Zion left the comfort of a prestigious beat at the New York Times *for a partnership with Warren Hinckle at* Scanlan's. *A drink with fight promoter Bob Arum at Sardi's bar led to the most unlikely IPO of all time, and the last new "hot issue" of the Go-Go 1960s.*

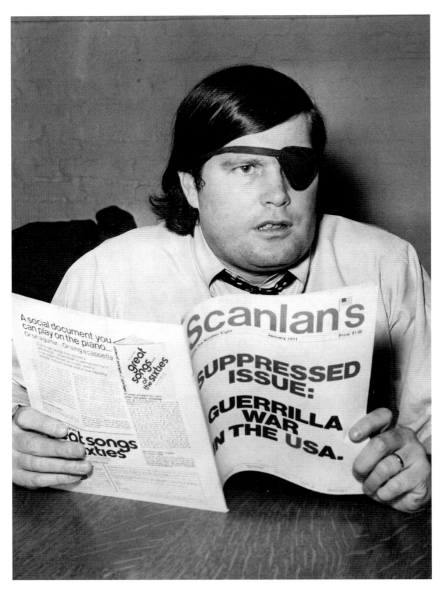

Warren Hinckle III was the brilliant, if erratic, editor of Ramparts *magazine, the high-flying journal of the radical left in the 1960s. Hinckle's free-spending ways bankrupted* Ramparts—*but that didn't stop him from getting Wall Street to fund his new venture—*Scanlan's *magazine. While* Scanlan's *might have weathered Hinckle's excesses, it couldn't survive President Nixon's wrath.*

After Hinckle and Zion cashed Plohn's check, they wasted little time spending the dough. While most literary startups might take a small, cramped office, *Scanlan's* took two offices on opposite coasts, as Hinckle couldn't imagine not working in his native San Francisco and Zion could not picture himself anywhere other than in his beloved Manhattan. And Hinckle and Zion did something else financially unthinkable: they refused to accept advertising. They believed first if journalists were not making enemies, they were just taking up space. They wanted to be free to antagonize and infuriate whomever they chose without the threat of economic reprisals. "We did everything we weren't supposed to," Hinckle proudly told *Time* magazine at the time. "No marketing studies. No direct-mail campaigns. No promotion. No ads. We didn't even do a dry-run issue." What Hinckle and Zion did do was spend half of the proceeds of the IPO before the first issue of *Scanlan's* hit the newsstands.

Scanlan's IPO perfectly represented the chaotic excesses of Wall Street as the Go-Go Era came to a crashing end. That the equity markets would fund a public company managed by Hinckle and Zion—neither of whom had ever been a director or officer of a public company or successfully managed any business enterprise, and one of whom had recently bankrupted a similar venture— whose only asset was an idea for a new muckraking, counterculture magazine defies any rational calculus. During its brief but eventful run, *Scanlan's* would make history and collide with the darker forces within the Nixon administration where it would meet its ruin.

THE FINANCIAL CONDITION of McDonnell & Co. deteriorated rapidly during the summer of 1969. Not helping matters was the erratic behavior of Murray McDonnell. Larry O'Brien, on the job barely six months, had reached the grim conclusion that the firm was adrift and his tenure as president likely to be short. The best solution, he thought, was a merger with another investment bank. Contributing to the chaos was another untimely death, this time from cancer. Thomas A. McKay, McDonnell & Co.'s senior vice president, treasurer, and a director, was only fifty-five years old.[35] To keep the N.Y.S.E. at bay over net capital rule concerns, McDonnell contributed an additional $1.6 million to the firm's capital.[36]

McDonnell's creditors had lost confidence in both Murray and O'Brien. First National City Bank—which had loans perhaps in excess of $100 million to various McDonnell entities and family members—with the support of the subordinated debt holders insisted on a change in senior management. (Those subordinate debt holders included Murray's mother, Anna McDonnell, and his sister, Anne McDonnell Johnson.) Led by Walter Wriston, the chairman of First National City Bank, the group brought in Paul McDonald, a seasoned executive from W.R. Grace & Company, to run day-to-day operations.[37] Part of the deal with the creditors was that the voting stock held by the McDonnell family would be placed in a voting trust, with Paul McDonald as sole voting trustee. McDonald did not have the authority, however, to approve a merger or sale of the company.

With his company teetering and stripped of all meaningful executive authority, Murray McDonnell seemed oblivious, pretending that nothing had changed. McDonnell spent a considerable amount of time chairing a high-profile committee (which included Dan Lufkin) on Catholic education at the behest of Cardinal Cooke to address the $30 million deficit the Archdiocesan school system was facing.[38] He was also spending more time at the bar at the New York Athletic Club that July, although he had always spent an inordinate amount of time there, so few took notice. Though his and his firm's cash reserves were clearly running on fumes, McDonnell nonetheless spent a quarter of a million dollars buying a racehorse at Saratoga that summer.

On July 24, 1969, McDonnell & Co. announced that it had sold one of its three N.Y.S.E. seats and that it had laid off seventy employees. It emphasized that no branch offices would be put up for sale. "I don't think our problems are any more severe than those of countless other houses on the street," a spokesman said. "We've gotten over our bind for the time being. We feel we're in much better shape now."[39] Two days later, Murray confirmed McDonnell & Co. was in merger discussions with several investment banks, including Scheinman, Hochstin & Trotta Inc. Scheinman, Hochstin had also made a $600,000 secured loan to McDonnell & Co. to provide desperately needed liquidity.[40]

The $600,000 loan was not nearly enough to steady McDonnell & Co. Among the many deep-pocketed friends McDonnell reached out to for another capital infusion was Dan Lufkin. Although Lufkin was fully occupied with the D.L.J. IPO process and the ongoing battle with the N.Y.S.E. over the terms under which it would permit member firms to go public, Lufkin took a deep dive on evaluating a rescue plan for McDonnell & Co. Lufkin's decision to help McDonnell was no doubt due in part to a sense of personal obligation: Lufkin's uncle, Elgood Lufkin, was married to McDonnell's aunt, Marie Murray, and Lufkin himself had been a close boyhood friend of Murray's brother, Sean, who had died tragically a year earlier.[41]

Dan Lufkin concluded that McDonnell & Co. would need at least $10 million of capital to stabilize. Lufkin himself was willing to put up a third and he had arranged for a co-investor, toy company heir Louis Marx Jr., to put up another third. However, both Lufkin and Marx had conditioned their commitments on further due diligence and on the participation of a third investor, Horace Flanigan, Murray McDonnell's father-in-law and the chairman of the Manufacturers Hanover Trust Company.[42]

Armed with the Lufkin and Marx proposal, Murray marched right down to the N.Y.S.E. to inform its chairman, Bunny Lasker, that rescue financing had been arranged. Lasker, eager to quell the rumors of McDonnell's demise, urged Murray to make a public announcement, which he did. Murray, with Larry O'Brien beside him, held a press conference on August 1, 1969, and declared that McDonnell had "completely resolved the temporary capital

problem and is on solid financial footing." "The company has made
arrangements for new capital in the minimum amount of $3,000,000
and up to a maximum of $10,000,000, depending upon the needs,"
the announcement continued. "McDonnell & Co.," they said, "is
now in the enviable position of having substantial capital support so
that it can continue its actions to streamline and modernize the
operations of the company in the interest of greater efficiency and
economy."[43] The announcement was complete fiction.

Horace Flanigan was never a fan of his son-in-law. He approved
neither of his high-profile society lifestyle nor his excessive booz-
ing, and was by no means onboard with putting millions of his own
money into McDonnell & Co. Dan Lufkin had lobbied Horace's
sons, Peter Flanigan and Robert Flanigan, a Colorado rancher, to
help enlist their father to consider the investment. "Horrible
Horace," as he was called at the bank, was unmoved.[44] The more
Lufkin and Marx continued to kick the tires at McDonnell & Co.,
the more concerned they got that $10 million might not be enough.
It appeared impossible to determine what might be enough as the
books were an absolute mess. "The more we looked into it, the
more things came out of the woodwork," Lufkin remembered.[45]
The bigger the operating loss revealed itself to be, the more "cost
savings" Murray claimed were obtainable, but he simply had no
credibility with prospective investors. Matters were not helped
when the story broke on August 6 that the S.E.C. was investigating
McDonnell's Washington, D.C., office at the urging of Congressmen Wright Patterson and John Moss for failing to correct errors
in customer accounts.[46] By Friday, August 8, the rescue deal was
dead.[47]

The timing could not have been worse. McDonnell had called
an offsite meeting of all senior McDonnell & Co. executives on
Sunday, August 10 at the Grand Summit Hotel in Summit, New
Jersey, to announce the details of the rescue financing and otherwise boost morale. But come Sunday, McDonnell was nowhere to
be found. He had checked himself into the hospital with "nervous
exhaustion," leaving Larry O'Brien alone to face the wrath of the

McDonnell & Co. managers. When O'Brien didn't have answers to pointed questions, the meeting turned ugly. Then, the doors to the conference room swung open, and McDonnell charged in, claiming he had just left a meeting with Dan Lufkin and the rescue deal had been finalized and all would be well. With slaps on the back and toasts to McDonnell, the meeting ended on a high note. Again, it was complete fiction.[48]

The next morning, Lufkin asked to see Larry O'Brien privately. Having heard of McDonnell's performance the evening prior at the Grand Summit Hotel, Lufkin told O'Brien that it was a complete fantasy and that Lufkin was distancing himself from the situation. Larry O'Brien asked Lufkin if anyone would blame him if he resigned as president of McDonnell & Co. Lufkin said no one would. O'Brien decided he would resign that day. McDonnell arrived in the office—quite late—was confronted by O'Brien about his misrepresentations to the executive team, and was left with O'Brien's resignation letter.[49] In his departing press release, O'Brien said: "When I came to McDonnell & Co. it was with the understanding that the firm would be in a position to broaden its horizons in a variety of ways. It has become apparent, however, that this will not be possible and, in fact, the company is retrenching into a smaller entity with concentration in its areas of traditional specialty. Considering the state of the economy and the stock market, the decision to retrench is a prudent one. Nevertheless, I find that McDonnell & Co. does not afford me the opportunity I thought it would."[50]

On the day of O'Brien's resignation, McDonnell & Co. also announced that it was selling ten of its twenty-six branch offices, as well as the McDonnell Mutual Fund, which had about $30 million in assets under management. It also announced a cost-saving plan designed to reduce research and sales and marketing expenses and head-count reductions in its corporate finance department. "In keeping with this plan to limit the nature of the company and its services," the company said, "the capital being provided to McDonnell & Co. will be made available through internal sources and personal investors." There was no mention that the previously announced financing had been withdrawn.[51]

More troubling news came out of the S.E.C. on August 13. McDonnell & Co.'s Boston office was suspended from trading O.T.C. stocks for ten days because of fraudulent activities of two of its brokers in promoting the stock of Roto American Corporation to customers for whom the stock was not a suitable investment. McDonnell & Co. was also required to make all its customers whole with respect to any losses on Roto American Corporation stock.[52]

Paul McDonald frantically tried to reduce expenses once it became clear there would be no rescue financing. To replace the deceased Frank McKay, he hired Henry Lindh, a cold-eyed accountant. "We're bleeding to death," were the first words out of Lindh's mouth when asked by an associate to summarize the state of McDonnell & Co. Lindh immediately decided to abandon the Data Architects SECURE back-office computer system, phase out the expensive temporary back-office arrangement with Shields & Company, and outsource the back-office function over the long Labor Day weekend to Automatic Computer Service, a division of Automatic Data Processing (A.D.P.), future U.S. senator Frank Lautenberg's firm. At last, with A.D.P. running the system, reliable numbers could be produced. Those numbers did not comfort Henry Lindh: McDonnell & Co. was losing $15,000 per day.[53]

On August 21, the company announced that it planned to sell or close an additional seven (seventeen in total) of its twenty-six branch offices.[54]

Meanwhile, efforts continued to find a merger partner or source of additional capital. Aristotle Onassis was reached out to again. Again, he passed. Henry Ford was also solicited again. He, too, passed. The McDonnell family agreed in September to convert $8.8 million in subordinated brokerage accounts into preferred stock and long-term subordinated debt. This didn't improve the firm's capital position sufficiently to entice outside investment, though it did succeed in keeping the N.Y.S.E. temporarily at bay over net capital rule concerns.[55]

■ ■ ■

ECONOMIC CONDITIONS AND market conditions in the summer of 1969 continued to dampen the outlook for the securities industry. The Dow had dropped nearly 20 percent year-to-date, hovering near 800, and interest rates continued to rise steadily. Trading volumes continued their slump, down over 10 percent for the year. With the volume discount showing its full effect, revenues on the reduced volumes were disproportionately down. Officially in a bear market and with the larger economy slowing, it would be expected that Wall Street's profitability would suffer, but outsiders had no idea how ill-equipped the investment banks were to weather a downturn.[56] After putting off needed investment in technology for years, the industry had spent nearly $100 million over the preceding year—with another $100 million budgeted—to bring its technology reasonably up-to-date. Bache & Co., the second-largest brokerage firm, had earned a mere $13,237 on revenues of $35 million during its most recently ended fiscal quarter, down from a profit of more than $2 million in the same period during 1968.

To address the revenue gap, Robert Haack knew that the N.Y.S.E.'s pending commission rate study and forthcoming rate proposal to the S.E.C. would include an increase in commission rates on small orders. The S.E.C., which was all in favor of vigorous competition when it led to a lowering of commissions for large institutional investors who were effectively subsidizing the small investor, balked whenever free market principles led to retail investors paying more. "Charges for smaller orders seem too low and provide little incentive for most firms to emphasize and expand service to the small investor,"[57] Haack wrote in a bulletin to Exchange members in late August. "In general, the Exchange and its consultants feel that any future commission structure should in no case reduce total commission revenue, but might have to provide for an overall increase."[58] Haack noted three preliminary conclusions from N.E.R.A.'s work to date. First, the current rate of return on securities transactions was insufficient to attract the capital investment needed by the industry to modernize. Second, commission rates on large orders were still too high relative to their cost of execution. Third, commission rates on small orders were too low relative to their cost of execution.[59]

The S.E.C., itself unaware of the true financial condition of the investment banks, thought that Haack was pleading poverty as an excuse to claw back the reduction in aggregate commissions as a result of the V.D. Hamer Budge gave Haack a very cold shoulder on his three conclusions, suggesting by way of comment to the *New York Times* that Haack and his consultants should spend a bit more time studying the issue. The S.E.C. did approve Haack's request to lengthen trading hours by another half hour, to 3:00 p.m., effective September 29, 1969.[60]

There was one firm seemingly immune to the market turbulence that was investing in all the areas where the other investment banks were cutting back—Merrill Lynch. "We have stepped up our advertising 20 percent this year to a record level and we're sticking to that," Donald Regan proudly told the *New York Times* in August.[61] Merrill Lynch was also hiring brokers at a breakneck pace, adding six hundred in 1969, an increase of nearly 20 percent. "The small investor is the backbone of this business and will continue to be despite the inroads of institutionalization," Regan said.[62] Merrill Lynch was increasing its research effort too. "The cost of research is such a small part of our overall operation that it is not a good place to economize," Regan declared.[63] Regan hired top graphic designers to conceive the new advertising campaign and real writers, not junior financial analysts, to prepare the copy. To pay for the increased advertising budget, Regan cut the base salaries of top executives, telling them that if they believed in the expansion strategy, as they said they did, they would more than make up for the salary decrease with the increase in value of their equity stakes in the firm.

Donald Regan's ambitions for Merrill Lynch weren't limited to dominating the brokerage business. "The investment counselor of the future," he told an audience in San Francisco, "will have a

broad conception of his responsibility; he will have to know something about life insurance, the money market, real estate, commodities, and the economy in general—as well as be knowledgeable
about securities." Regan had already conceived of the financial su-
permarket, all those products—joined with commercial banking,
eventually, with the chipping away of Glass-Steagall—under the
roof of one institution. With the end of the fixed commission cartel, after the consolidation and elimination of the weak, inefficient
competitors, the only available avenues for growth and profitability
would be capital-intensive trading and product-line expansion. In
these Merrill Lynch would be the leader in the decades to come.

CHAPTER NINE

"IT'S A FREE-FOR-ALL"

■

Firms Fail and More on the Brink

Throughout August, concern at the N.Y.S.E. grew regarding the viability of the nation's third largest brokerage, Francis I. duPont & Co. On August 8, Charles Moran, senior managing partner of Francis I. duPont & Co., confirmed reports that the firm would be closing 8 of its 111 branch offices and had dismissed 200 of its 5,700 employees.[1] Francis I. duPont & Co. had doubled its workforce in 1968, by reason of both an aggressive expansion and acquisition strategy and to bail out its floundering back-office operations. At the same time, Francis I. duPont & Co. announced that it had mutually agreed to terminate merger discussions with Laird, Bissell & Meeds, Inc., a Delaware-based investment bank. "These consolidations have been in the wind for a long time," Wallace C. Latour, a senior partner of Francis I. duPont & Co., told the press. "The marketing decision has been to move smaller offices with more limited potential into larger more dynamic production offices that offer more potential."[2]

On September 11, the Francis I. duPont & Co. board ousted Moran, elevating Latour to the position of senior managing partner. Latour told the press that Moran "asked to be relieved of some of his onerous duties."[3] The duPont family had invested approximately $20 million in the firm over the prior year to keep it afloat. This largesse convinced many that the fabulous wealth of the duPont family could always be counted on to steady the firm.

. . .

DESPITE THE PUSHBACK from Hamer Budge at the S.E.C., Robert Haack continued to pitch for higher commission rates on small transactions. Haack was not about to advertise his fears of a looming financial crisis involving some of the largest and most prestigious investment banks—McDonnell & Co., Hayden, Stone, Inc., Francis I duPont & Co. Instead, he presented the rate increase as an imperative to preserve access to the equity markets to the small investor. He took the stage at the Association of Stock Exchange Firms annual conference at the Hilton Hotel in Midtown Manhattan on September 5, 1969, and announced that the N.Y.S.E. planned to press for higher commission rates on small transactions. "Far from discouraging investment by individuals," Haack said, "cost-related commission rates could increase direct ownership because firms would have an incentive to provide more emphasis and depth in services to the small customer."[4] Hamer Budge, also in attendance at the conference and still not buying any of it, commented that Haack's proposed commission rate change came "very much as a surprise to the commission and its staff."[5]

But even leaders in the institutional investor community were having second thoughts about the impact of the volume discount, growing concerned about the solvency and long-term viability of the investment banks. Consolidation in the securities industry—through distressed as well as opportunistic combinations—was accelerating. On September 5, Hornblower & Weeks-Hemphill, Noyes announced a merger with Lester, Ryons & Co., a Los Angeles–headquartered firm with fourteen offices in California, to form the seventh-largest investment bank.[6] A few weeks later, Reynolds & Co. announced that it would acquire Atlanta-based Courts & Co.[7] On the heels of that deal, Paine, Webber Jackson & Curtis acquired the southeastern powerhouse brokerage of Abbott, Proctor & Paine, with nineteen branch offices in Virginia, North Carolina, Tennessee, and West Virginia.[8] And before year-end, Auchincloss, Parker & Redpath and Thompson & McKinnon, Inc. announced they would merge, the combined company to have fifty-eight branch offices.[9] If only a handful of firms survived, their concentrated market power and political power had many institutional investors concerned. John Bogle, chairman of the Investment Company Institute, stated in his speech to the annual International Mutual Fund Dealers' Conference on September 15 that reductions in brokerage commissions might not be in the best interest of institutional investors. "Our industry's prime commitment must be to the liquidity and the reliability of the central marketplace," Bogle said. "In turn, therefore, we have a vested interest in a sound and profitable securities industry, with the efficient independent broker as an essential part of the picture."[10]

The growing concern over the poor financial results of investment banks in 1969 tempered the Club's opposition to members going public. New capital from a less than ideal source was better than more firms slouching toward insolvency. On September 18, 1969, the board of governors of the N.Y.S.E. announced its proposed conditions for allowing member firms to go public.[11] The proposal required that any member with publicly traded equity and any parent company of a member had to have as its "primary purpose" the business of brokering and dealing in securities (as opposed, for example, to investing in securities like a mutual fund). In addition, the proposal required that a majority of the voting stock of Exchange members be owned by persons who were Exchange members or employees of a member firm. In addition, any holder of 5 percent or more of a member firm that was not itself a member firm or any employee of one had to have the ownership approved by the board of governors of the Exchange. In addition, in a move to prevent mutual funds and other institutional investors from buying member firms, the proposal prohibited any customer accounting for 5 percent or more of a member firm's revenues from owning more than 5 percent of that firm's stock without approval of the board of governors of the Exchange. The proposal also limited firms to selling no more than 20 percent of their stock in the first two years after their IPOs. The proposal required approval by the

S.E.C. and by Exchange members in order to become effective. The vote of Exchange members was scheduled for November 20.

The proposal was a long way from being acceptable to either the Justice Department or the S.E.C., who saw those ownership conditions and limitations as nothing more than the Club preserving its price-fixing cartel. The time it would take to revise the new rules so they would pass muster with the regulators would delay for months the infusion of much-needed capital into the investment banks.

IN THE MEANTIME, the problems at Hayden, Stone Inc. continued. On September 25, the N.Y.S.E. levied a $100,000 fine, the largest fine in history, on Hayden, Stone for failure to keep accurate records and file its financial statements in a timely way.[12] Alfred J. Coyle, president of Hayden, Stone, assured the public that the company's problems were behind it. Coyle released a statement that the firm's "sound financial position is reflected in its audited financial statement, filed with the N.Y.S.E. on September 18, 1969, and soon to be mailed to its customers."[13] With the fine paid, the N.Y.S.E. removed all operating restrictions it had imposed on Hayden, Stone during its investigation of the firm's affairs. The fine, Haack hoped, would satisfy the S.E.C. And the lifting of restrictions, he further hoped, would allow the firm to improve its financial situation.

The New York Regional Office of the S.E.C., however, was most unsatisfied. It remained deeply concerned about Hayden, Stone's solvency notwithstanding the new clean bill of health from the Exchange.[14] And its own investigation of Hayden, Stone's books revealed it to be in violation of the net capital rule by a substantial margin. The Exchange had allowed Hayden, Stone to include as a liquid asset, essentially as cash, for purpose of the net capital calculation an expected tax refund of over $4 million despite the fact that the Internal Revenue Service had yet to approve the refund.[15] In fact, Hayden, Stone hadn't even filed its tax return claiming the refund. Kevin Thomas Duffy, the head of the S.E.C.'s New York Regional Office, was so alarmed by the lax practices of the N.Y.S.E.

in enforcing the net capital rule that he wrote a letter to Hamer Budge recommending that the S.E.C. rescind the Exchange's net capital rule exemption and bring in-house to the S.E.C. that compliance function.[16] Robert Haack didn't know about Duffy's letter; but with it, another ball had dropped.

A fourth Wall Street firm of note fell victim to the crisis on October 13, 1969. Amott, Baker & Co. was overcome by its back-office woes. The firm, with about 7,000 customers, announced that it would be liquidating. All of its branch offices would be acquired by Charles Plohn & Co. in order "to enable us to devote all our efforts to clearing up the delivery of any securities or balances which may not have been accomplished as yet for some of our clients."[17] The board of governors of the N.Y.S.E. announced it had set aside $500,000 from the Special Trust Fund to assure all customers of Amott, Baker would be made whole. But Charles Plohn & Co., the *Scanlan's* IPO underwriter and co-recipient of the largest fine ever levied by the N.Y.S.E., was hardly an ideal suitor for the shotgun marriage, as its financial condition was not much better than Amott, Baker's.

SPORTS-OBSESSED WALL STREET had one pleasant and surprising diversion in the fall of 1969: the previously hapless New York Mets were in the World Series. Only in its eighth season that year, the franchise's previous campaigns had been abysmal. The Mets finished dead last in the National League in five of those seasons and second-to-last in the other two, barely avoiding another last-place finish in 1968. But the 1969 Mets were different from their earlier incarnations, and the difference was pitching. They had a talented young staff that included Tom Seaver, Nolan Ryan, Jerry Koosman, Tug McGraw, and Gary Gentry. The team won 100 games in 1969 despite a team batting average of .242. They swept the Atlanta Braves in three games to win the National League pennant in the league championship series, then faced the Baltimore Orioles, who had won 106 regular-season games, in the World Series. After dropping the first game to the Orioles, the Mets won the next four games, closing out the series with a 5 to 3 win at Shea Stadium on October 16.

Four days later, while the employees of Morgan Guaranty Trust were cheering manager Gil Hodges as he led the Mets ticker-tape parade motorcade down Broadway, someone stole $1 million of securities from the Morgan Guaranty back-office cage—literally walking out with a stack of stock and bond certificates unnoticed. "It's a free-for-all," said Murray Gross, an assistant U.S. Attorney in New York at the time. "Everybody's stealing. It's organized crime, it's employees, clerks, messengers, those who work in the cage or come to the cage, margin clerks, bookkeepers, men, women, day shift, night shift."[18] Robert Morgenthau, the U.S. Attorney for the Southern District of New York and Mr. Gross's boss, estimated that over $45 million of securities had been stolen from the back offices in the prior year.[19]

AT MCDONNELL & CO., the fire sale continued as the new management team desperately tried to raise funds. On October 17, the company announced it had sold its mutual fund business to Scheinman, Hochstin & Trotta, the firm that had lent it $600,000 in July. The sale price barely exceeded the loan amount. Later that month, McDonnell announced it was selling six more branch offices, five of them—in Chicago, Boston, Detroit, Denver, and Los Angeles—to Shearson, Hammill & Co., and the sixth, in San Francisco, to an undisclosed purchaser.[20] This left McDonnell & Co. with only the palatial 400 Park Avenue office, the Paris office, and the firm's headquarters at 120 Broadway. At the beginning of 1969, it had twenty-six branch offices. A McDonnell & Co. spokesman said the firm was essentially exiting the retail brokerage business to focus on institutional sales, rights offerings, and bond trading.[21]

On the evening of October 22, 1969, the back-office crisis claimed its fifth notable Wall Street firm: Gregory & Sons, a medium-size firm with 3,000 retail customers and a respected corporate finance business.[22] It was also the leading broker for New York State savings banks. The heat being brought down by the New York Regional Office of the S.E.C. on the N.Y.S.E. for its lax enforcement of the net capital rule in the case of the Hayden, Stone phantom tax refund proved to be the proximate cause of Gregory & Sons's swift demise.

Gregory & Sons was not too big to fail, and, with the S.E.C.'s New York Regional Office laser-focused on lax net capital rule enforcement, the board of governors of the Exchange knew that any further shenanigans might shake Hamer Budge out of inaction down in Washington. Gregory & Sons was hoping the Exchange would give it full net capital credit for restricted securities, certainly a possibility under the historically liberal interpretation of the rule by the Exchange. In truth, Gregory & Sons was insolvent and nearing default on its loan obligations. The Exchange suspended Gregory & Sons' operations and appointed Lloyd McChensey, the Exchange's chief examiner, as liquidator of the firm. The Exchange also announced that it was making available $5 million from its Special Trust Fund to Gregory & Sons customers.[23]

The Special Trust Fund had total assets of only $11 million cash on hand and another $15 million in commitments from member firms. Accordingly, the $5 million pledged for Gregory & Sons represented a material diminution of its bailout capacity. It was clear that if a larger firm failed, the Special Trust Fund might prove inadequate. And many insiders wondered whether those $15 million in commitments would be honored in a worsening crisis, given the financial condition of many of the member firms making those commitments. Ominously, the Exchange also announced that day that the sixty-office, St. Louis-based Dempsey-Tegeler & Co. firm would be operating under restriction as a result of concerns about its accounting and bookkeeping. The Exchange was requiring Dempsey-Tegeler to divest itself of certain unprofitable branch offices and make senior level management changes.[24]

ON OCTOBER 21, Irving Pollack, the director of the S.E.C.'s Trading and Markets Division, sent a letter to Robert Haack raising concerns about nine provisions of the N.Y.S.E.'s member firm public ownership proposal.[25] In particular, the S.E.C. was focused on the restriction on 5 percent ownership of a member firm by a customer. The S.E.C. also questioned why the Exchange included a grandfather clause in its proposal that allowed existing publicly owned investment banks to become members only if they had been in business for at least five years prior to January 1, 1969. This seemed tailored to allow First Boston Corporation, long a publicly-traded company, to become a member, but to exclude the brokerage affiliates of mutual funds, such as Investors Diversified Services, which had purchased the failing investment bank John Nuveen & Co., the broker-dealer subsidiary of Nuveen Corporation, in a distressed sale a month earlier, and Kansas City Securities, which had announced a desire to become a member of the N.Y.S.E.[26] To the S.E.C., this restriction, together with the requirement that member firms be majority controlled by Exchange members or employees, seemed designed more to thwart ownership by institutional investors than to prevent bad actors from owning member firms. In addition, the S.E.C. believed the 20 percent limit on stock sales during the first two years after an IPO made no sense, as access to the public markets to improve the capital position of member firms should not be arbitrarily restricted. Of course, starving growing firms of equity capital did preserve the status quo, which is what the Club had in mind.

The regulatory pressure on the N.Y.S.E. over its public ownership proposal increased on October 29, when Richard W. McLaren, the head of the U.S. Justice Department's Antitrust Division, in a speech at the Waldorf Astoria to the Investment Bankers Association, characterized the proposal as "a private club approach to exchange membership [that] appears to be short-sighted as well as contrary to the purposes of the Securities Exchange Act and the principles of the antitrust laws."[27] McLaren said the ownership restrictions "are obviously designed to prevent institutional investors from gaining membership on the exchange."[28] It had become clear to Haack that regulatory approval of the Exchange's proposal would not be forthcoming in time for the scheduled member vote in November, which would have to be postponed. This meant that there would be no desperately needed capital coming from the public until 1970, at the earliest.

ON NOVEMBER 5, the N.Y.S.E. officially responded to the S.E.C.'s objections to its public ownership proposal. In a letter from Robert Haack to the S.E.C.'s Irving Pollack, the Exchange contended that the prohibition on a customer owning 5 percent of a member was justified as a means of enforcing the Exchange's prohibition on rebates of fixed commissions to customers. "Where the stockholding was substantial, a significant rebate could result," Haack wrote. "The anti-rebate sections of the exchange constitution are deemed necessary to maintain a minimum commission structure," he added. "There would be no effective minimum without a prohibition against rebates."[29] In short, the Club was justifying maintaining an anticompetitive cartel in order to preserve its price fixing.

Regarding the 49 percent aggregate ownership limit for persons who were not members or employees of members, Haack noted that the limitation allowed for an increased percentage to be sold after the member firm had been public for three years and would allow for sufficient equity capital to be raised by member firms.[30] The Club was holding the line on this rather insignificant condition even if it meant delaying by months member firms accessing the public equity markets and starving the industry of desperately needed capital.

On November 17, the Antitrust Division of the Justice Department formally declared that the ownership limitations in the N.Y.S.E.'s public ownership proposal violated federal antitrust laws. The Justice Department requested that the S.E.C. not permit any member of the N.Y.S.E. to go public until the Exchange's proposal had been modified to reflect the Justice Department's concerns and recommended that the S.E.C. hold public hearings on the Exchange's proposal. "The New York Stock Exchange has advanced no persuasive rationale phrased in terms of the public interest to support its proposed limitations on membership by publicly-held corporations," the Justice Department asserted.[31] "This raises a strong inference that the limitations are primarily designed to exclude institutional investors from membership."[32] The Justice Department, noting that it continued to believe that fixed commission rates themselves violated the federal antitrust laws, strongly argued that as long as fixed rate commissions were in effect, the Exchange should not be permitted to exclude institutional investors from membership unless a showing could be made that there was a "compelling need" to do so in order to properly regulate the securities markets.

The following day, the N.Y.S.E. formally postponed the membership vote on the public ownership proposal at the request of the S.E.C. "The exchange, of course, will delay action on the proposed constitutional amendments to give the commission, as it requests, an opportunity to adequately review and comment," Robert Haack stated. "We are hopeful that the commission will submit any comments to us as promptly as possible."[33]

At the same time Haack was battling the S.E.C. and the Justice Department over the public ownership proposal, he was antagonizing them by advocating raising fixed commission rates for small transactions. "One of the key changes in the commission structure must be an increase in rates on small orders," Haack stated in a speech to the Stock Transfer Association on November 21, 1969.[34] "The truth of the matter is that the growth of direct share ownership depends in great measure on the development and servicing of small orders by brokerage firms which in turn requires commissions offering adequate incentives," Haack said.[35] Haack indicated that the N.Y.S.E. would be presenting a new rate schedule for approval by the S.E.C. early in 1970.

WITH FIVE SIZABLE firms having already failed in the back-office crisis, the S.E.C. in New York was no longer taking at face value the assurances of the N.Y.S.E. regarding the adequacy of its

Special Trust Fund. The New York Regional Office thought Hayden, Stone Inc. would be the next to fail and, given its size, feared the consequences would be disastrous. On November 7, Hamer Budge received an alarming letter from the New York Regional Office regarding the financial condition of Hayden, Stone.[36] The letter implored Budge to take three immediate actions: first, force Hayden, Stone to curtail its activities and request the N.Y.S.E. appoint a liquidator for the firm; second, require the Exchange to assess members for a substantial increase in the size of the Special Trust Fund, as it was inadequate to address the coming bailouts that would inevitably be required; and third, urge that Congress pass legislation insuring brokerage accounts, as a run on the entire industry was a very real possibility. Budge did none of these things and simply passed the letter on to the Division of Trading and Markets.[37]

On November 12, the S.E.C.'s Division of Trading and Markets sent a memorandum to all of the S.E.C. Commissioners indicating that Hayden, Stone was in serious financial distress, operating at a $10,462,000 operating loss for the first nine months of 1969 and with a large amount of its capital being withdrawn by insiders.[38] The firm had also committed to move into a new headquarters building at an incremental cost of $6,200,000. The Division recommended that the Commission require the N.Y.S.E. to propose a business plan for Hayden, Stone that would prevent its collapse, including preventing any further withdrawal of capital. The Division also recommended requiring the Exchange to pledge the Special Trust Fund to guarantee no customer losses at Hayden, Stone. However, the Hamer Budge–led Commission took no formal action, either directly or indirectly by direction to the N.Y.S.E., to protect the customers of Hayden, Stone. The New York Regional Office could hardly believe the S.E.C. in Washington would do nothing to prevent a Hayden, Stone collapse and leave it to the N.Y.S.E., Hayden, Stone's chief enabler, to prevent a systemic crisis.

The New York Regional Office, realizing that its head office was not prepared to take formal action against Hayden, Stone, began to pressure the firm on its own throughout December to seek an equity infusion or risk curtailment of its operations. They tried a second time to convince Washington to instruct the N.Y.S.E. to begin contingency planning for a forced reduction in the size of Hayden, Stone's operations on December 17.[39] Again, the head office in Washington ignored the recommendations of the New York Regional Office.

To help ease the growing concerns that the Special Trust Fund was insufficient after the failures of Pickard, Amott, Baker & Co. and Gregory & Sons, on December 19, the board of governors of the N.Y.S.E. authorized a year-end transfer of $5 million from its operating income into the Special Trust Fund.[40] This was the first additional contribution since the fund was first established in 1963 after the Salad Oil Scandal. The New York S.E.C. knew that Hayden, Stone alone would bankrupt the fund even with the additional $5 million.

THE FEDERAL GOVERNMENT'S mishandling of corporate wrongdoing wasn't limited to the S.E.C.'s inaction. The Justice Department's prosecution of Roy Cohn was bungled badly. Robert Morgenthau decided to prosecute Roy Cohn in two separate trials. The first would deal with the charges in the second indictment brought in January 1969: the bribery of New York City's appraiser in the Fifth Avenue Coach Lines condemnation proceeding and the alleged blackmailing by Cohn of Lawrence Weisman, the former president of Fifth Avenue Coach Lines and his alleged co-conspirator in that bribery scheme. The trial began in late September and lasted eleven weeks.

Weisman was Morgenthau's star witness in the trial, and he spent eight days on the stand. He confessed to his part in the bribery scheme and said that Cohn had later threatened to expose him if he didn't sell his interest in Fifth Avenue Coach Lines to the Victor Muscat investor group. Under cross-examination, however, it was revealed that Weisman had made a hefty profit on the sale of his shares. It was also shown that Weisman remained close friends with Cohn for years after the alleged blackmail. Weisman had subsequently hired Cohn in two litigation matters and invited him to his wedding. Cohn's lawyer, Joseph E. Brill, even brought to the courtroom a silver lead pitcher Weisman had given to Cohn in late 1968 as a present with an engraved inscription that read: "To R.M.C., second best lawyer in the United States, with regards from L.I.W., Number One!"

The biggest prosecution error, however, was the promiscuous granting of immunity to anyone who could tie Roy Cohn to a crime. Weisman was forced to admit under cross-examination that he had been granted immunity from prosecution by Morgenthau in exchange for his testimony against Cohn. Another key witness, the appraiser, Bernard Reicher, also admitted on cross-examination that he had been given a plea deal by Morgenthau for agreeing to testify against Cohn. Morgenthau's last witness was Edward Krock, Victor Muscat's right-hand man. He, too, had made a plea deal with Morgenthau in exchange for his testimony.

The trial was delayed in late November because Brill had suffered a heart attack. Cohn's partner, Thomas Bolan, took over as Cohn's lead defense attorney.

Cohn had decided that Bolan would not be delivering the closing argument, however. In a move of unprecedented gall and guile, Cohn—who did not take the stand to testify in his own behalf and accordingly could not be cross-examined—announced to the court that he would be delivering the closing argument. Morgenthau's office objected vehemently to the ploy, but Judge Inzer Wyatt could find no legal grounds to prohibit Cohn from proceeding.

In a two-day, five-hour summation, Roy Cohn captivated the jury and the dozens of press overflowing the standing-room-only courtroom. Cohn methodically took apart Morgenthau's case. "This is the first time in my life I have addressed a jury on behalf of a defendant in a criminal case," Cohn began.[41] "When I went to law school, little did I dream that my first would be on my own behalf." Cohn picked apart Weisman's testimony, ridiculing his accusation of blackmail. Cohn carried around the silver pitcher with the affectionate inscription as he spoke to the jury. He also read aloud a note from Weisman after the alleged extortion: "Roy, I'll always be able to count you as one of my friends." "Of course," Cohn added, "that's just the sort of letter you write to your friendly blackmailer."[42]

Cohn next attacked the testimony of Bernard Reicher, noting major inconsistencies in his story. Cohn also hammered home the fact that he was legally entitled to receive in discovery all of the data he supposedly bribed Reicher to obtain. "Why would anyone do that?" Cohn asked the jury.[43]

Cohn closed by summarizing the case against him as being based upon the testimony of perjurers, blackmailers, and scoundrels. He expressed his faith in the jury system of the United States, "a country a lot of people like to knock, but it's the greatest country in the world."[44]

After deliberating six hours, the jury returned its verdict: not guilty on all counts. Cohn stood up with a broad smile and made a deep bow to the jurors. He was then embraced by his co-defendants and scores of well-wishers in the courtroom. "This is just about the [most] relieved and happiest moment of my life," Cohn told the press. "God bless America! Thank God we put juries between the type of tyranny that Morgenthau perpetrates on his personal enemies."[45]

Five days after Cohn's acquittal, President Nixon fired Robert Morgenthau, making good on Maurice Stans's promise to Roy Cohn. Morgenthau, a Democrat, was ousted over the objections of New York's senators, Jacob Javits and Charles Goodell, both Republicans. Governor Nelson Rockefeller also publicly supported retaining Morgenthau, an unprecedented rebuke to a president of their own party.[46]

DONALD WEEDEN HAD grown progressively frustrated and angry with Washington's bungling: the Cohn trial debacle, the regulatory mismanagement of the back offices, and the seemingly endless hearings and jawboning—but no action—at the S.E.C. on eliminating fixed commissions. All of the issues the S.E.C. was struggling with—fixed commission rates, public ownership of Exchange member firms, institutional access to exchanges, off-Exchange trading in listed stocks—were sideshows, Weeden believed. He believed the solution for the problems in the stock markets was right in front of everyone's noses: the competitive structure of the corporate bond markets.

Prior to World War II, trading in corporate bonds was overwhelmingly a retail market and, not surprisingly, the overwhelming majority of the volume of trading in corporate bonds took place on the N.Y.S.E. After World War II, with the rise of institutional investors, the corporate bond market bifurcated: retail corporate bond investors continued to transact their relatively small-dollar trades on the N.Y.S.E., but institutional investors transacted the vast majority of their large-dollar trades off the Exchange floor in privately negotiated trades with other market makers. The commission rates for retail investors were fixed by the Exchange; those paid by the institutional investors were negotiated. Any Exchange member could transact in listed bonds either on or off the Exchange.

Before December 1969, Donald Weeden and his brothers had mostly stayed out of the battles in Washington affecting the industry. While they had assisted Milton Cohen and his staff during the preparation of the Special Study Report and testified in the rate hearings, they had rebuffed requests to join Harold Silver in his litigation against the N.Y.S.E. They lived with the heavy-handed tactics of the N.Y.S.E. and adapted. Weeden & Co.'s profits increased by taking advantage of every inefficiency the Exchange created with its monopolistic conduct. They mostly kept quiet while the S.E.C. sat on its hands and left the irrational status quo undisturbed. Frankly, the irrational status quo was pretty good for Weeden & Co.'s business. But the unfairness of equity market structure and the stupidity of its rules had become too much for Donald Weeden. He was embarrassed by the back-office catastrophe and angry at the recklessness of the undercapitalized and failing Wall Street firms who made and benefited from those rules.

By December 1969, Donald Weeden had had enough. He sat down with his brothers and his lawyer and drafted a letter to the S.E.C.[47] More than any other document, Weeden's December 19, 1969, letter to the S.E.C. provided a cohesive framework for a modern marketplace: the "Central Market Place" (which would later be called the "National Market System"):

> Left to their own devices, without concerted action by the New York Stock Exchange, markets in listed stocks should logically evolve into a simple combination of the present auction market servicing broker-handled executions of public orders and a negotiated market of well-capitalized market makers catering mainly to institutions. This is the direction that the corporate bond market took in the 1930s and 1940s when increased institutional trading in those securities demanded something more than just an auction market. What evolved was a combination market place that preserved the auction market while at the same time encouraged the growth of market makers, both inside and outside the exchange structure. This system protected the individual investor and the brokerage function related to that type of business, yet was capable of providing the liquidity and depth necessary for expanded institutional trading.[48]

In conclusion, urging the S.E.C. to require the N.Y.S.E. to scrap its monopolistic rules, Weeden wrote:

> The combined system for trading listed stocks which we envision should be more efficient and less expensive than the present system since it would reduce the number of high-cost hands through which an institutional block order must travel. A lot of the fat in the present system would be eliminated, and along with it, the unnatural compensation that accrues to many individuals and firms. Marginal producers and well-established firms, including ours, might find the going so rough that merger or liquidation becomes their only course. It is understandable or defensible that the New York Stock Exchange lends them support through its policies and actions. The

system the Exchange seeks to perpetuate is moribund. The forces acting on the market place for listed stocks are irreversible and will ultimately prevail.

We urge the Commission to resist the temptation to compromise in favor of the status quo. Compromise will only perpetuate present barriers and increase fragmentation of a growing market. Worse still, it will magnify the many distortions that presently plague the industry, distortions that grow harder to eliminate the longer they remain. Why prolong the process of adjustment? How much more responsible in the long run for the Commission to set free the forces of competition and permit a reasonably quick adjustment to the reality of institutional dominance in the listed stock market—a needed adjustment that would not increase the burden of regulatory surveillance of the true Central Market Place.[49]

For the next six years, a path he had not sought lay before Weeden. He would spend many of his days and nights traveling the country making speeches and testifying in hearing rooms advocating for a fair and rational marketplace.

ANOTHER MAVERICK WAS gearing up for a public crusade that December. H. Ross Perot's crusade involved collecting postcards. Perot had observed with growing distaste the antics of the Vietnam anti-war protest movement. It represented everything that Perot thought was wrong with young Americans: lack of patriotism, a disdain for free enterprise, sloppy appearance, and a lack of discipline. To counter a massive anti-war march on Washington in November, Perot paid for the printing and distribution of 25 million postcards reading "Mr. President, you have my support in your efforts to bring about a just and lasting peace," to be mailed back to the organization Perot formed for the purpose of receiving them, "United We Stand."[50] While Perot's postcard drive garnered a bit of national press, it hadn't made the media splash Perot had hoped for. Nothing if not persistent, Perot soon cooked up another venture.

To the extent Americans had heard of Ross Perot at the time, it was likely as a result of the blockbuster IPO of the computer company he founded, E.D.S., in September 1968. Offered at $16.50 per share, it was soon trading at ten times that price, and Ross Perot became the world's first tech billionaire. Perot was born and raised in east Texas and after graduating from Annapolis in 1953 and serving his four years of active duty in the Navy, took a job at I.B.M. in Dallas selling computer systems. He was the greatest salesman in I.B.M.'s storied history. He sold so many computers that he repeatedly refused promotions, as taking a salaried executive position would have dramatically reduced his compensation. He was selling so many computers that I.B.M. had to take drastic action to rein in his pay, cutting his commission rate by 80 percent and assigning him a "reverse quota"—an annual sales amount above which he would receive no commission.

In 1962, Perot achieved this reverse quota on January 19. Disgusted with I.B.M. stifling him, he quit a few weeks later and in June 1962 formed E.D.S. with $1,000 of capital. In 1965, after the Medicare legislation was passed, E.D.S. won the contract from Texas Blue Shield to automate the payments processing for the program. Soon, E.D.S. had similar contracts in ten other states. By 1968, New York investment bankers were beating a path to Perot's door begging to take him public. Perot, the homespun Eagle Scout suspicious of everything eastern, particularly Wall Street, turned them away—all but one. For reasons no one can quite explain, Ross Perot took a strong liking to a tall, tough-talking young Italian American banker, Frank Langone, from the second-tier investment bank R. W. Pressprich and Company.

R. W. Pressprich would take E.D.S. public and Frank Langone would become a legend on Wall Street and a billionaire himself many times over. Langone would manage successful companies like Home Depot, and he went on to become a governor of the N.Y.S.E.

On December 15, 1969, Ross Perot called a press conference to announce that United We Stand would charter a plane to take humanitarian supplies and Christmas presents to American prisoners of war held in North Vietnam.[51] He told the press he had sent a telegram to Pham Van Dong, the Premier of North Vietnam, asking for permission to land in Hanoi, but had not yet been given a response. In any event, Perot said, the plane would depart Los Angeles International Airport the following week. Perot also announced that United We Stand would be sponsoring trips by the wives and children of American prisoners of war to go to the Paris peace talks and lobby North Vietnamese officials for their release.[52] On December 19, Perot summoned the press again. United We Stand would now be sending 150 wives and children to Paris and two planeloads of supplies of Christmas presents to Hanoi aboard Boeing 320-C jets leased from Braniff Airways. He conceded that he had not heard from the North Vietnam government as to whether he'd be allowed to land the planes.[53]

The following day, Hanoi responded. North Vietnam promised that the American prisoners would receive all gifts sent via existing protocols—they suggested the postal route through Moscow—but under no circumstances would Perot's planes be given clearance to land in Hanoi.[54] Undeterred, Perot told the press the planes would be taking off for Bangkok the next day. "We have sent a return cable to the North Vietnamese explaining that the purpose of our trip is to improve the relationship between the people of the United States and the people of North Vietnam," he told the *New York Times*. "Allowing private American citizens to bring Christmas directly to these men would be a major step toward improving relationships between our people. We are still confident that once the North Vietnamese fully understand the purpose of our mission and the desirable effect it will have between the people of both countries they will allow us to enter."[55]

On December 21, Perot left Love Field in Dallas aboard the first of the two chartered jets, which he christened the "Peace on Earth," en route first to Los Angeles to load the supplies and thereafter to Bangkok. The second plane, which Perot named the "Goodwill Toward Men," would leave the following day.[56] On December 24,

Perot and a contingent of Red Cross volunteers and reporters aboard the Peace on Earth landed in Bangkok, Thailand, with 75 tons of Christmas gifts, food, and medical supplies.[57] He met with North Vietnamese officials to convince them of the merit of his mission. The North Vietnamese, however, hadn't budged. On Christmas day, 150 family members of American POWs landed in Paris aboard a Boeing 707 chartered by Perot seeking to meet with the North Vietnamese delegation at the Paris peace talks in order to obtain the release of their loved ones. The North Vietnamese refused to meet with them. After only six hours on the ground in Paris, they boarded the plane and returned to New York.[58] Perot spent Christmas in Laos. The following day, he met with North Vietnamese diplomats there, but with the same result. That afternoon, he announced he was abandoning the mission to North Vietnam, but would seek to have the supplies delivered on his behalf by the Soviet Union.[59] On December 27, back in Bangkok, Thailand, Perot held another press conference, this time announcing that the Peace on Earth would be flying to Moscow to deliver the aid packages. Perot had hoped to fly from Bangkok to Rome where he had obtained an audience with Pope Paul VI to promote his mission before flying to Moscow, but the western route was denied him when Burma and India, at the request of the Soviets, refused to allow Perot to fly across their airspace.[60] So, on December 28, Perot flew east, over the arctic circle, for a twelve-hour layover in Anchorage, Alaska, before resuming the easterly journey to Copenhagen, Denmark.[61] Two days later, on New Year's Eve, Ross Perot, still in Copenhagen, announced that the Soviets had formally denied his visa application and that he and his planes would be returning home.[62] Perot spent $1,500,000 on the aborted mission, a financial debacle notwithstanding its public relations boon.[63]

Back in Dallas, Perot's senior management team at E.D.S. was planning a different kind of mission for Perot in 1970: conquering Wall Street through its back offices. It, too, would be a debacle—and a far more expensive one.

∎ ∎ ∎

1969 WAS AN unmitigated disaster on Wall Street, and it held little optimism for 1970 at year-end. The Dow was down over 15 percent for the year. Bond indices were down even more sharply, most by more than 20 percent. Interest rates were at levels not seen since the Civil War. Consumer confidence was falling and most economists were predicting a recession in 1970. Three prominent Wall Street firms had failed in 1969. Two of them, Amott & Baker and Gregory & Sons, were N.Y.S.E. members. Several significantly larger firms—McDonnell & Co., Hayden, Stone, Inc., Francis I. du-Pont & Co., Goodbody & Co., and Dempsey-Tegeler & Co.—were struggling to remain solvent. While the implementation of C.C.S. enabled the industry to get control of the paperwork, the financial consequences of the back-office chaos were now being suffered, in the midst of the worst bear market in decades.

Washington was irreversibly on course to reform the anticompetitive practices of the N.Y.S.E. that had been tolerated for decades. The volume discount and end of give-ups were only the beginning. Competitive commission rates and institutional access to the exchanges were simply a matter of time. So was public ownership of member firms. That would come in 1970, and with it would go the control of the Club over access to capital and its supercharging power to change the competitive landscape and power structure on Wall Street.

As bad as 1969 had been on Wall Street, few outside of the inner circle at the Exchange and a handful of staff at the New York Regional Office of the S.E.C. knew how diminished the financial condition of many of the industry giants had become. And as downbeat as the prognostications for 1970 were, none of the experts predicted the carnage the new year would bring to Wall Street—or the bailout it would hustle from Washington.

PART IV
1970

The Bailout

CHAPTER TEN

"THE RESULT COULD BE A
MAJOR CATASTROPHE"

McDonnell & Co. Fails

Back home, Ross Perot began the new year of 1970 focused on an enormously important and equally difficult strategic initiative that he believed would propel E.D.S.'s growth throughout the 1970s. Wall Street's back-office crisis was E.D.S.'s next golden opportunity, thought Perot. He would do for the financial services industry what he had done for Medicare—standardize data management and rationalize systems, all using E.D.S. services. Perot would become the back-office operator/savior for all of Wall Street, reaping billions along the way.

Perot's first call was to the one man he trusted on Wall Street: Frank Langone. He asked Langone which man knew the most about the back-office operations on Wall Street. Langone answered, without hesitation: Lee Arning, the senior vice president of the N.Y.S.E. in charge of operations.[1] Perot reached out to Arning and suggested they meet in Dallas to discuss ways E.D.S. might assist in cleaning up the back-office mess. Arning did all he could to conceal his enthusiasm and agreed to meet as soon as Perot was ready.[2]

What Lee Arning told the E.D.S. people in Dallas did nothing but confirm their belief that E.D.S. could swoop in and capture not just the back-office operations of Wall Street firms, but possibly the entire clearing and settlement functions of the N.Y.S.E. itself.[3] All of these computer systems—of the member firms, the Exchange,

C.C.S. and its clearing and settlement operations—were different and not integrated. No one in his right mind would design a data management system like this, Perot thought to himself. Perot knew what needed doing: scrap it all and build a new one from scratch—integrated and efficient—and owned and operated by E.D.S. But to accomplish this, Perot needed to convince all of those constituencies to hand this enormous responsibility over to E.D.S. This challenge was made more complicated by the stark reality that E.D.S. had never built or operated even a single computer system for a Wall Street firm. What Ross knew he needed was the first customer. So, at Lee Arning's urging, Ross Perot came to New York in January 1970 to meet with the brass of the N.Y.S.E. and pitch his vision of an integrated, automated data processing system for the entire securities industry and, more importantly, to co-opt the Exchange leadership to be emissaries and salesmen of E.D.S. to find that all-important first customer.[4]

Perot was not the only one to see opportunity for riches in 1970 out of the chaos of the back-office crisis. On the thirty-fourth floor of the General Motors Building in Midtown Manhattan, four men, all in their thirties, had recently raised $3 million of new equity capital to build a state-of-the-art, fully computerized back-office operation. Their back office would have the capacity to process all transactions for their ten-year-old investment bank many times over, giving their eponymous firm—Cogan, Berlind, Weill & Levitt, Inc.—a competitive advantage in acquiring distressed brokerage firms at fire-sale prices.[5]

Sandy Weill had started as a runner at Bear, Stearns before moving to Burnham and Company. Across the hallway in Weill's apartment in Queens lived Arthur Carter, then a junior banker with Lehman Brothers.[6] The two became friends and began to talk about forming their own firm. Arthur Carter brought another friend into these discussions, Roger Berlind, a broker at Eastman Dillon.[7] Berlind convinced a colleague at Eastman Dillon, Peter Potoma, to join in the venture and, in 1960, Carter, Berlind, Potoma & Weill was launched in a tiny office at 37 Wall Street.[8]

As a favor to Sandy Weill as much as anything, Tubby Burnham, chairman of Burnham and Company, not expecting much trading volume, agreed to clear the firm's trades through Burnham's back office.[9] Within a year, they outgrew the office at 37 Wall Street and moved to more spacious quarters at 60 Wall Street.[10] In 1962, Peter Potoma was asked to leave the firm. He had developed a drinking problem and also violated N.Y.S.E. trading rules.[11] In 1963, two partners were added to the team: Arthur Levitt Jr., son of New York State comptroller Arthur Levitt Sr., and a brash, Harvard-educated Bostonian, Marshall Cogan.[12] The firm initially focused on retail brokerage, but by the mid-1960s saw that institutional sales were the wave of the future. In addition, Marshall Cogan was early in seeing that the conglomerators would be a source of enormous fees in both merger and acquisition advisory business and block sales and trading. He also had an uncanny ability to meet and befriend corporate heavy hitters, landing Charlie Bluhdorn of Gulf & Western as a major client of the firm.[13]

In September 1968, the partners had a falling-out with Arthur Carter, who wanted to take the firm into principal investing in merchant banking and leveraged buyouts rather than traditional fee-based investment banking businesses. His partners disagreed, Carter was asked to leave, and "Cogan" replaced "Carter" on the letterhead. (Cogan came first because the firm had become known on Wall Street by its acronym, C.B.W.L.) A few months later, Tubby Burnham arranged a dinner with the C.B.W.L. partners and gave them the bad news that because of the firm's explosive growth, the Burnham back office could no longer handle its volume of transactions.[14] They needed to look elsewhere for back-office support. They thought Tubby Burnham was motivated by jealousy of the young firm's success—it had nearly the same volume of business as Burnham and Company and was growing much faster.[15]

In the middle of Wall Street's back-office crisis, this was a potentially catastrophic development. The four partners frantically reached out to other Wall Street firms—Loeb Rhoades, Lehman

Brothers, and Bache & Co.—but all turned down their requests for back-office services.[16]

Adversity, among other things, breeds innovation, commitment, and efficiency. The C.B.W.L. partners decided they would never be held hostage by another firm. They would build their own back office. They recruited Frank Zarb, the second in command of the back-office operations of Goodbody & Co. Zarb agreed to an interview and got right to the point: "If you guys can get me a million dollars, I'll build you the best clearing firm on Wall Street."[17] Ironically, building a technologically state-of-the-art back office from scratch in 1969, when done by an expert like Zarb, was much less expensive than upgrading an existing back office with obsolete technology. They got him $3 million, and by January 1970, C.B.W.L. was looking to acquire more product to push through Frank Zarb's shiny new electronic plumbing.[18]

TWO FIRMS WERE at the top of C.B.W.L.'s list of possible acquisition targets. C.B.W.L. correctly believed that McDonnell & Co. would be forced to sell its remaining crown jewel assets—the Paris and 400 Park Avenue branch offices—at fire-sale prices. McDonnell & Co. sold its mutual fund business to Scheinman, Hochstin & Trotta, Inc., but C.B.W.L. had no opportunity to bid on this since Scheinman, Hochstin & Trotta's $600,000 loan on the business allowed them to essentially preempt the sales process with a credit bid.[19] Despite its shedding of offices and the sale of its mutual fund business, McDonnell & Co.'s net capital position worsened in February 1970. Its operations were not improving either. Nearly 25 percent of all complaints received by the S.E.C. in early 1970 came from disgruntled McDonnell & Co. customers. McDonnell & Co.'s new chief executive, Paul McDonald, begged, successfully, for the N.Y.S.E. to give him more time to get into capital compliance.[20] First National City Bank, overextended with loans to McDonnell & Co., was also threatening to pull the plug and call the loans.[21] Paul McDonald promised the bank he would find an equity investor or merger partner by March, but none would emerge.[22] And Paul McDonald had a new problem that February. McDonnell & Co.'s external auditors, Lybrand, Ross Bros & Montgomery, informed McDonald that McDonnell & Co.'s accounting records were such a mess it would be unable to deliver an opinion on its financial statements.[23]

The other firm that C.B.W.L. believed would need to shed assets was Francis I. duPont & Co., which had rapidly, some said recklessly, expanded during the 1960s. On January 15, 1970, Francis I. duPont & Co. announced it was closing nine branch offices, located domestically in Massachusetts, California, Florida, and New York and overseas in London, Paris, Kuwait, and Lebanon.[24] On February 4, Francis I. duPont & Co. disclosed that it had lost $7.7 million in 1969 despite having near-record revenues of $116,832,000.[25] The next day brought more bad news. The N.Y.S.E. announced that it had fined Francis I. duPont & Co. $50,000; its senior partner, Edmund duPont, $25,000; its former managing partner, Charles Moran, $25,000; and the former partner in charge of the firm's back office, Alfred J. Coffey, $10,000.[26] The fines related to failing to respond properly to customer complaints. In response to the fines, Francis I. duPont & Co. released a statement: "The charge of poor handling of customer complaints involves a period of time when the famous paperwork logjam was at its peak and procedures for handling such matters were admittedly but unavoidably unsatisfactory. Since that time we've installed new procedures and new management which are working extremely well."[27]

C.B.W.L. had not spent much time analyzing the assets of Hayden, Stone Inc. By March, Hayden, Stone's financial condition was grave. The firm reported to the New York Regional Office of the S.E.C. that it had excess net capital of $1,954,000 as of January 31, 1970. Its official report to the N.Y.S.E. showed a $3.2 million net capital deficit.[28] Hayden, Stone's internal accounting records would later reveal that it had been in violation of the net capital rule throughout February as well.[29] Desperate for capital, the lifeline for the firm came from, of all places, from Oklahoma.

On March 3, Hayden, Stone announced that it had received loans in the form of publicly-traded equity securities with an aggregate value of $17,480,000.[30] These loans would be subordinated to Hayden, Stone's other obligations, thereby qualifying the loans for capital treatment under the Exchange's net capital rule. Six individual investors and IHC, Inc., a diversified industrial company based in Oklahoma, provided the subordinated loans. In addition to the interest on the loans, the investor group received an option to purchase 35 percent of the stock of Hayden, Stone at a favorable price. The investor group was led by Jack E. Golsen, chairman and president of LSB Industries, Inc., an Oklahoma City–based industrial company that manufactured bearings, machine tools, and air-conditioning equipment.[31]

The stock loaned by this investor group consisted of $4,900,000 worth of shares of Carousel Fashions, Inc. (owned by IHC, Inc.), $4,890,000 of shares of Four Seasons Nursing Centers of America, Inc., $4,372,000 of shares of CMI Corporation, $2,117,500 of shares of Woods Corporation, and $1,200,000 of shares of LSB Industries, Inc. Hayden, Stone was the principal investment banker for all of these companies.[32] Hayden, Stone closed on the loan on March 13, 1970. Alfred J. Coyle, Hayden, Stone's chairman and president, hailed the transaction, saying it would give the firm "the base to expand its major investment banking and brokerage role and to continue its progress of recent years."[33]

Almost immediately after the closing, the values of the stocks began to decline. Within a year, Four Seasons Nursing Centers would be bankrupt, its stock worthless, and each of the other stocks would suffer substantial losses.

THE DOUBLE BLOW of lower commissions and tanking stock prices was decimating the liquidity and capital of many firms. The Club pressured the N.Y.S.E. leadership to somehow find a way to get an increase in commission rates. The S.E.C. had the opposite in mind. As the rate hearings continued in 1970, the Commission staff requested that the N.Y.S.E. and the other major exchanges submit briefs by February 2 reflecting a rate structure on an unbundled basis. Gene Rotberg at the S.E.C. wanted the exchanges to show whether in fact trading commissions subsidized research and, if so, to what extent. With the N.E.R.A. study nearly complete, Robert Haack was eager to formally submit a permanent commission rate proposal to the S.E.C. to shift the agenda away from an à la carte rate approach.

The board of governors of the N.Y.S.E. met on February 12 under tight security to vote on a proposed permanent commission rate schedule to send to the S.E.C. for approval.[34] The rate schedule approved by the governors provided for increases of up to 100 percent on small transactions, but rate cuts of up to 37.5 percent on certain large, institutional transactions. The commission for the average-sized trade would rise about 68 percent. The net effect of the changes would be an increase in commissions of about 10 percent.[35]

In the formal statement filed with the S.E.C. for its approval of the new rate schedule, Robert Haack painted a grim picture of the brokerage business: "Four of every ten New York Stock Exchange member firms doing a public business lost money on securities commission income (including net margin interest income) in the first half of 1969. Their cumulative loss amounted to $58,000,000. Losses ranged up to $5,700,000, with thirteen firms losing over $1,000,000 and fifty-one losing over $250,000."[36] Haack highlighted how significant the losses of many firms were relative to their capital: "Among the 156 firms that experienced losses in 1969, fully one-quarter had losses equivalent to over 25 percent of capital and over one-third had losses in the 11 percent to 25 percent range."[37] One out of ten N.Y.S.E. member firms—over forty firms in total—experienced losses representing more than 25 percent of their capital in 1969.

Haack focused the S.E.C. commissioners on N.E.R.A.'s finding that an overall average profitability of 15 percent on capital devoted to the stock trading execution business was appropriate for the industry. His proposed permanent rate schedule would result in that rate of return. He provided a copy of the N.E.R.A. report to each of the commissioners on a confidential basis.[38]

The rate proposal also addressed the issue of allowing access to the Exchange by non-member broker-dealers. The proposal included a 25 percent discount on commissions charged to non-members, reduced to a 20 percent discount for transactions involving more than 500 shares.[39]

In the rate proposal, the Exchange did not address the issue of allowing institutional investors to become members. "By taking these complicated and important issues one by one," Haack said in a statement released in connection with the board approval, "we will be able to arrive at solutions dictated by facts and logic, rather than emotion and instinct. We are confident that the exchange will be in a position to speak to the institutional question in an informed way once these other issues have been satisfactorily resolved."[40]

Hamer Budge expressed two concerns about the proposal. First, he wanted assurances from Haack that the Exchange members would continue to serve the small investor—which Haack committed to do. Second, he believed that the S.E.C. was not equipped with the resources to perform a rate regulation function and had doubts that Congress would provide the necessary funds to do so.[41]

Once the rate proposal became public, support and opposition among N.Y.S.E. members broke predictably along the lines of retail versus institutional business models. D.L.J., Salomon Brothers, and Smith Barney & Co., Inc., each of which did a predominantly institutional business, publicly opposed the plan. Billy Salomon sent a letter to all Exchange members urging them to oppose the plan. "If adopted," he asserted, "the proposed new rate structure could result in serious damage to the investment process and the structure of the financial community, which would affect every shareholder of listed common stocks and every corporation whose shares are listed on the New York Stock Exchange."[42] Robert A. Powers, president of Smith, Barney, also urged that the new plan not be implemented and voiced harsh criticism of the secrecy of the board of governors' deliberations and lack of input from members. "We thought we were members of the New York Stock Exchange, but apparently we're not treated like one." Powers asserted: "Nobody knew anything about this thing until Saturday morning when we read it in the newspapers."[43]

Retail-heavy firms like Bache & Co., Francis I. duPont & Co., and Goodbody & Co. enthusiastically supported the proposal. "We believe that significant increases in commissions, along the general lines proposed by the New York Stock Exchange, are vitally necessary if the retail investor is to receive the sales, operations, and research service he deserves," Harold P. Goodbody, the senior partner of Goodbody & Co., stated.[44] Harry A. Jacobs, Jr., president of Bache & Co., announced that "Bache & Co. strongly supports this move on the part of the New York Stock Exchange and hopes that the S.E.C. will approve it unchanged."[45]

Merrill Lynch, which was strong in both retail and institutional businesses, thought rates should be even lower. It had no issue with the additional volume discount, but thought the rate increase on small orders was excessive. Donald Regan called those rate increases "seriously out of balance," but noted that "there is obviously nothing we can do about it at present."[46]

WHILE THE CLUB angled for an increase in commission rates to stanch the bleeding, adverse developments continued. Dempsey-Tegeler & Co. had fallen out of net capital rule compliance at year-end and hastily sought a capital infusion to prevent the N.Y.S.E. from appointing a liquidator. On January 20, the firm announced it had received a capital infusion in the form of a subordinated account from the King Resources Company, a Denver-based oil exploration company that Dempsey-Tegeler had taken public in 1967. Dempsey-Tegeler also announced that day that it would be shedding thirty-three of its remaining sixty branch offices in order to preserve liquidity.[47]

On January 28, Blyth & Co., a leading investment bank, announced that it was resigning its membership from the N.Y.S.E. in order to permit it to be acquired by I.N.A. Corporation, a large insurance company. The acquisition would have run afoul of the Exchange's prohibition on a member being owned by a company not engaged principally in the securities business. The reason for the transaction was Blyth's need to access more capital to expand its business. "Let me assure you it's not a shotgun marriage," Paul Devlin, Blyth's chairman told reporters. "We had no capital problem. You're either going to have to get bigger or smaller in this business. We're going to get bigger, and that means permanent capital."[48]

Not be outdone by I.N.A. Corporation, The Prudential Insurance Company, the world's largest insurance company, followed a few weeks later with an announcement that it intended to buy an investment bank unless there was a "drastic reduction" in commission rates.[49]

FRANCIS I. DUPONT & CO., was hardly alone in announcing dismal 1969 earnings. Bache & Co., Inc. announced it had lost more than $7,000,000 during the nine months ended October 31, 1969 (its loss for the fiscal year would be $8,741,000).[50] On February 10, Merrill Lynch announced that while it was profitable for 1969, its profits had plunged 41 percent from 1968. It had earned $32,299,732 in 1969 as compared to $54,486,076 in 1968.[51] On February 24, Goodbody & Co. announced that it had lost $832,000 in 1969, as compared to a profit of $4,096,000 for 1968.[52] The Third Market firms were not immune from the downturn either. Even Weeden & Co. announced a loss for 1969 of $2,950,061, as compared to a profit of $2,423,752 in 1968.[53]

THE NEGOTIATIONS WITH the S.E.C. over the two remaining controversial conditions under which N.Y.S.E. member firms could go public made little progress in the early months of 1970. The

S.E.C. continued to object to the prohibition on a customer owning more than 5 percent of the stock of a member firm and the 49
percent cap on public ownership. On February 26, the S.E.C. for
the first time formally announced it would allow N.Y.S.E. firms to
go public if those two conditions were dropped.[54] In addition, the
S.E.C. agreed in principle to permit a condition that required any
parent of a member firm have as its "primary purpose" the conduct
of a broker-dealer business, subject to review of the Exchange rule
defining "primary purpose."

On March 5, 1970, the board of governors of the N.Y.S.E. approved a series of amendments to its constitution to permit public
ownership of Exchange member firms and submitted those
amendments to a vote of members concluding on March 19,
1970.[55] The provisions objected to by the S.E.C. were removed
from the final amendments. The board of governors of the N.Y.S.E.
also proposed a rule defining "primary purpose" to be met if at
least 50 percent of consolidated revenues were derived from
broker-dealer businesses.

The Department of Justice was not ready to hang the bunting. It
concluded that the "primary purpose" rule was an illegal restraint
of trade designed to prevent mutual funds and other institutional
investors from becoming Exchange members. The N.Y.S.E., with
the approval of the S.E.C., went ahead anyway, and the battle with
the Department of Justice would go on.

On March 19, the members of the N.Y.S.E. approved the public
ownership amendments by a vote of 1,013 to 70.[56] To hopefully
prevent, or at least delay, the Justice Department attack upon the
"primary purpose" rule, the board of governors also announced
that day that it was establishing an ad hoc committee chaired by
Bunny Lasker to study the possibility of allowing institutional investors to become members of the Exchange.[57] On March 26, the
board of governors of the Exchange formally adopted the rule providing for the 50 percent of revenue presumption of compliance
with the "primary purpose" test, and submitted the rule to the
S.E.C. for its approval.[58] This final regulatory hurdle was a formality

since the S.E.C. had agreed it would not object to the adoption of the rule. (The S.E.C. did reserve the right to require that it be rescinded pending Justice Department action.)

On March 30, D.L.J. announced that it planned to price its public offering on April 9. Formal approval of the Exchange's public ownership rule had delayed the offering and necessitated an amendment to the offering registration statement. The S.E.C. would need to review the amendment and declare the registration statement effective before sales could be consummated. When the registration statement was first filed in May 1969, it assumed an offering price of $30 per share. At the end of March 1970, given the depressed state of the investment banking business, market insiders were expecting a price in the low twenties.[59] The registration statement disclosed that 80 percent of D.L.J.'s revenues were from securities commissions, 60 percent from N.Y.S.E. commissions—and commission rates, particularly on institutional trading of large blocks, were going nowhere but down.

THE WHISPERING FROM the S.E.C. staff to the staff of the N.Y.S.E. was that it would take at least six months—and possibly up to two years—for the S.E.C. to complete its evaluation of the new rate structure proposed by the N.Y.S.E. Meanwhile, the industry was hemorrhaging money. On March 14, the Cost and Revenue Committee of the N.Y.S.E. met and authorized Bunny Lasker, Robert Haack, and Ralph DeNunzio, the thirty-eight-year-old executive vice president of Kidder Peabody & Co. and newly elected vice-chairman of the Exchange, to negotiate some interim relief on rates from the S.E.C. The trio agreed to ask the S.E.C. to allow a special transaction fee on trades involving less than 1,000 shares.[60] On March 19, the board of governors of the Exchange approved a $15 temporary surcharge on all such transactions. In a letter to the Exchange membership explaining the decision, Robert Haack stated that: "Allowing for the normal three-week waiting period of S.E.C. comments, if the commission interposes no objection, the new charge could be given final approval by our board on April 12 and take effect shortly thereafter."[61]

Also on that day, the Board of Estimate of the City of New York unanimously approved a project for a new skyscraper with over 1.5 million square feet of office space. Occupying 135,000 of those square feet, it was announced, would be the new home of the N.Y.S.E. It would contain three times more space than its current location (built in 1903) and would be located at the eastern end of Wall Street. The seven-acre site was to be created with landfill removed from the World Trade Center location to build out into in the East River near Pier 13.[62]

The cost of constructing the building to house the new N.Y.S.E. was estimated to be $155 million, and it was expected to take five years to complete. That skyscraper was to be part of a thirty-acre development for new commercial and residential structures along the East River, complementing the Battery Park City development on the Hudson River side of downtown Manhattan. The City agreed to lease the office space to the N.Y.S.E. for fifty years, with options to renew for four ten-year terms and one additional nine-year term, for ninety-nine years in total. The City of New York also agreed to reroute FDR Drive under the new skyscraper. The mayor at the time, John Lindsay, held a press conference at City Hall to announce the new lease. "Approval of this proposal is a major step in the continuing revitalization of lower Manhattan and an important landmark in the history of our city," said Lindsay. "The decision is a wise one for the stock exchange and an important display of faith in the continuing economic vitality and prosperity of our city." It would prove to be one of the shortest-lived development projects in New York history—another victim of the back-office crisis.[63]

ON MARCH 12, 1970, Paul McDonald, the president of McDonnell & Co., called an emergency meeting with the firm's principal lender, First National City Bank. Presenting at the meeting were McDonnell & Co.'s external auditors, Lybrand, Ross Bros. &

Montgomery. The auditors were there to explain why Lybrand was unable to certify McDonnell & Co.'s 1969 financial statements. The reason was a mountain of record-keeping errors and irregularities. Also at the meeting was John Cunningham, the second in command of the N.Y.S.E. whose duties had recently expanded to keeping tabs on the ever-expanding list of troubled firms.[64]

McDonald told the assembled executives that there was little chance of saving the firm from insolvency and liquidation, given its dire financial condition and the reality that without certified financial statements the possibility of a rescue financing was very remote. He also told them that he was unwilling to continue as president unless he received assurances from the N.Y.S.E. that it would not take regulatory action against him personally for allowing the firm to continue to operate in violation of the net capital rule. In addition, McDonald told the men that the S.E.C. was investigating the firm and its former president, Murray McDonnell, for violating the Securities Act of 1933 for failing to register securities—now worthless—sold to employees in late 1968 and early 1969 as the firm's back-office and capital problems worsened. In addition, the S.E.C. was investigating salesmen in McDonnell & Co.'s 400 Park Avenue and Asbury Park, New Jersey, branch offices for numerous fraudulent activities. So long as McDonnell & Co. had a reasonable possibility of surviving, the S.E.C. was willing to delay bringing charges formally in order to give it time to sell itself or merge, but its tolerance for further delay was nearing its end. John Cunningham listened politely to Paul McDonald and then told him unequivocally that the Exchange would not provide him any such exculpation.[65]

The meeting broke up soon thereafter, and John Cunningham returned to the Exchange and briefed Robert Haack on the latest developments at McDonnell & Co. The two men came to the same conclusion very quickly. The Exchange needed to shut down and liquidate McDonnell & Co. Not even John Coleman, if he were so inclined, could have delayed the demise of McDonnell & Co.[66]

An emergency meeting of the board of governors of the Exchange was quickly called that afternoon, and the liquidation of

McDonnell & Co. was approved with little debate.[67] It was uncertain what the cost of liquidation would be, but the governors agreed that McDonnell & Co. customers would need to be made whole through the Exchange's Special Trust Fund. A total of $7 million of the $26 million Special Trust Fund had already been committed to bail out the three sizable member firms that had earlier gone insolvent—Pickard & Company, Amott, Baker & Co., and Gregory & Sons. Cunningham told the governors he estimated that $6 million would be required to be provided by the Special Trust Fund to McDonnell & Co.[68] (This would prove to be an optimistic projection.)

The governors braced for what would follow: the public announcement of the largest failure of a Wall Street investment bank since the Great Depression.

Shortly after 10:00 a.m. on Friday the thirteenth of March, the bells rang out on *Dow Jones Newswire* machines throughout Wall Street and beyond indicating that a major business story was breaking.[69] The machines then printed out the news that McDonnell & Co. was being liquidated by the N.Y.S.E. In truth, much of the firm had already been carved up and disposed of. What had been twenty-six branch offices were down to three—120 Broadway and Park Avenue in New York and one in Paris, France. While it once had 1,500 employees, only 270 remained on March 13. Of the 40,000 retail customers at its peak, barely 3,000 remained.[70] The slow wasting of McDonnell & Co. and the months of rumors predicting its demise cushioned the systemic blow of its failure. Most institutional counterparties had already stopped trading with McDonnell & Co. The Exchange had already decided how McDonnell & Co.'s remaining accounts would be parceled out to other firms. The immediate concern of the other Wall Street investment banks was poaching the few remaining talented bankers and brokers at McDonnell. A ceaseless flurry of calls for the top talent began shortly after the *Dow Jones* story hit the wires and continued all day.

The S.E.C. reacted almost immediately. Kevin Duffy, the New York regional administrator for the S.E.C., called a press conference to announce that formal charges would shortly be brought against McDonnell & Co. and certain of its officers, but refused to specify what those charges would be.[71]

Murray McDonnell, the firm's deposed president, in his remaining capacity as chairman put out a statement that morning: "It is with deep regret that we have decided to close McDonnell & Co. after sixty-five years on Wall Street. The firm, started by my father, has had a long tradition of integrity and reliability and it is in that spirit that we have made our decision."[72]

While the failure of McDonnell & Co. was not a surprise to either the board of governors of the Exchange or the New York Regional Office of the S.E.C., it came as a complete surprise to Congress and the White House. The prestige and high profile of the McDonnell family predictably brought a rush of press coverage. The back-office crisis on Wall Street was no longer an inside story buried in the business section; it was front-page news. Within days, new rumors emerged that another major investment bank was soon to be shuttered by the N.Y.S.E. Francis I. duPont & Co. and Hayden, Stone were the most frequently mentioned, but also Bache & Co., the industry's second largest firm. Among the giants, only Merrill Lynch seemed immune from the rumors. Nine firms, unnamed by the Exchange, remained under regulatory restrictions on their operations. The business press, wary of worsening the crisis, had an unwritten agreement with John Cunningham not to refer to any rumored failing firms by name. Robert Haack urged the S.E.C. to approve the $15 transaction surcharge on an expedited basis to calm fears of further financial deterioration of member firms.

On March 23, 1970, the *New York Times* raised the specter of a systemic crisis. "Of special concern is the crisis of public confidence that could ensue if one or more of the securities industry's giant houses were to become insolvent," wrote Terry Robards. "Such a crisis could cause a run on other houses, according to one theory, and the result could be a major catastrophe."[73] To quell the anxiety arising out of the *New York Times* story, Robert Haack released an unusual statement, disclosing that all of the N.Y.S.E.'s top twenty-five member firms in terms of revenue, comprising over half of the

Exchange's dollar volume of business, were in compliance with the net capital rule.[74] He reiterated that the Exchange continuously monitored the financial condition of member firms, particularly when they were in danger of violating capital requirements. Given the Exchange's liberal interpretation of the net capital rule for favored firms, including McDonnell, no one on Wall Street took comfort from Haack's announcement, but the intended audience was not Wall Street, but rather the unsuspecting investing public. Haack's statement didn't clarify that "compliance" was determined after myriad exceptions and indulgences that allowed insolvent firms, up to the moment they were closed down, to assert they were technically in compliance with the net capital rule, as applied by the Club.

The possible systemic fallout from the collapse of McDonnell & Co. was not overlooked by Congress. On the Monday following its receivership, Representative John E. Moss of California, who had introduced Senator Muskie's broker-dealer insurance legislation in the House of Representatives, scurried to get the bill moving through the House.[75] He wrote a letter to Representative Haley O. Staggers of West Virginia, chairman of the House Foreign and Interstate Commerce Committee, requesting that committee hearings be held immediately on the bill. Staggers did not agree on a timetable for hearings, but did appoint staff to investigate the issue. "We have to see what the trouble is," Staggers told the press. "I think in all probability it's mismanagement rather than anything else. We cannot rush in and say we're going to subsidize the stock market and subsidize some of the big boys who want to make a killing. We have to have some facts."[76]

Senator Harrison A. Williams Jr., chairman of the Senate Subcommittee on Securities, announced publicly that his committee would hold hearings on the Muskie bill within a month.[77]

With concern over fallout from the McDonnell & Co. failure unabated, Haack announced on March 25 that the N.Y.S.E. would make available a loan to the Exchange's Special Trust Fund of up to $30 million, subject to approval by the Exchange's board of governors and members.[78] With the cost of liquidating McDonnell & Co. not quantifiable with any degree of certainty, even if the $6 million already committed proved to be sufficient, only $13 million would remain in the Special Trust Fund, nowhere near the amount that might be needed if a very large firm failed. Haack did not disclose from what sources the loan would be extended, only that it would come from funds available to the Exchange. Haack also announced that the board of governors had established a special committee, formally named the Surveillance Committee, but better known as the "Crisis Committee," to monitor troubled firms and the sufficiency of the Special Trust Fund. The Crisis Committee was comprised of Bunny Lasker; Ralph DeNunzio; Felix Rohatyn; Solomon Litt; Robert L. Stott Jr., managing partner of Wagner, Stott & Co., a specialist firm; and Stephen M. Peck, senior partner of Weiss, Peck & Greer.[79]

The S.E.C. in Washington, also concerned now about the financial stability of Wall Street firms, gave interim approval on April 2 to the N.Y.S.E.'s proposed $15 per transaction surcharge on trades involving 1,000 or fewer shares, but only for a ninety-day period. Hamer Budge stated that: "Data obtained by the Commission confirms the loss experience of these firms. We are concerned with the financial problems of the industry and the losses sustained in the past year and during the first quarter of 1970."[80] Robert Haack said he was "very pleased at the S.E.C.'s quick and constructive response."[81] As a condition of the approval, the Exchange was required to order its members to suspend practices that discriminated against small investors, such as maintaining minimum account balances and minimum trade sizes.

The fee supplement came too late for Baerwald & DeBoer, a small N.Y.S.E. member firm that announced that day that it would liquidate, unable to maintain compliance with the net capital rule. The N.Y.S.E.'s Special Trust Fund would need to advance $900,000 to Baerwald & DeBoer to make its customers whole.[82]

■ ■ ■

ON APRIL 13, the S.E.C. formally revoked McDonnell & Co.'s broker-dealer license, suspended Murray McDonnell from the securities industry for one year, and permanently barred him from taking any managerial position with any other securities firm without permission of the S.E.C. The S.E.C. found a slew of violations by the firm and its employees, including violations of the antifraud provisions of the securities laws, record-keeping violations, margin rule violations, and failures to properly supervise employees. In addition to Murray McDonnell, fourteen other McDonnell & Co. executives were to be subject to disciplinary proceedings before the Commission.[83]

KARLA JAY SPENT most of her limited free time in early 1970 attending meetings of what were then considered to be radical feminist groups—the Redstockings, the Women's International Terrorist Conspiracy from Hell (WITCH), and Media Women.[84] WITCH engaged in zany street theatre events inspired by those Abbie Hoffman organized—like his dollar bill–throwing episode at the N.Y.S.E. in 1967. At its first event, on Halloween 1968, WITCH members dressed up as sorceresses and marched through the financial district, casting spells on the Exchange and prominent Wall Street banks.

While attending a meeting of Media Women at Susan Brownmiller's apartment, Karla agreed to be one of the ringleaders of the takeover of the *Ladies Home Journal* offices on March 18.[85] The office was occupied until editors agreed to reform sexist practices and dedicate more pages to covering the feminist movement. In the last week of March, Karla organized her own event to bring attention to the issue that had most motivated her activism—sexual harassment. Karla thought the best place to stage it was outside the Wall Street subway station where Francine Gottfried ran the gauntlet back in September 1968.[86]

To give the men of Wall Street a taste of their own medicine, Karla held the "First National Ogle-In." Karla and her cohorts whistled and catcalled at shocked bankers and brokers hurrying to work, commenting in graphic detail on their body parts and sexual acts they might enjoy. Trailing behind them were WABC-TV camera crew and Marlene Sanders, a prominent reporter (and mother of controversial legal commentator Jeffrey Toobin). The outrageous footage struck a chord with the media and the public.[87]

Days later, Karla was invited on the Barry Gray radio show, the top-rated talk show in New York at the time, to discuss the Ogle-In and what had motivated her to do it. After the appearance, Karla was deluged with letters from women who had suffered indignities similar to those of Francine Gottfried or worse.[88] It would take over a decade before the courts would fully recognize workplace sexual harassment as a civil rights violation.

CHAPTER ELEVEN

"I THINK IT WOULD BE DISASTROUS"

■

The Bailout Bill Moves Along— and Enter Ross Perot

With the end of give-ups, the cozy relationship between N.Y.S.E. members and the fund managers was over. The interests of the Exchange members and the mutual fund industry were now directly at odds over commission rates. These two behemoths of Wall Street were on a collision course. The mutual fund managers wanted either substantially reduced commission rates or membership on the N.Y.S.E, either by directly joining or by buying an investment bank—in either case so they would pay drastically reduced commissions. The result of either strategy would be a devastating loss of revenue for N.Y.S.E. members, who were already losing money at an alarming rate in the spring of 1970.

After the board of governors' "sneak attack" February rate proposal to the S.E.C. that substantially lowered commissions on block trades, the block trading houses were furious with Bunny Lasker and were not going to be blindsided again. The man those members selected to lead the charge against mutual fund membership was John L. Loeb Sr., the senior partner of Loeb, Rhoades & Co. and a prominent Establishment figure on Wall Street and in Washington.

On April 9, John Loeb released to the press a letter he had sent Bunny Lasker regarding mutual fund membership. "It is our judgment that institutional ownership and control of members of the exchange would strike a damaging blow to the operations of the exchange and the securities industry and would be detrimental to the national interest. It would drive out of business many independent broker-dealers, who are the main source of the business brought to the floor of the exchange and whose existence is essential to the free function of the securities markets and availability of broad, public financing to the nation's business."[1]

At the news conference he called to discuss the letter, Loeb added: "In my opinion you'd wipe out the little people in the business and you'd get a concentration of power. If you don't keep a network of small brokers, then you will reduce access for the individual investors who really make up the liquidity of this market. Much more is at stake in the question of institutional membership than the sharing of commission dollars or the privileges of membership. The stakes are the very continuation of the exchange as basically an agency market for the public, operated by professionals whose interests lie primarily in the transacting of securities trading for the general public."[2] Loeb closed by urging Lasker to stand firm on the "primary purpose" requirement for ownership of Exchange members.

Many of the Exchange members who backed Loeb also organized a frontal public attack on the February 13 rate proposal. While the bellyaching about the plan and the secretive process that led to it made headlines back in February, the block trading houses did not believe at the time they could kill the proposal. But in April, after the collapse of McDonnell & Co., they believed they could kill it. Loeb, along with Salim L. Lewis, the senior partner of Bear, Stearns & Co., led this charge as well, attacking the work for the N.Y.S.E. by N.E.R.A., its economic expert. "I think the trouble with the N.E.R.A. proposals was that the discount is at much too low a figure and that also it soaks the little guy," Loeb told the *New York Times* on April 12.[3] "I think it's a dead issue. All I know is that N.E.R.A. was wrong." Lewis added that "I personally don't think the N.E.R.A. report will become a reality."[4]

▪ ▪ ▪

SENATOR EDMUND MUSKIE knew immediately after McDonnell & Co.'s collapse that his dormant broker-dealer insurance bill from a year earlier would be perhaps the most important legislation of 1970. Originally directed at O.T.C. dealers without access to the N.Y.S.E.'s Special Trust Fund, with the failure of McDonnell & Co., Muskie feared that other N.Y.S.E. firms, possibly even ones larger than McDonnell & Co., were at risk of failing. Perhaps the Special Trust Fund would be insufficient to protect the investing public. To respond to the criticisms of his bill by the N.Y.S.E., Muskie introduced an amendment on April 9.[5] The principal changes in the amended bill were to modify the method for determining how much premium firms would pay. The first bill based the assessment on net capital; the revised bill allowed the insuring agency to take into account all relevant actuarial factors in determining the rate any particular firm would pay, including its liabilities and the risk of its business relative to its net capital.[6]

The Exchange knew the Special Trust Fund as currently funded would prove to be inadequate for what lay ahead but was still hoping to avoid additional regulation. It hoped to develop enhancements to the Special Trust Fund by way of a private insurance program in lieu of the federal government–sponsored insurer proposed by Muskie. Muskie countered that his plan would be less expensive for the industry, as borrowing backed by full faith and credit of the United States would come with much lower interest costs than funds coming from the shaky credits predominating in the securities industry at the time.[7] Muskie highlighted the fact that the Special Trust Fund was nearly depleted, with only $3 million of cash-on-hand and another $10 million available under lines of credit, hardly enough to absorb potential losses of more failures on the scale of McDonnell & Co.

On Monday April 13, the N.Y.S.E. Crisis Committee met to consider ways to increase the Special Trust Fund to deflect the growing concerns about its funding. The goal was to raise at least an additional $75 million. One idea to raise the needed funds was to levy a charge on all transactions, essentially taking a portion of the newly approved $15 transaction surcharge and applying it to the Special Trust Fund. "If there isn't $75 million available in one form or another, there isn't anything to oppose the Muskie bill with," one participant in the meeting told the *New York Times*.[8] It was also leaked to the *New York Times* that the source of the $30 million to be made available by the N.Y.S.E. to loan to the Special Trust Fund was the money in the building fund previously dedicated to the Exchange's planned new headquarters at the large-scale redevelopment on the East River in the financial district, thereby dooming that project.[9]

Robert Haack publicly took issue with Senator Muskie's characterization of the Special Trust Fund as nearly depleted. In a telegram to Muskie on April 14, Haack contended that the "exchange's trust fund is not near depletion. Presently the program of $25,000,000 established in 1964 has between $17,500,000 and $18,000,000 available. Of this amount, $10,000,000 is represented by lines of credit established in 1964 with four New York banks.[10] In addition, the exchange has announced that it has initiated steps to make available, if necessary, a loan of up to $30,000,000 from its general funds."[11] In his closing, Haack noted that the N.Y.S.E. would be formally proposing an alternative to the Muskie bill during the upcoming Senate hearings: "We will suggest at the hearings before the Securities Subcommittee on Friday an alternative to S. 2348 which continues self-regulation with government oversight and assistance as this is the approach which needs to be considered."[12]

The alternative was to be developed by an industry task force led by Ralph DeNunzio. On April 15, DeNunzio sent a letter to Hamer Budge signed as well by top officials of AMEX, the Association of Stock Exchange Firms, the Investment Bankers Association, the N.A.S.D., the Boston Stock Exchange, the Midwest Stock Exchange, the Pacific Coast Stock Exchange, and the Philadelphia-Baltimore-Washington Stock Exchange, describing the industry's commitment to developing a private insurance program for securities customers.[13]

ON THURSDAY APRIL 16, at 10:00 a.m. in room 5302 of the New Senate Office Building, the Senate Subcommittee on Securities began hearings on the Muskie bill with Hamer Budge as the first witness. In an unprecedented appearance, Budge brought with him all of the other S.E.C. commissioners—Hugh Owens, Richard B. Smith, James J. Needham, and Sydney Herlong—as well as the general counsel of the S.E.C., Philip Loomis, and the director of the Division of Trading and Markets, Irving Pollack. Budge had been shaken out of his neglect of the crisis, the Senate having succeeded where the S.E.C.'s New York Regional Office had repeatedly failed.[14] During his testimony, Budge acknowledged an "urgent need" for an insurance program to protect customers of insolvent brokerage firms, but refused to state a preference between a government-sponsored program or a private one run by the securities industry. "For the reasons set forth," Budge said, "the Commission believes that a program of insurance should be adopted at the earliest possible time. While we have some questions as to the proposed bill in its present form, we believe that with appropriate changes it could provide the answer. This should not, however, preclude efforts by the industry to come up with its own solution for the adoption of an adequate and workable insurance program, which may provide a less costly and more efficient approach. The point that must be emphasized is that it is urgent the remedial measures be adopted promptly."[15]

The chairman of the subcommittee, Senator Harrison Williams of New Jersey, asked Budge what the effect would be if two or three of the larger brokerage firms became insolvent. Budge answered bluntly: "I think it would be disastrous, Mr. Chairman."[16] Williams followed up: "You don't believe, then, that the present stock exchange trust fund is sufficient to protect investors in that unlikely but unhappy event?" Budge again answered directly: "I do not."[17]

When asked, Budge confessed that he did not know any specifics about the proposed industry-sponsored private insurance program, but expressed doubts that sufficient private-sector insurance could be obtained absent some form of federal government guarantee or subsidy. "I don't know anyone who could write this kind of insurance to cover all the brokers and dealers in the country," Budge testified. "I don't think the industry can purchase that type of insurance. They would either have to finance it themselves, which I assume is contemplated in their industry proposal, or they would have to be financed initially by the Federal Government."[18] Budge also disclosed that the Nixon administration had not reached any determination as to the relative merits of a private insurance program versus a governmental one.

What was not asked of Budge was why he, the chairman of the S.E.C., knowing that the Special Trust Fund was inadequate and knowing by way of the New York Regional Office that at least one very large firm—Hayden, Stone—was at risk of imminent collapse, neither took action nor sounded the alarm to Congress or the investing public to address the looming financial catastrophe on Wall Street.

The next witness called was Donald T. Regan, president of Merrill Lynch. Regan wasted no time in advertising that Merrill Lynch was the nation's healthiest investment bank, calling out its $275 million of capital and its net capital ratio of 7.35-to-1, more than twice the capital required by the S.E.C., and mentioning that it did not invest any of its capital in equity securities or other risky investments.[19] Regan declared that any insurance program, whether obtained from the private sector or government supported, would treat only the symptoms of the industry's problems and not their causes. So, instead, Regan offered a three-pronged regulatory overhaul. First, he proposed lowering the net capital ratio from 20-to-1 to 12-to-1. Second, he recommended that allowable regulatory capital should only be true equity capital; subordinated notes and customer accounts should not be included. Third, he proposed that regulatory capital should be prohibited from being used for speculation. With these reforms, Regan argued that the need for customer insurance would be essentially eliminated. Nonetheless, because of the current public alarm over the solvency of the securities firms, Regan testified that Merrill Lynch supported the creation of an insurance program, but preferred one financed without taxpayer assistance. Regan would not, however, rule out the need for government support. "I recognize, though, the force of the argument raised by some of you that some governmental part in all this would help public confidence. It is a point I would prefer to leave open until these hearings have progressed and we are all better informed."[20]

After Donald Regan, the subcommittee heard from John E. Leslie, chairman of the board of Bache & Co., the nation's second-largest brokerage firm.[21] Like Regan, Leslie offered up his own proposals for reform. First, Leslie stated that all broker-dealers doing business with the public should be required to provide annual and quarterly financial disclosures similar to those required by S.E.C. rules for exchange-listed companies. Second, he argued for higher commission rates to put the industry on a firmer financial footing. Third, Leslie asserted that regulatory capital standards needed to be enhanced so that "permanent" capital only was credited. Fourth, Leslie argued for more rigorous regulatory oversight of the operations of broker-dealers.[22] Unlike Regan, Leslie was willing to support the Muskie bill. Senator Williams, at the conclusion of Leslie's opening statement, asked: "Mr. Leslie, in your conclusion you certainly subscribed to the aims of this legislation, is that correct?" "Very definitely," Leslie responded.[23]

The last witness called that day was Wallace C. Latour, managing partner of Francis I. duPont & Co. Unlike Merrill Lynch and Bache & Co., Francis I. duPont & Co. was, to say the least, not in sound financial condition. Wallace Latour was not about to give any hint of his firm's dire condition, however. His testimony was a classic of unintentional hilarity. "Let me say here and now in the clearest, most positive language at my command that Francis I. du Pont & Co. stands strong, vigorous, and viable, as a leader in the industry should."[24] Latour would not endorse the Muskie bill and wouldn't even concede the need for a private industrywide insurance program. He believed it to be too early to commit to any particular course of action until the N.Y.S.E. Crisis Committee and the industrywide task force chaired by Ralph DeNunzio made their recommendations. "If an investor's insurance plan should prove to be the only, or even the most effective way, we would support such a 'confidence fund' enthusiastically," Latour proclaimed.[25] "But while constructive alternatives are still being asked for and considered, I might say that my firm warmly endorses the creation of an industrywide task force to work out suggestions for a self-regulatory program that would fortify the financial protection available to the investing public."[26] He closed his statement with a plea for higher commission rates: "In the final analysis, however, in our judgment nothing that my firm could do alone or in concert with the industry, and no legislation before this distinguished committee currently, could contribute more quickly or more definitely to the health of the securities industry and, therefore, directly to the welfare of the investing public than the prompt adoption of a modern, realistic commission rate structure."[27]

Latour's idea of a "modern, realistic commission rate structure" did not involve competitive rates, only higher rates, maintained by a price fixing cartel, sanctioned by federal law.

The following morning, the subcommittee reconvened at 10:15 a.m. with N.Y.S.E. president Robert Haack as the first witness, joined by Exchange officers John Cunningham, Charles Klem, Donald L. Calvin, and Mahlon Frankhauser.[28] Haack opened his remarks by endorsing the objectives of the Muskie bill, but conceded having "some problems" with it. Haack asserted that "a blending of government resources with industry self-regulation is the most effective and practical way to provide the greatest measure of protection to the investing public." What Haack proposed was to continue the current oversight regime of self-regulatory bodies—the N.Y.S.E. and the other registered national securities exchanges, together with the N.A.S.D.—overseen by the S.E.C., but with customer accounts protected through the creation of an industry-funded insurance program backstopped, in the case of a systemic crisis involving the failures of multiple large firms, with lines of credit from the U.S. Treasury. "If the Congress were to establish legislation which would create authority for standby lines of credit which could be drawn upon by the self-regulatory organizations, the major problem that I presently see in the area could be overcome," Haack stated.[29] "I suggest, therefore, that the subcommittee consider legislation which would authorize the establishment of lines of credit to registered self-regulatory agencies for use in the event of a potential broker or dealer insolvency."[30]

As Haack envisioned the program working, to be eligible for a loan, the registered organization would have to make a filing with the S.E.C. The statute would establish a borrowing base tied to the earnings and assessment authority of the organization. The exchanges that have a trust fund would use those funds before drawing on the line of credit. If an organization did not have a trust fund, it could, when necessary, use the line of credit. Unlike the Muskie bill, Haack's plan would not have dollar limits on the customer account balances insured and coverage would extend not only to customers but all other counterparties of the failed firm.

Haack informed the senators that this proposed scheme would be considered by the recently created industrywide task force, but that it had not been formally endorsed by any exchange or other self-regulatory organization. Haack also disclosed that the N.Y.S.E.'s Special Trust Fund had between $7.5 million and $8 million in cash available, together with undrawn lines of credit of $10 million. He also disclosed that the Special Trust Fund had a contingent liability of $6 million not reserved for in those available liquidity amounts that related to a guarantee of a loan made to a member firm in liquidation (McDonnell & Co.).[31]

Haack then proceeded to criticize various provisions of the Muskie bill. First, he noted the complexity that would result with a new regulatory body in addition to the S.E.C., the national securities exchanges, and the N.A.S.D. He further noted that the annual assessment contemplated to fund the new insurance entity was $25 million—more than the entire budget of the S.E.C. for 1970.[32]

In response to Haack's proposal, Senator Muskie stated: "What you are proposing is a situation in which the Federal Government will have little authority to avoid the catastrophe but would have the privilege of coming in when the catastrophe struck."[33]

This was precisely what Haack had in mind.

Following the N.Y.S.E. representatives, Ralph S. Saul, president of AMEX, was called, accompanied by Frank C. Graham Jr., chairman of AMEX, Paul Kolton, executive vice president, and James W. Walker Jr., senior vice president in charge of legal and governmental affairs.[34] Saul essentially endorsed the Haack proposal, calling it "an imaginative and creative approach for blending government resources with the resources of self-regulation."[35] Saul also informed the subcommittee that he believed the industry could have a final, actionable plan to implement the "lines of credit" proposal outlined by Haack by July 1, 1970.

The last witness called that day was Robert M. Gardiner, chairman of the legislation committee of the Association of Stock Exchange Firms, accompanied by Dr. Leon T. Kendall, president of the association, and Richard O. Scribner, its general counsel. Gardiner stated that while he believed some form of enhanced investor protection was needed by the industry, he was unable to endorse any particular approach at that time and would wait until the industrywide task force made its recommendations. "The problems to which the group must address itself are not capable of simple solution," Gardiner said. "Many alternatives must be analyzed, and we are not prepared to hazard a guess today as to which one or what combination should be adopted."[36]

The subcommittee adjourned the hearings with the agreement that additional hearings would be necessary, at a time to be agreed. (It would reconvene on June 18.)

■ ■ ■

AFTER HIS SENATE testimony, Hamer Budge, now aligned with the S.E.C.'s New York Regional Office, turned up the heat on the N.Y.S.E. On April 27, the *New York Times* reported that the S.E.C. had raised serious objections to how the Exchange was interpreting its net capital rule.[37] In particular, the *Times* noted the S.E.C.'s dissatisfaction over the Exchange's manipulation of the rule to avoid putting firms out of business, even though the practice put the public at risk.[38] On April 28, the S.E.C.'s Director of Trading and Markets sent a letter to the N.Y.S.E. questioning whether N.YS.E-member firms should remain subject to the net capital rule as interpreted by the N.Y.S.E. or instead revert to direct oversight by the S.E.C. with respect to net capital rule compliance.[39] This was the final ball dropping. Since late 1969, the S.E.C.'s New York Regional Office had been warning the Commission about how lax the N.Y.S.E. was in applying the net capital rule, relaying numerous instances where the N.Y.S.E. was more of an enabler of the circumvention of the rule than it was an enforcer of it. This letter sent shock waves through the leadership of the Exchange. For John Coleman and the rest of the Club, loss by the N.Y.S.E. of the power to enforce the net capital rule would be a forfeiture of perhaps its most consequential prerogative. The careful planning and execution by Coleman and his allies over decades to accumulate and maintain power in the hands of the Exchange insiders, the old guard, was unraveling.

AT THIS MOMENT of high anxiety on Wall Street, outside events would intervene again, bringing with them violence and mayhem. President Nixon gave a nationally-televised address on the evening of April 30 and informed the nation that the North Vietnamese communist forces had escalated hostilities in sanctuaries in the neutral country of Cambodia following American troop withdrawals. Accordingly, Nixon announced that the U.S. military would be conducting missions in Cambodia to neutralize the North Vietnamese operating in those sanctuaries.

The student anti-war movement reacted to President Nixon's speech with fury, calling the actions an "invasion" of Cambodia and an "expansion of the war." At Kent State University in Ohio, drunken students smashed windows of businesses in downtown Kent and attacked local police officers trying to restore order. The following night, student radicals set fire to the university's R.O.T.C. building and slashed the hoses of the firemen attempting to extinguish the blaze. The Ohio National Guard was called in to quell the violence. On the Monday after Nixon's speech, 2,000 angry students gathered to confront the National Guardsmen. The Guard ordered the students to disperse and fired tear gas. When the students refused to disperse, the National Guardsmen advanced. Unfamiliar with the campus, a group of Guardsmen found themselves hemmed in by the chain-link fence of an athletic practice field in front of them and an angry mob of protestors gathering behind them. What happened next remains hotly disputed. The adjutant general of the Ohio National Guard later told reporters that a sniper had fired on the Guardsmen. This allegation remains unproved. Many Guardsmen later testified that they felt in fear for their lives as the angry mob of radicals surrounded them. A volley of shots was fired by the Guardsmen, leaving four students dead and nine others wounded.

On May 8, hundreds of students from New York University and other local colleges gathered at Broad and Wall Streets outside the N.Y.S.E. to protest the Kent State shootings and demand an immediate withdrawal of all remaining American military forces in Vietnam.[40] The congestion and disorder caused by the demonstration that Friday morning wreaked havoc on the commute and the already frayed nerves of bear market Wall Street. There were hundreds of additional commuters into the financial district that spring, as construction work was at maximum manpower on the rapidly rising twin towers of the new World Trade Center, four blocks northwest of the N.Y.S.E.

At noon, thousands of financial district employees and construction workers from the World Trade Center site emptied into the streets around the Exchange. All morning, the agitated student radicals had been haranguing the bankers and brokers as capitalist enablers of the oppression and slaughter in Vietnam. Used to this sort of thing, as the Exchange had seen a near-continual kick line of crazies in recent years going back to Abbie Hoffman in 1967, the suits mostly ignored the protestors. The hungry construction workers, however, were mostly not in a live-and-let-live mood. An outmatched line of New York City police did their best to protect the protestors, then gathered on the steps of Federal Hall across from the Exchange, from two hundred or so charging construction workers in overalls and yellow and red hard hats carrying American flags, screaming "Kill the Commie Bastards!" In about two minutes, despite being outnumbered five to one, the hard hats beat the living daylights out of the student radicals, targeting those with the longest hair for the most severe beatings, the *New York Times* reported.[41]

As bloodied students ran for their lives, out of the financial district toward City Hall, cheering construction workers followed in hot pursuit. As they approached City Hall, the construction workers noticed that the American flag above the building was flying at half mast, at the direction of Mayor John Lindsay, to mourn the dead Kent State students. This did not sit well with the hard hats, mostly outer-borough ethnics, many of whom had fought in Vietnam and nearly all of whom had family or friends who had (or still were).

They paused from tormenting the longhairs and directed their efforts to demanding the stars and stripes above City Hall be raised to full staff. A group broke through a police guard and, led by a sympathetic mailman, charged up to the roof of City Hall and raised the flag themselves. Their cohorts cheered wildly. Shortly thereafter, an aide to Mayor Lindsay, Sid Davidoff, climbed out on the roof and lowered the flag again, causing a near-riot outside. A large contingent of police had arrived by this time, most of them from the same neighborhoods as the construction workers and sharing their low opinion of the liberal Lindsay administration.[42]

The officer in charge sought out Deputy Mayor Richard A. Aurelio (Lindsay was still at Gracie Mansion, having never made it downtown that day) and told him that if he didn't raise the flag back to full staff again, he was going to have a full-fledged riot on his hands. Across the street, at Pace College, a throng of construction workers, seeing a peace sign banner hanging from the roof, stormed into that building, tore down the banner, and were burning it in the street. Seeing the rapidly deteriorating situation for himself, Deputy Mayor Aurelio quickly gave the okay. Two plainclothes policemen, Pat Mascia and Bob Ruction, joined by City Hall janitor John Zissel, walked on the mansard roof and again raised the flag. As soon as it reached its full height, the assembled construction workers took their hard hats off, placed them over their hearts, and spontaneously broke into a rousing rendition of the "Star-Spangled Banner." Aurelio couldn't help but notice the grinning policemen, helmets at their hearts, enthusiastically singing along. Only six of the construction workers were arrested by police; seventy student protestors were hospitalized with injuries.[43]

Almost immediately after the press reported on the "hard hat riot," as they named it, calls came flooding in to the office of Peter J. Brennan, president of the 200,000-member Building and Construction Trades Council of Greater New York, the union that represented many of the workers building the World Trade Center. The calls ran 20-to-1 in favor of the construction workers involved in the melee. "The unions had nothing to do with it," Brennan told reporters. "The men acted on their own. They did it because they were fed up with violence by the anti-war demonstrators who spat at the American flag and desecrated it."[44] Brennan denied reports that workers had attacked the student protestors with wrenches and pipes, as had been reported. "If they tangled with those who were spitting on the flag, they did so with their fists," Brennan said.[45]

Seeing how strong the public opinion was for counter-demonstrations supporting President Nixon's efforts to bring peace with honor in Vietnam, the construction union leaders saw an opportunity to increase their own popularity with the public, always an asset in any future labor dispute. The union members would stage daily demonstrations in Lower Manhattan in support of President Nixon. On Monday, May 11, the first union-backed rally was held, although the union leadership denied any involvement in organizing it. "It was their own action," said Thomas W. Gleason, president of the International Longshoremen's Association, when asked about his men's participation in the demonstration. "We knew nothing about it."[46] Thus began two straight weeks of lunch-hour demonstrations by the workers in support of Nixon and at least as enthusiastic denunciations of Mayor Lindsay. The most numerous banners each day read "Lindsay is a Commie."

The climax came on Wednesday, May 20, when over 150,000 construction workers and longshoremen marched from City Hall to Battery Park, a sea of American flags, singing "God Bless America," "You're a Grand Old Flag," "Yankee Doodle Dandy," "Over There," and other patriotic anthems. The march was organized by Peter Brennan's Building and Construction Trades Council of Greater New York.[47] The unofficial leader of that march was Joe Kelly, a thirty-one-year-old father of two daughters and a newborn son, and a member of Local 1 of International Union of Elevator Constructors working at the World Trade Center site, who carried a large, gold-fringed American flag with a gold eagle with outstretched wings on top of a large pole at the head of the parade. "The Pope to the Catholic Church is the same as the President is to the American people," Kelly told the *New York Times*. "He's the one who decides. He's infallible when he speaks of religion as far as the Catholic Church goes. I'm not saying Nixon is infallible. But he's Commander-in-Chief of the armed forces. He's in charge." The march was peaceful, except for the throwing of beer cans at anti-war students flashing peace signs at the passing marchers. One of those students, Cliff Sloane of Brooklyn, a freshman at the University of Michigan, told a *New York Times* reporter, "I'm scared. If this is what class struggle is all about, there's something wrong somewhere."[48]

President Nixon was ecstatic over the huge union-led rally in support of his administration's Vietnam policies. The following day, Nixon called Peter Brennan and invited him and twenty-two other union officials involved with the march to the White House the following Tuesday. In the Oval Office, Peter Brennan presented President Nixon with his own hard hat labeled "Commander in Chief" and left one for General Creighton W. Abrams, commander of United States military forces in Vietnam, which had four stars painted on it. Brennan told the president: "The hard hat will stand as a symbol, along with our great flag, for freedom and patriotism to our beloved country. We pray that our fighting men will be able to exchange their steel helmets very soon for hard hats and join with all of us in building a greater America, morally and physically, for all Americans."[49]

AMIDST THE MAYHEM in Lower Manhattan, the board of governors of the N.Y.S.E. approved amendments to the Exchange's constitution to authorize the increase of the Exchange's Special Trust Fund to $55 million on May 18, the increase to be funded by the $30 million previously earmarked to finance the new headquarters for the Exchange on the East River. "It is apparent that expansion of the Special Trust Fund program was needed to reflect in full the growth of the industry and the increasing size and scope of member organizations in the six years since the program was established," Robert Haack said in a membership bulletin.[50]

Throughout May, the bear market slide continued. On May 4, after the Dow Jones closed at 709.74, its lowest level since August 1963, the Federal Reserve Board reversed course, lowering the margin requirement on stock purchases from 80 percent to 65 percent.[51] The Fed's action did not stop the slide. On May 25, the Dow dropped 20.81 points, its steepest fall since the day President Kennedy was assassinated, to 641.36. It dropped again the following day to 631.16, the lowest close since November 19, 1962. In response to the stock market collapse, President Nixon, at the urging of Bunny Lasker, invited forty-five major business leaders from across the country to a White House dinner on Wednesday, May 27. At the dinner, Fed chairman Arthur Burns spoke, promising a healthy increase in the money supply to keep the economy growing and, hopefully, to elevate stock prices. Nixon also spoke. While the dinner was friendly, the Wall Street attendees, who included Bunny Lasker, Robert Haack, Dan Lufkin, Donald Regan, Billy Salomon, John Loeb, and Ralph Saul, left with most of the same anxieties they arrived with.[52]

The cutbacks and layoffs at the financially-troubled firms continued in May. At Hayden, Stone, Inc., across-the-board pay cuts between 10 and 15 percent were implemented for all employees. In addition, there was a senior management shake-up, with Donald R. Stroben assuming the roles of chairman and chief executive officer and Alfred Coyle demoted to chairman of the executive committee.[53] Francis I. duPont announced it was laying off 5 percent of its workforce.[54] Goodbody & Co. announced that it had let go four hundred employees.[55] Charles Plohn & Co. announced the closing of six of its seven branch offices and the firing of most of its sales force.[56]

ALL SPRING, THE decline in stock prices and depressed trading volume eroded the already-shaky capital positions of many investment banks. The N.Y.S.E., facing the real possibility that the S.E.C. would rescind its authority to enforce the net capital rule, began moving proactively and aggressively to encourage mergers and equity infusions to avoid another failure. Two habitually troubled firms, Glore Forgan Straats Inc. and Francis I. duPont & Co., were at the very top of the Exchange's matchmaking list. Lee Arning, the Exchange official tasked by Robert Haack and John Cunningham with arranging these shotgun marriages, told Archie Albright, the chief executive officer of Glore Forgan, that his firm must merge with Francis I. duPont & Co. or he would institute proceedings to suspend its operations. A similar ultimatum was delivered to Wallace Latour, the chief executive officer of F.I. duPont & Co.[57]

On Saturday May 30, Archie Albright and Russ Forgan, Glore Forgan's chairman, drove to Wallace Latour's home in Bronxville, New York, to meet with him and Edmund duPont, Francis I. duPont & Co.'s chairman, to discuss a merger of the two firms.[58] On the face of it, the transaction made solid business sense. Glore Forgan was a "major" underwriting firm, which meant that it would be invited to participate in many more and higher quality securities offerings than Francis I. duPont & Co. Francis I. duPont & Co. had a vast broker network through which such securities could be distributed. Francis I. duPont & Co. also had the duPont name, which carried social cache as well as the implied financial backing of one of America's wealthiest families. Glore Forgan had become, with the election of President Nixon, the most politically well-connected investment bank in the country. Its former chief executive officer, Maurice Stans, was a major fundraiser for Richard Nixon's 1968 presidential campaign and had become Nixon's Secretary of Commerce. Glore Forgan's outside counsel was William Casey, another senior Nixon advisor who in 1971 would be named chairman of the S.E.C. (Ten years later, President Reagan would appoint Casey as director of the Central Intelligence Agency.) At the conclusion of the meeting, the senior executives agreed in principle to a merger, the combined entity to be named F. I. duPont, Glore Forgan & Co.[59]

The next day, the due diligence team at Glore Forgan, led by Norm Swanton, began to uncover unforeseen issues regarding Francis I. duPont & Co.'s operations, especially the sorry state of its back office. Late that evening, the senior executives of both firms reconvened at Glore Forgan's New York City offices to discuss Norm Swanton's diligence issues. Edmund duPont listened impatiently as Swanton walked through his list of particulars. When Swanton finished, Edmund duPont asked if a commitment of $20 million more in equity capital by the duPont family would alleviate Swanton's concerns? Archie Albright and Russ Forgan said that would be fine, indeed, and ended the meeting ecstatic. Norm Swanton, however, was livid. He told Albright and Forgan that it would take at least $50 million of new capital to ensure the solvency of Francis I. duPont & Co. Glore Forgan itself faced a looming capital deficiency as many of its senior partners, including Maurice Stans, were pulling out their capital as a result of retirement or fears of the firm's long-term prospects. In addition, the inevitable inefficiencies at the outset of a large merger would take time and capital to resolve. Albright and Forgan, convinced that the combination of the merger synergies and the duPont family's deep pockets would be enough to offset the current capital problems of both firms, told Swanton in no uncertain terms to stand down. Reduced to tears, Norm Swanton resigned on the spot.[60]

On June 2, 1970, rumors of the impending merger were confirmed to the *Wall Street Journal* by Wallace Latour.[61] The reaction from the Street was uniformly positive. The combination of Glore Forgan's underwriting prowess with Francis I. duPont & Co.'s retail brokerage army was thought to be capable of rivaling Merrill Lynch for industry dominance.[62] Upon reading of the impending merger, Hirsch & Co., a medium-sized firm facing the difficult and expensive prospect of updating its outmoded back office, reached out to Lee Arning to see if the new F. I. duPont, Glore Forgan & Co. would have any interest in restarting negotiations with respect to its acquisition. Francis I. duPont & Co. and Hirsch had engaged in preliminary discussions regarding an acquisition months before, but Francis I. duPont & Co. had terminated the discussions. Arning, armed with the inside information that Hirsch & Co., despite its operational challenges, had the strongest capital position of all three firms with a net capital ratio of 10-to-1, twice the minimum, strongly pushed the idea.[63] It then became a three-way merger. The combined firm would have 141 branches with over 2,100 brokers.[64]

Mumbling and disheveled, Bill Casey may have been God's oddest-looking creation since the aardvark, but he was a brilliant, crafty, and politically savvy lawyer. Casey waited until the last minute to send the draft merger agreement over to the N.Y.S.E. for its approval, allowing momentum for the deal to build. Bob Bishop, the day-to-day numbers man monitoring net capital rule compliance at the Exchange, scoured the agreement, looking for a section providing for a new capital infusion. There was none. Bishop had reviewed the pro forma financial statements for the surviving combined company and knew there was a several million-dollar capital hole in the balance sheet. Bishop then called up Wallace Latour and informed him that the Exchange would not approve the merger without a capital infusion. Bishop did not believe this to be an existential crisis for the merger, as he, like most everyone else, believed that Edmund duPont could simply call a few of his cousins and the necessary funds would promptly appear. This was an illusion Edmund duPont made no effort to dispel. The truth, however, was that the duPont family was not willing to put another dime in the family investment bank. Edmund himself was loaded to the gills with personal debt to finance his previous capital contributions to the firm to foster the illusion of unlimited family resources.[65]

Enter Ross Perot.

It had been a challenging year so far for the tech mogul. On April 22, E.D.S. lost a third of its market value when its stock dropped from $150 per share to $100.[66] Perot, who owned 81 percent of the company, suffered a paper loss that day of $445 million. While the price decline was not due to any fundamental change in the business prospects of E.D.S.—investors simply concluded that equities generally and growth technology stocks in particular were overvalued—Perot knew that only a new and large growth opportunity—like operating the computers that ran Wall Street's back offices—would bring back the stock's lost luster.

Francis I. duPont & Co. had recently hired Rudolph A. Smutney, a banker formerly of R. W. Pressprich, Ken Langone's firm. R. W. Pressprich had improbably taken E.D.S. public in an amazing coup that put Langone on the Wall Street map. Smutney wanted nothing more than to take away business from his old firm, preferably from its best client, Ross Perot, and Smutney had an ingenious pitch to do just that.[67]

Like many Wall Street firms that were partnerships in those days, Francis I. duPont & Co. had implemented a perfectly legal tax dodge to arbitrage the higher income tax rates paid by individuals as compared to corporations. All of the back-office computers and related assets used by Francis I. duPont & Co. were owned by a separately-taxed corporation owned by the firm. The corporation, named Wall Street Leasing, would then lease the computer systems back to Francis I. duPont & Co., allowing its partners to take a tax deduction at a higher rate when the firm was profitable. The computer assets didn't count toward the firm's net capital in any event, so their loss from the balance sheet wouldn't affect regulatory compliance. Smutney's idea was to sell the stock of Wall Street Leasing to Ross Perot for cash and E.D.S. stock, which obviously would count toward net capital, solving the Exchange's issue. At the same time, Ross Perot would get the foothold he wanted on Wall Street—in the hottest newly-organized giant firm, no less. Bill Casey loved the idea. Wallace Latour and Edmund duPont thought it was genius. Lee Arning and Bob Bishop thought the same. Ross Perot was equally thrilled. On July 6, 1970, the merger was completed. Ross Perot was finally on Wall Street.[68]

Soon after the merger, E.D.S. signed an eight-year contract with F.I. duPont, Glore Forgan Inc. to run its back office for a minimum of $8 million per year (more, if volume increased). E.D.S., which had no experience running a Wall Street back office, won the contract, beating out A.D.P. despite the fact that A.D.P. submitted a lower bid and had vast experience on Wall Street. Unlike E.D.S., however, A.D.P. was unwilling to make a capital investment in F. I. duPont, Glore Forgan.[69]

THE HOUSE SUBCOMMITTEE on Commerce and Finance met on the morning of June 4 to discuss the House version of Muskie's broker-dealer insurance bill.[70] Representative Moss opened the hearing by noting that he had sent a letter on June 1, 1970, to Ralph DeNunzio, in his capacity as chairman of the industrywide task force, hoping to receive the proposal from the task force prior to commencing the subcommittee's hearings, but he had received no response.[71] Moss concluded that despite the absence of an industry proposal, the urgency of the matter required that the hearings nonetheless proceed. As the first witness, Moss called Hamer Budge, who was joined by the S.E.C.'s General Counsel, Philip A. Loomis Jr., and its Director of the Division of Trading and Markets, Irving M. Pollack.[72] Budge opened his testimony by stating the urgent need for some method of protecting public investors whose cash and securities were held by broker-dealers. He noted that approximately $3 billion was held by those firms on behalf of their customers and many billions more of securities. He noted as well the substantial risk to these customers posed by the failure of a large investment bank. He further stated that the N.Y.S.E.'s Special Trust Fund and similar funds of other exchanges could be exhausted by the failure of even a single additional large investment bank.[73]

Budge proposed an insurance program whereby an independent non-profit corporation could be formed with a board of directors comprised of representatives of industry self-regulatory organizations and the general public and overseen by the S.E.C. Beyond that, Budge was unwilling to give details of what the S.E.C.'s preferred scheme would be. "As you know, the Congress in the 1930s decided that this industry should be a self-regulated one with oversight power in the Commission," Budge stated. "Because of that we would like to examine the industry proposal if it is submitted promptly. But if it is not, we will shortly be prepared to give you our comments in detail—in fact, in the form of legislation, should you so desire."[74]

Following his testimony, Budge received a telephone call from Ralph DeNunzio, who told him that the industrywide task force had agreed to set up an insurance company, initially funded by the industry with at least $50 million in cash but contemplated to have access to more funds by way of credit lines from the U.S. Treasury Department. It would be substantially similar to what Budge proposed in his testimony. "The industry is in agreement on all of the substantive points," DeNunzio told the *New York Times*. "Out of a lot of opposing points of view has come agreement on every one of the major elements. This is complete cooperation."[75]

The subcommittee reconvened the following morning, with Representative Moss informing everyone that the staff of the S.E.C. and the staff of the subcommittee had met after the prior day's hearing, the outcome of which enabled Moss to "report that I, personally, and the staff are convinced that both the S.E.C. and the industrywide task force have made progress toward coming up with a workable scheme of broker-dealer insurance. Although the task force has not yet been able to set a firm date for the completion of their work," Moss noted, "it would now appear that they are likely to have a final proposal, in legislative form, within the next two weeks."[76] On that basis, Moss adjourned the hearings until June 15, a time he hoped sufficient to allow the industrywide task force to submit its final proposal to the subcommittee. He instructed the staff of the subcommittee to meet with the industrywide task force to help expedite its proceedings.

CHAPTER TWELVE

"THERE'S MORE LARCENY PER SQUARE FOOT AT THE NEW YORK STOCK EXCHANGE THAN ANY PLACE IN THE WORLD"

The Club Props Up Insolvent Firms— Until They're the Taxpayers' Problem

The inner circle of the N.Y.S.E. leadership—those members of the Club with the best knowledge of the deteriorating financial condition of many of its largest members—was growing more fearful by the day over the congressional hearings and how Ralph De-Nunzio, one of their own, was far out on a very shaky limb. If the true financial condition of many Exchange members was known, the hearings would certainly turn punitive, possibly Pecora-like. Felix Rohatyn was elevated to the position of unofficial chairman of the Crisis Committee in no small measure because of his skillful December 1969 testimony before Representative Emanuel Celler's House Judiciary Committee on the antitrust implications of the wave of conglomerate mergers. Felix's brains and charm made him a favorite of Harold Geneen, chief executive officer of ITT Corporation, and he advised on most of ITT's conglomerate mergers of the 1960s Go-Go years. If a time came when DeNunzio had to be replaced as the de facto congressional liaison of the Exchange,

Rohatyn would be the substitute, it was decided. As a merger and acquisition investment banker and not a specialist or trader, Rohatyn was not really in the inner circle of the Club and could be thrown under the bus, if necessary, without hurt feelings among those who really mattered. For the rest of 1970, the Crisis Committee would meet for lunch every Monday on the sixth floor of the N.Y.S.E. and every Thursday at 8:45 a.m. Emergency meetings often were called on weekends and held at Bunny Lasker's fifth-floor suite at the Carlyle Hotel. The group was in touch by telephone daily and, in times of great peril, met in person daily.

THE HOUSE SUBCOMMITTEE reconvened on June 15, with Ralph DeNunzio appearing as the day's first witness.[1] DeNunzio was accompanied by two lawyers from Sullivan & Cromwell, John R. Raben and John Maynard, who served as counsel to the industrywide task force. DeNunzio submitted to the subcommittee a draft bill that would give effect to the industrywide task force's insurance proposal. The insuring entity DeNunzio's bill contemplated would be a federally chartered non-profit corporation—also named Securities Investor Protection Corporation—with a board of twelve directors, one appointed by the president of the United States, one appointed by the Secretary of the Treasury, five members appointed by the N.Y.S.E., three members appointed by the next three largest stock exchanges (one each), and two appointed by the N.A.S.D. All by-laws and rules of S.I.P.C. would be subject to S.E.C. approval. S.I.P.C. would insure customer brokerage accounts up to $50,000. Claims of other counterparties would not be covered. Every broker-dealer registered under the Securities Exchange Act of 1934 would be required to become a member of S.I.P.C., unless exempted by the S.E.C.[2]

Under the industrywide task force's proposal, S.I.P.C. would initially be funded in the amount of $75 million from assessments of its broker-dealer members and privately obtained credit lines within 120 days of enactment, and thereafter by way of further assessments and private lines of credit until $150 million was available. Initially, $3 million of cash on hand would be transferred by the trust funds of the various national stock exchanges ($2.6 million of which would come from AMEX) to S.I.P.C., together with $7 million from the initial assessments of S.I.P.C. members. This would provide the equity to enable S.I.P.C. to obtain $65 million in credit lines from private-sector banks. These bank lines would ultimately be reduced to zero after additional S.I.P.C. member assessments, after taking into account operating expenses, reached $65 million. S.I.P.C. would be entitled by law to borrow up to $1 billion from the U.S. Treasury so long as the S.E.C. certified to the U.S. Treasury that the projected assessments by S.I.P.C. of its members afforded a reasonable probability that the loan would be repaid and that the loan was essential for the protection of investors and maintenance of confidence in the U.S. securities markets.[3]

S.I.P.C. would establish its own rules as to the basis upon which members would be assessed, expected to initially be 0.125 percent of gross revenues. But in no event could a firm's assessment exceed 0.25 percent of its gross revenues from its securities business (or 0.50 percent, if S.I.P.C. had loans outstanding owing to the U.S. Treasury). The draft bill also provided that to the extent a broker-dealer's compliance with the net capital rule was overseen by a securities exchange, that exchange would continue to be the regulatory body determining such compliance. This would set into law the power John Coleman had obtained for the N.Y.S.E. in 1942 using his political influence with FDR's S.E.C., power the Exchange was at that very moment at risk of losing.[4]

Two staff lawyers for the subcommittee, Theodore Focht and Michael Taylor, questioned DeNunzio and the Sullivan & Cromwell lawyers regarding the proposed bill. They highlighted for the subcommittee that the rates paid by S.I.P.C. members would be established by resolutions of its board, not by by-law or regulation, with the result that the S.E.C. would not have the power to approve such rates. The only power the S.E.C. would be granted in this regard was the right to hear appeals by member firms who thought their

rates too high, in which case, if it so decided, the S.E.C. could reduce a firm's rate. Noting that the bill would give statutory effect to
the N.Y.S.E.'s oversight of net capital rule compliance, Focht and
Taylor confirmed with DeNunzio that the bill was intended to invest in the S.I.P.C. board, which would be controlled by the stock
exchanges, the power to set the examination standards for net capital rule compliance, effectively creating a second buffer between
the Club and the S.E.C.[5]

The next morning, Hamer Budge appeared before the subcommittee, again accompanied by Philip Loomis and Irving Pollack, to
submit a proposed bill setting forth the S.E.C.'s insurance plan.[6]
Budge indicated that he had not received the industrywide task
force bill until very recently, and the S.E.C. had prepared its own
bill in the event the DeNunzio bill proved unworkable by the subcommittee. For the sake of brevity, Budge limited his remarks to
highlighting the material differences between the S.E.C.-proposed
bill and DeNunzio's proposed bill. Budge's first criticism of the
DeNunzio bill was its lack of any further oversight power granted
to the S.E.C. to limit broker-dealer use of customer securities and
cash account balances. Next, Budge stated that the S.E.C. ought to
have full approval rights over the assessments of S.I.P.C. members,
not simply the power to reduce assessments. Budge further noted
that the maximum allowed assessment of 0.50 percent of revenues
would not be sufficient to pay interest on a $1 billion U.S. Treasury
loan with a market rate of interest (i.e., 6 percent), not to mention
amortize principal. Budge proposed no statutory cap on assessments. Budge also proposed that the board of S.I.P.C. be comprised
of five public representatives and ten industry representatives,
rather than two public representatives and ten industry representatives. Budge concluded that if his differences with the DeNunzio
bill could not be resolved, the insurance corporation could simply
be an organ of the S.E.C.[7]

During the resumed questioning the following morning, Budge
indicated that of the proposed governance structures—the Muskie
bill's creation of a new corporation with the S.E.C. commissioners

as its directors and DeNunzio's bill's creation of a new corporation with a board controlled by the stock exchanges, but with public representation—Budge actually preferred the approach of the De-Nunzio bill, so long as the S.E.C. had sufficient oversight over S.I.P.C. and enhanced regulatory authority over customer securities and cash account balances. Budge further indicated that he did not want the new insurance entity—whether a new corporation or the S.E.C. itself—to assume separate, duplicative regulatory authority over broker-dealers, preferring instead to continue the existing self-regulatory model and leverage the staff and resources of the N.Y.S.E., the other exchanges, and the N.A.S.D. He noted that the N.Y.S.E. alone had 3,000 employees, while the S.E.C. had only 1,400.[8]

At the conclusion of questioning, Chairman Moss, noting that the S.E.C. and the industrywide task force had not had any meaningful opportunity to compare each other's proposed bills and attempt to reconcile the same, adjourned the subcommittee at 11:55 a.m., but before doing so admonished the S.E.C. and the industry-wide task force to work expeditiously to come up with a compromise bill. Representative Moss insisted on passing a bill into law in that legislative session.[9]

Later that day, President Nixon made his first public comment on the broker-dealer insurance legislation. While not getting into the competing proposed bills, President Nixon indicated that he would sign legislation that "would guarantee the investor against losses that could be caused by financial difficulties of brokerage houses."[10]

The next day, the action moved to the Senate side of the Capitol with Ralph DeNunzio appearing before the Subcommittee on Securities.[11] Appearing together with John Raben and John Maynard of Sullivan & Cromwell, DeNunzio described the terms of the industrywide task force's bill, as he had three days earlier to the House subcommittee. DeNunzio told the Senate subcommittee that he had met with the S.E.C. the day before to discuss in detail the areas of difference between his bill and the S.E.C. bill and that he had scheduled a meeting of the industrywide task force for the following Monday to seek a compromise acceptable to the S.E.C.

Denunzio told the subcommittee that the four principal areas of disagreement were: who would determine assessments and whether they would be capped; how much the initial funding for S.I.P.C. would be; what additional regulatory authority would be given to the S.E.C.; and the corporate governance of S.I.P.C. The enhancement of S.E.C. regulatory authority related to limiting the use by broker-dealers of cash and securities in customer accounts. The S.E.C. wanted broad rule-making authority, with the actual rules to be established later by S.E.C. regulation, and the industrywide task force wanted to know what the rules would be up front, in the legislation or at least limited by the legislation.[12]

Senator Muskie told DeNunzio that the Senate subcommittee would be proceeding with its own legislation, whether or not the industrywide task force and the S.E.C. reconciled their differences. He introduced a substitute bill that day that reflected his current thinking.[13]

WHILE THE INSURANCE bill was being hashed out in Washington, another body blow struck Wall Street. The Penn Central Transportation Company, formed in 1968 by the merger of the Pennsylvania Railroad and the New York Central Railroad, unexpectedly filed for bankruptcy on June 21. While the company had been struggling since the merger—it had to withdraw a proposed $100 million offering of debentures a month earlier for lack of demand—most financial market participants thought its liquidity needs would continue to be met by the short-term commercial paper market until its financial position stabilized and it could again access long-term credit. The Nixon administration pledged to have the Defense Department guarantee up to $200 million of short-term bank loans in June, which many believed signaled further federal government support, if needed. Yet on June 19, Daniel Z. Henkin, Assistant Secretary of Defense for Public Affairs, announced that the Department of Defense would not be providing the loan guarantees.

The D.O.J. announcement sent the price of Penn Central's commercial paper into free fall. Since millions of Penn Central's commercial paper needed to be refinanced weekly, its inability to do so precipitated its bankruptcy filing two days later. This, in turn, sent the rest of the commercial paper market tumbling. The cost to refinance short-term notes skyrocketed, leaving issuers to turn to their backstop commercial bank credit lines to affect the refinancing of their commercial paper. The result was a dangerously strained banking system, exacerbated by the actions of Federal Reserve Board chairman Arthur Burns, who had been steadily reducing the supply of credit in order to curb inflation.

To his credit, Arthur Burns immediately saw the gravity of the risk posed by the Penn Central bankruptcy combined with the deteriorating financial condition of the Wall Street investment banks. Burns promptly reversed course and flooded the financial system with liquidity. The Fed announced that it would extend credit to any member banks willing to lend to issuers of maturing commercial paper. It also suspended Regulation Q, which capped the interest rates banks paid on large-dollar certificates of deposit, enabling banks to obtain more funds to bolster their short-term liquidity. The Fed also began large open-market purchases of securities and offered to lend directly to firms unable to refinance their commercial paper. The Fed actions worked, and the commercial paper market began to settle back into normal activity.

One firm, Goldman, Sachs & Co., the largest market maker in commercial paper, nearly went under as a result of the Penn Central debacle. With only approximately $50 million in capital at the time, the losses on its large inventory of commercial paper for the three hundred issuers for whom it made markets might have bankrupted the firm absent the Fed intervention. In addition, Goldman, Sachs would face years of litigation as a result of continuing to sell Penn Central commercial paper to customers nearly up to the time of the bankruptcy filing.

■ ■ ■

AT HAYDEN, STONE, the financial situation rapidly deteriorated throughout June. The investment by the Oklahoma group did not stabilize the firm's capital because the securities in the subordinated accounts declined in value from approximately $17.5 million in March to less than $6.5 million in June. The aggressive cost-cutting program announced in May involving the closing of several branch offices, the layoff of four hundred employees, and a 15 percent pay cut for its remaining employees was simply too little too late. Hayden, Stone reported an $8 million net capital deficiency to the N.Y.S.E. in June.[14]

In order to convince the board of governors of the Exchange to permit it to continue to operate, Hayden, Stone was required to adhere to a strict eight-point agreement. It was required to immediately raise $7.8 million of new capital by selling securities not qualifying for net capital credit. It was to aggressively implement additional cost savings initiatives so that it would be profitable at a 7.5 million share per day N.Y.S.E. trading volume. Next, it could not have aggregate underwriting commitments at any one time outstanding in excess of $1.5 million. It was also required to "buy in" all short stock differences, and no capital could be withdrawn from the firm until July 1971, which would be subject to enhanced reporting obligations to the Exchange. In order to accelerate an anticipated $5 million tax refund from the Internal Revenue Service, it was required to change its fiscal year-end to June 30 or September 30 (from December 31). Lastly, it was required to execute an undated liquidating agreement permitting the N.Y.S.E. to dissolve the firm if it failed to comply with any of the other terms of the agreement.[15]

The N.Y.S.E.'s strict terms came with a substantial financial benefit, however. The Exchange provided Hayden, Stone with a $5 million bridge loan, to be repaid upon the earlier of receipt of the proceeds of the tax refund or December 29, 1970. If the loan was not repaid when due or if Hayden, Stone fell out of net capital rule compliance or was otherwise found by the N.Y.S.E. to not be able to operate in a safe and sound manner, the Exchange would be permitted to liquidate the firm.[16]

On June 24, Alfred Coyle called Peter Flanigan, President Nixon's senior economic advisor, asking that he intervene on Hayden, Stone's behalf with the I.R.S. to permit the expedited tax refund by means of the fiscal year change. The expedited refund had been denied by the New York I.R.S. office and was under appeal to the Treasury Department in Washington. Flanigan reached out to senior Treasury Department official Charles Walker. Flanigan told Walker that Hayden, Stone was in dire financial condition and the expedited tax refund might make the difference as to its survival. He further speculated to Walker as to what the systemic effects of a failure of a major Wall Street firm like Hayden, Stone might be. Flanigan requested that Walker reach out to Coyle and set up a meeting with Hayden, Stone's accounting firm, Haskins & Sells, to attempt to resolve the matter quickly. Walker agreed to do so. Flanigan instructed Walker to have no further contact with the White House on this matter and told him the White House would not discuss the matter any further with Alfred Coyle or anyone else on behalf of Hayden, Stone.[17]

On June 25, Hayden, Stone announced that it was taking steps to raise $7.8 million of additional capital.[18] No mention was made of the other requirements of its agreement with the N.Y.S.E. or that it was subject to liquidation at the discretion of the Exchange if it failed to live up to that agreement. Hayden, Stone also confirmed that the firm had been in discussions to merge with Merrill Lynch, but that such talks had terminated.[19]

THROUGHOUT JUNE, MEMBERS of the board of governors of the N.Y.S.E met quietly with the leaderships of the largest member firms of the Exchange, both the block trading houses and those with large retail brokerage businesses. They attempted to obtain agreement on a revised commission rate structure to present to the S.E.C. in lieu of the February 13 plan. The revised plan would involve smaller volume discounts on block trades and smaller rate increases on small transactions.

Anticipating the filing of a new rate schedule, Haack used the opportunity to request a ninety-day extension from the S.E.C. of the $15 transaction surcharge, set to expire on July 6, and to plead poverty on behalf of the industry. In a letter to Hamer Budge, contemporaneously made public, Haack asserted: "Throughout 1970 there has been a progressive and serious deterioration in the overall profitability of member firms. Not only were there progressively fewer firms in the black, but there has been a steady shrinkage in the dollar amount of their profits. The service charge has fallen far short of its predicted impact. With the erosion in stock volume, the added revenue appears to be a fraction of the amount anticipated."[20]

On June 29, the board of governors of the Exchange met and voted to approve a revised commission rate schedule, which was submitted to the S.E.C. the following day.[21] The revised plan removed all additional volume discounts and limited the increases for small transactions—those involving values of $5,000 or less—to 50 percent. In the February plan, commissions on certain small transactions would have risen more than 100 percent. In addition, the Exchange repeated its request for a ninety-day extension of the $15 commission surcharge that had been in effect since April 6. Under the new plan, the N.Y.S.E. anticipated an industrywide aggregate annual revenue increase of $520 million, or 35 percent, as compared to $438 million, or 15 percent, under the February 13 plan.[22]

On the same day, it was reported that the S.E.C. and Ralph De-Nunzio's industrywide task force had reached agreement on one of their outstanding issues—the maximum annual fee paid by broker-dealers to S.I.P.C. The industrywide task force originally wanted a cap of 0.125 percent during times when no loan from the U.S. Treasury was outstanding to S.I.P.C. They settled on 0.25 percent. It was further reported that DeNunzio and Hamer Budge had told Senator Muskie that both sides believed their remaining outstanding differences could be solved promptly.[23]

Representative John Moss was growing concerned that the N.Y.S.E. was pleading poverty to the S.E.C. to garner approval of the surcharge extension and a more lucrative revised fee schedule while at the same time telling Congress there were no additional firms in violation of the net capital rule or otherwise in severe financial distress. Moss sent a letter to the S.E.C. requesting that it hold public hearings prior to approving the surcharge extension or the new rate schedule.[24] Senator Harrison Williams, chairman of the Securities Subcommittee, sent a telegram to the S.E.C. the following day, also requesting public hearings: "I am well aware of the financial plight now affecting the entire securities industry. However, both the N.Y.S.E. rate schedule and a continuation of the surcharge would adversely affect millions of small investors. I therefore urge the S.E.C. to hold public hearings on both these measures before taking action. It is only in the manner that all interested parties may be heard."[25]

On July 2, the S.E.C. announced that it would hold public hearings on both the extension of the surcharge and the new rate schedule.[26] The hearings on the surcharge would begin on Monday, July 13 and those on the new rate schedule would commence on Monday, July 20.

THE OPERATIONAL IMPROVEMENTS from C.C.S. were steadily reducing the paperwork strain. In May, 72 percent of all eligible trades were settled through C.C.S. without physical delivery of certificates.[27] Nonetheless, the strain on Bob Bishop and Lee Arning resulting from one firm after another falling out of net capital rule compliance was becoming unbearable. Bishop had the day-to-day interaction with the failing firms on net capital rule compliance, which involved a great deal of unpleasant directives and threats of liquidation. He was constantly complained about to Lee Arning and to members of the Crisis Committee. In turn, the members of the Crisis Committee, particularly Felix Rohatyn, would complain to Bishop that he was going too easy on the failing firms.

Bishop was monitoring more than 500 firms, 167 of which were on some sort of regulatory restraint. There were only about 200 employees, including support staff, dedicated to this herculean undertaking. With belt-tightening all around, there was no budget to increase staff. In fact, Bishop and Arning were under tremendous pressure to cut costs. In July, the board of governors appointed a Special Capital Committee to recommend changes to the net capital rule to strengthen the capital structures of member firms, further stressing the Exchange staff. The prime directive that summer, though, was to prevent another major firm from failing before S.I.P.C. was up and running. Severely complicating that objective was the fact that there were three very large firms on the brink—Hayden, Stone; F.I. du-Pont, Glore Forgan & Co.; and Goodbody & Co.

The public announcements of these three large firms in July, however, betrayed no financial concerns. On Monday, July 6, the three-way merger of Francis I. duPont & Co., Glore Forgan Staats, Inc., and Hirsch & Co. closed, and the consolidated firms opened for business as F. I. duPont, Glore Forgan & Co. The combined firm had 126 branches in 105 cities in the United States and abroad. Wallace C. Latour, the chief executive officer of the combined firm, was predicting that it would be profitable almost immediately. "I think we have a chance to break even in our first quarter," he told reporters. "We will be waiting to see."[28]

THE HOUSE SUBCOMMITTEE on Commerce and Finance reconvened on July 7 to hear public representatives testify on the broker-dealer insurance bills. Hans R. Reinisch, president of the National Shareholders Association, criticized the proposed bills for not requiring greater disclosure from member firms, as well as excluding from the assessment revenue base underwriting fees and mutual fund sales fees.[29] The following day, the subcommittee heard from Richard Ney, the former actor who was at the time a successful, if unconventional, financial advisor and author of the 1970 bestseller *The Wall Street Jungle*. Ney spent the morning lambasting Wall Street in colorful language. "I greet you not as an outsider but as an investment adviser," he told the subcommittee, "a member in good standing of the establishment—though perhaps not as welcome on the floor of the N.Y.S.E. as I might like to be—this, not because I know what I know but because I have dared to tell the public what I know: Which is that there is more larceny per square foot on the floor of the N.Y.S.E. than any place else in the world."[30]

The next day, Hamer Budge again appeared before the House Subcommittee on Commerce and Finance, accompanied by the four other members of the S.E.C. and its general counsel, Philip A. Loomis Jr., and Irving M. Pollack, the director of the S.E.C.'s Division of Trading and Markets.[31] Budge informed the subcommittee that morning that the S.E.C., the Treasury Department, and the industrywide task force had agreed on a compromise bill late the night before, a draft of which Budge submitted to the subcommittee. Also on hand to describe the bill were Bruce K. MacLaury, Deputy Under Secretary of the Treasury for Monetary Affairs, and William Bryan, Assistant to the Director, Office of Debt Analysis. Ralph DeNunzio, accompanied by John R. Raben and John Maynard of Sullivan & Cromwell, also appeared before the subcommittee in support of the revised compromise bill.[32]

The bill provided for insurance coverage on customer accounts of up to $50,000. S.I.P.C. would have a fifteen-member board of directors, ten members appointed by the exchanges and other self-regulatory bodies and five public members from which the chairman of the board would be chosen. All by-laws, rules, and regulations of S.I.P.C. would be approved by the S.E.C. The Commission would also have the power to require S.I.P.C. to adopt by-laws, rules, and regulations at its request. All securities brokers and dealers would be required to be members of S.I.P.C., except as exempted by the S.E.C. The bill would also make clear that the S.E.C. had the power to regulate broker-dealer use of customer cash and securities on deposit with firms, and it provided for a $1 billion loan facility from the U.S. Treasury to S.I.P.C. to be drawn at such time as the S.I.P.C. funds on hand and private credit lines were exhausted. The annual assessments on S.I.P.C. members would be 0.25 percent of commission revenues during periods when no loans from Treasury were outstanding and up to 0.5 percent when any such loan was outstanding. Within 120 days, S.I.P.C. would receive $3 million from transfers from stock exchange trust funds—other than the N.Y.S.E. Special Trust Fund—as well as $7 million from the first annual assessment of members and private credit lines of $65 million. Within five years, it was expected that assessments would allow S.I.P.C. to obtain a permanent funding level of $150 million, no more than 60 percent of which could be in the form of private credit lines. The revised bill also provided for a special transaction fee of $0.20 per $1,000 of transaction value, if the S.E.C. deemed it necessary to repay any Treasury loan.[33]

After two hours of testimony, the subcommittee adjourned at noon to reconvene the following morning. Due to conflicts resulting in the unavailability of both Hamer Budge and Ralph DeNunzio that day, Representative Moss delayed the hearings until the following Wednesday, July 15.[34]

WHEN BUDGE WAS recalled as the first witness before the House subcommittee on the morning of July 15, he delivered a bombshell. He submitted to the subcommittee a letter he had received the day before from N.Y.S.E. president Robert Haack designed to explain why none of the N.Y.S.E. Special Trust Fund would be immediately transferred to S.I.P.C. The reason was that the Exchange would agree to assume responsibility to make whole the customers of not only the four N.Y.S.E. firms currently in liquidation—Amott Baker, Gregory & Sons, McDonnell & Co., and Berwald & DeBoer Budge—but also six other member firms that were, wrote Haack, "as a practical matter also in liquidation."[35] The letter did not identify the firms by name in order to avoid runs on them, but the six unnamed firms were Kleiner, Bell; Mayerson & Company; Fusz-Schmelzle; Orris Brothers & Co.; Blair & Co.; and

Dempsey-Tegeler. It was estimated by the Exchange that the ten firms in liquidation would likely cost the Exchange $60 million, with Blair & Co. and Dempsey-Tegeler estimated to account for nearly $50 million of the total. (The other N.Y.S.E. firm that had failed in the back-office crisis, Pickard & Company, had already been liquidated and its customers made whole.) Unmentioned were the three systemically important firms also on the brink (Hayden, Stone; Goodbody; and F.I. duPont, Glore Forgan), for the Special Trust Fund would be rendered insolvent if any of those failed. That was obvious, and if it were known, the entire bill would be rewritten—with tougher regulations requiring less leverage at investment banks and more financial responsibility for them for the cost of protecting customers at failing firms.

In addition to the shock of hearing that six N.Y.S.E. member firms were secretly in liquidation, suspicions immediately arose that the Exchange was carrying additional firms, keeping them afloat through loose enforcement of the net capital rule. The Exchange, of course, was doing precisely that—propping up any firm whose insolvency would result in total depletion of the Special Trust Fund before S.I.P.C. was up and running. Then the liquidation of failed firms would be S.I.P.C.'s problem. There was no way to know for sure if the six firms referred to were just the least expensive to liquidate, and now neither Budge nor Congress trusted the Exchange to give them a straight answer. However, it was Budge's job, as chairman of the S.E.C., to make sure a crisis like this never happened. Accordingly, he was just as incentivized to soft-pedal the state of affairs to Congress as the Exchange was to soft-pedal it to the S.E.C. Budge in his testimony cleverly put the issue of other insolvent firms right back in the Exchange's lap. Budge told the House subcommittee that the N.Y.S.E. has to "accept responsibility for any firms which are not in capital compliance or who may not be in capital compliance at enactment of this bill."[36]

When Ralph DeNunzio and his Sullivan & Cromwell lawyers appeared after Budge, the subcommittee's counsel, Theodore Focht, pressed him as to whether "it is fair for us to assume that there is no serious immediate problem with respect to other firms."[37] DeNunzio was evasive: "Mr. Focht, I don't really see how I can elaborate on that very much. We appreciate that that letter is a communication from the Exchange that specifically comments on four firms in one category and six of another. Certainly I know of no—I am sure those statements are factually correct. I really wouldn't want to comment as to whether or not there are any other problems besides that."[38] Representative Moss immediately instructed Focht to request from Robert Haack information regarding any other firms in financial distress and whether the N.Y.S.E. intended to retain financial responsibility for any firms other than the ten identified that might become insolvent or fall out of compliance with the net capital rule after July 14, 1970, and prior to the effectiveness of the S.I.P.C. legislation.[39]

THE FOLLOWING DAY, the Senate Subcommittee on Securities called witnesses from the U.S. Treasury, the S.E.C., and the industrywide task force to explain the compromise bill. First to appear was Secretary of the Treasury David M. Kennedy, accompanied by Bruce K. MacLaury, Deputy Under Secretary for Monetary Affairs.[40] Secretary Kennedy explained the need for the S.E.C. to be able to implement a discretionary transaction fee of a maximum of $0.20 per $1,000 transaction value of sales of equity securities whenever any portion of the $1 billion U.S. Treasury line of credit was drawn. The maximum assessment of 0.50 percent ($25 million, based on 1969 revenue) would be insufficient to service even $500 million of a Treasury loan at 7 percent interest ($35 million), an optimistic interest rate given the 7 ¾ percent interest rate seven-year Treasuries were yielding at the time. This fee would yield an additional $38 million, based on 1969 data. The fee, of course, would function as a tax on the investing public rather than be borne by the investment banks themselves.[41]

After Kennedy, the subcommittee heard from Hamer Budge, accompanied by the General Counsel of the S.E.C., Philip A.

Loomis Jr., and Irving Pollack, Director, Division of Trading and Markets.[42] Senator Muskie began the questioning of Budge by asking whether Budge was satisfied the N.Y.S.E. had sufficient resources to make whole the customers of the ten firms known to be insolvent. Budge gave a very lawyerly response: "Senator, the representations which have been made to the Commission by the N.Y.S.E. would cause us to conclude that the Exchange has adequate resources presently to take care of the liquidation of any firms which are now in net capital violation."[43] Muskie, of course, knew this left a lot of ground uncovered: for example, firms that were technically in net capital rule compliance as a result of liberal interpretation of the rule by the Exchange, firms that misrepresented their numbers to the Exchange, and firms that fell out of compliance after July 14, 1970.

Senator Muskie put the question more directly to Budge: "How can we satisfy ourselves as to the extent of that situation in a way that would reassure you and the administration and ourselves that we are not getting ourselves into something really serious? We would hate to see the payout window of this new corporation active the day after it comes into existence."[44] To this, Budge gave a frank answer: "Well, I don't believe that there can be any assurance, Senator. This industry was beset with a combination of circumstances. In 1967 and 1968, the volume just skyrocketed. The industry then started to gear up but it did so too late and that is why it got into the back-office difficulties. It expended a great deal of money, it employed a host of people, it made long-term commitments for hardware, for leases of all kinds, long-term expenditures, and all of a sudden, the volume in the market went way down. In addition, the drop in the market affected the capital position of the firms themselves. That combination of circumstances has made it very difficult for the industry to serve the public. And that has been the concern of the Commission in the other areas where we have wanted the public to be served—in any place where the industry found they were losing money, they simply stopped taking care of those customers. I don't think there can be any assurance that the brokerage firms will not fail. I would assume that that is the purpose of this legislation. Certainly they are having financial difficulties at this time."[45]

Senator Muskie then honed in on the regulatory weak link—the delegation of oversight of the net capital rule to the N.Y.S.E. "So that exemption is applied, pursuant, I gather, to the self-regulatory principle, but can be withdrawn at any time that the Commission deems it advisable and in the public interest," Muskie correctly observed. "Now if I am right in my understanding of it, why hasn't it been withdrawn in any case under the present circumstances which prompted this legislation?"[46] Budge misleadingly responded that the N.Y.S.E. net capital rule was more stringent than the S.E.C. net capital rule.[47] The truth, as Budge knew, was that the loose interpretation of the rule by the Exchange resulted in firms being deemed in compliance when any reasonable interpretation would have resulted in ratios well in excess of 20-to-1. Budge also claimed that the S.E.C. lacked the resources to properly enforce the net capital rule: "I think the New York Stock Exchange alone has twice as many employees as the S.E.C. We are not staffed to go into the brokerage houses all over the country to perform this function."[48]

Next, Muskie raised questions as to the wisdom of an addition to the bill not previously identified, one that permitted the S.I.P.C. board—controlled by the securities industry—to request that subordinated loans be made to firms not being liquidated.[49] Muskie was concerned that the Club would request loans to its favored few, not necessarily those firms most needing a capital infusion. While the S.E.C. would need to approve a subordinated loan, no request could be made to it unless it was first approved by the S.I.P.C. board. "It is at that point that the possibility of favoritism might arise, the members of the board could take the initiative and they could take it on a selective basis that might reflect favoritism or discrimination," Muskie observed.[50] Budge was candid again in response: "That certainly could be true in the original selection, I think you are correct Senator."[51]

Senator Harrison Williams of New Jersey read to Budge a quote from Merrill Lynch chief executive Donald Regan from Regan's July 9, 1970, testimony to another Senate committee in an unrelated hearing regarding the broker-dealer insurance bill. Regan said: "We have never thought there was much merit in the idea that the taxpayer should be on the hook perhaps for as much as a billion dollars for such insurance—referring to the insurance we are discussing. Indeed, we believe the securities business perhaps above all other businesses should have the strength, the determination, and perhaps the willingness to pay its own way."[52] Budge responded that "the industry, I think, tried very diligently to develop a private insurance program but as far as I know they were not successful in so doing." Senator Williams commented that "I think Mr. Regan also has an element of disagreement with the proposition that the strong should be assessed to cover the weak."[53]

Ralph DeNunzio and John Raben and John Maynard from Sullivan & Cromwell were the last witnesses to appear.[54] Senator Muskie questioned DeNunzio as to whether the N.Y.S.E.'s Special Trust Fund had sufficient assets to cover the ten identified insolvent firms. DeNunzio responded that "the Exchange feels it has, and has so indicated to the Commission."[55] He was asked what would happen to any sums in the Special Trust Fund left over after the firms for which the Exchange had responsibility were wound up and customers made whole. DeNunzio responded that the current intention was that any such amounts would be deposited into S.I.P.C., but that would be at the discretion of the board of governors of the N.Y.S.E. If it were determined to contribute such amounts to S.I.P.C., the compromise bill contemplated that those amounts would be credited against future assessments—effectively a refund. (Muskie's concerns about a windfall from the Special Trust Fund were short-lived: its assets were depleted—and then some—before S.I.P.C.'s creation.)

DeNunzio was then asked whether he knew of any firms other than the ten identified that were operating in violation of the net capital rule. He answered: "To the best knowledge of the N.Y.S.E., there are no other firms operating in violation of the net capital requirements." Muskie probed beyond net capital rule violators, asking: "Do you think that that is a full measure of the possible difficulties that we ought to be aware of and sensitive to?" DeNunzio replied: "I think this, if business conditions continue as they have been in the last several months, if volume continues to stay very low, if the public continues to be on the sidelines as far as this market is concerned, and if we have any prolonged period of activity such as we have had, it is possible there will be some other firms. It is very difficult to predict this or calculate this in advance."[56]

A WEEK AFTER the hearings ended, Theodore H. Focht, counsel to the House Subcommittee on Commerce and Finance, received a reply letter from Robert Haack as to whether the N.Y.S.E. Special Trust Fund would assume responsibility for any firms beyond the ten insolvent firms identified. The answer, in so many words, was no. Haack wrote: "I believe we outlined the responsibility of the Special Trust Fund in connection with member firms now in some sort of liquidation in our July 14 letter to the Chairman of the S.E.C. It is difficult to define the role of the Trust Fund further because of the uncertainty of such important factors as the length of the current severe decline in market activity or when Congress will pass the Security Investors Protection Corporation legislation and when that bill will become effective. In this regard, I would like to emphasize that in supporting S.I.P.C. and the concept and establishment of an industrywide fund, the Exchange has obviously had to de-emphasize the buildup of its own Trust Fund. S.I.P.C. will have the powers to assess members, as well as extensive borrowing ability, thus curbing the ability of the Exchange to build up the Exchange's Trust Fund as we had originally planned to do. As a result, prompt action on S.I.P.C. is essential in order that the transition period between the present Exchange Trust Fund and the establishment of S.I.P.C. be of the most modest duration, as well as to provide continuing reassurance to the investing public."[57]

Not long after the conclusion of the hearings, both Democrats and Republicans in Congress began voicing doubts over the compromise bill. Six questions were most frequently raised. First, was the industry contribution of $75 million initially and $150 million after five years sufficient to avoid tapping into the $1 billion taxpayer-funded Treasury backstop loan facility? Second, should the tax on equity transactions—paid by customers—be permitted? (Why shouldn't increased assessments be levied on Wall Street firms instead?) Third, why should all firms without regard to their financial condition be allowed to be insured through S.I.P.C.? (When the F.D.I.C. was created, banks needed to pass an examination to assure they weren't insolvent as a condition to obtaining deposit insurance.) Fourth, why should S.I.P.C. make subordinated loans to firms not taken over by S.I.P.C.? (Acting as a "lender of last resort" to financially distressed firms is a completely different function than liquidating firms declared insolvent and making whole customers.) Fifth, should the insurance entity be a private corporation? (Why not simply have the S.E.C. operate an insurance vehicle as a division of the Commission?) Lastly, if S.I.P.C. was to be formed, why should its board be controlled by industry representatives as opposed to public representatives appointed by the president, the Secretary of the Treasury, or the S.E.C.?

While the hearings may have ended, the answers to these questions would continue to be debated by the members of the congressional committees.

AT THE SAME time the congressional hearings on S.I.P.C. were taking place, the S.E.C. was holding hearings on the commission rates. During the week of July 13, the S.E.C. heard testimony regarding the extension of the $15 transaction surcharge. In addition to the N.Y.S.E. representatives advocating for the extension, the S.E.C. heard from Hans Reinisch, who had testified in the House S.I.P.C. hearings the prior week. Reinisch criticized the S.E.C. for approving the surcharge back in April without public hearings and called the Exchange's claims of financial hardship "scare tactics."[58]

On July 20, the public hearings on the revised fee schedule began. The N.Y.S.E. put forth Irwin Stelzer, president of N.E.R.A., to explain the new rates. Unfortunately, Stelzer was forced to concede under questioning from Sheldon Rappaport of the S.E.C. staff that the new rates did not reflect the "cost basis analysis" that N.E.R.A. indicated back in February was appropriate for rates for a quasi-public utility like the N.Y.S.E.[59] Rappaport highlighted for Stelzer the language from the February N.E.R.A. report that stated any departure from the cost basis of setting commissions would have to be justified by a "special study" demonstrating "the putative benefits to the public." Stelzer said the special study requirement was satisfied by the "lifelong study" of the seventeen august members of the board of governors of the N.Y.S.E. Again, the S.E.C. staff avoided confrontation with witnesses and quietly took notes.[60]

Ralph DeNunzio appeared before the S.E.C. the following day. Sheldon Rappaport asked DeNunzio why the sales commission for a 1,000-share order at $40 per share was $429.00 under the new rate schedule but would have been only $243.74 under the February plan. Like Irwin Stelzer, DeNunzio could not provide a reasoned basis for the large disparity.[61]

On July 24, Charles H. Brunie, partner in Oppenheimer & Co., closed the week's testimony. Brunie told the S.E.C. that the future of the entire capitalistic system could be threatened if securities commission rates were not raised sufficiently. When asked what he thought a reasonable rate structure would be, Brunie said he didn't believe reasonableness was the proper standard. The goal, he said, ought to be "to create a viable securities industry. . . . I am afraid a viable securities industry is much more important to me than the reasonableness of the rate. . . . You're taking a grave chance with the capitalistic system," he added. "I don't see that it's worth it."[62]

Gene Rotberg was more amused than angered by the fact that after months of hearings and N.E.R.A. pricey analysis, the N.Y.S.E. had thrown in the towel on trying to develop a reasonable basis for a fixed commission rate structure that would pass muster under the antitrust laws. Rotberg knew from the start it couldn't be done. And, in the final analysis, the N.Y.S.E. didn't do a very good job faking it. The game was now over.

THE DISTRESSED MERGERS and acquisitions wave continued unabated during July. On July 7, Thompson & McKinnon Auchincloss, Inc. announced it would acquire fifteen branch offices of Blair & Co., Inc. At the same time, Blair announced that it was closing an undisclosed number of other branch offices to refocus its operations. On July 10, Mitchum, Jones & Templeton, a Los Angeles–based investment bank, announced that it was acquiring nine West Coast branches of Dempsey-Tegeler & Co.[63] After the sale, Dempsey-Tegeler would be left with only sixteen branches. In late 1969, before the financial crisis, it had had sixty branch offices. Less than a week later, Dempsey-Tegeler announced that it was suspending operations and hoped to reorganize as a smaller entity. The following week, it was reported that Dean Witter & Co. was in talks to merge with Paine, Webber, Jackson & Curtis, although this deal would never happen.[64]

Word of the largest proposed Wall Street merger of the year was leaked to the press on July 21. It was reported that Hayden, Stone, Inc. and Walston & Co. were in discussions.[65] By early July, Hayden, Stone had concluded it could not survive as an independent company. It held preliminary talks with a number of other firms, including Merrill Lynch, Bache & Co., Reynolds, Shearson and Loeb Rhoades. By mid-July, only Walston & Co., Inc., the fourth largest investment bank, was still interested. The merged firm—to be called Walston Hayden Stone, Inc.—would combine Walston's 100 branch offices, 1,700 brokers, and 200,000 customer accounts with Hayden, Stone's 55 branch offices, 900 brokers, and 150,000 customer accounts. It would also combine Walston's $49 million of net capital with Hayden, Stone's $38 million. With this merger, one of the three systemically important troubled firms would be rescued, a major triumph for Lee Arning and a tremendous shot in the arm for Ralph DeNunzio's and the Crisis Committee's efforts to pass the S.I.P.C. legislation in a form favorable to the industry.

THE PLAINTIFF'S BAR continued to find creative theories to hold the N.Y.S.E. responsible for losses arising out of the back-office crisis. In early August, Howard D. Morgenbesser, the holder of a subordinated account at the insolvent Baerwald & DeBoer, filed suit against the Exchange alleging that it was negligent in its supervision of Baerwald & DeBoer by failing to enforce the net capital rule.[66] Morgenbesser argued that if he had known the firm was in violation of the net capital rule on a timely basis, he would have withdrawn his account and not lost the $150,000 contained therein. He was also seeking $3 million in punitive damages. While the Exchange was using the Special Trust Fund to make whole holders of regular accounts, it was not protecting holders of subordinated accounts.

SENATOR MUSKIE WAS growing increasingly frustrated about the lack of transparency from the N.Y.S.E. regarding the number of its member firms in financial distress. At the July 16 hearing of the Securities Subcommittee, Muskie had asked Ralph DeNunzio for detailed information about firms in net capital rule violation or otherwise in financial difficulty. Muskie, having not gotten a response, sent DeNunzio a sharply worded warning letter on August 6. "I have not received a reply from you and I am very concerned over the delay," Muskie wrote, and he threatened to stop all work in the Senate on the securities customer insurance bill until DeNunzio complied with the information request.[67]

On the House side, Representative John Moss was equally frustrated with the cat-and-mouse game the Exchange was playing by assuring the solvency of the Special Trust Fund while at the same time balking at taking responsibility for firms that were insolvent. By even the most optimistic estimates, more than $35 million of the

$55 million Special Trust Fund assets had been spent or earmarked for known customer losses. Those numbers further assumed no amounts would be spent for any firms that failed after Dempsey-Tegeler, which Moss knew was an absurd assumption. Moss reminded the Exchange that it had advertised for years that investors who do business with a N.Y.S.E.-member firm would not lose money if that firm goes bankrupt.

In a letter to Representative Moss on August 12, John Cunningham said that was not true: "The Exchange does not have, and never has had, an obligation to come forward and make good any losses that customers may suffer because of the failure of an exchange member, nor does the Exchange assure that there cannot be such losses." He asserted that the Special Trust Fund was not a "guarantee fund" and its use was always at the discretion of the Special Trust Fund's trustees. To John Moss, the Exchange's evasion of responsibility was beginning to smell like a wet dog.

ON AUGUST 7, the S.E.C. hearings on the revised N.Y.S.E. fee proposal concluded. The Commission staff gave no indication as to when they would respond or what the process would be in finalizing a "permanent" fee structure. The Antitrust Division of the Department of Justice, which had mandated, at a minimum, that fixed commissions be "reasonable," likewise was mum as to whether the revised proposal—or the original February 13 proposal, for that matter—met the reasonableness standard.

On the last day of August, the S.E.C. announced that it would allow the $15 surcharge on orders of up to 1,000 shares to continue indefinitely. It released a brief statement stating that: "Upon the basis of its review of monitoring program data and other relevant information developed in the Commission rate hearing, the Commission has concluded that present conditions do not warrant termination of the surcharge at this time. Accordingly, the Commission has determined to permit the continuation of the surcharge until such time as circumstances warrant its termination."[68]

CHAPTER THIRTEEN

"HENCEFORTH ALL TRADES IN HAYDEN, STONE'S NAME WILL BE DESIGNATED CBWL-HAYDEN, STONE"

■

Back from the Brink

On Monday August 10, the N.Y.S.E. announced that Dempsey-Tegeler & Co. was to be formally liquidated, with up to $15,000,000 committed from the Special Trust Fund to protect Dempsey-Tegeler's customers.[1] Norman Swanton, the former Glore Forgan Staats, Inc. executive who resigned in protest over the Francis I. duPont & Co. merger, was appointed by the N.Y.S.E. to be the liquidator of Dempsey-Tegeler. On the same day, it was also announced that Blair & Co., once an up-and-coming aggressive firm that led many of conglomerate Textron's securities offerings, was to be shuttered, selling its fifty branch offices in a fire sale liquidation.[2] Both Dempsey-Tegeler and Blair were on the list of failing firms provided to Senator Muskie and Representative Moss and for which the Exchange would retain responsibility for bailing out their customers. Accordingly, this news did not fundamentally change the outlook for passage of the S.I.P.C. legislation. The Exchange declined to answer any questions from the press regarding the remaining resources of the Special Trust Fund following the Dempsey-Tegeler and Blair insolvencies.

Two days later, another troubled firm, Brand, Grummet & Sei-gel, Inc., announced that it had entered into a tentative agreement to be acquired by Thompson & McKinnon, Auchincloss, Inc.[3] It was another shotgun wedding arranged by the Crisis Committee.

Under intense press scrutiny and with many firms voicing concern over counterparty risk, on August 13, the N.Y.S.E. publicly disclosed the list of ten member firms in "formal or informal liquidation."[4] In addition to the six firms already publicly known to be in liquidation—Amott, Baker; Gregory & Sons; McDonnell & Co.; Baerwald & DeBoer; Dempsey-Tegeler; and Blair & Co.—the Exchange identified Kleiner, Bell & Co.; Orvis Brothers & Co.; Mayerson Co.; and Fusz-Schmelzle Co.[5]

All of the four newly identified firms were small, independently posing no systemic risk. In addition, Robert Haack announced that the Special Trust Fund had expended or committed $30.7 million to date to liquidate these firms, leaving $24 million. He gave no indication whether any of the newly identified firms would need to access any of that remaining $24 million available in the Special Trust Fund. "The Exchange has told both the S.E.C. and the Congressional committees involved in the pending customer protection legislation that it is committed to protecting customers of these ten firms through its Special Trust Fund," Haack stated.[6] "We have stated that we believe the money available to the Trust Fund is sufficient to complete the delivery of public customer accounts from these ten firms," he added.[7] He continued: "To our knowledge, there are no N.Y.S.E. member firms in business with major current paperwork problems. This is significant because experience indicates that firms in financial difficulties but with current and correct records can transfer customer accounts if necessary either at no cost or very little cost to the Special Trust Fund."[8] Haack was silent as to whether any other firms were currently in violation of the net capital rule. He also made no mention of the three major firms—Hayden, Stone; Goodbody; and F.I. duPont, Glore Forgan—teetering on insolvency.

. . .

DURING THE FIRST week of August, the Oklahoma consortium led by Jack E. Golsen that had rescued Hayden, Stone in March replaced the stock in their subordinated accounts with cash, in order to prevent Hayden, Stone from liquidating the stock in the market at deflated market prices to maintain the agreed minimum account values.[9] While this normally would have been viewed as positive news for Hayden, Stone—volatile common stock replaced with cash—instead it was taken as a lack of confidence in Hayden, Stone's financial condition. After the Hayden, Stone–Walston merger talks had leaked early in the negotiations, almost continuously thereafter rumors spread that the talks were breaking down. To quell the rumors, on August 11, the two firms put out a statement that the talks were "proceeding according to plan" and that they anticipated signing a merger agreement the first week of September.[10] A meeting with the Hayden, Stone creditors was held at the Racquet and Tennis Club on Park Avenue in Midtown Manhattan shortly thereafter to discuss the deal. The creditors would be required to consent to the deal and extend the maturity of their loans. In the end, Walston balked at a merger, afraid of the dubious record keeping and potential undisclosed liabilities at Hayden, Stone. Walston's proposal would have resulted in Hayden, Stone's subordinated lenders—including Jack Golsen's Oklahoma group—receiving less than 100 cents on the dollar. Golsen had made it clear after the meeting at the Racquet Club that he was not supportive of the Walston merger or any other deal that required him to take a loss.[11]

On August 19, in a head-spinning announcement, Hayden, Stone disclosed not only that the proposed merger with Walston had been abandoned, but that it had instead entered into a definitive merger agreement with C.B.W.L. As part of the transaction, Walston would acquire eighteen of Hayden, Stone's domestic branches, with the remainder of Hayden, Stone being divided into a "good bank" and a "bad bank," with the unwanted "bad" assets and certain liabilities being isolated in a new shell corporation to be liquidated, and the remaining "good" assets, including the remaining twenty-eight Hayden, Stone branch offices, being merged with C.B.W.L. to form a new firm to be named CBWL-Hayden, Stone, Inc.[12] Like the Walston deal before it, the announcement of the new deal was well received on Wall Street, as C.B.W.L. was well-capitalized and operated mainly institutional trading, asset management, and research businesses, with little overlap with Hayden, Stone's well-regarded underwriting business and retail brokerage network. It was estimated at the time of the announcement that only 1,100 of Hayden, Stone's 2,400 employees would be offered employment after the merger.[13] It was also announced that Hayden, Stone's elegant headquarters on the ninth floor at 25 Broad Street, where the firm had been since Charles Hayden moved from Boston to New York in 1906, would be shuttered with all retained employees moving to C.B.W.L.'s offices in the General Motors Building on Fifth Avenue.[14] Additionally, none of Hayden, Stone's senior management would be given any meaningful role in the combined firm. As for Hayden, Stone's subordinated creditors, the merger agreement did not require them to take a haircut on their loans, but did require them to extend the maturity of their loans after the merger, waiving the right to require repayment upon the change of control.[15] What was not disclosed was the N.Y.S.E.'s $5 million bridge loan to Hayden, Stone using the Special Trust Fund to keep it afloat. This would be leaked to the press two weeks later by congressional staffers.

THE SAME DAY as the Hayden, Stone transaction was announced, the N.Y.S.E. announced that it had suspended two firms—First Devonshire Corporation and Charles Plohn & Co.— because of net capital rule violations.[16] Neither firm was named as one of the ten firms the N.Y.S.E. had identified to Congress as failing. Notably, the Exchange took no extraordinary action to save either firm. The management of First Devonshire was surprised at how swiftly the Exchange acted, issuing a statement that the suspension came "as a complete surprise" and that the firm believed it "had complied with all requirements of the exchange."[17] Equally surprising was the absence of any announcement that the Exchange's Special Trust Fund would protect the customers of First Devonshire or Charles Plohn & Co.

Charles Plohn & Co., the firm that had taken *Scanlan's Monthly* and so many other speculative companies public, had used extraordinary measures to try to stay afloat, some legal—Charles Plohn sold his wife's vast silverware collection for $500,000 and contributed the proceeds to the equity of the firm—some illegal—the firm pledged fully paid customer securities as collateral for loans to the firm.

In Washington, the silence from the N.Y.S.E. was deafening. If the Exchange knew First Devonshire or Charles Plohn & Co. was on the brink, why wasn't that disclosed by Ralph DeNunzio in his House and Senate testimony? If the Exchange did not know, its oversight was woefully deficient—and what other unpleasant surprises were lurking? Dishonesty or incompetence were the only explanations as far as Senator Muskie and Representative Moss were concerned.

On the same day it learned First Devonshire and Charles Plohn & Co. were suspended, the S.E.C. sent a letter to Robert Haack: "So that we may consider what, if any, action will be required, we are desirous of learning the precise nature and extent of the Exchange's financial commitment to customers and creditors of [First Devonshire Corporation]. While we understand that you might believe that it is premature at this time for the Exchange to make such a commitment, it is the Commission's view that conditions are such that we must have this information." The Exchange responded the following day: "No financial commitment has been made by the Exchange or the Special Trust Fund to the customers and creditors of [First Devonshire Corporation]." Unsatisfied with this response, the S.E.C. followed up with another letter on August 21: "In view of your statement that 'no financial commitment has been made by the Exchange or the Special Trust Fund to the customers or creditors of [First Devonshire Corporation],' it is imperative that we be informed as soon as possible, whether and if so, to what extent, the Exchange is prepared to make a financial commitment in the event [First Devonshire Corporation] is unable to satisfy promptly the claims of customers for their funds and securities." To this letter the Exchange responded on August 25, 1970, that it was in fact not prepared to make any financial commitment, and any assistance at some future date would be decided by the trustees of the Special Trust Fund in the exercise of their fiduciary duties.

On August 27, 1970, the S.E.C. charged both First Devonshire Corporation and Charles Plohn & Co. with violations of securities laws.[18] It also petitioned the court to have bankruptcy receivers appointed for both firms under federal bankruptcy laws, removing their liquidation from oversight by the N.Y.S.E.[19] The S.E.C. took the view that if the Exchange was not assuming financial responsibility for customer losses at those firms, it should not control the distribution of their assets.

SENATOR MUSKIE WAS furious over being blindsided by the First Devonshire and Charles Plohn & Co. bankruptcies. He was even more livid that the N.Y.S.E. refused to take responsibility for making their customers whole. Muskie was determined to proceed with his version of a broker-dealer insurance bill—that gave control over the insurance corporation to the S.E.C., not Wall Street. Muskie was also determined to report a bill out of the Securities Subcommittee to the full Senate Banking Committee by Labor Day. He requested a final closed-door drafting session on his bill for Friday, August 28, the last working day before the Labor Day weekend.[20] The industrywide task force hoped to delay the proceedings and preserve their more favorable compromise bill. They did not want Muskie's bill reported to the full committee and, by some means, convinced enough members of the subcommittee to leave early for the long weekend to deny him the presence of the necessary six senators to constitute a quorum to conduct business.[21]

While respected by his Senate colleagues, Ed Muskie was not beloved, for he could at times be an excruciating human being. An outraged Muskie called in the press to the empty hearing room. "They told me if I didn't call off the session, they would do everything they could to see it wasn't held," Muskie told reporters.[22] "I don't know that they called anyone else, I'm not going to imply that they did," he continued. "But I want to make clear my position. I'm ready. I'm here. I'm ready to write the bill. Legislation is not written by the stock exchanges; it's written by Congress."[23] The chairman of the Securities Subcommittee, Senator Harrison Williams of New Jersey, home to a great many Wall Streeters, was the recipient of a disproportionate amount of financial industry campaign contributions. Williams indicated that he would "try to see" that the broker-dealer insurance bill got reported after the Labor Day recess.[24]

Over the Labor Day weekend, another sizable firm failed: Robinson & Co., Inc. with approximately 8,000 customers. It filed for federal bankruptcy protection on the morning of Tuesday, September 1 when the courts reopened. Robinson had resigned its N.Y.S.E. membership in July, so technically its failure was not a responsibility of the Exchange.[25]

Three days later, Orvis Brothers & Co., one of the firms identified as being "informally in liquidation," made it formal. After completing the sale of five of its branch offices to Halle & Stieglitz, Inc. and four others to E. F. Hutton & Co., the N.Y.S.E. appointed William J. Ragusin, a former D.L.J. executive, to liquidate its remaining assets.[26]

Muskie and Moss were more determined than ever that the N.Y.S.E. bear financial responsibility for all firms that were failing or in violation of the net capital rule—responsibly interpreted—prior to the passage of the S.I.P.C. legislation. This included Robinson & Co., Inc. They were not buying the Exchange's argument that since the firm sold its seat on the Exchange in a fire sale in July, it was off the hook. The vast majority of customer accounts were created long before then, and Robinson had made no public announcement that it had surrendered its membership. However, Muskie and Moss were also awake to the possibility that a large firm, possibly even a systemically important firm, might fail, bankrupting the Special Trust Fund and endangering the commercial banking system and economy generally. They were aware this put them between the proverbial rock and a hard place.

LATE SUMMER, 1970 was the most treacherous time for the N.Y.S.E. since the Whitney scandal of 1938. This time, however, firms of much more consequence than Whitney's were on the brink of failure. And just like in 1938, the N.Y.S.E. had closed ranks to protect its own, obfuscating with regulators and Congress. The 1970 crisis was even more fraught, as the Exchange needed something from Congress beyond being left alone. In 1970, Wall Street needed a bailout.

John Coleman had risen to the chairmanship of the N.Y.S.E. in the wake of the Richard Whitney scandal and the reforms of the Exchange's governance that followed. He learned patience and strategic retreat, when necessary, were critical to maintaining power in the long run. The reformers would have their day, unwelcome changes would inevitably come, but soon the do-gooders would move on. Then, slowly, unnoticed, the Club might reassert itself, clawing back power by cleverly circumventing the reforms. Coleman had accomplished this decades earlier by usurping power from the board of governors and shifting it to committees of the board that did not have public representation, by keeping the professional full-time president of the Exchange well paid, co-opted, and in the dark about many things and, most importantly, by usurping from the S.E.C. the power to enforce the net capital rule. August 1970 was time for another strategic retreat. Ralph DeNunzio was over his skis with Congress. Senator Muskie and Representative Moss were not happy with him over the Exchange's failure to disclose the true financial condition of First Devonshire Corporation, Charles Plohn & Co., and Robinson & Co., Inc. The time had come for DeNunzio to step back and for Felix Rohatyn to step forward. There was no announcement. No memo or transcript of this decision was left behind because the truths that matter most are always whispered. DeNunzio, well aware that pride is the burden of a foolish person, raised no objection.

Felix Rohatyn was a master at self-promotion, at least as skilled at that as he was with merger and acquisition advice. Unbridled in his business, social, and political ambitions, the refined, French-speaking Rohatyn had charmed and schemed his way onto the board of governors of the N.Y.S.E. in 1968. He was the antithesis of John Coleman's Irish ward boss persona. Felix imagined himself portrayed as the savior of Wall Street in its hour of maximum crisis. John Coleman was happy to give him the spotlight—so long as Coleman was kept out of it and Felix delivered the government bailout. Felix would make good on both counts.

From that point forward, virtually every press account that discussed the N.Y.S.E. response to the back-office crisis focused on Felix Rohatyn, and Felix, being who he was, managed to have nearly all those pieces extoll his brilliance and calm under fire. Perhaps a sentence or two would be spared for Bunny Lasker, but hardly a mention of Ralph DeNunzio and never a word about John Coleman.

THE C.B.W.L. MERGER agreement with Hayden, Stone required that all of Hayden, Stone's subordinated lenders keep their money in the company post-merger. There were more than a hundred subordinated lenders that would need to agree. Hayden, Stone management had scheduled a meeting with the subordinated lenders on Thursday, September 3, 1970, again at the Racquet and Tennis Club, to discuss terms of the merger and the creditworthiness of the post-merger company. After the earlier unsuccessful negotiations between the Walston team and the Hayden, Stone creditors, there was great anxiety in advance of this meeting. The night before, C.B.W.L. and Hayden, Stone officials learned that the Chicago Board of Trade planned on announcing the suspension of Hayden, Stone the following morning over financial concerns, which would have spooked the creditors and possibly scuttled the merger. That night, Robert Haack and Felix Rohatyn flew to Chicago and successfully convinced the Chicago Board of Trade to delay the suspension for a week. The creditors meeting went ahead as planned. Initially, there were three holdouts— London investor Donald Eldridge, venture capital investor Arthur Rock in San Francisco, and Jack Golsen in Oklahoma City. Haack was dispatched to London to win over Eldridge, and Stephen Peck, partner in the specialist firm of Weiss, Peck & Greer, was sent to convince Rock. By Thursday, September 10, both had agreed to the deal. That left Jack Golsen.[27]

Jack Golsen believed, with good reason, that Hayden, Stone had lied to him about the firm's financial condition when he made his loan back in March. He also believed the N.Y.S.E. was well aware at the time that Hayden, Stone was in violation of the net capital rule, but kept quiet so as not to scare off investors—suckers like him. He wanted to blow up the deal so that the world would learn what bad actors they all were.[28] With the Chicago Board of Trade extension expiring at 9:00 a.m. Chicago time on Friday, September 11, the N.Y.S.E. set 10:00 a.m. New York time as the deadline for a deal with Golsen.[29] If Golsen held out, Hayden, Stone would be suspended from operating by the N.Y.S.E. A systemically important firm would fail.

On Thursday night, Roger Berlind and Marshall Cogan chartered a private Learjet from Teterboro Airport in New Jersey to Oklahoma City. It was Marshall Cogan's first time in a private plane.[30] Severe thunderstorms delayed their takeoff until after midnight. They finally landed around 4:30 a.m. local time in Oklahoma City. They had convinced Jack Golsen to meet with them at his office at 6:00 a.m.[31] For the next two hours, Berlind and Cogan bullied, cajoled, and finally begged Golsen to take the deal. With less than an hour until the deadline, Bunny Lasker, chairman of the N.Y.S.E., and Felix Rohatyn, on behalf of the Crisis Committee, called in to the meeting to reinforce the message to Golsen that the failure of Hayden, Stone might well take down the Exchange and with it possibly the financial system. Golsen remained unmoved. Ace Greenberg from Bear, Stearns called. A fellow Oklahoman, Greenberg thought a plea from him might be better received than those from one of the East Coast crowd. Golsen demurred. Bunny Lasker, petrified over what was about to happen, called the White House and begged President Nixon to intervene. The White House called Golsen's office. Chief of staff H. R. Haldeman asked Golsen to hold for President Nixon. Golsen refused to talk to Nixon.[32]

Marshall Cogan had one last idea. He asked everyone to leave the office except himself and Golsen. "Now listen to me, Jack," Cogan began. "You will be responsible for killing more Jews than Eichmann if you don't go along with the deal. You will do drastic harm to the legacy of Jews on Wall Street."[33] Golsen had felt that part of the reason that Hayden, Stone had taken advantage of him was that it was a W.A.S.P. firm and he was a Jew. The appeal to ethno-religious pride by Cogan, a fellow Jew from a Jewish-controlled firm, won Golsen over. At 9:55 a.m., New York time, Golsen signed on to the deal. On the floor of the N.Y.S.E., it was announced from the rostrum that "Henceforth, all trades in Hayden, Stone's name will be designated CBWL-Hayden, Stone." An enormous cheer came up from the floor.[34]

In addition to the concessions from Golsen and the other subordinated lenders, CBWL-Hayden, Stone obtained further support from the N.Y.S.E. The Exchange purchased $6 million of illiquid assets from the "bad bank," named H. S. Equities, Inc. The Exchange also indemnified CBWL-Hayden, Stone for up to $1.6 million in losses from the liquidation of H. S. Equities, Inc. Lastly, the Exchange agreed to liquidate thousands of Hayden, Stone customer accounts on behalf of H. S. Equities, Inc., where record-keeping errors were so profound that that C.B.W.L. refused to accept responsibility.[35]

As difficult as the CBWL-Hayden, Stone deal was, its closing was no time for celebration by Lee Arning, Bob Bishop, and the Crisis Committee. Hayden, Stone was the smallest of the systemically important failing firms. Goodbody & Co., the fifth largest investment bank with a hundred branch offices and 250,000 customer accounts, was in desperate need of a merger partner. F. I. duPont, Glore Forgan—larger than Hayden, Stone and Goodbody & Co. combined—was rapidly running out of cash as well.

IN WASHINGTON, SENATOR Muskie hadn't forgotten about the customers of First Devonshire and Charles Plohn & Co. If the N.Y.S.E. thought its financial accommodation to CBWL-Hayden, Stone would be its last such deal, Muskie was going to see to it that it was very mistaken. During the two weeks after Labor Day, Senator Muskie and the other nine senators on the Securities Subcommittee worked on a greatly modified version of the broker-dealer insurance bill. That version of the bill was approved by the full Senate Banking Committee on September 15, 1970.[36] Among the more important changes was an increase in the annual assessment to 0.5 percent of the prior year's revenues, which was expected to grow the insurance fund to $150 million within five years and replace the $65 million private lines of credit.[37] Thereafter, and so long as the insurance fund was at least $100 million, the annual assessment would be reduced to 0.25 percent of gross revenue. Gross revenue was broadly defined in the bill to include eleven sources of income: securities commissions; execution and clearance; trading revenue; net underwriting profit; interest charged to customers; advisory fees and management fees; proxy solicitation fees; service charges; dividends and interest on firm investment accounts; fees for puts and calls; and income from other investment banking services. The assessment for each firm would be determined by risk factors weighted by the S.E.C. If at any time any portion of the $1 billion U.S. Treasury facility was borrowed, the S.E.C. could implement a surcharge on securities transactions with a value of $5,000 or more in the amount of $0.20 per $1,000 value, if deemed necessary to assure repayment of the Treasury loan.[38] In addition, the board of S.I.P.C. would be comprised of the chairman of the S.E.C., the chairman of the Federal Reserve Board, the Secretary of the Treasury, and two public members appointed by the president with the advice and consent of the Senate. No industry representation on the board was provided for. Membership in S.I.P.C. would be obligatory for any broker or dealer who held cash or securities on behalf of any customer. The provision in the DeNunzio-S.E.C. bill allowing for subordinated loans by S.I.P.C. to broker-dealer members prior to their liquidation was stricken from the bill. Stricken, too, was the interposing of S.I.P.C. between the exchanges and the S.E.C. in net capital rule compliance oversight.

On September 17, the House Commerce and Finance Subcommittee unanimously passed the broker-dealer insurance bill, with two notable differences from the Senate bill.[39] In the House version, the board of S.I.P.C. would be comprised of five members selected by the securities industry and two public members appointed by the president during any period when no loans were outstanding from the U.S. Treasury. If a Treasury loan were outstanding, four more presidential appointees would be added, constituting a majority. In addition, the House version required all brokers and dealers to become members of S.I.P.C., other than those who sold only mutual funds or variable annuity contracts, whether or not they held cash or securities on behalf of customers.

ON THE SAME day the Senate Banking Committee approved Muskie's bill, a class action lawsuit was filed in the federal district court in Manhattan by Ivan Kempner, a customer of First Devonshire Corporation, on behalf of all its customers against the N.Y.S.E. alleging that it had "represented and promised to all customers of member firms that it had established a trust fund to secure such customers against loss in the event any such member found itself in financial difficulty" in order "to induce customers to do business with such member firms, thereby adding to the revenues and profits of the defendant and its member firms."[40] Kempner further alleged that the N.Y.S.E. was aware that First Devonshire Corporation was in violation of the net capital rule long before it suspended operations and allowed the firm to operate notwithstanding the hazard such operation posed to unsuspecting customers.[41]

The customers of Robinson & Co., too, were lining up to sue the N.Y.S.E., as they felt the Exchange had an obligation to warn them when it became aware that Robinson was insolvent. The latest the Exchange could have become aware of this, their suits asserted, was when the firm approached the Exchange to approve the sale of its seat on the Exchange, together with other substantial assets, to Phillips, Appel & Walden, Inc. in mid-July.[42] Robinson ceased to be a member on July 24 when that sale closed. Bob Bishop provided an affidavit that, as of July 24, Robinson was in compliance with the net capital rule "and there was no threat of loss of money or securities to such customers due to the financial condition of Robinson."[43] However, the S.E.C. was suing Robinson and certain of its officers, claiming the firm was in violation of the net capital rule as early as April and misled the public about its true financial condition. Bishop also denied that the Exchange had any obligation to use the Special Trust Fund even if Robinson were still a member, adding that the "Exchange has consistently described the fund as a discretionary fund and not an insurance fund or a protection fund."[44] Bishop's affidavit further referred to the Exchange's 1964 Annual Report that described the Special Trust Fund: "The Exchange would decide in any case which customers, if any, would be assisted—and to what extent. Of course, in no event would any customer have any claim against the Exchange or against the Special Trust Fund."[45]

Of particular concern to the Exchange was that the Robinson customers were seeking an injunction preventing any use of the Special Trust Fund until they were assured that it wouldn't be depleted pending resolution of their suits. Federal Judge Inzer B. Wyatt (the same judge who presided over the Roy Cohn acquittal) ultimately refused to grant the injunction. "This court cannot rewrite the trust instrument," he wrote in his opinion. "The trust was set up with specific provisions vesting any expenditures of trust assets in the sole discretion of the trustees. This is within the power of the creator of the trust."[46] In addition, he noted that the trustees were not party to the lawsuit. He allowed the suit against the Exchange to continue, however.[47]

More litigation bad news came that week with a decision out of the Seventh Circuit in Milwaukee. The N.Y.S.E. lost an appeal with the court finding that the Exchange's antitrust exemption did not apply to its rule against customer rebates.[48] Citing the *Silver* decision, the Seventh Circuit held that the antitrust exemption must be narrowly applied—just because the S.E.C. approved rates didn't mean it approved the prohibition of rebates. Absent evidence the S.E.C. explicitly and comprehensively reviewed and approved the rebate rule, it wasn't immune from antitrust attack. This opened the door for antitrust attack on all the Exchange's anticompetitive rules. Even fixed commissions themselves, it seemed, might be challengeable by private plaintiffs. The less substantive review the S.E.C. undertook in reviewing rates, the better the case could be made that the Commission did not intend to immunize them from attack. And if the S.E.C. did not undertake a comprehensive review of rates using a customary public utility "reasonableness" analysis— which it never did because the N.Y.S.E. never wanted it to and the S.E.C. obliged—fixed rates may have violated the antitrust laws for decades.

Hans Randolph Reinisch of the National Shareholders Association thought just that. On October 5, relying on the *Thill* decision, he filed an antitrust class action lawsuit seeking $3 billion for illegal price fixing.[49] The AMEX and five of the largest brokerage firms— Merrill Lynch; Bache & Co.; Walston & Co. Inc.; Paine, Webber, Jackson & Curtis; and F. I. duPont, Glore Forgan & Co.—were also named as defendants in the lawsuit. The suit alleged that the defendants entered into an illegal cartel to fix commissions "so as to avoid and completely sidestep the cost-reducing spur of competition that should exist in the execution and processing of an order, getting it to and through the process of clearing on the floor of such exchange."[50] The suit asserted that the N.Y.S.E. was not

lawfully entitled to an antitrust exemption as the S.E.C. is not a
rate-setting body under the Securities Exchange Act of 1934. With
this lawsuit, the Exchange faced not only the loss of fixed commission revenue going forward, but the possibility of enormous damages relating to commissions collected over many years. (In June
1971, the suit was dismissed by Judge Inzer Wyatt on grounds that
it was not properly brought as a class action.)

THROUGHOUT OCTOBER, the staff of the S.E.C. prepared an
extremely confidential report based on its investigation of the
N.Y.S.E.'s enforcement of the net capital rule. The confidential report revealed that, during 1969, the Exchange loosened its interpretation of the rule, which, in effect, caused it to be less stringent
than the S.E.C. rule. The report pointed out that this not only dis-
guised capital deficiencies during 1969 and 1970, but very likely
established a climate that permitted capital problems in the industry to become even more acute than otherwise would have been
the case.[51] As a result of the S.E.C. investigation and report, the
Exchange was pressured to increase the haircuts applied to securities in calculating its net capital.[52] The haircuts for equities listed
on AMEX or actually traded in the O.T.C. market were increased
to 40 percent from 30 percent. The haircut for N.Y.S.E.-listed stocks
remained at 30 percent, but if equities of one issuer exceeded 10
percent of a firm's total net capital, a 45 percent haircut would be
applied. The haircut on equities listed on other exchanges or less
liquid O.T.C. stocks was increased to 50 percent from 30 percent
and excluded the most illiquid securities entirely. In addition, securities in subordinated accounts could not be counted as capital
unless they couldn't be withdrawn for at least a year. And when
such amounts were withdrawn, they had to be paid out equally over
twelve months.

■ ■ ■

THE S.E.C. ISSUED its response to the N.Y.S.E. rate proposal on October 22, 1970—and it was a bombshell. It determined that fixed rate commissions on transactions in excess of $100,000 were "unreasonable" as a matter of law.[53] This determination was a deathblow as far as antitrust compliance was concerned. The era of negotiated commission rates had begun, at least in the institutional market. The average mutual fund order was $150,000. The bifurcated market of negotiated rates for institutional trades and fixed rates for retail trades akin to the bond market as recommended by Donald Weeden was now a reality. In addition, the Commission held that the rate increases on trades involving 100 to 400 shares were also unreasonable and should be cut back by up to 50 percent.[54] Furthermore, the Commission insisted that the final rate schedule on 400-share or smaller orders be the maximum rates, not the minimum, and required those rates to be based on dollar value rather than number of shares. Furthermore, the Commission said it would prohibit any limitation on the size of customer accounts or orders and would not allow any additional fees or charges on small accounts. The Commission made it clear that its response was not subject to negotiation.[55]

The N.Y.S.E. was unwilling to accept these provisions. Despite being "non-negotiable," the Club fully intended to do everything within its power to preserve fixed commissions for as much business as possible.

CHAPTER FOURTEEN

"CARRIE NATION TIPPLING IN THE BASEMENT"

※

To the Brink Again and Back

On September 17, Goodbody & Co. agreed to be acquired by Shareholders Capital Corporation, a major publicly-traded mutual fund company, for a surprisingly low price of $9.4 million.[1] "We believe our clients, staff and employees will benefit substantially from broadened financial services, the permanent capital, and improved access to public capital markets which the combination will provide," said Goodbody's managing partner, Edward N. Bagley, putting a brave face on the obvious fire sale.[2]

Goodbody & Co., although much less valuable than Shareholders Capital Corporation, would constitute a significant majority of the combined firm's revenues, and since the "primary purpose" rule was calculated based on whether a majority of an entity's revenues (not profits) came from securities businesses, the merger complied with the N.Y.S.E.'s new rule. As a result of the proposed merger, Goodbody & Co. was to become the second publicly-traded member of the N.Y.S.E., after D.L.J. Again, Lee Arning and Bob Bishop appeared to have pulled off a miraculous shotgun wedding, leaving only F.I. duPont, Glore Forgan & Co. as a large firm in danger. But like the earlier Walston-Hayden, Stone engagement, Goodbody & Co. would be left at the altar.

The merger ran into trouble before the ink on the merger agreement was dry, but not because of concerns over an institutional shareholder owning a N.Y.S.E. member. Goodbody's fiscal year-end was August 30, just over two weeks before the merger agreement was signed. Goodbody's auditors, Ernst & Ernst, had completed the audit work by the second week of October and filed a preliminary report with respect to Goodbody's financial condition on October 15. Under the terms of the merger agreement, Shareholders Capital Corporation executives likewise received a copy of this preliminary report and were aghast. Goodbody's books and records were in such a state that a traditional balance sheet couldn't be prepared. Instead, "suspense accounts" of $4.1 million and $8.6 million were established to reconcile cash balances and short securities positions, respectively. Stock record differences totaled $12.8 million long and $9 million short. Aged dividends and interest receivable amounted to $5 million and customers owed the firm $2.2 million that was unsecured by any collateral. Customer securities that were fully paid and, accordingly, should have been segregated, but weren't, totaled $53.2 million.[3]

Goodbody was in violation of the net capital rule and clearly had been for months. This was not news to the upper echelon of the Club but certainly was to Shareholders Capital Corporation, which terminated the merger agreement literally the next day. Goodbody had never been mentioned by Robert Haack or Ralph DeNunzio to Congress as one of the failing firms. In fact in August 1970, the Exchange approved Goodbody's opening of a new branch office— always taken as a sign in those days that a firm was sound financially. In truth, Goodbody had for months been a special project of the Crisis Committee, but as the fifth largest investment bank, it was too big to fail, so extraordinary secrecy was used in handling its rescue. Bunny Lasker, Ralph DeNunzio, Felix Rohatyn, Lee Arning, and Bob Bishop all breathed much easier when the September 17 merger agreement was signed. When it was torn up on October 16, publicly, rumors of Goodbody's impending collapse spread like wildfire. The Crisis Committee went into full crisis mode.

The first line of defense was to quickly find another merger partner for Goodbody. This, miraculously, was accomplished when

Arthur L. Carter, the deposed former partner of Roger Berlind, Sandy Weill, and Arthur Levitt Jr. and the original "C" in C.B.W.L., appeared, prepared to execute an agreement in record time. Carter, through his new company, Utilities and Industries Corporation, was itching to get his hands on another major Wall Street firm.[4] Goodbody's 95 branch offices and 250,000 customers would put Carter in control of a firm larger even than the newly-merged CBWL-Hayden, Stone, Inc. Carter proposed a transaction whereby Utilities and Industries Corporation would invest $15 million in Goodbody for a 44 percent profit interest and a 56 percent voting interest, and Robert and Laurence Tisch, through Loew's Theatres, Inc., would invest $5 million for a 12 percent non-voting preferred profit-sharing interest. The remaining economic and voting equity interests would be distributed among Goodbody's existing partners.[5] Arthur Carter and James E. Hogle, chairman of Goodbody, put out a joint press release on October 16, which said: "Details of the investment have been presented to the N.Y.S.E., which has expressed no objection."[6] The transaction required approval of the Exchange as well as the S.E.C. and was also conditioned on subordinated lenders of at least $31 million of the total of $35 million agreeing to extend their loans to Goodbody for at least a year. Importantly, no definitive agreement had been signed by the Carter-Tisch group.

The Carter-Tisch group's deal with Goodbody began to fall apart over the weekend of October 24–25. The subordinated lenders were balking about extending, and it became clear to Arthur Carter that $20 million of new capital would not be enough to solve Goodbody's financial issues. On Monday, October 26, Carter pulled out of the deal.[7] In a stroke of unbelievably bad timing, the S.E.C., as part of its public notice disclosure requirements in the approval process for the Carter-Tisch deal, revealed that the N.Y.S.E. had informed Goodbody that it would be suspended from operating if the capital infusion did not take place by November 5, 1970.[8] The Commission also revealed that the Carter-Tisch group was the only party that had expressed any interest in investing in Goodbody.

On Tuesday, October 27, with the news that the Carter-Tisch deal had fallen apart not yet publicly known, Bunny Lasker called an emergency meeting of the Crisis Committee to which he invited top officials of the thirty largest investment banks for the purpose of arranging an industry bailout of Goodbody.[9] Lasker outlined five options he concluded were available: First, let Goodbody fail—this was out of the question as a financial disaster would inevitably result. Second, assess the entire membership of the Exchange to fund a bailout—this, too, was out of the question as there was not time to call a membership meeting. Third, form a consortium of ten or so large investment banks to provide a loan to Goodbody. Fourth, split Goodbody up among a number of houses. Fifth, find one investment bank to buy all of Goodbody & Co. with the Exchange providing some financial guarantee. The meeting participants quickly concluded that options three and four could not be accomplished in the nine remaining days before the November 5 deadline, given the complexity of such multi-party negotiations.[10]

Only three firms expressed any willingness to even entertain buying Goodbody: Reynolds & Co.; Paine, Webber, Jackson & Curtis; and Merrill Lynch.[11] It was apparent to all that the only firm of the three that the others were willing to risk the survival of Wall Street on was Merrill Lynch. The talks quickly settled into what terms Donald Regan would insist on to take Goodbody.

Donald Regan quietly appraised the situation and concluded it presented a tremendous opportunity for Merrill Lynch. Under normal circumstances in those days, the Antitrust Division of the Department of Justice would never allow the number one market share firm—by a wide margin—to acquire the number five market share firm. But because of the panic on Wall Street over the meltdown all predicted would result from a Goodbody free fall into bankruptcy, the Justice Department informally assured Regan that it would apply the "failing firm" doctrine to the acquisition and not object to it.[12] Merrill Lynch had branch offices in nearly every city Goodbody had them. Accordingly, Regan saw enormous cost savings in closing those duplicative offices while retaining Good-body's 250,000 customers.[13] Nonetheless, Don Regan's terms were steep.

Merrill Lynch proposed loaning Goodbody $15 million prior to the November 5 deadline as a first step and thereafter acquiring all of Goodbody's equity in a second step as promptly as possible in exchange for guaranteeing its customer accounts.[14] The Exchange agreed to guarantee the payment of up to $20 million of contingent liabilities, if they ultimately become payable, and agreed to indemnify Merrill Lynch against the first $10 million of litigation expenses and judgments that might arise against Goodbody after the closing of the acquisition.[15] The Exchange proposed backstopping those obligations by a special assessment authority to be granted to the Exchange by way of an amendment to the Exchange's constitution to be approved by the board of governors of the N.Y.S.E. at a special meeting called for November 4—the day before the Exchange's deadline for the Goodbody capital infusion—and by vote of Exchange members promptly thereafter.[16] Regan had one other unusual condition—if any of the other top twenty largest N.Y.S.E. member firms were suspended or voluntarily withdrew from the Exchange because of financial concerns prior to the closing date for the second-step acquisition, Merrill Lynch could unwind the entire deal.[17] If another systemic threat emerged that quickly, Donald Regan was not going to allow Merrill Lynch to have to weather the storm with Goodbody weighing it down.

On November 4, the board of governors of the Exchange approved the constitutional amendment to permit the transaction. On November 5, Merrill Lynch formally executed the definitive merger agreement and provided the $15 million subordinated loan in the form of U.S. Treasury securities to Goodbody.[18] The vote of Exchange members on the constitutional amendment was expected to occur in the first week of December.[19] At a press conference at Merrill Lynch's 70 Pine Street headquarters to announce the definitive merger agreement, Donald Regan stated that "Merrill Lynch entered into the affair at the request of the N.Y.S.E., which advised

Merrill Lynch that no assistance to Goodbody from other sources could be found. At the time of its entry, Merrill Lynch made clear that it was acting out of concern for the customers of Goodbody, who otherwise would have been put in financial jeopardy."[20]

In the aftermath of the Merrill Lynch–Goodbody deal, there was serious dissatisfaction expressed by a sizable minority of the membership of the Exchange who thought Donald Regan had outsmarted Felix Rohatyn and the rest of the Crisis Committee with the $30 million backstop. To preempt an organized opposition to the approval of the constitutional amendment, Robert Haack put out an unusual urgent plea to vote in favor of the amendment to Exchange members on November 12. "The shock waves of Goodbody's failure would be felt in some measure by every other firm, no matter how large," Haack wrote. "Public confidence in this industry could be lost for many years to come."[21]

ON OCTOBER 29, 1970, the New York Regional Office of the S.E.C. sent a memorandum to the members of the Commission in Washington detailing the continuing serious financial problems at F. I. duPont, Glore Forgan & Co.[22] As of its latest fiscal year-end, September 28, 1970, the firm had long stock record differences of $20,630,000 and short stock record differences of $33,132,000.[23] In addition, the firm had a net negative cash difference of $8,600,000. Furthermore, its margin accounts were under margined by $7,800,000.[24] It was clear to Hamer Budge—as well as to the Crisis Committee—that the rescue of F.I. duPont, Glore Forgan was essential to resolving the crisis.

The firm had lost another $550,000 in October and had essentially run out of cash, exhausting all internal options to raise capital. When Robert Bishop of the N.Y.S.E. saw F. I. duPont, Glore Forgan's financial statements for October, he informed Lee Arning, Robert Haack, and the members of the Crisis Committee that a bailout was needed immediately. Robert Haack called Edmund duPont to the Exchange and insisted he seek capital from the last remaining likely source—the duPont family. Haack and Edmund duPont traveled to Wilmington, Delaware, to meet with Lammot duPont Copeland Sr., chairman of the board of directors of E. I. duPont & Co., to ask for an investment. To the shock and horror of Haack, Copeland emphatically refused to invest even a penny.[25] Haack and the Crisis Committee now faced the real possibility of an F. I. duPont, Glore Forgan bankruptcy, which, pursuant to Donald Regan's merger agreement with Goodbody, would also mean a Goodbody bankruptcy, as Merrill Lynch would certainly terminate the merger agreement by invoking the "no top twenty firm failure" condition. The simultaneous failures of the second and fifth largest Wall Street firms would undoubtedly set off a chain reaction of additional failures, which would not be confined to the securities industry. The commercial banking system would also be at risk.

On November 5, the same day Merrill Lynch signed the Goodbody merger agreement, Robert Bishop ordered Wallace Latour at F. I. duPont, Glore Forgan to liquidate all securities in subordinated accounts to raise cash.[26] Those securities included 100,000 shares of E.D.S. stock that Ross Perot had contributed to F. I. duPont, Glore Forgan as part of his investment in the firm.[27] The timing for this could not have been worse, as E.D.S. at that very moment was in the market with a 500,000-share secondary offering underwritten by R. W. Pressprich, Ken Langone's investment bank.[28] Lee Arning from the N.Y.S.E. called Langone to see if the offering could be upsized to 600,000 shares to accommodate a sale of the F. I. duPont, Glore Forgan stake. Langone was shocked by the inquiry; he, like nearly everyone on Wall Street at the time, believed the earlier Perot investment had stabilized the firm. He told Arning he could sell the extra 100,000 shares without significantly affecting the price, but that he had to inform Ross Perot of the inquiry. Lee Arning had worse news for Langone: the proceeds of the 100,000 E.D.S. stock shares would not be enough to steady F. I. duPont, Glore Forgan. An additional $5 million of capital was needed.[29] Langone told Arning he better call Perot himself. Lee Arning called Ross Perot and explained the gravity of the situation

and asked Perot to include the 100,000 shares in his secondary offering and loan F. I. duPont, Glore Forgan $5 million. Perot ex-
pressed no emotion, saying he would think about it.

Within days, Lee Arning received updated financials from F. I.
duPont, Glore Forgan. It turned out that a $5 million loan would
not suffice—$10 million would be needed.[30] With no other option,
Lee Arning called Perot and told him the request was now $10
million, not $5 million. Perot couldn't believe what he was hearing.
How could a firm not realize it needed another $5 million only
days earlier? Perot gave Arning his answer there and then: he would
not invest further in F. I. duPont, Glore Forgan. Arning immediately informed Robert Haack, Bunny Lasker, and Felix Rohatyn of
Perot's response. Lasker knew Perot was their only option. Congress would not create S.I.P.C. if it knew F. I. duPont, Glore Forgan
and Goodbody would need to be bailed out. Many members of the
N.Y.S.E. would rather resign membership than pay the assessments
that would be needed for the bailout of those two firms—Morgan
Stanley, Kuhn Loeb, and Dillon Read were already threatening to
do so over the guarantees provided to Merrill Lynch in the Goodbody deal.[31]

Bunny Lasker set in motion a lobbying plan at the highest levels
to bring Ross Perot back to the table.

ROSS PEROT WAS hardly Bunny Lasker's only problem. Congress watched the Goodbody saga unfold with incredulity and an-
ger. Three months earlier, the N.Y.S.E. had assured Congress that
only the ten firms identified by the Exchange were at risk of failing.
Since then, four unnamed firms had failed—First Devonshire Corporation, Charles Plohn & Co., Robinson & Co., Inc., and now
Goodbody & Co. The Exchange refused to assist the customers of
the first three firms, but now was going so far as to amend its constitution to assist Goodbody customers. On November 16, the
broker-dealer insurance bill reported out by the House Committee
on Interstate and Foreign Commerce was scheduled to be voted on

by the House of Representatives, but Representative John Moss pulled the bill off the calendar pending answers to his concerns.[32] He suggested that changes would be made to the House bill, including raising the maximum annual assessments of S.I.P.C. and eliminating industry control of the S.I.P.C. board when no Treasury loans are outstanding.[33] To try to prevent the strengthening of the bill, Robert Haack promised to respond to all the congressmen's questions in person during a closed-door hearing the following morning.[34]

The congressmen were not persuaded by Haack's explanations on the morning of November 17 and instead announced that the bill would be amended on the floor of the House to double the maximum annual assessment from 0.50 percent of industry gross revenue to 1 percent of industry gross revenue, and the N.Y.S.E. must publicly commit to bail out, if needed, the customers of First Devonshire Corporation, Charles Plohn & Co., and Robinson & Co., Inc.[35]

The adverse modification of the House version of the broker-dealer insurance bill was not even the low point of Haack's day. That would come at his speech before the 1,200 members of the New York Economic Club at their dinner at the Waldorf Astoria that evening.

WITH A CONTENTIOUS rate proceeding pending in front of the S.E.C., a member vote on a constitutional amendment providing for a costly special assessment of Exchange members in connection with the collapse of Goodbody also pending, Congress insisting the Exchange members take costly financial responsibility for three other failed firms, F. I. duPont, Glore Forgan within days of bankruptcy, dozens of other member firms teetering on the edge of insolvency, and the industry as a whole losing money, it is safe to assume that not a soul would have predicted that Robert Haack, president of the N.Y.S.E., would address the assembled business leaders of New York and call for the end of fixed commissions, which would inevitably drive dozens more member firms out of business, either by way of insolvency or into the arms of the handful of large, well-capitalized firms. Yet that is exactly what Robert Haack did on November 17, 1970.

He opened his speech before the New York Economic Club with a disclaimer stating that the views he was about to express were his alone and did not necessarily represent those of the board of governors of the Exchange, but quickly got to the point: "Notwithstanding my own previous personal and strong support of fixed commissions, I believe that it now behooves our industry leaders to rethink their personal judgments on negotiated rates. While I question whether or not the industry is presently sufficiently strong financially to completely disregard fixed minimum rates, I personally think it might well consider full negotiated rates as an ultimate objective."[36]

Haack didn't leave it at that. "Bluntly stated," Haack continued, "the securities industry, more than any other industry in America, engages in mazes of blatant gimmickry." Speaking of the Exchange, Haack critically referenced its "numerous archaic and anachronistic practices and procedures."[37] "Whatever vestiges of a private club atmosphere remain at the New York Stock Exchange must be discarded," Haack proclaimed. "In the near future, I will be presenting definitive proposals to our board . . . which hopefully, will lead to a major restructuring of the New York Stock Exchange. The Exchange must, in my opinion, do all that it can to be a most efficient, businesslike organization, responsive to the needs of the public and the membership, if it is to continue to serve as the marketplace it has been for 178 years."[38]

In closing, Haack said, "I would entreat our members to harmonize the many diverse interests which make up the brokerage business, for it is my fear that we are tearing ourselves asunder and risking loss of our central marketplace in the process. If our industry blunts its differences for the common good, and positions itself more competitively, this country will continue to enjoy the significant benefits of having a premier marketplace for securities."[39]

■ ■ ■

THE RESPONSE TO Haack's speech in the press fueled its provocation. "If Mr. Haack had dropped a bomb on the trading floor," the *Wall Street Journal* commented, "he hardly could have caused more commotion."[40] The response from the Club was immediate and predictable. "All kinds of hell broke loose," Lee Arning recalled.[41] The official response from the N.Y.S.E. came by way of a terse press release from Bunny Lasker, chairman of the Exchange: "The policy of the New York Stock Exchange is made by the board of governors and not by the president, who is responsible for the administration of the Exchange under the constitution."[42] Privately, Lasker was furious. He was not a fan of Haack even before the speech, thinking him effete, spineless, and ineffectual.[43] John Coleman thought Haack should be summarily dismissed.[44] John Loeb Sr. and Clifford Michel of Loeb, Rhodes & Co., long unhappy with Haack, had a month earlier sounded out Ralph Saul of AMEX about taking the job at the Big Board. They now advocated that the board of governors make him a formal offer.[45] Gus Levy was more measured. He told the press: "I'm for fixed rates. Bob is a close friend of mine. He did not discuss the speech with me. He's entitled to his opinion, but I happen to disagree with him."[46] Cooler heads prevailed, as a majority of the governors agreed that the negative press and adverse reaction from Congress and the S.E.C. that would result from firing Haack would pose an unacceptable risk at that time with all the Exchange had to deal with.

Haack's only official punishment was a dressing-down by the board of governors, leaked to the press, but his diminished power was soon apparent.[47] He was removed as the principal negotiator of the rate schedule with the S.E.C., replaced by Bunny Lasker.[48] Lasker pleaded with the S.E.C. and lobbied his friends in Congress to pressure the S.E.C. to raise the dollar threshold for unfixing commission rates and to permit larger rate increases on 400 and fewer share orders. Those negotiations were complicated by the resignation of S.E.C. chairman Hamer Budge, who had come under strong criticism, much of it emanating from the New York Regional Office, for the failure of the Commission to have taken more aggressive measures to prevent the wave of insolvencies on Wall Street. President Nixon requested that Budge stay on as chairman until the end of the congressional session, given the uncertainty surrounding the broker-dealer insurance bill.[49]

One casualty of the Haack speech was John Cunningham, Haack's right-hand man and the executive vice president of the N.Y.S.E. Cunningham had crossed swords with Bunny Lasker frequently and was also criticized for being heavy-handed with many member firms in implementing C.C.S., although his defenders credited his approach with getting the system operational. In any event, on November 22, 1970, Cunningham's resignation was announced.[50] The letter indicated that Cunningham had submitted his resignation on November 16—the day before Haack's speech—although many believe that date was a contrivance to save Haack and the board of governors the embarrassment of linking his departure to the controversy. In truth, Haack had been encouraging Cunningham to find another job for some time out of fear Bunny Lasker or another disgruntled governor would have him fired.[51]

Some, however, supported Haack's speech. Billy Salomon, managing partner of Salomon Brothers, publicly praised Haack and gave his support to ending fixed commission rates: "When there is reflection, people will probably be happy these things are out in the open."[52] Donald Regan was more colorful in his praise of Haack's speech: "Part of the preparation is to rid ourselves of useless weight. The first relic to be chucked overboard is the fixed commission structure. Wall Street is hiding behind a protective pricing system, while it preaches free competition and free markets. That is like catching Carrie Nation tippling in the basement. We say that competition is good for everyone."[53]

BUNNY LASKER'S LOBBYING campaign to change Ross Perot's mind about the $10 million investment in F. I. duPont, Glore

Forgan focused on one person—President Nixon. Both Lasker and Perot had raised substantial sums for Nixon's 1968 campaign, so Lasker concluded that getting Nixon to intervene with an appeal to Perot's patriotism was his best bet. Lasker was a frequent guest at the Nixon White House so access to the president was not a problem. Lasker called the president and told him that without a Perot investment, F. I. duPont, Glore Forgan would fail—which, in turn, would cause Merrill Lynch to pull out of the Goodbody merger resulting in Goodbody's failure.[54] The likely outcome of this, Lasker told Nixon, would be the collapse of dozens of other firms and the collapse of trading of securities, seizing up the flow of capital to American businesses and likely endangering the commercial banking system. A deep recession—or worse—would inescapably result, Lasker warned. In short, a financial crisis not seen since the Great Depression.[55]

Nixon listened to Lasker's dire predictions and believed every word of them. He was not in an optimistic mood in late November 1970. The Democrats had gained twelve seats in the House of Representatives in the November 3, 1970, midterm election, and Nixon's reelection chances were looking uncertain.[56]

Nixon charged his attorney general, John Mitchell, with the urgent task of bringing Ross Perot around.[57] Mitchell knew Lasker well and quickly grasped the seriousness of the situation. He called Perot and conveyed the strong concern of the president about the crisis and the gratitude the president would have if Perot could find a way to come up with $10 million. He would be a hero, perhaps the savior of the American economy, preventing another Great Depression. Perot told Mitchell he was very sorry about the straits F. I. duPont, Glore Forgan found itself in, but he did not cause them, and his "no" was final.[58]

President Nixon, miffed and surprised, thought that if appeals to Perot's Americanism didn't work, perhaps an appeal to him as a Texan might. Nixon reached out to former Texas governor John Connally, a conservative Democrat then in talks with Nixon regarding a cabinet position (he would be named Secretary of the

Treasury in 1971), and asked him to have a go at Ross. Connally, eager to demonstrate his effectiveness to Nixon, immediately called Perot. Like Mitchell, Connally got nowhere.[59] Next, Nixon tried out his chief White House economic advisor, former Dillon, Read & Co. partner Peter Flanigan. Flanigan struck out as well. Out of options, John Mitchell tried one last time, pleading with Perot. Somehow, he got Perot to agree that if Mitchell called every other possible investor in F. I. duPont, Glore Forgan and none would bite, Perot would reconsider.[60] Mitchell, in good faith, called every possible firm he could think of. None bit.[61] Perot, undoubtedly hearing from Langone and others that Mitchell had in fact made a broad market check, kept his word. Perot laid out his proposal to Mitchell. Mitchell knew Perot was a clever and tough negotiator, but he marveled at the audacity of Perot's offer.

If Merrill Lynch could get an exemption from the antitrust laws to acquire Goodbody, why couldn't he get an exemption from the tax laws, Perot reasoned, given that President Nixon was trotting out all his administration's heavy artillery. The structure of Perot's deal was as follows: Perot would borrow $10 million from his bank, use the proceeds to acquire tax-free municipal bonds, and contribute those municipal bonds to F. I. duPont, Glore Forgan in the form of a subordinated loan. Within ninety days of the making of such loan, F. I. duPont, Glore Forgan would be required to convert to a corporation, and Perot would have the right to exchange $1.5 million of the municipal bonds in his subordinated account for 51 percent of the stock of the corporation, giving him voting control. As Perot did not want the 100,000 shares of E.D.S. stock owned by F. I. duPont, Glore Forgan dumped on the market, the existing partners of F. I. duPont, Glore Forgan would be required to collectively contribute $5 million of new capital to the firm.[62]

The tax issue with this structure was that the Internal Revenue Service had ruled that interest expense on a loan was not tax deductible to the extent the proceeds of the loan were used to buy tax-free municipal bonds. That, Perot told Mitchell, was his problem to solve, as Perot would not do the deal without a letter ruling from the I.R.S. that an exception would be made in the case of Ross Perot.[63]

John Mitchell solved that problem. He made it clear to the I.R.S. that neither he nor the president cared what the I.R.S.'s position was, Ross Perot was going to get that tax letter. After a bit of hand-wringing, the bureaucrats held their noses and hand-delivered the letter to a waiting Ross Perot in the lobby of the Internal Revenue Service headquarters in Washington, D.C.[64]

WALLACE LATOUR'S PARTNERS at F. I. duPont, Glore Forgan proved a more difficult constituency. A clique of partners thought selling Ross Perot control and 51 percent of all future profits for $1.5 million was an outrage and was threatening to hold out, and a unanimous vote of the partners was needed to convert from a partnership to a corporation. Hearing of this, Bunny Lasker was apoplectic. Reminiscent of Keith Funston's threat in November 1963 to blackball any partner of Ira Haupt & Co. who did not go along with the bailout plan, Lasker called Edmund duPont on the carpet at the N.Y.S.E. and made it clear to him that any partner of his who didn't go along with Perot's plan would never work on Wall Street again. Word of the dressing-down spread and the insurrection was quickly quelled.[65]

On November 25, rumors were swirling around Wall Street that F.I. duPont, Glore Forgan would fail imminently.[66] Fearing the deal with Perot might not hold, Wallace Latour called a press conference for 4:30 p.m. on November 25, 1970, to announce the transaction.[67] The announcement of the press conference only intensified the rumors. The rumor-mongering got so bad that AMEX officials sanctioned two floor members for spreading the rumor that the duPont family planned to pull their capital out of the firm the minute the Merrill Lynch–Goodbody deal closed. At the press conference, Latour announced the capital infusion by Perot, which ended the rumors of impending collapse.[68]

Despite achieving its intended effect, Latour's announcement was reckless and possibly illegal. Perot had not yet signed an agreement to do the deal, and the logistics of preparing and executing definitive documentation would likely take three weeks. This, Wallace Latour did not tell the press. He also materially misrepresented the terms of the deal. Latour said that "a group headed by H. Ross Perot" would be making a capital infusion of at least $15 million, omitting the fact that $5 million was required by Perot to come from existing partners. Latour also said that Perot's $15 million capital infusion would be in the form of a subordinated loan that would not give Perot equity ownership in the firm, not mentioning that ninety days after closing Perot could convert $1.5 million of the subordinated loan into 51 percent of the equity of the firm.

Shortly after Latour's press conference, Sam Freedman, an E.D.S. employee in New York heading up the financial due diligence team for Perot on the F. I. duPont, Glore Forgan deal, made a panicked call to Perot, who was in New York, staying at the Waldorf Astoria hotel. Perot had Freedman come right over and the executive laid out for Perot in detail irrefutable proof that the financial statements of F. I. duPont, Glore Forgan that Perot had been provided were inaccurate and that the company's true financial condition was far, far worse than he had been told.[69] Perot saw in black and white that Wallace Latour and Edmund duPont had misled him. But he also realized immediately that he had been successfully played. The deal was announced. He had given his word to President Nixon.

If he pulled out of the deal now, the Club would spin the story to paint Perot as an opportunist, the recipient of a sweetheart deal from the I.R.S. that shortchanged American taxpayers by capitalizing on a pending financial crisis. The worst-case scenario outlined by John Mitchell might well come to pass and every aspect of Ross Perot's conduct leading up to the meltdown of Wall Street and the inevitable commercial banking crisis and economic recession that would result would be scrutinized in excruciating detail. He would no longer be the heroic, patriotic Texan championing the cause of the Vietnam POWs. He would be portrayed by the Wall Street crowd to their friends in the press and Congress as the villain, the opportunist, the coward. This, Ross Perot could not endure, the $10 million be damned. He thanked Freedman and told him to mention nothing of it to anyone else. On December 15, 1970, Ross Perot and every partner of F. I. duPont, Glore Forgan signed the definitive agreement. A smiling Bunny Lasker told the press the financial crisis was over: "I think we can safely say that we are aware of no major firm that is in danger at the present time."[70]

THE CRISIS WOULD not really be over, however, if the broker-dealer insurance bill didn't pass before the congressional recess. A new Congress would be sworn in in January 1971 and the procedural realities were such that if the bill did not pass both houses by year-end, it might be March 1971—or later—before it became law. With dozens of firms barely hanging on, a run on investment banks by their customers could have literally happened at any minute. Wall Street breathed easier on December 1, 1970, when the U.S. House of Representatives passed its version of the bill by a vote of 359 to 3.[71] There was some debate on the composition of the S.I.P.C. board, and Manny Celler and Representative H. R. Gross, a Republican of Iowa, proposed an amendment to provide for public rather than industry control of the board, but the amendment failed.[72]

On December 10, 1970, the Senate passed its version of the bill, which differed from the House bill in that it provided for public control of the S.I.P.C. board and, by way of a floor amendment, set forth detailed requirements for brokers and dealers with respect to custody and use of customer securities and enhanced the qualification requirements for new brokers and dealers.[73] A conference committee was appointed to reconcile the bills, with instructions to report in time for year-end passage by both houses.

More good news came that week when the members of the N.Y.S.E. approved the constitutional amendment to provide for the assessments that might be necessary to fund the indemnity given to Merrill Lynch in connection with the Goodbody acquisition. It was approved by a vote of 1,027 to 164, a margin of greater than six to one. On December 11, 1970, Merrill Lynch closed the acquisition.[74]

THE HOUSE-SENATE CONFERENCE committee on the broker-dealer legislation completed its work on a compromise bill on December 18.[75] The S.I.P.C. board of directors would be controlled by the public and governmental representatives, four to three. Of the seven members, one member, a Treasury Department official, would be designated by the Secretary of the Treasury; one member, a member of the Federal Reserve Board, would be designated by the Federal Reserve Board; and five members would be appointed by the president with the advice and consent of the Senate, three of which would be representatives of the securities industry and the remaining two chosen from the general public.[76]

The detailed requirements regarding custody and use of customer securities and admission of new brokers and dealers were excluded from the compromise bill, but the S.E.C. was granted broad powers to enact regulations with respect to such matters and required the S.E.C. to set a reserve requirement against customer cash, in the form of cash or U.S. Treasury securities. In addition, a provision was added requiring the S.E.C. to make a study of unsafe and unsound practices by brokers and dealers and deliver a report thereon to the Congress within a year with recommendations for additional legislation. The final bill did not require the N.Y.S.E. to bail out the customers of First Devonshire Corporation, Charles Plohn & Co., or Robinson & Co., Inc., but Robert Haack gave written assurance to the Senate Banking Committee that the Exchange would do so. Senator Muskie made it clear that if the Exchange did not make good on this promise, there would be a wide-ranging Senate investigation of the N.Y.S.E.[77]

On December 21, the House passed the compromise bill. The next day, the Senate followed suit, despite a threatened filibuster by Republican Edward Brooke of Massachusetts and Democrat William Proxmire of Wisconsin over the failure to include the detailed requirements regarding custody and use of customer securities in the final bill.[78] A last-minute letter to Senator John Sparkman of Alabama, chairman of the Senate Banking and Currency Committee, from S.E.C. member Hugh Owens pledging prompt enactment of strict regulations regarding custody and use of customer securities persuaded Brooke and Proxmire to abandon their threatened filibuster.

On December 29, Ross Perot settled the score with Edmund duPont and Wallace Latour. In a terse press release that day, F. I. duPont, Glore Forgan announced that Edmund duPont, son of the founder of the firm, had been replaced as chairman with John W. Allyn, a partner in the Chicago office and the principal owner of the Chicago White Sox, and that Latour had been replaced with Harold A. Rousselot. Sources told the *New York Times* that the removals were "connected with the complex and sometimes tense negotiations involving the Perot financing" and also related to Mr. duPont's "inability to bring together certain financing from the duPont family."[79]

On December 30, 1970, President Nixon signed the Securities Investor Protection Act creating S.I.P.C. and providing for the bailout of the securities industry.[80] Nixon also announced the members of its initial board of directors: Bruce K. MacLaury, Undersecretary of the Treasury for Monetary Affairs; J. Charles Partee, Adviser to the Federal Reserve Board; Byron D. Woodside, a former S.E.C. commissioner, who would be chairman of the S.I.P.C. board; George J. Stigler, Professor of Economics at the University of Chicago; Glenn E. Anderson, President and Director of the Carolina Securities Corporation; Andrew J. Melton Jr., Chairman of the Executive Committee of Smith Barney & Co.; and Donald T. Regan of Merrill Lynch, who never wanted the government bailout.

■ ■ ■

BUNNY LASKER, Ralph DeNunzio, John Coleman, and the rest of the Club knew that from that point on, the numbers wouldn't matter. Since the U. S. Treasury had agreed to backstop S.I.P.C. for $1 billion, it would come up with $100 billion, if need be, rather than allow a U.S. government–sponsored insurance company to fail. For agreeing to hold the customers of First Devonshire Corporation, Charles Plohn & Co., and Robinson & Co., Inc. harmless, the N.Y.S.E. bought itself out of a number of class action lawsuits and a United States Senate investigation. The Exchange would later assess its members $20 million for that purpose. Congress and the country's attention quickly turned back to Vietnam, the radicals in the anti-war movement, and the deep divisions in American society.

All things considered, it was a great deal for Wall Street. There would be no Pecora-like hearings. There was bipartisan agreement on that. The Democrats didn't want hearings that would embarrass Larry O'Brien, who had been elected chairman of the Democratic National Committee again weeks after resigning from McDonnell & Co. Neither did the Republicans: Peter Flanigan, Nixon's chief White House economic adviser, married to Murray McDonnell's sister and facilitator of Hayden, Stone's tax returns, would no doubt have been grilled at such hearings; Maurice Stans, Nixon's Secretary of Commerce and former managing partner of Glore Forgan, would not have fared well either; John Mitchell, attorney general, who orchestrated Ross Perot's favorable tax ruling, certainly didn't want an inquiry; and Bill Casey, soon to be confirmed as chairman of the S.E.C., most definitely did not want questions asked regarding what he knew about F.I. duPont, Glore Forgan's net capital rule compliance. Not a single executive from a Wall Street firm or the N.Y.S.E. was indicted.

In 1933, as the pound of flesh taken in exchange for the bailout of the commercial banks through the creation of the F.D.I.C., commercial banks were required to divest themselves of all their investment banking operations and became subject to stricter prudential regulation limiting their risk-taking. There were no meaningful additional regulations limiting risks at the investment banks imposed as a condition to S.I.P.C. In order to join the F.D.I.C., commercial banks were subject to inspections in order to demonstrate that they were solvent before given membership. No such condition was imposed to becoming a member of S.I.P.C.—the good, the bad, and the ugly were all welcomed with open arms. None of this slowed down Nixon or the Democratic Congress in pushing through the bailout bill in December 1970. The Club proved that it's easier to fool people than to convince them they've been fooled.

Although Wall Street avoided a catastrophic outcome—and the most knowledgeable in the Club knew how close they had come to a collapse of the N.Y.S.E. and with it the banking system and the entire economy—the toll taken by the back-office crisis was enormous. More than a hundred N.Y.S.E. member firms went out of business, by merger or insolvency, between 1968 and 1970, seventy-three in 1970 alone. Many hundreds of small brokerage firms throughout the country also shut their doors. Nearly 17,000 jobs were lost on Wall Street and tens of thousands more in supporting industries. The capital lost by partners, shareholders, and lenders has never been definitively calculated, but it is estimated to be in the tens of billions of dollars.

Most significantly, "moral hazard" and "implicit government guarantee" became operative phrases on Wall Street thereafter. The seeds had been sown for even greater risk-taking—and government bailouts—a generation later.

EPILOGUE

"Nobody Knows Anything"

Representative Haley Staggers was not convinced that the N.Y.S.E. and the S.E.C. had been completely forthright with Congress during the hearings over the Securities Investor Protection Act. In early 1971, he authorized the Special Subcommittee on Investigations under his Committee on Interstate and Foreign Commerce to perform an in-depth review of S.E.C. records to get a better idea of what had happened and what should be done to prevent it from happening again. The results of that investigation convinced Staggers that more examination was warranted. He directed Representative John Moss to have his Subcommittee on Commerce and Finance begin such an inquiry. On December 28, 1971, Moss published the subcommittee's report, which included a number of legislative recommendations, including abolishing fixed commissions; opening membership on national securities exchanges to institutional investors; eliminating anticompetitive practices such as the N.Y.S.E.'s Rule 394, which prohibited members engaging in transactions off the Exchange in Exchange-listed stocks; increasing criminal penalties for violation of the securities laws; increasing capital requirements; bolstering accounting and auditing standards; and creating national systems of securities depositories and clearing and settlement.

On the same day, S.E.C. Chairman William Casey delivered to the Senate and the House of Representatives the S.E.C.'s Study of Unsafe and Unsound Practices of Brokers and Dealers that was mandated by the Securities Investor Protection Act. Casey's report diagnosed most of the same underlying causes as Moss's report. In terms of S.E.C. actions, Casey recommended tightening the net capital rule to lower the maximum allowed ratio to 15-to-1, prohibiting withdrawals of capital and requiring contraction of business when the ratio exceeded 12-to-1, prohibiting expansion of business when the ratio exceeded 10-to-1, increasing haircuts on securities, and instituting immediate charges to capital for net short differences. Casey also recommended S.E.C. rule-making to require immediate buy-ins to settle net short differences, mandate quarterly physical inventory counts, segregate customer cash and securities, toughen new entry requirements for brokers and dealers, require use of C.U.S.I.P. numbers and Depository Trust Company global certificate services, and implement an industrywide O.T.C. market clearing and settlement system. Casey requested legislative changes to allow the S.E.C. to regulate transfer agents, to grant the S.E.C. broader powers to require approval of all rules by securities exchanges, and to give the S.E.C. power to require harsher sanctions by the securities exchanges for rule violations.

IN NOVEMBER 1972, the S.E.C. enacted the first major new rule in response to the various investigations and recommendations arising out of the back-office crisis. To protect customer cash and securities, the Commission adopted Rule 15c3-3, which requires that each investment bank must tally up at least once per week what the firm owes to its customers and what customers owe the firm, and if the amount owed by the firm exceeds the amount owed to it, the firm must deposit cash and securities representing such excess into a special reserve bank account for the exclusive benefit of customers and segregated from the firm's other accounts. While weaker than many reformers had hoped, the rule represented the first attempt to prevent customer cash from being essentially free working capital for investment banks.

In 1975, the S.E.C. finally revoked the N.Y.S.E.'s exemption from the S.E.C. net capital rule, adopting an industrywide rule with a maximum 15-to-1 ratio and with specifically-mandated haircuts and limitations on withdrawals of capital. In 2004, the S.E.C. fundamentally changed the net capital rule for the largest broker-dealers— those with $5 billion of capital or more—allowing for holding company regulation and modeling of risk rather than using the traditional calculation. The S.E.C. called this novel approach its Consolidated Supervised Entities, or C.S.E., program. All five eligible broker-dealers—Bear, Stearns; Lehman Brothers; Merrill Lynch; Goldman, Sachs; and Morgan Stanley—selected the new approach. While intended to better measure aggregate risk of the corporate families these investment banks were members of, the modeling in practice allowed these firms to substantially increase leverage—in some cases resulting in net capital ratios as high as 40-to-1. Many market observers believe the weakening of the net capital rule through the C.S.E. program was a significant cause— and some believe the most significant cause—of the 2008 financial crisis.

THE INTENSE LOBBYING by Bunny Lasker and Ralph DeNunzio to raise the dollar threshold for unfixed commission rates from $100,000 as proposed by the S.E.C. in October 1970 worked— temporarily. In a February 11, 1971, letter to the N.Y.S.E., the S.E.C. ordered the Exchange to eliminate fixed commissions on all transactions with a value in excess of $500,000, effective April 1, 1971. The $500,000 threshold left over 90 percent of commission revenue fixed. But on September 11, 1973, the S.E.C. lowered that ceiling to $300,000 and announced that all fixed commissions would be abolished on April 30, 1975. It formally adopted a rule to that effect, Rule 19b-3, on January 23, 1975.

Commission rates fell quickly after May Day 1975 on Wall Street and continued falling. Before May Day, the average commission paid was about $0.80 per share. Today, it is about $0.03 per share. With the advent of the internet, fully electronic trading became available for anyone with a computer, and the "day trader" was spawned. Despite doom-prophets predicting the impoverishment of Wall Street, May Day fairly closely marked the beginning of another golden age on Wall Street, with enormous fixed income trading profits, a rise in hostile takeovers, and the emergence of sophisticated corporate finance tools like the high yield bond and index options and futures and bespoke derivatives.

What the end of fixed commissions did destroy was the Third Market. By 1978, the volume of N.Y.S.E.-listed stocks traded in the Third Market was less than 3 percent of the volume on the Exchange. As the S.E.C. historical society would later note: "It was the distortion of the market created by N.Y.S.E.'s fixed commission rates that opened the way for the Third Market: by knocking out that prop, the S.E.C. ended up hurting the N.Y.S.E.'s old nemesis more than the exchange itself." Most importantly, the end of fixed commissions democratized capital. In 1975, about 15 percent of American households owned stocks; today, approximately 50 percent do. The end of fixed commissions also effectively ended the decade-old debate over institutional membership, as the cost of owning a seat on the Exchange and operating a broker-dealer no longer offset trading commission costs.

THE N.Y.S.E. FINALLY agreed to create a computerized trade reporting system in 1972. It was a first step toward fully automated trade execution. In April 1978, the Intermarket Trading System (I.T.S.) was launched, electronically linking the N.Y.S.E., AMEX, and the remaining seven regional exchanges. The I.T.S. electronically sent orders, but did not electronically execute trades—paper from the teletype machines went to a specialist for execution. In 1981, the N.Y.S.E. allowed the N.A.S.D.A.Q.'s Computer Assisted Execution System (C.A.E.S.), which handled N.Y.S.E.-listed securities, to connect with I.T.S., the first time the Exchange directly participated in fully automated execution. In 1984, a system called "Super DOT" was introduced that allowed orders up to 2,000 shares to be electronically routed to a specialist. Between 1982 and 1995, the N.Y.S.E. spent more than $1 billion on cell phones, computers, and handheld terminals. By the end of the century, it could handle 1.4 billion shares a day, with Super DOT handling 90 percent of the volume. During the 2008 financial crisis, the N.Y.S.E. volume exceeded 9 billion shares. Forty years earlier, 10 million share days overwhelmed the system, causing the back-office crisis.

Today, algorithms do the majority of buying and selling on the N.Y.S.E. In truth, there is no technological reason why all trading on the Exchange isn't computerized, as is the case on most other exchanges. The major reason there is any human presence on the floor of the Exchange is public relations. The backdrop of a noisy, active trading floor, the ringing of opening and closing trading bells, is irresistible theater, what people think capitalism ought to look like, a marvelous set for the business news television cameras, and, as Keith Funston would no doubt agree, priceless free advertising for listing on the N.Y.S.E.

THE SECURITIES INVESTOR Protection Corporation has to date functioned effectively and has maintained its solvency, even through the 2008 financial crisis and even though customer account coverage has been substantially increased, currently insuring up to $500,000 per customer account, up to $250,000 of which can be cash. The first N.Y.S.E. member firm S.I.P.C. liquidated was Weis Securities, Inc. in 1973. The liquidation of Adler, Coleman in 1995 was the largest S.I.P.C. handled up to that time, with over 50,000 customer accounts. (The Coleman family had sold the firm a year earlier and its new owner ran the business into the ground unbelievably quickly.) This was dwarfed in 2008, when Lehman Brothers, with over 110,000 customer accounts, was liquidated. Over $92 billion in customer account assets were handled during the Lehman liquidation. Later that same year, Bernard L. Madoff Investment Securities LLC was liquidated as well, with over $10.5 billion recovered for customers. Since inception, S.I.P.C. has advanced $2.9 billion of its own funds to make whole over 773,000 customers.

JOSEPH MEEHAN DIED at his home in Southampton, New York, on November 23, 1972, the ninth anniversary of the agonizing weekend when he did not know whether his firm would survive. The funeral Mass at St. Vincent Ferrer in Manhattan was celebrated by Cardinal Cooke. William F. Buckley Jr. was the lector. His pall-bearers included Henry Ford II; William Clay Ford; George F. Baker Jr., grandson of the founder of First National City Bank; and, of course, John A. Coleman.

JOHN COLEMAN's influence waned after the back-office crisis. With the S.E.C. laser-focused on net capital rule compliance and Congress threatening more investigations, all the markers in the world could not buy you a look-the-other-way at the N.Y.S.E. anymore. After he fell ill with heart trouble in 1975, he made fewer appearances at the Exchange. He died on February 23, 1977. Cardinal Cooke celebrated his funeral Mass as well, this time at St. Patrick's Cathedral.

MURRAY McDONNELL'S deal with the S.E.C. banned him from the securities business for one year. When that period expired, Charlie Allen at Allen & Company hired Murray as a broker covering international clients, the job he would hold for the rest of his life. Left in much reduced circumstances by the collapse of McDonnell & Co., Murray needed to start over, not exactly at the bottom, but men are judged not only by where they land but how far they've fallen, and Murray had fallen far indeed. There were many who thought Murray would never recover; some feared he might take his own life or drown himself in the bottle. Murray surprised a great many. He embraced humility after being humbled, quit the country squire routine, quit the booze, and became a beloved friend to many on Wall Street who, before his fall, were not particularly fond of Murray. He is one of the few men who had more friends after he lost fantastic wealth than when he had it. Murray McDonnell died on New Year's Day 1991 at age sixty-eight.

DONALD WEEDEN's concept of multiple markets for a particular stock, with each of those markets competing with the others for order flow—the national market system—was adopted by Congress and the S.E.C. as the ideal market structure in the mid-1970s and remains so today. It wasn't until 2007, however, that the S.E.C. forced a real-time electronic interface among all markets. By the late 1970s, Weeden & Co.'s profitability was hurt by the emergence of new market participants—the discount brokers, led by Charles Schwab. In 1979, Weeden & Co. merged with Mosley, Hallgarten & Estabrook, a N.Y.S.E. member firm. In 1985, Donald Weeden left Mosley, Hallgarten, Estabrook & Weeden, bought the Weeden name back, and formed his own firm doing an institutional brokerage business. In 2019, that firm was sold to Piper Sandler Companies. Today, Donald Weeden is retired and lives in Danbury, Connecticut.

ROBERT HAACK announced on October 21, 1971, that he would not seek to continue as president of the N.Y.S.E. after his contract term expired on July 31, 1972. There had been delayed consequences from the Economic Club speech. The board of governors of the Exchange decided that they would restructure corporate governance to provide for a full-time chairman of the board with expanded powers and reduced powers for the president. Haack wanted no part of that, which is what the Club hoped and expected. The president's position would remain vacant until 1980 when John Phelan Jr. was selected. After he left the Exchange, Haack joined a number of corporate boards, including that of Merrill Lynch. He died on June 14, 1992, at age seventy-five.

DAN LUFKIN left D.L.J. in 1971. He had made his fortune and thought his talents would be more useful elsewhere. While any number of federal government appointments would have been his for the asking, he believed he would have the most impact acting locally. That same year, he became Connecticut's first commissioner of the Department of Environmental Protection. From that time to the present, he has been active in leadership of many organizations dedicated to preserving the environment. Lufkin continued to keep his hand in business through his investment firm, Questor Partners, and even returned to D.L.J. briefly later in the 1970s during a period of difficulty at the firm. He lives today at his home in Connecticut.

RALPH DeNUNZIO was elected chairman of the N.Y.S.E. in 1971 after Bunny Lasker's term. Whatever ill will DeNunzio may have generated with Congress during the S.I.P.C. hearings in 1970 was soon forgotten, for in 1978, the Senate confirmed DeNunzio as a director of S.I.P.C. He also continued his ascent at Kidder, Peabody & Co., becoming Al Gordon's replacement as chief executive officer in 1976 and also replacing Gordon with the added role of chairman of the board in 1986 upon the firm's sale to General Electric Company. The following year, DeNunzio was forced out by G.E. management in the wake of the Martin Siegal insider trading scandal where DeNunzio was criticized for failure to properly supervise the star investment banker-*cum*-criminal. DeNunzio went on to form his own investment firm, Harbor Point Associates, Inc., and joined a number of boards, including that of Nike, Inc. DeNunzio is now retired, living in Riverside, Connecticut.

MARSHALL COGAN initially emerged as the most powerful presence at CBWL-Hayden, Stone, but he had a fundamental disagreement with Sandy Weill over business strategy. Weill wanted the firm to focus more on the traditional agency model—brokerage, underwriting, advisory businesses—while Cogan, like Arthur Carter before him, wanted to pursue leveraged buyouts. Cogan left the firm in 1973. The following year, he completed his first buyout—of General Felt Industries Inc. Later acquisitions would include Knoll International Holdings Inc., Foamex International Inc., and United Auto Group. Cogan also owned the famous 21 Club restaurant in New York from 1985 to 1995. When asked how, as a twenty-something kid, he was able to get his phone calls returned at the then–little known C.B.W.L. by the likes of Charles Bluhdorn, Jimmy Ling, and Jerry Tsai, Cogan seemed surprised at the question: "I thought my ideas were good—they were good. You realize that no one has a monopoly on good ideas. In fact, I learned pretty young that, very often, nobody knows anything." Today, Marshall Cogan lives in New York City—and at age eighty-five is still doing deals.

DONALD REGAN was elected vice-chairman of the board of governors of the N.Y.S.E. in 1973. He used the position to continue his advocacy for an end to fixed commissions, indifferent to its unpopularity among many of his fellow governors. In 1981, Regan stepped down as chairman of Merrill Lynch, which he had joined in 1946, to become President Ronald Reagan's Secretary of the Treasury. His stewardship of Merrill Lynch through the turbulent times on Wall Street during the late 1960s and 1970s was remarkable. When he left, the firm had become a bulge bracket underwriter in addition to increasing its dominance as the leading brokerage firm. It had successfully entered into many consumer financial product markets thought impossible for investment banks to compete in, like checking accounts and credit cards, taking market share away from traditional commercial banks. In 1985, Regan changed jobs with President Reagan's chief of staff, James A. Baker III. It was to prove a bruising experience. Some accused Regan of trying to run the government as if it were Merrill Lynch. "The President no longer has advisors," Ed Rollins, Reagan's White House political director, quipped. "He has Donald Regan, and Donald Regan has advisors." The following year, the Iran-Contra scandal broke and the president's popularity tumbled. Worse for Don Regan, he got on the wrong side of First Lady Nancy Reagan, who thought Don Regan had forgotten who worked for whom in the Reagan White House. She plotted successfully to have him fired in 1987. In 1988, Regan published his memoirs, which did a number on Nancy Reagan, revealing that she consulted regularly with an astrologer in San Francisco, Joan Quigley, and used her persuasive powers over her husband to conform policymaking decisions to Ms. Quigley's prognostications. Needless to say, the press had a field day. After the memoir sensation, Regan spent a quiet retirement in Williamsburg, Virginia, where he passed away on June 11, 2003.

FELIX ROHATYN received an unexpected call from New York governor Hugh Carey in May 1975 requesting an immediate meeting at the governor's office in New York City. Wasting no time, Carey laid out his problem to Rohatyn in simple terms: New York City had $3 billion in short-term debt coming due in the next fifteen months, and Carey had run out of ideas as to how it might be paid. Felix gave an equally quick diagnosis: New York City, with its profligate ways, had no credibility on Wall Street; Carey and New York State did. Carey's political analysis of the mess was exactly the same as Rohatyn's financial analysis. Carey named Rohatyn to his four-member crisis advisory committee. Rohatyn's mentor at Lazard, Andre Meyer, cautioned Felix: "Public service is like having a young mistress. You should be careful. It's tempting." Ultimately a new state entity was created—the Municipal Assistance Corporation, known as the "Big M.A.C.," with nine directors, five appointed by Governor Carey and four appointed by Abe Beame, the mayor of New York City. Among Carey's appointments were John Coleman and Felix Rohatyn, who served as chairman. To make the whole plan work, Rohatyn concluded that federal financial support of some sort was necessary, as even New York State's credit wasn't sufficient. President Ford was not initially supportive, birthing the most famous tabloid headline of all time: "Ford to City: Drop Dead." Pressured by Fed chairman Arthur Burns, Ford relented, and short-term credit lines were provided. Despite many nasty and at times public and personal battles with labor and political leaders—Beame's successor, Ed Koch, would frequently complain to the press, "Who elected Felix mayor?"—by 1980, the city's budget was balanced. In 1996, Felix took the heat for his visible leadership at the N.Y.S.E. during the back-office crisis and at the Big M.A.C. Senate Republicans, not fond of Felix's advocacy for federal government bailouts, blocked his confirmation for the vice-chairmanship of the Federal Reserve Board. As a consolation, President Clinton appointed Rohatyn ambassador to France in 1997 after Pamela Harriman died. After four years in Paris, Felix returned to New York, settling into a role as senior advisor at Lazard and senior statesman, generally. Rohatyn died in Manhattan at age ninety-one on December 14, 2019.

ROY COHN's second criminal trial on the Fifth Avenue Coach Lines charges began in late September 1971 and lasted three weeks. It can only be described as a disaster for the government. Seven of the ten counts against Cohn were either dropped by prosecutors during the trial or dismissed by Judge Charles H. Tenney prior to giving the case to the jury. It took the jury less than an hour to acquit Cohn of the remaining charges. After the acquittal, Cohn took on an almost mythical, if diabolical, status. He encouraged the portrayals of him as an untouchable anti-hero, tough enough to take on the United States of America three times and win. He promoted himself as an outsider, a fearless and cunning advocate, willing to take on any opponent. The "Legal Executioner," *Esquire* magazine called Cohn on the cover of its December 1978 issue. Throughout the 1970s, Roy Cohn held court daily at long lunches at his table at the 21 Club and most nights could be found at Studio 54 or another hot celebrity haunt of the moment. His client list was a who's-who of the rich, famous, and infamous— Rupert Murdoch, Si Newhouse, Charlie Allen, Donald Trump, George Steinbrenner, Bianca Jagger, Terrence Cardinal Cooke, and the heads of the Gambino, Genovese, and Buonanno crime families. Cohn's power reached its apex in 1980 with the election of Ronald Reagan as president. Both Reagan and his wife, Nancy, were close, personal friends of Cohn's, and Cohn had raised many times more money for Reagan than he had for Nixon a dozen years earlier. In 1986, Cohn's ways finally caught up with him. He was disbarred for ethics violations weeks before he died of AIDS at age fifty-nine. He spent his final days writing his autobiography— co-authored with Sidney Zion. It was published posthumously.

ROSS PEROT's Wall Street headaches got worse. In January 1971, a congressional investigation into the Penn Central bankruptcy revealed that a senior F. I. duPont, Glore Forgan partner, Charles J. Hodge, had manipulated stocks with Penn Central's CFO using margin loans from Penn Central's banks. The two also arranged for a Penn Central subsidiary to illegally buy an airline, Executive Jet Aviation Inc. Worse, Executive Jet had provided prostitutes to favored flyers—including Hodge—and charged the women's services to the company. Perot was incensed. He told the Crisis Committee he was not going ahead with the F. I. duPont, Glore Forgan debt conversion and demanded full repayment of his loan.

Felix Rohatyn and Bunny Lasker begged him to reconsider. Perot relented after he was given 90 percent of the firm's equity and the N.Y.S.E. agreed to indemnify him for up to $15 million of any further liabilities. The following year, Perot made another major Wall Street bet, investing $15 million in Walston & Co. As if a bad dream, what had occurred at F.I. duPont, Glore Forgan was repeated at Walston. By 1973, it was failing and looking to Perot to bail it out. Again, Perot took the plunge, merging Walston with F. I. duPont, Glore Forgan. By 1974, it was all over for Perot on Wall Street. The N.Y.S.E.'s $15 million was spent and Perot himself had sunk an estimated $100 million in those firms. Perot announced he was liquidating the combined firm, but promised that all customers would be made whole and no bailout from S.I.P.C. would be required. While all the equity holders and debt holders, mostly notably Perot himself, were wiped out, Perot was true to his word, and no customers lost money. Perot reemerged on the national scene in 1991 when he publicly opposed the Gulf War. He announced on CNN's *Larry King Live* on February 20, 1992, that he would run for president. By June, Perot was leading in many polls by double-digits, but he did not do well as a front-runner. By July, Perot was polling at only 20 percent. In the end, Perot received 18.9 percent of the popular vote and no electoral votes. Perot ran again as a third-party candidate in 1996, but was not a factor, finishing with just 8 percent of the popular vote. He lived relatively quietly for the rest of his life in Texas, dying of leukemia on July 2, 2019.

WARREN HINCKLE and SIDNEY ZION, the last of the hot issue IPO entrepreneurs of the gonzo Go-Go Era, did not have long careers as public company executives, although for a brief period in the summer of 1970 it looked as if *Scanlan's* might make of go of it, as relentlessly bashing Nixon proved a successful business plan. The September issue of *Scanlan's* contained an editorial entitled "Nixon and the Bums" chronicling the misdeeds of the Wall Street "hard hat riot" union officials who were invited to the White House. This infuriated President Nixon, who ordered White House counsel John Dean to investigate *Scanlan's*. The union bosses were none too happy either. When the October issue of *Scanlan's*, devoted entirely to extremist groups waging guerrilla war in America, was sent to the printer, Barnes Press in New York City, the workers there, members of the Amalgamated Lithographers of America union, refused to process the print job, calling its contents "un-American." Hinckle found a substitute printing firm in San Francisco that agreed to print the issue. But two days later, with no explanation, that printer returned the *Scanlan's* check uncashed and declined the job. After dozens of calls to printers all across the country, Hinckle and Zion found a printer in Los Angeles, Medallion Printers, that agreed to print the issue. But Medallion Printers, too, backed out after its union workforce refused to work the job, also calling the magazine "un-American." By the end of October, the delays in printing the issue had cost *Scanlan's* more than $100,000. Sidney Zion had a friend well connected with a disreputable union local in New Jersey who told him President Nixon had reached out to Peter Brennan, and the word was sent to the print shop unions throughout America to put the screws to *Scanlan's*. During the first week of December, Warren Hinckle finally found a printer in Canada, which made a shipment of 6,000 copies of the magazine to distributors in Oakland and San Francisco. Almost immediately, U.S. customs agents raided the warehouses holding the magazines and seized them, claiming they were unlawful on the grounds that they were "materials advocating treason or forcible resistance to the nation's laws." On the same day, Montreal police seized 80,000 copies at the printer's warehouse and the Royal Canadian Mounted Police seized 22,000 more copies in a truck on its way to the U.S. The Canadian press inquired as to why Canadian law enforcement was seizing copies of an American liberal muckraking magazine. The Chief of Police in Montreal answered bluntly: "The United States Government asked us to stop it." Once the magazines were finally released in Canada under pressure from the media, Hinckle and Zion were told by the magazine's national distributor that it was dropping *Scanlan's* from distribution. They soon received calls from magazine dealers in thirty cities, including Chicago, Detroit,

Philadelphia, and Los Angeles, refusing to stock the issue. Off the record, most of these dealers told Zion the same story: government officials had visited them and told them it would not be good for the country—or them—if they sold the magazine. The "guerrilla war" issue was *Scanlan's* last. The magazine never recovered from the three-month delay in publication and Nixon's get-even campaign against it. The money was gone. Vendors and writers went unpaid. After only eight issues, the company filed for bankruptcy. Sidney Zion died of cancer in New York City on August 2, 2009. Warren Hinckle died on August 25, 2016, in San Francisco.

NOTES

Prologue

1. Norman C. Miller, *The Great Salad Oil Swindle* (New York: Coward McCann, Inc., 1965), pp. 94–95.
2. Miller, *The Great Salad Oil Swindle*, p. 91.
3. Miller, *The Great Salad Oil Swindle*, pp. 150–156.
4. John Brooks, *Business Adventures* (Hodder & Stoughton, 2014), chapter 6.
5. Miller, *The Great Salad Oil Swindle*, pp. 160–165.
6. "Sharp Stock Downturn Linked to Suspension of Wall St. Houses," *New York Times*, November 22, 1963; "Firm Is Dealing Through Other Brokers—Haupt Keeps Doors Closed," *New York Times*, November 22, 1963.
7. "The Day JFK Died We Traded Through Tears as NYSE Shut After Selloff," *Bloomberg News*, November 22, 2013.
8. "The Day JFK Died We Traded Through Tears as NYSE Shut After Selloff."
9. Interview with Michael J. Meehan II, May 2, 2019, at the Brook, New York City.
10. "The Vanishing Salad Oil: A $100 Million Mystery," *New York Times*, January 6, 1964; "Last Rites for President John F. Kennedy Remembered by Catholic Priest Rev. Oscar L. Huber," *Huffington Post*, November 19, 2019.

Chapter One

1. Eric J. Weiner, *What Goes Up* (Hachette Book Group USA, 2005), p. 94.
2. Weiner, *What Goes Up*, p. 92.
3. Weiner, *What Goes Up*, p. 90.
4. Weiner, *What Goes Up*, p. 96.
5. Chris Welles, *The Last Days of the Club* (E. P. Dutton & Co., Inc., 1975), p. 146.
6. Welles, *The Last Days of the Club*, p. 42.
7. Welles, *The Last Days of the Club*, pp. 50–51.
8. Interview with Michael J. Meehan II, October 3, 2019, at the Brook, New York City.
9. Welles, *The Last Days of the Club*, p. 50.
10. Donald E. Weeden, *Weeden & Co.: The New York Stock Exchange and the Struggle over a National Securities Market* (Weeden Securities Corp., 2002), p. 46.
11. Weeden, *Weeden & Co.*, p. 1.
12. Weeden, *Weeden & Co.*, Portfolio II, plate 6.
13. Welles, *The Last Days of the Club*, p. 52.
14. "Coast Exchange to Add Fund Unit," *The New York Times*, May 13, 1965.

15. Alan D. Morrison, Aaron Thegeya, Carol Schenone, and William J. Wilhelm Jr., "Investment-Banking Relationships: 1933–2007," *Review of Corporate Finance Studies* 7, no. 2 (2018), pp. 194–244.

16. Morrison et al, "Investment-Banking Relationships: 1933–2007."

17. Herbert P. Janicki and Edward Simpson Prescott, "Changes in the Size Distribution of U.S. Banks: 1960–2005," *Economics Quarterly* 92, no. 4 (Fall 2006).

18. Janicki and Prescott, "Changes in the Size Distribution of U.S. Banks: 1960–2005."

Chapter Two

1. Joel Seligman, *The Transformation of Wall Street*, 3rd Ed. (Wolters Klower, 2003), p. 165.

2. Paul A. Gompers and Josh Lerner, "The Really Long-Run Performance of Initial Public Offerings: The Pre-Nasdaq Evidence," *Journal of Finance* 58, no. 4 (August 2003).

3. Seligman, *The Transformation of Wall Street*, p. 240.

4. Seligman, *The Transformation of Wall Street*, p. 291.

5. Seligman, *The Transformation of Wall Street*, p. 295.

6. Seligman, *The Transformation of Wall Street*, p. 296.

7. Letter from G. Keith Funston to William Carey, dated December 6, 1961; Letter from G. Keith Funston to Milton H. Cohen, dated November 16, 1962.

8. Milton Cohen, "Reflections on the Special Study of Securities Markets," *Commercial and Financial Chronicle* 197, no 6272.

9. Seligman, *The Transformation of Wall Street*, p. 296.

10. "Report of the Special Study of Securities Markets, Part 1" (U.S. Government Printing Office, April 3, 1963).

11. "Report of the Special Study of Securities Markets, Part 5" (U.S. Government Printing Office, September 17, 1963).

12. "Report of the Special Study of Securities Markets, Part 5."

13. "Report of the Special Study of Securities Markets, Part 5."

14. Seligman, *The Transformation of Wall Street*, p. 318.

15. Seligman, *The Transformation of Wall Street*, p. 321.

16. Seligman, *The Transformation of Wall Street*, p. 323.

17. Eugene Goldman, "LBJ Tapes Show President's Admiration for Manny Cohen and Litmus Tests for Regulators," white paper, August 2003. Available at http://3197d6d14b5f19f2f440-5e13d29c4c016cf96cbbfd197c579b45.r81.cf1.rackcdn.com/collection/papers/2000/2003_0801_Goldman_LBJ_tapes.pdf.

18. Address by Manuel F. Cohen, Chairman of the Securities and Exchange Commission, before American Society of Corporate Securities, Inc., Colorado Springs, Colorado, June 28, 1966.

19. Christopher Elias, *Fleecing the Lambs* (Henry Regnery Company, 1971), p. 64.

20. "Study of Unsafe and Unsound Practices of Brokers and Dealers—Report and Recommendations of the Securities and Exchange Commission" (U.S. Government Printing Office, December 1971), p. 151.

21. Hurd Baruch, *Wall Street: Security Risk* (Acropolis Books, 1971), pp. 156–157.

22. Baruch, *Wall Street: Security Risk*, p. 158.

23.   Baruch, *Wall Street: Security Risk*, pp. 174–176.
24.   Robert J. Cole, "John A. Coleman, Philanthropist, Big Board Chairman, Dies at 75," *New York Times*, February 25, 1977.
25.   Cole, "John A. Coleman, Philanthropist, Big Board Chairman, Dies at 75."
26.   Robert Sobel, *A History of the New York State Exchange 1935–1975* (Weybright and Talley, 1975), p. 106.
27.   Richard Phalon, "A 50-Year Man on Wall Street; Prominent Specialist Began His Career as a Page Boy," *New York Times*, June 23, 1966.
28.   Muriel Siebert with Alice Lee Ball, *Changing the Rules* (The Free Press, 2002).
29.   Ron Insana, *Traders' Tales* (John Wiley & Sons, Inc., 1996), p. 11.
30.   Insana, *Traders' Tales*.
31.   Baruch, *Wall Street: Security Risk*, p. 176.
32.   "Net Capital Requirements for Brokers and Dealers—Interpretation and Guides," Securities Exchange Act, release No. 8024; Accounting Series release No. 107, January 18, 1967.
33.   "Net Capital Requirements for Brokers and Dealers."
34.   "Study of Unsafe and Unsound Practices of Brokers and Dealers," pp. 49–80.
35.   "Study of Unsafe and Unsound Practices of Brokers and Dealers."
36.   "Study of Unsafe and Unsound Practices of Brokers and Dealers."
37.   "Study of Unsafe and Unsound Practices of Brokers and Dealers."
38.   "Study of Unsafe and Unsound Practices of Brokers and Dealers."

Chapter Three

1.   Winthrop H. Smith, Jr., *Catching Lightning in a Bottle: How Merrill Lynch Revolutionized the Financial World* (John Wiley & Sons, Inc., 2013), p. 177.
2.   Smith, *Catching Lightning in a Bottle*, p. 178.
3.   Smith, *Catching Lightning in a Bottle*, pp. 178–179.
4.   "Study of Unsafe and Unsound Practices of Brokers and Dealers," p. 283.
5.   "DTCC Finds 1.3 million Soaked Securities in Sandy-Flooded NY Vault," Reuters, November 14, 2012.
6.   Chuck Boyer, "The System 360 Revolution," IBB.com/Observer, 2004.
7.   Welles, *The Last Days of the Club*, p. 286.
8.   George Schussel and Jack May, "Wall Street Automation: A Primer," *Datamation* 16, no. 4 (April 1970).
9.   Vartanig G. Vartan, "Funston Will Step Down as Stock Exchange Chief," *New York Times*, September 13, 1966.
10.   Vartanig G. Vartan, "10 Big Board Governors Named to Recommend Funston Successor," *New York Times*, September 16, 1966.
11.   Varfanig G. Vartan, "Haack Is Elected to Funston Post," *New York Times*, April 26, 1967.
12.   Vartanig G. Vartan, "The Big Board: Boom in Volume Overshadows Uncertainty on Fees," *New York Times*, February 26, 1967; Vartanig G. Vartan, "Margin of Profit Dips for Brokers," *New York Times*, July 6, 1967.
13.   Vartanig G. Vartan, "Stock Exchanges to Close at 2 P.M. for Rest of Week," *New York Times*, August 8, 1967.

14. Vartanig G. Vartan, "A Short Day on Big Board with Much Work," *New York Times*, August 9, 1967.
15. Vartanig G. Vartan, "Shorter Trading Session Continues Another Week," *New York Times*, August 11, 1967.
16. John Kifner, "Hippies Shower $1 Bills on Stock Exchange Floor," *New York Times*, August 25, 1967.
17. "The Exchange Community in 1975: A Report on Its Potentials, Problems and Prospects," an Economics Study by the New York Stock Exchange, December 1965.
18. "Automation Gets Big Board Review," *New York Times*, October 24, 1967.
19. Alec Benn, *The Unseen Wall Street of 1969–1975* (Quorum Books, 2000), pp. 13–14; Vartanig G. Vartan, "Big Board Clears Debt Issues for Fins in Policy Discussion," *New York Times*, November 17, 1967.
20. Vartanig G. Vartan, "Brokerage Houses Fear a Back-Office Logjam if the Pace of Trading Surges," *New York Times*, September 24, 1967.
21. Vartanig G. Vartan, "Big Board Names Two Top Aides," *New York Times*, November 3, 1967.

Chapter Four

1. Seligman, *The Transformation of Wall Street*, pp. 384–385.
2. Weeden, *Weeden & Co.*, p. 6.
3. Weeden, *Weeden & Co.*, p. 6.
4. Weeden, *Weeden & Co.*, p. 7.
5. Seligman, *The Transformation of Wall Street*, p. 385.
6. Seligman, *The Transformation of Wall Street*, p. 401.
7. Vartanig G. Vartan, "Big Board Seeks Changes on Fees," *New York Times*, January 3, 1968.
8. Vartan, "Big Board Seeks Changes on Fees."
9. Seligman, *The Transformation of Wall Street*, p. 401.
10. Vartanig G. Vartan, "The Back Office Blues," *New York Times*, January 13, 1968.
11. H. J. Maidenberg, "Clerical Workers Avoid Back-Office Woes," *New York Times*, June 13, 1968.
12. Vartanig G. Vartan, "Stock Exchange to Shut at 2 P.M., Starting Monday," *New York Times*, January 19, 1968.
13. Vartan, "Stock Exchange to Shut at 2 P.M., Starting Monday."
14. Robert E. Semple Jr., "Nixon Announced for Presidency," *New York Times*, February 2, 1968.
15. Terry Robards, "S.E.C. Cites Cohn in Bus Line Case," *New York Times*, February 10, 1968.
16. Terry Robards, "S.E.C. Cites Cohn in Bus Line Case."
17. John J. Abele, "Stock Exchange Staff Men Help Pickard Clear VP," *New York Times*, February 20, 1968.
18. "Review of SEC Records of the Demise of Selected Broker-Dealers: Staff Study for the Special Subcommittee on Investigations of the Committee on Interstate and Foreign Commerce House of Representatives, Ninety Second

Congress, First Session"; (U.S. Government Printing Office, July 1971), pp. 136–140.

19. "System at Goodbody Is Speeding Reports on Trading," *New York Times*, March 5, 1968.
20. Welles, *The Last Days of the Club*, pp. 133–134.
21. Robert D. Hershey Jr., "Institutions Join Rush to Grab New Issues," *New York Times*, May 26, 1968.
22. Vartanig G. Vartan, "Wall Street and Banks Assail Paper Woes," *New York Times*, April 3, 1968.
23. Seligman, *The Transformation of Wall Street*, p. 404.
24. Seligman, *The Transformation of Wall Street*, p. 404.
25. Seligman, *The Transformation of Wall Street*, p. 403.
26. Seligman, *The Transformation of Wall Street*, p. 404.
27. Vartanig G. Vartan, "Big Board Approves Rule to Exit Logjam," *New York Times*, April 19, 1968.
28. Vartanig G. Vartan, "Certificate Automation Is Ready," *New York Times*, May 17, 1968.
29. "Study of Unsafe and Unsound Practices of Brokers and Dealers," p. 227.
30. "Sean M'Donnell, 34, of Investment Firm," *New York Times*, June 5, 1968.
31. Welles, *The Last Days of the Club*, p. 176.
32. "Review of SEC Records of the Demise of Selected Broker-Dealers," p. 122.
33. Welles, *The Last Days of the Club*, p. 181.
34. Welles, *The Last Days of the Club*, p. 186.
35. Elias, *Fleecing of the Lambs*, pp. 63–64.
36. Welles, *The Last Days of the Club*, pp. 188–189.
37. Elias, *Fleecing the Lamb*, p. 65.
38. Welles, *The Last Days of the Club*, p. 193.
39. Interview with Michael J. Meehan, II, May 2, 2019, at the Brook, New York City.
40. Welles, *The Last Days of the Club*, p. 181.
41. John Carry, *Golden Clan* (Houghton Mifflin Company, 1977), p. 177.
42. Welles, *The Last Days of the Club*, p. 176.

Chapter Five

1. Seligman, *The Transformation of Wall Street*, p. 405.
2. Vartanig G. Vartan, "Haack Asks Firms to Use Restraint to Reduce 'Fails,'" *New York Times*, June 8, 1968.
3. Vartan, "Haack Asks Firms to Use Restraint to Reduce 'Fails.'"
4. Vartan, "Haack Asks Firms to Use Restraint to Reduce 'Fails.'"
5. Eileen Shanahan, "Margin on Stocks Increased to 80%," *New York Times*, June 8, 1968.
6. Vartanig G. Vartan, "Big Board Weighs Commission Plan," *New York Times*, June 11, 1968.
7. John J. Abele, "Give-Ups to End," *New York Times*, June 28, 1968.
8. Eileen Shanahan, "S.E.C. Is Accusing Firm on Records," *New York Times*, June 14, 1968.

9. John J. Abele, "Over-the-Counter Trading 'Bedlam,'" *New York Times,* June 14, 1968.

10. Eileen Shanahan, "Brokers Warned by S.E.C. to Cut Back on Stock Jam," *New York Times,* June 18, 1968.

11. Vartanig G. Vartan, "Exchange Closings Helpful, Industry Tells S.E.C.," *New York Times,* June 21, 1968.

12. "Study of Unsafe and Unsound Practices of Brokers and Dealers," p. 227.

13. "Study of Unsafe and Unsound Practices of Brokers and Dealers," p. 228.

14. Robert A. Wright, "Big Board Introduces Computers to Facilitate Stock Transfers," *New York Times,* June 29, 1968.

15. Eileen Shanahan, "Big Board Witness Yields in Attack on Commissions," *New York Times,* July 2, 1968.

16. Eileen Shanahan, "Broker Opposed Change in Fund Fees," *New York Times,* July 3, 1968.

17. Eileen Shanahan, "Brokers Detail Fee Stratagem," *New York Times,* July 4, 1968.

18. Eileen Shanahan, "Bache, Reynolds Firms Testify to S.E.C. on Fund Sale Methods," *New York Times,* July 9, 1968.

19. Eileen Shanahan, "Give Ups Backed in Research Role," *New York Times,* July 11, 1968.

20. Eileen Shanahan, N.A.S.D. Accepts End of "Give Ups," *New York Times,* July 18, 1968.

21. Eileen Shanahan, "Broker Says Fund's Commission on Purchases Went to Sponsor," *New York Times,* July 19, 1968.

22. Eileen Shanahan, "Broker Describes Rebate by Fund," *New York Times,* July 20, 1968.

23. Eileen Shanahan, "Holders of One Fund Help Pay Another's Cost S.E.C. Is Told," *New York Times,* July 23, 1968.

24. Eileen Shanahan, "Payment of Give-Ups at Issue in S.E.C. Study of Commissions," *New York Times,* June 24, 1968.

25. Eileen Shanahan, "Mutual Fund Complex Opposes Fixed Commissions on Trading," *New York Times,* August 1, 1968.

26. *S.E.C. vs. Fifth Avenue Coach Lines Inc.*, No. 67 Civ.4182, United States District Court, S.D. New York, July 26, 1968.

27. "Study of Unsafe Unusual Practices of Brokers and Dealers," p. 228.

28. "Study of Unsafe Unusual Practices of Brokers and Dealers," p. 228.

29. "Brokers Warned by S.E.C. Again," *New York Times,* July 30, 1968.

30. "Study of Unsafe and Unsound Practices of Brokers and Dealers," p. 228.

31. Robert D. Hershey Jr., "By-Ins Ordered by the Big Board," *New York Times,* August 3, 1968.

32. Vartanig G. Vartan, "Exchanges to Restrict Sell-Order Acceptances," *New York Times,* August 16, 1968.

33. "Study of Unsafe and Unusual Practices of Brokers and Dealers," p. 228.

34. "Study of Unsafe Unusual Practices of Brokers and Dealers," p. 228.

35. Eileen Shanahan, "Big Board Urges Commission Cut on Large Trees," *New York Times,* August 9, 1968.

36. Robert E. Bedingfield, "Commission Cuts Irk Some Firms," *New York Times*, August 9, 1968.
37. Eileen Shanahan, "Commission System Is Defended," *New York Times*, August 20, 1968.
38. Shanahan, "Commission System Is Defended."
39. Shanahan, "Commission System Is Defended."
40. Eileen Shanahan, "Big Board Cautions Commissions Pay for Research Data," *New York Times*, August 21, 1968.
41. Eileen Shanahan, "Basis Questioned for Broker Fees," *New York Times*, August 22, 1968.
42. Eileen Shanahan, "Midwest Market Hits Give-Up Ban," *New York Times*, August 24, 1968.
43. "Amex President Opposes Elimination of Fixed Fees," *New York Times*, August 27, 1968.
44. Edwin L. Dale, Jr., "New Plan Mostly Affects the Large Traders and Mutual Funds," *New York Times*, September 5, 1968.

Chapter Six

1. Terry Robards, "S.E.C. Accuses Merrill Lynch on Inside Data," *New York Times*, August 28, 1968.
2. Richard Phalon, "Merrill Lynch Penalized by S.E.C. in Insider Case," *New York Times*, November 27, 1968.
3. "Crisis in the Securities Industry, a Chronology: 1967–1970," Prepared for the Subcommittee on Commerce and Finance, Committee on Interstate and Foreign Commerce, House of Representatives" (New York Stock Exchange Inc., August 1971), pp. 14–15.
4. "Study of Unsafe and Unsound Practices of Brokers and Dealers," p. 229.
5. Leonard Sloane, "Boom and Bust on Wall Street," *New York Magazine*, October 14, 1968.
6. Sloane, "Boom and Bust on Wall Street."
7. Vartanig G. Vartan, "Hack Sees End to 4-Day Week and Curbs on Brokers' Volume," *New York Times*, October 2, 1968.
8. Vartan, "Hack Sees End to 4-Day Week and Curbs on Brokers' Volume."
9. "Text of Nixon's Letters on Securities Industry," *New York Times*, October 2, 1968.
10. William Laubert, "The Hotshot One-Man Roy Cohn Lobby," *Life*, September 5, 1969.
11. Vartanig G. Vartan, "Market Closing Set to Continue," *New York Times*, October 11, 1968.
12. Vartanig G. Vartan, "Haack Endorses Revised Fee Plan," *New York Times*, October 21, 1968.
13. "Big Board Votes to Reduce Fees," by Vartanig G. Vartan, *New York Times*, October 25, 1968.
14. Welles, *The Last Day of the Club*, p. 196.

15. Welles, *The Last Day of the Club*, p. 196.
16. Welles, *The Last Day of the Club*, p. 195.
17. Welles, *The Last Day of the Club*, p. 196.
18. Welles, *The Last Day of the Club*, p. 196.
19. "Review of SEC Records of the Demise of Selected Broker-Dealers," p. 127.
20. "Interview with Michael J. Meehan II, May 2, 2019, at the Brook, New York City.
21. Eileen Shanahan, "Fixed Brokerage Fee Scored," *New York Times*, October 11, 1968.
22. Shanahan, "Fixed Brokerage Fee Scored."
23. Shanahan, "Fixed Brokerage Fee Scored."
24. Edward Ranzal, "U.S. Indicts Cohn Charging Fraud and a Conspiracy," *New York Times*, November 23, 1968.
25. Vartanig G. Vartan, "5-Day Trading Week Here to Stay—Unless," *New York Times*, December 8, 1968.

Chapter Seven

1. Terry Robards, "Funds Set Aside by Hayden Stone," *New York Times*, January 15, 1969.
2. Robert Metz, "Market Place: Paperwork Jam Still a Problem," *New York Times*, January 17, 1969.
3. Seligman, *The Transformation of Wall Street*, p. 414; Terry Robards, "Wall St. Defends Fixed-Fee System," *New York Times*, January 20, 1969.
4. Terry Robards, "Big Board to Study Commission Rates," *New York Times*, January 23, 1969.
5. Edward Ranzal, "Cohn Is Indicted in Bribery Case," *New York Times*, January 18, 1969.
6. Ranzal, "Cohn Is Indicted in Bribery Case."
7. Leonard Sloane, "Wall Street Is the Newest Frontier," *New York Times*, January 19, 1969.
8. Lyndon Baines Johnson Library Oral History Collection—Interview of Lawrence O'Brien by Michael L. Gillette, September 23, 1987.
9. Interview of Lawrence O'Brien by Michael L. Gillette.
10. Welles, *The Last Days of the Club*, p. 199.
11. Sidney Zion, *The Autobiography of Roy Cohn* (Lyle Stuart, Inc., 1988), pp. 219–221.
12. James Ridgeway, "The Ramparts Story: . . . Um; Very Interesting," *New York Times Magazine*, April 20, 1969.
13. James Ridgeway, "The Ramparts Story."
14. "New Penalties Set in Ruling by S.E.C. on Brokerage Fails," *New York Times*, January 31, 1969.
15. Terry Robards, "Lehman Brothers Censored by S.E.C.," *New York Times*, February 7, 1969.
16. Walter Rugabar, "Budge of S.E.C. Promoted to Head Regulatory Unit," *New York Times*, February 23, 1969.
17. H. J. Maidenberg, "Rand Corp. Hired to Help Wall Street Paper Mess," *New York Times*, February 13, 1969.

18. Terry Robards, "Automated Transfer Plan Put into Action for Stocks," *New York Times*, February 25, 1969.
19. Terry Robards, "Automated Transfer Plan Put into Action for Stocks,"
20. "S.E.C. Curb Is Set for Anthony & Co.," *New York Times*, February 28, 1969.
21. Eileen Shanahan, "Stock Theft Ring Hinted by Haack," *New York Times*, February 27 1969.
22. Eileen Shanahan, "Haack Says F.B.I. Denied Aid to Curb Stock Theft," *New York Times*, March 5, 1969.
23. Shanahan, "Haack Says F.B.I. Denied Aid to Curb Stock Theft."
24. "Murphy Bill Asked Fingerprint Data," *New York Times*, March 10, 1969.
25. Murray Illson, "F.B.I. Rounds Up 4 in $14 Million Theft of Securities Here," *New York Times*, May 30, 1969.
26. Terry Robards, "duPont Nears Corporate Status," *New York Times*, March 11, 1969.
27. "Review of S.E.C. Records of the Demise Of Selected Broker-Dealers," p. 77.
28. "Review of S.E.C. Records of the Demise Of Selected Broker-Dealers," p. 77.
29. "Review of S.E.C. Records of the Demise Of Selected Broker-Dealers," p. 77.
30. Terry Robards, "Brokerage Fails Lowest in a Year," *New York Times*, April 23, 1969.
31. William D. Smith, "Will Market Get Massage and Close 'Technology Gap,'" *New York Times*, March 30, 1969.
32. "1969 American Report of the National Association of Securities Dealers Inc.," pp. 14–16; "Automated System to Grow Unlisted Quotes Is Shown," *New York Times*, May 16, 1969.
33. Terry Robards, "A.B.A Would Drop Stock Certificate to Use Punchcard," *New York Times*, June 17, 1969.
34. Terry Robards, "Big Board Association Endorses Punch-Card Stock Certificates," *New York Times*, June 30, 1969.
35. Terry Robards, "Big Board Asserts S.E.C. Lacks Authority on Rates," *New York Times*, May 2, 1969.
36. Robards, "Big Board Asserts S.E.C. Lacks Authority on Rates."
37. Robards, "Big Board Asserts S.E.C. Lacks Authority on Rates."
38. Terry Robards, "Fees Still Split, Haack Tells S.E.C.," *New York Times*, May 3, 1969.
39. Robards, "Fees Still Split, Haack Tells S.E.C."

Chapter Eight

1. Terry Robards, "Big Board Defied by Member Firm," *New York Times*, May 23, 1969.
2. Interview of Dan Lufkin by Amy Blitz, Harvard Business School Director of Media Development for Entrepreneur Management, April 2002.
3. Interview of Dan Lufkin by Amy Blitz.
4. Eric J. Weiner, *What Goes Up: The Uncensored History of Modern Wall Street as Told by the Bankers, CEOs and Scoundrels Who Made It Happen* (Back Bay Books, 2005), p. 77.

5. Interview of Dan Lufkin by Amy Blitz.

6. Interview of Dan Lufkin by Amy Blitz.

7. Alec Benn, *The Unseen Wall Street of 1969–1975—and Its Significance for Today* (Praeger, 2000), pp. 3–5.

8. Benn, *The Unseen Wall Street of 1969–1975*, p. 5.

9. "Committee Selected by Stock Exchange to Weigh Question," *New York Times,* September 22, 1964.

10. Vartanig V. Vartan, "Big Board Reviews Rule to Bar Public Ownership of Members," *New York Times,* November 16, 1966.

11. Interview of Dan Lufkin by Amy Blitz.

12. Benn, *The Unseen Wall Street of 1969–1975*, p. 6.

13. Robards, "Big Board Defied by Member Firm."

14. Wiener, *What Goes Up*, p. 123.

15. Wiener, *What Goes Up*, p. 123.

16. Robards, "Big Board Defied by Member Firm."

17. Robards, "Big Board Defied by Member Firm."

18. "Weeden Files a Statement for Offering of Its Shares," *New York Times,* June 17, 1969.

19. John J. Able, "Change in Rules," *New York Times,* June 26, 1969.

20. "Big Board Approves Public Ownership of Member Firms," *New York Times,* July 18, 1969.

21. 1969 National Report of the National Association of Securities Dealers, Inc., pp. 18–19.

22. "23rd Annual Report of The Securities and Exchange Commission, Fiscal Year Ended June 30, 1957" (U.S. Government Printing Office, Washington, 1958), p. 17.

23. Terry Robards, "Exchanges Plan 2:30 P.M. Closing," *New York Times,* June 28, 1969.

24. Robards, "Exchanges Plan 2:30 P.M. Closing."

25. "Fund Group Seeks Western Broker," *New York Times,* July 10, 1969.

26. "Fund Group Seeks Western Broker."

27. Robert J. Cole, "Nuveen Quitting Stock Exchanges," *New York Times,* July 15, 1969.

28. Terry Robards, "Big Board to Let Brokers Go Public," *New York Times,* July 18, 1969.

29. Robards, "Big Board to Let Brokers Go Public."

30. "Form S-2 Registration Statement of Scanlan's Literary House Inc.," File No. 2-34010, Filed with the Securities and Exchange Commission on July 18, 1969.

31. Sidney Zion, *Read All About It! The Collected Adventures of a Maverick Reporter* (Summit Books, 1982), pp. 43-44.

32. Terry Robards, "Plohn's Two Edges: Sharp and Blunt," *New York Times,* September 28, 1969.

33. Robards, "Plohn's Two Edges: Sharp and Blunt"; Thomas W. Ennis, "Charles T. Plohn, Sr., Partner in Wall Street Concerns in 1960s," *New York Times,* July 24, 1984.

34. Zion, *Read All About It!*, p. 44.
35. Welles, *The Last Days of the Club*, p. 187.
36. Welles, *The Last Days of the Club*, p. 198.
37. Welles, *The Last Days of the Club*, p. 200.
38. Gene Currivah, "Catholic Schools Face Crisis Here," *New York Times*, June 18, 1969.
39. "McDonnell & Co. Discloses Steps Taken for Economy," *New York Times*, July 25, 1969.
40. Robert J. Cole, "Brokerage House Seeks a Merger," *New York Times*, July 28, 1969.
41. Welles, *The Last Days of the Club*, p. 201.
42. Welles, *The Last Days of the Club*, p. 201.
43. Terry Robards, "McDonnell & Co. Finds Financing," *New York Times*, August 2, 1969.
44. Welles, *The Last Days of the Club*, p. 202.
45. Welles, *The Last Days of the Club*, p. 203.
46. "McDonnell Office in Washington Being Investigated by the S.E.C.," *New York Times*, August 7, 1969.
47. Welles, *The Last Days of the Club*, p. 203.
48. Interview of Lawrence F. O'Brien by Michael L. Gillette, September 23, 1987.
49. Interview of Lawrence F. O'Brien by Michael L. Gillette.
50. Terry Robards, "O'Brien Quits McDonnell as Firm Cuts Back More," *New York Times*, August 12, 1969.
51. Robards, "O'Brien Quits McDonnell as Firm Cuts Back More."
52. "McDonnell Branch Punished by S.E.C.," *New York Times*, August 14, 1969.
53. Welles, *The Last Days of the Club*, pp. 204–205.
54. Terry Robards, "McDonnell & Co. Plans to Close, Sell or Consolidate 17 Offices," *New York Times*, August 22, 1969.
55. Welles, *The Last Days of the Club*, pp. 205–206.
56. Charles J. Role, "When Wall Street Catches the Flu, 26 Million Americans Ache," *New York Times*, August 13, 1969.
57. Terry Robards, "Haack Cites Need for Higher Fees," *New York Times*, August 27, 1969.
58. Robards, "Haack Cites Need for Higher Fees."
59. Robards, "Haack Cites Need for Higher Fees."
60. Terry Robards, "S.E.C. Asks Delay," *New York Times*, August 29, 1969.
61. Elizabeth McFowler, "Small Buyer Is Still King at Merrill," *New York Times*, August 24, 1969.
62. McFowler, "Small Buyer Is Still King at Merrill."
63. McFowler, "Small Buyer Is Still King at Merrill."

Chapter Nine

1. Robert E. Bedingfield, "Francis I. duPont to Close 7 Units," *New York Times*, August 9, 1969.
2. Bedingfield, "Francis I. duPont to Close 7 Units."

3. Terry Robards, "Latour Elected F.I. duPont Chief," *New York Times*, September 12, 1969.

4. Terry Robards, "Haack Advocates Increased Rates," *New York Times*, September 6, 1969.

5. Robards, "Haack Advocates Increased Rates."

6. "Hornblower Slates Take-Over," *New York Times*, September 6, 1969.

7. Terry Robards, "Brokerage Firms Planning Merger," *New York Times*, November 12, 1969.

8. Robards, "Brokerage Firms Planning Merger."

9. William D. Smith, "Thomson & McKinnon Sets Link; Auchincloss Agrees," *New York Times*, December 16, 1969.

10. "Stock Fee Cuts Seen Fund Peril," *New York Times*, September 16, 1969.

11. Terry Robards, "Big Board's Chief Acts to Let Brokers Go Public," *New York Times*, September 19, 1969.

12. Terry Robards, "Penalty Imposed on Hayden, Stone," *New York Times*, September 26, 1969.

13. Robards, "Penalty Imposed on Hayden, Stone."

14. "Review of S.E.C. Records of the Demise of Selected Broker-Dealers," pp. 36–37.

15. "Review of S.E.C. Records of the Demise of Selected Broker-Dealers," pp. 104–105.

16. "Review of S.E.C. Records of the Demise of Selected Broker-Dealers," pp. 104–105.

17. Terry Robards, "Plohn Will Get Amott's Assets," *New York Times*, December 19, 1969; "Review of S.E.C. Records of the Demise of Selected Broker-Dealers," p. 51.

18. Robert J. Cole, "How Crime Is Infiltrating Wall Street," *New York Times*, November 30, 1969.

19. Robert J. Cole, "Morgenthau Hits Wall Street Thefts," *New York Times*, November 26, 1969.

20. Terry Robards, "McDonnell & Co. Seeks to Sell Fund Unit to Scheinman Firm," *New York Times*, October 18, 1969.

21. Terry Robards, "McDonnell & Co. Seeks to Sell Fund Unit to Scheinman Firm."

22. Leonard Sloane, "Gregory & Sons Gets Liquidator," *New York Times*, October 23, 1969.

23. Sloane, "Gregory & Sons Gets Liquidator."

24. Terry Robards, "Restrictions Put on Dempsey Firm," *New York Times*, October 24, 1969.

25. "Agencies Assail Exchange Plan to Curb Firm's Going Public," *New York Times*, October 20, 1969.

26. Terry Robards, "Investors Diversified Services Purchases John Nuveen and Co.," *New York Times*, September 16, 1969.

27. "Agencies Assail Big Board's Plan," *New York Times*, October 30, 1969.

28. "Agencies Assail Big Board's Plan."

29. John J. Abele, "Big Board Plans Offerings Rules," *New York Times*, November 6, 1969.

30. Abele, "Big Board Plans Offerings Rules."
31. "Big Board Exclusions," *New York Times*, November 18, 1969.
32. "Big Board Exclusions."
33. Terry Robards, "Exchange Delays Vote," *New York Times*, November 18, 1969.
34. Terry Robards, "Stock Fee Shifts Backed by Haack," *New York Times*, November 22, 1969.
35. "Review of S.E.C. Records of the Demise of Selected Broker-Dealers," pp. 105–106.
36. "Review of S.E.C. Records of the Demise of Selected Broker-Dealers," p. 106.
37. "Review of S.E.C. Records of the Demise of Selected Broker-Dealers," p. 106.
38. "Review of S.E.C. Records of the Demise of Selected Broker-Dealers," p. 107.
39. "Review of S.E.C. Records of the Demise of Selected Broker-Dealers," p. 107.
40. Terry Robards, "Big Board Plans a Fund Transfer," *New York Times*, December 20, 1969.
41. Arnold H. Lubasch, "Cohn Sums Up in His Own Defense," *New York Times*, December 10, 1969.
42. Arnold H. Lubasch, "Cohn Ridicules a Key Witness in Ending Defense Summation," *New York Times*, December 11, 1969.
43. Lubasch, "Cohn Ridicules a Key Witness in Ending Defense Summation."
44. Lubasch, "Cohn Ridicules a Key Witness in Ending Defense Summation."
45. Arnold H. Lubasch, "Cohn Is Acquitted in Bus Bribe Case," *New York Times*, December 13, 1969.
46. Richard L. Madden, "Senate Asked to Confirm Republican for Post," *New York Times*, December 18, 1969.
47. "Reprint of a Letter Submitted to the Securities and Exchange Commission, by Donald E. Weeden, Executive Vice President of Weeden & Co.," December 19, 1969, "Appendix A, *Weeden & Co.*
48. "Reprint of a Letter Submitted to the Securities and Exchange Commission."
49. "Reprint of a Letter Submitted to the Securities and Exchange Commission."
50. "Texas Millionaire Pays for a Postcard Drive," *New York Times*, November 15, 1969.
51. Linda Greenhouse, "A Flight to Aid P.O.W.'s Planned," *New York Times*, December 16, 1969.
52. Greenhouse, "A Flight to Aid P.O.W.'s Planned."
53. Jon Nordheimer, "Texan Says He'll Send Families of Prisoners to Paris for Plea," *New York Times*, December 20, 1969.
54. "Hanoi Says Gifts Reach P.O.W.'s but Bars Airlift," *New York Times*, December 21, 1969.
55. John Nordheimer, "Perot Still Confident," *New York Times*, December 21, 1969.
56. "Flight Leaves to Aid P.O.W.'s Despite Cool Response in Hanoi," *New York Times*, December 22, 1969.
57. John Nordheimer, "Texan Seeking to Meet Hanoi Premiere," *New York Times*, December 25, 1969.
58. John Nordheimer, "Perot Plane in Laos," *New York Times*, December 26, 1969.
59. Henry Giniger, "U.S. Wives Get Vague Hanoi Pledge," *New York Times*, December 26, 1969.

60. "Texan Concedes Failure of His P.O.W. Aid Plan," *New York Times*, December 27, 1969.

61. "Perot Planning Flight to Moscow to Get Gifts to Hanoi P.O.W.'s," *New York Times*, December 28, 1969.

62. Jon Nordheimer, "Texan Heads for Copenhagen, Still Attempting to Aid P.O.W.'s," *New York Times*, December 30, 1969.

63. "Soviet Denies Perot a Visa to Send Gifts," *New York Times*, January 1," 1970.

Chapter Ten

1. Benn, *The Unseen Wall Street of 1969–1975*, p. 70.
2. Benn, *The Unseen Wall Street of 1969–1975*, p. 71.
3. Benn, *The Unseen Wall Street of 1969–1975*, p. 71.
4. Benn, *The Unseen Wall Street of 1969–1975*, p. 71.
5. John J. Abele, "Cogan, Berlind, Long Unstructured, Gets Boss," *New York Times*, January 18, 1970 .
6. Weiner, *What Goes Up*, p. 74.
7. Weiner, *What Goes Up*, p. 75.
8. Weiner, *What Goes Up*, p. 79.
9. Weiner, *What Goes Up*, p. 79.
10. Weiner, *What Goes Up*, p. 80.
11. Weiner, *What Goes Up*, p. 81.
12. Weiner, *What Goes Up*, p. 82.
13. Weiner, *What Goes Up*, p. 85.
14. Abele, "Cogan, Berlind, Long Unstructured, Gets Boss."
15. Weiner, *What Goes Up*, p. 137.
16. Weiner, *What Goes Up*, p. 138.
17. Weiner, *What Goes Up*, p. 138.
18. Abele, "Cogan, Berlind, Long Unstructured, Gets Boss."
19. "Scheinman Acquires McDonnell Fund," *New York Times*, January 27, 1970.
20. Welles, *The Last Days of the Club*, p. 206.
21. Welles, *The Last Days of the Club*, p. 206.
22. Welles, *The Last Days of the Club*, p. 206.
23. Welles, *The Last Days of the Club*, p. 207.
24. "Frances I. duPont Closing 9 Branches," *New York Times*, January 16, 1970.
25. Terry Robards, "Frances I. duPont List Big '69 Loss," *New York Times*, February 5, 1970.
26. "F.I. duPont Fined by the Big Board," *New York Times*, February 6, 1970.
27. "F.I. duPont Fined by the Big Board."
28. "Review of SEC Records of the Demise of Selected Broker-Dealers," p. 108.
29. "Review of SEC Records of the Demise of Selected Broker-Dealers," p. 108.
30. John J. Abele, "Capital Lined Up by Hayden, Stone," *New York Times*, March 4, 1970.
31. Abele, "Capital Lined Up by Hayden, Stone."
32. Abele, "Capital Lined Up by Hayden, Stone."

33. Abele, "Capital Lined Up by Hayden, Stone."
34. Terry Robards, "Big Board Votes on a New Fee Scale," *New York Times*, February 13, 1970.
35. Robards, "Big Board Votes on a New Fee Scale."
36. "Excerpts from Big Board Statement on Stock Fees," *New York Times*, February 14, 1970.
37. "Excerpts from Big Board Statement on Stock Fees."
38. "Excerpts from Big Board Statement on Stock Fees."
39. "Excerpts from Big Board Statement on Stock Fees."
40. Robards, "Big Board Votes on a New Fee Scale."
41. Eileen Shanahan, "Big Board Backs Small Investor," *New York Times*, February 16, 1970.
42. Terry Robards, "Salomon Assails Stock-Fee Change," *New York Times*, February 19, 1970.
43. "Smith Barney Asks Delay for Big Board's Fee Rise," *New York Times*, February 18, 1970.
44. "Goodbody Lists Loss of $832,000," *New York Times*, February 25, 1970.
45. Terry Robards, "Merrill Lynch Faults Fee Plan," *New York Times*, February 17, 1970.
46. Robards, "Merrill Lynch Faults Fee Plan."
47. Terry Robards, "Dempsey-Tegeler Gets Loan; 33 of Its 60 Branches to Close," *New York Times*, January 21, 1970.
48. Terry Robards, "Investment Banking Firm Resigns Its Membership on the Big Board," *New York Times*, January 29, 1970.
49. "Prudential Urges Brokers to Cut Rates," *New York Times*, March 5, 1970.
50. Terry Robards, "Bache & Co. Deficit for the Year May Be Brokerage Firm Record," *New York Times*, March 17, 1970.
51. Terry Robards, "Merrill Lynch Profit Down by 41% in 1969," *New York Times*, February 11, 1973.
52. "Goodbody Lists Loss of $832,000."
53. John J. Abele, "Weeden Reports First Lost Since '46," *New York Times*, April 7, 1970.
54. Terry Robards, "S.E.C. Backs Ownership by Public of Stock Firms," *New York Times*, February 27, 1970.
55. Terry Robards, "Governors of Big Board Back Changes on Public Ownership," *New York Times*, March 6, 1970.
56. Terry Robards, "Big Board Firms Back Public Ownership," *New York Times*, March 20, 1970.
57. Robards, "Big Board Firms Back Public Ownership."
58. Terry Robards, "Big Board Adopts Going-Public Plan," *New York Times*, March 27, 1970.
59. Terry Robards, "Donaldson Offering Planned for April 9," *New York Times*, March 31, 1969.
60. Terry Robards, "Big Board Wants Transaction Fee," *New York Times*, March 16, 1970.

61. Terry Robards, "Exchange Governors Approve Interim $15 on Charge Trades," *New York Times,* March 20, 1970.

62. Maurice Carroll, "City Approves East River Site for Stock Exchange," *New York Times,* March 20, 1970.

63. Carroll, "City Approves East River Site for Stock Exchange."

64. Welles, *The Last Days of the Club,* p. 207.

65. Welles, *The Last Days of the Club,* pp. 207–208.

66. Welles, *The Last Days of the Club,* p. 208.

67. Welles, *The Last Days of the Club,* p. 208

68. Terry Robards, "Brokerage House Decides to Close," *New York Times,* March 14, 1970.

69. Welles, *The Last Days of the Club,* p. 208.

70. Welles, *The Last Days of the Club,* p. 208.

71. Terry Robards, "Fears Fulfilled as Big Broker Fails," *New York Times,* March 15, 1970.

72. Welles, *The Last Days of the Club,* p. 208.

73. Robards, "Brokerage House Decides to Close."

74. Terry Robards, "More Failures Portended as Wall Street Woes Rise," *New York Times,* March 23, 1970.

75. "Big Board Reports Capital Rules Met," *New York Times,* March 24, 1970.

76. Eileen Shanahan, "Insurance Plan for Firms Asked," *New York Times,* March 18, 1970.

77. Shanahan, "Insurance Plan for Firms Asked."

78. "Big Board Plans to Bolster Fund," *New York Times,* March 26, 1970.

79. "Big Board Plans to Bolster Fund."

80. Terry Robards, "S.E.C. Allows Stock Surcharge for 40 Days Starting Monday," *New York Times,* April 3, 1970.

81. Robards, "S.E.C. Allows Stock Surcharge for 40 Days Starting Monday."

82. "Review of S.E.C. Records of the Demise of Selected Broker-Dealers," p. 57.

83. William D. Smith, "M'Donnell & Co. Charged by S.E.C.," *New York Times,* April 14, 1970.

84. Karla Jay, *Tales of the Lavendar Menace: A Memoir of Liberation* (New York: Basic Books, 1999).

85. Karla Jay, *Tales of the Lavendar Menace,* p. 115.

86. Karla Jay, *Tales of the Lavendar Menace,* p. 133.

87. Karla Jay, *Tales of the Lavendar Menace,* p. 133.

88. Karla Jay, *Tales of the Lavendar Menace,* pp. 133–134.

Chapter Eleven

1. Terry Robards, "Loeb Backs Limiting Big Board Members," *New York Times,* April 10, 1970.

2. Robards, "Loeb Backs Limiting Big Board Members."

3. Terry Robards, "Big Change Urged in Stock-Fee Plan," *New York Times,* April 13, 1970.

4. Robards, "Big Change Urged in Stock-Fee Plan."
5. "Federal Broker-Dealer Insurance Corporation-Hearings Before the Subcommittee on Securities of the Committee on Banking and Currency, United States Senate, Ninety-First Congress, Second Session (U.S. Government Printing Office, 1970), pp. 82–103.
6. "Federal Broker-Dealer Insurance Corporation-Hearings Before the Subcommittee on Securities of the Committee on Banking and Currency."
7. "Federal Broker-Dealer Insurance Corporation-Hearings Before the Subcommittee on Securities of the Committee on Banking and Currency."
8. Terry Robards, "Rise in Big Board's Fund from $7.5-million to $75-million Weighed," *New York Times*, April 14, 1970.
9. Robards, "Rise in Big Board's Fund from $7.5-million to $75-million Weighed."
10. "Federal Broker-Dealer Insurance Corporation Hearings Before Subcommittee on Securities," pp. 5–6.
11. "Federal Broker-Dealer Insurance Corporation Hearings Before Subcommittee on Securities," pp. 5–6.
12. "Federal Broker-Dealer Insurance Corporation Hearings Before Subcommittee on Securities," pp. 5–6.
13. Terry Robards, "Task Force Is Set to Help Investors If a Broker Fails," *New York Times*, April 16, 1970.
14. "Federal Broker-Dealer Insurance Corporation Hearings Before Subcommittee on Securities," p. 7.
15. "Federal Broker-Dealer Insurance Corporation Hearings Before Subcommittee on Securities," p. 17.
16. "Federal Broker-Dealer Insurance Corporation Hearings Before Subcommittee on Securities," p. 17.
17. "Federal Broker-Dealer Insurance Corporation Hearings Before Subcommittee on Securities," p. 18.
18. "Federal Broker-Dealer Insurance Corporation Hearings Before Subcommittee on Securities," p. 22.
19. "Federal Broker-Dealer Insurance Corporation Hearings Before Subcommittee on Securities," pp. 26–27.
20. "Federal Broker-Dealer Insurance Corporation Hearings Before Subcommittee on Securities," p. 28.
21. "Federal Broker-Dealer Insurance Corporation Hearings Before Subcommittee on Securities," p. 34.
22. "Federal Broker-Dealer Insurance Corporation Hearings Before Subcommittee on Securities," pp. 35–37.
23. "Federal Broker-Dealer Insurance Corporation Hearings Before Subcommittee on Securities," p. 37.
24. "Federal Broker-Dealer Insurance Corporation Hearings Before Subcommittee on Securities," p. 39.
25. "Federal Broker-Dealer Insurance Corporation Hearings Before Subcommittee on Securities," p. 45.
26. "Federal Broker-Dealer Insurance Corporation Hearings Before Subcommittee on Securities," p. 45.

27. "Federal Broker-Dealer Insurance Corporation Hearings Before Subcommittee on Securities," p. 45.

28. "Federal Broker-Dealer Insurance Corporation Hearings Before Subcommittee on Securities," p. 169.

29. "Federal Broker-Dealer Insurance Corporation Hearings Before Subcommittee on Securities," p. 176.

30. "Federal Broker-Dealer Insurance Corporation Hearings Before Subcommittee on Securities," p. 176.

31. "Federal Broker-Dealer Insurance Corporation Hearings Before Subcommittee on Securities," p. 178.

32. "Federal Broker-Dealer Insurance Corporation Hearings Before Subcommittee on Securities," p. 185.

33. "Federal Broker-Dealer Insurance Corporation Hearings Before Subcommittee on Securities," p. 193.

34. "Federal Broker-Dealer Insurance Corporation Hearings Before Subcommittee on Securities," p. 201.

35. "Federal Broker-Dealer Insurance Corporation Hearings Before Subcommittee on Securities," p. 201.

36. "Federal Broker-Dealer Insurance Corporation Hearings Before Subcommittee on Securities," pp. 210–215.

37. Eileen Shanahan, "S.E.C. Challenges Rules on Solvency," *New York Times*, April 27, 1970.

38. Shanahan, "S.E.C. Challenges Rules on Solvency."

39. "Study Of Unsafe and Unsound Practices of Brokers and Dealers," p. 232.

40. Homer Bigart, "War Foes Here Attacked by Construction Workers," *New York Times*, May 9, 1970.

41. Bigart, "War Foes Here Attacked by Construction Workers."

42. Bigart, "War Foes Here Attacked by Construction Workers."

43. Bigart, "War Foes Here Attacked by Construction Workers."

44. Emmanuel Perlmutter, "Head of Building Trades Unions Here Says Response Favors Friday's Action," *New York Times*, May 12, 1970.

45. Perlmutter, "Head of Building Trades Unions Here Says Response Favors Friday's Action."

46. Perlmutter, "Head of Building Trades Unions Here Says Response Favors Friday's Action."

47. Homer Bigart, "Huge City Hall Rally Backs Nixon's Indochina Policies," *New York Times*, May 21, 1970.

48. Bigart, "Huge City Hall Rally Backs Nixon's Indochina Policies."

49. Robert Semple, Jr., "Nixon Meets Heads of 2 City Unions, Hails War Support," *New York Times*, May 27, 1970.

50. Terry Robards, "Big Board Votes to Expand Fund," *New York Times*, May 19, 1970.

51. Eileen Shanahan, "Stock Margin Cut to 65% from 80% by Reserve Board," *New York Times*, May 6, 1970.

52. "Burns Reassures Business Lenders," *New York Times*, May 28, 1970.

53. Terry Robards, "Major Brokerage Houses Tighten Belt Some More," *New York Times*, May 8, 1970.

54. Robards, "Major Brokerage Houses Tighten Belt Some More."

55. Robards, "Major Brokerage Houses Tighten Belt Some More."

56. Robards, "Major Brokerage Houses Tighten Belt Some More."

57. Benn, *The Unseen Wall Street of 1969–1975*, p. 53.

58. Benn, *The Unseen Wall Street of 1969–1975*, p. 53.

59. Benn, *The Unseen Wall Street of 1969–1975*, pp. 55–57.

60. Benn, *The Unseen Wall Street of 1969–1975*, pp. 61–62.

61. Benn, *The Unseen Wall Street of 1969–1975*, p. 63.

62. Terry Robards, "F.I. duPont Sets a Major Merger," *New York Times*, June 4, 1970.

63. "Benn, *The Unseen Wall Street of 1969–1970*, pp. 64–66.

64. Terry Robards, "F.I. duPont and Hirsch Join Merger Trend," *New York Times*, June 9, 1970.

65. Benn, *The Unseen Wall Street of 1969–1975*, p. 69.

66. "Perot's Stock Falls $445-Million in Day," *New York Times*, April 23, 1970.

67. Benn, *The Unseen Wall Street of 1969–1975*, pp. 71–72.

68. Benn, *The Unseen Wall Street of 1969–1975*, pp. 72–73.

69. Welles, *The Last Days of the Club*, p. 250.

70. "Securities Investor Protection, Hearings Before the Subcommittee on Commerce and Finance of the Committee on Interstate and Foreign Commerce House of Representatives Ninety-First Congress, Second Session (U.S. Government Printing Office, 1970), p. 1.

71. "Securities Investor Protection, Hearings Before the Subcommittee on Commerce and Finance of the Committee on Interstate and Foreign Commerce House of Representatives," pp. 2–3.

72. "Securities Investor Protection, Hearings Before the Subcommittee on Commerce and Finance of the Committee on Interstate and Foreign Commerce House of Representatives," p. 149.

73. "Securities Investor Protection, Hearings Before the Subcommittee on Commerce and Finance of the Committee on Interstate and Foreign Commerce House of Representatives," pp. 150–152.

74. "Securities Investor Protection, Hearings Before the Subcommittee on Commerce and Finance of the Committee on Interstate and Foreign Commerce House of Representatives," p. 154.

75. Terry Robards, "Brokerage Firms to Insure Public Failures," *New York Times*, June 5, 1970.

76. "Hearings Before the Subcommittee on Commerce and Finance," pp. 161–162.

Chapter Twelve

1. "Securities Investor Protection, Hearings Before the Subcommittee on Commerce and Finance," p. 163.

2. "Securities Investor Protection, Hearings Before the Subcommittee on Commerce and Finance," pp. 163–182.

3. "Securities Investor Protection, Hearings Before the Subcommittee on Commerce and Finance," pp. 163–182.
4. "Securities Investor Protection, Hearings Before the Subcommittee on Commerce and Finance," pp. 163–182.
5. "Securities Investor Protection, Hearings Before the Subcommittee on Commerce and Finance," pp. 194–196.
6. "Securities Investor Protection, Hearings Before the Subcommittee on Commerce and Finance," p. 197.
7. "Securities Investor Protection, Hearings Before the Subcommittee on Commerce and Finance," pp. 197–211.
8. "Securities Investor Protection, Hearings Before the Subcommittee on Commerce and Finance," pp. 215–236.
9. "Securities Investor Protection, Hearings Before the Subcommittee on Commerce and Finance," p. 237.
10. "Nixon Endorses Stock Insurance," *New York Times*, June 18, 1970.
11. "Federal Broker-Dealer Insurance Corporations, Hearings Before the Committee on Banking and Currency," p. 221.
12. "Federal Broker-Dealer Insurance Corporations, Hearings Before the Committee on Banking and Currency," pp. 221–238.
13. "Federal Broker-Dealer Insurance Corporations, Hearings Before the Committee on Banking and Currency," p. 239.
14. "Review of S.E.C. Records of the Demise of Selected Broker-Dealers," p. 108.
15. "Review of S.E.C. Records of the Demise of Selected Broker-Dealers," p. 108.
16. "Review of S.E.C. Records of the Demise of Selected Broker-Dealers," p. 108.
17. Memorandum for the Files, From Peter Flanigan, dated June 24, 1970.
18. "Capital Is Sought by Hayden, Stone," *New York Times*, June 26, 1970.
19. "Capital Is Sought by Hayden, Stone."
20. Terry Robards, "Haack Cites Drop in Firms' Profits," *New York Times*, June 25, 1970.
21. Terry Robards, "New Commission Rates Are Sought by Big Board," *New York Times*, June 30, 1970.
22. Robards, "New Commission Rates Are Sought by Big Board."
23. Robards, "New Commission Rates Are Sought by Big Board."
24. Robards, "New Commission Rates Are Sought by Big Board."
25. Eileen Shanahan, "$520-Million Asked," *New York Times*, July 1, 1970.
26. Eileen Shanahan, "S.E.C. to Hold Hearings on $15 Stock Surcharge," *New York Times*, July 3, 1970.
27. "Delivery of Stock 72% Computerized," *New York Times*, June 15, 1970.
28. Terry Robards, "Wall Street Watches as Merged Firm Opens," *New York Times*, July 6, 1970.
29. "Securities Investor Protection, Hearings Before the Subcommittee on Commerce and Finance," p. 239.
30. "Securities Investor Protection, Hearings Before the Subcommittee on Commerce and Finance," p. 254.
31. "Securities Investor Protection, Hearings Before the Subcommittee on Commerce and Finance," p. 315.

32. "Securities Investor Protection, Hearings Before the Subcommittee on Commerce and Finance," p. 315.

33. "Securities Investor Protection, Hearings Before the Subcommittee on Commerce and Finance," pp. 316–330.

34. "Securities Investor Protection, Hearings Before the Subcommittee on Commerce and Finance," p. 357.

35. "Securities Investor Protection, Hearings Before the Subcommittee on Commerce and Finance," pp. 330–331.

36. "Securities Investor Protection, Hearings Before the Subcommittee on Commerce and Finance," p. 395.

37. "Securities Investor Protection, Hearings Before the Subcommittee on Commerce and Finance," p. 395.

38. "Securities Investor Protection, Hearings Before the Subcommittee on Commerce and Finance," p. 395–396.

39. "Federal Broker-Dealer Insurance Corporation Hearings Before the Subcommittee on Securities," p. 242.

40. "Federal Broker-Dealer Insurance Corporation Hearings Before the Subcommittee on Securities," pp. 242–255.

41. "Federal Broker-Dealer Insurance Corporation Hearings Before the Subcommittee on Securities," p. 255.

42. "Federal Broker-Dealer Insurance Corporation Hearings Before the Subcommittee on Securities," p. 262.

43. "Federal Broker-Dealer Insurance Corporation Hearings Before the Subcommittee on Securities," p. 263.

44. "Federal Broker-Dealer Insurance Corporation Hearings Before the Subcommittee on Securities," pp. 263–264.

45. "Federal Broker-Dealer Insurance Corporation Hearings Before the Subcommittee on Securities," p. 265.

46. "Federal Broker-Dealer Insurance Corporation Hearings Before the Subcommittee on Securities," p. 265.

47. "Federal Broker-Dealer Insurance Corporation Hearings Before the Subcommittee on Securities," p. 266.

48. "Federal Broker-Dealer Insurance Corporation Hearings Before the Subcommittee on Securities," p. 276.

49. "Federal Broker-Dealer Insurance Corporation Hearings Before the Subcommittee on Securities," p. 276.

50. "Federal Broker-Dealer Insurance Corporation Hearings Before the Subcommittee on Securities," p. 276.

51. "Federal Broker-Dealer Insurance Corporation Hearings Before the Subcommittee on Securities," p. 279.

52. "Federal Broker-Dealer Insurance Corporation Hearings Before the Subcommittee on Securities," p. 279.

53. "Federal Broker-Dealer Insurance Corporation Hearings Before the Subcommittee on Securities," p. 296.

54. "Federal Broker-Dealer Insurance Corporation Hearings Before the Subcommittee on Securities," p. 299.

55. "Federal Broker-Dealer Insurance Corporation Hearings Before the Subcommittee on Securities," p. 303.

56. "Securities Investor Protection, Hearings Before the Subcommittee of Commerce and Finance," p. 397.

57. Eileen Shanahan, "Broker Cost Rise Is Traced to '60s," *New York Times*, July 15, 1970.

58. Eileen Shanahan, "Research Lacking on Big-Board Fees," *New York Times*, July 21, 1970.

59. Shanahan, "Research Lacking on Big-Board Fees."

60. Eileen Shanahan, "Big Board Tells Why Fees Differ," *New York Times*, July 22, 1970.

61. Eileen Shanahan, "Broker Favors Rise in Charges," *New York Times*, July 25, 1970.

62. Eileen Shanahan, "Broker Favors Rise in Charges."

63. Leonard Sloane, "Brokerage Move Set," *New York Times*, July 8, 1970.

64. "Paine Webber Ends Talks With Witter," *New York Times*, August 8, 1970.

65. Leonard Sloane, "Hayden, Stone Reported Planning Link to Walston," *New York Times*, July 22, 1970.

66. Eileen Shanahan, "Wall Street Warned on Insurance Bill," *New York Times*, August 7, 1970.

67. Eileen Shanahan, "Exchange's Fund Spurs Questions," *New York Times*, April 24, 1970.

68. "S.E.C. Will Keep Surcharge Plan," *New York Times*, September 1, 1970.

Chapter Thirteen

1. Terry Robards, "Dempsey Gets Liquidator; Blair Sells All Branches," *New York Times*, August 11, 1970.

2. Robards, "Dempsey Gets Liquidator; Blair Sells All Branches."

3. "Stock Firm Aims at Consolidation," *New York Times*, August 13, 1970.

4. Terry Robards, "Big Board Lists Liquidating Firms," *New York Times*, August 14, 1970.

5. Robards, "Big Board Lists Liquidating Firms."

6. Robards, "Big Board Lists Liquidating Firms."

7. Robards, "Big Board Lists Liquidating Firms."

8. Robards, "Big Board Lists Liquidating Firms."

9. Terry Robards, "Stock Withdrawn at Hayden, Stone," *New York Times*, August 5, 1970.

10. "Walston's Merger with Hayden Nears," *New York Times*, August 12, 1970.

11. Terry Robards, "Cogan, Berlind to Absorb Key Part of Hayden, Stone," *New York Times*, August 20, 1970.

12. Robards, "Cogan, Berlind to Absorb Key Part of Hayden, Stone."

13. Robards, "Cogan, Berlind to Absorb Key Part of Hayden, Stone."

14. Terry Robards, "Hayden, Stone Quitting Offices Downtown for Skyscraper Home," *New York Times*, August 21, 1970.

15. Weiner, *What Goes Up*, p. 143.

16. Terry Robards, "2 Big-Board Firms Draw Suspensions on Finances," *New York Times*, August 19, 1970.
17. Robards, "2 Big-Board Firms Draw Suspensions on Finances."
18. John J. Abele, "Plohn Receiver Asked by S.E.C.," *New York Times*, August 28, 1970.
19. Abele, "Plohn Receiver Asked by S.E.C."
20. "Muskie Charges Pressure by Wall Street on Bill," *New York Times*, August 29, 1970.
21. "Muskie Charges Pressure by Wall Street on Bill."
22. "Muskie Charges Pressure by Wall Street on Bill."
23. "Muskie Charges Pressure by Wall Street on Bill."
24. "Muskie Charges Pressure by Wall Street on Bill."
25. Benn, *The Unseen Wall Street of 1969–1975*, p. 36; Baruch, *Wall Street Security Risk*, pp. 221–223.
26. "Liquidator Named for Orvis Brothers," *New York Times*, September 5, 1970.
27. Weiner, *What Goes Up*, p. 143.
28. Weiner, *What Goes Up*, p. 143.
29. Welles, *The Last Days of the Club*, p. 247.
30. Interview with Marshall Cogan, New York City, February 27, 2020.
31. Weiner, *What Goes Up*, p. 144.
32. Weiner, *What Goes Up*, p. 145.
33. Weiner, *What Goes Up*, p. 144.
34. Weiner, *What Goes Up*, p. 144.
35. Baruch, *Wall Street Security Risk*, pp. 74–75; Welles, *The Last Days of the Club*, p. 245.
36. "Broker-Failure Insurance Bill Gains; Devonshire Customer Suing Exchange," *New York Times*, September 16, 1970.
37. "Broker-Failure Insurance Bill Gains."
38. "Broker-Failure Insurance Bill Gains."
39. Eileen Shanahan, "Insurance Bill on Brokers Gains," *New York Times*, September 18, 1970.
40. "Broker-Failure Insurance Bill Gains."
41. "Broker-Failure Insurance Bill Gains."
42. Terry Robards, "Big Board Refuses to Help Firm's Customers," *New York Times*, September 28, 1970.
43. Terry Robards, "Suit Challenged on Big Board Aid," *New York Times*, September 30, 1970.
44. Robards, "Suit Challenged on Big Board Aid."
45. Robards, "Suit Challenged on Big Board Aid."
46. Terry Robards, "Robinson Group Rebuffed by Court on Trust Fund," *New York Times*, October 9, 1970.
47. Robards, "Robinson Group Rebuffed by Court on Trust Fund."
48. Terry Robards, "Legal Cases Test Exchange Form," *New York Times*, September 20, 1970.
49. Terry Robards, "Big Board Sued for $3-Billion," *New York Times*, October 6, 1970.

50. Robards, "Big Board Sued for $3-Billion."
51. Memorandum to Chairman Burns, Board of Governors of the Federal Reserve System, from John D. Stoffels, Regarding Composition of "Capital" of Brokerage Firms, dated October 29, 1970.
52. "Changes Planned in Exchange Rule," *New York Times*, October 7, 1970.
53. Eileen Shanahan, "S.E.C. Says Rise Sought in Stock Fees is Too Big," *New York Times*, October 23, 1970.
54. Shanahan, "S.E.C. Says Rise Sought in Stock Fees is Too Big."
55. Eileen Shanahan, "How Tough Is S.E.C.?" *New York Times*, October 24, 1970.

Chapter Fourteen

1. Terry Robards, "Mutual Fund Group Buying Goodbody; Big Board Seeks Fuller Member Data," *New York Times*, September 18, 1970.
2. Robards, "Mutual Fund Group Buying Goodbody."
3. Baruch, *Wall Street Security Risk*, p. 237.
4. Terry Robards, "Goodbody's Fund Quest Is Clarified by Big Board," *New York Times*, October 21, 1970.
5. Eileen Shanahan, "Goodbody Faces Capital Deadline," *New York Times*, October 27, 1970.
6. Terry Robards, "Merger Plans Called Off by Goodbody and Fund," *New York Times*, October 17, 1970.
7. Shanahan, "Goodbody Faces Capital Deadline."
8. Shanahan, "Goodbody Faces Capital Deadline."
9. Benn, *The Unseen Wall Street of 1969–1975*, p. 38.
10. Benn, *The Unseen Wall Street of 1969–1975*, p. 38.
11. Terry Robards, "Merrill Lynch Deciding on Goodbody Acquisition," *New York Times*, October 24, 1970.
12. Benn, *The Unseen Wall Street of 1969–1975*, p. 39.
13. Baruch, *Wall Street Security Risk*, p. 232.
14. Terry Robards, "Merrill Lynch to Rescue Firm," *New York Times*, October 30, 1970.
15. Robards, "Merrill Lynch to Rescue Firm."
16. Benn, *The Unseen Wall Street of 1969–1975*, p. 39.
17. Benn, *The Unseen Wall Street of 1969–1975*, p. 39.
18. Terry Robards, "Merrill Lynch Signs Goodbody Acquisition," *New York Times*, November 6, 1970.
19. Robards, "Merrill Lynch Signs Goodbody Acquisition."
20. Robards, "Merrill Lynch Signs Goodbody Acquisition."
21. Terry Robards, "Exchange Urges Members to Back Goodbody Rescue," *New York Times*, November 13, 1970.
22. "Review of S.E.C. Records of the Demise of Selected Broker-Dealers," p. 80.
23. "Review of S.E.C. Records of the Demise of Selected Broker-Dealers," p. 80.
24. "Review of S.E.C. Records of the Demise of Selected Broker-Dealers," p. 80.
25. Benn, *The Unseen Wall Street of 1969–1975*, p. 78.

26. Benn, *The Unseen Wall Street of 1969–1975*, p. 78.
27. Benn, *The Unseen Wall Street of 1969–1975*, p. 79.
28. Benn, *The Unseen Wall Street of 1969–1975*, p. 79.
29. Benn, *The Unseen Wall Street of 1969–1975*, p. 80.
30. Benn, *The Unseen Wall Street of 1969–1975*, p. 80.
31. Benn, *The Unseen Wall Street of 1969–1975*, p. 82.
32. Eileen Shanahan, "Big Board Queried on Aid to Brokers," *New York Times*, November 17, 1970.
33. Shanahan, "Big Board Queried on Aid to Brokers."
34. Shanahan, "Big Board Queried on Aid to Brokers."
35. Eileen Shanahan, "Congress Assured on Failed Houses," *New York Times*, November 18, 1970.
36. "Competition and the Future of the New York Stock Exchange," Remarks of Robert W. Haack, President of the New York Stock Exchange at the Economic Club of New York, Waldorf Astoria, New York, November 17, 1970.
37. "Competition and the Future of the New York Stock Exchange."
38. "Competition and the Future of the New York Stock Exchange."
39. "Competition and the Future of the New York Stock Exchange."
40. Welles, *The Last Days of the Club*, p. 16.
41. Benn, *The Unseen Wall Street of 1969–1975*, p. 128.
42. Welles, *The Last Days of the Club*, p. 20.
43. Welles, *The Last Days of the Club*, p. 20.
44. Interview with Michael J Meehan, New York City, May 2, 2019.
45. Benn, *The Unseen Wall Street of 1969–1975*, p. 128.
46. Terry Robards, "Wall Street Shaken by Haack Speech," *New York Times*, November 19, 1970.
47. Terry Robards, "Big Board Governors Confront Haack on Fee Issue," *New York Times*, November 20, 1970.
48. Eileen Shanahan, "Big Board Urges Spur on New Fees," *New York Times*, November 21, 1970.
49. Eileen Shanahan, "Budge Will Leave S.E.C. When Congress Adjourns," *New York Times*, November 14, 1970.
50. Terry Robards, "No. 2 Man Leaves Stock Exchange," *New York Times*, November 23, 1970.
51. Benn, *The Unseen Wall Street of 1964–1975*, pp. 126–127.
52. Robards, "Wall Street Shaken by Haack Speech."
53. John J. Abele, "Regan Says Fixed Rates Should Be 'First Relic' Discarded in Changes," *New York Times*, December 3, 1970.
54. Benn, *The Unseen Wall Street of 1964–1975*, p. 83.
55. Benn, *The Unseen Wall Street of 1964–1975*, p. 83.
56. Benn, *The Unseen Wall Street of 1964–1975*, p. 83.
57. Benn, *The Unseen Wall Street of 1964–1975*, p. 84.
58. Benn, *The Unseen Wall Street of 1964–1975*, p. 84.
59. Benn, *The Unseen Wall Street of 1964–1975*, p. 84.
60. Benn, *The Unseen Wall Street of 1964–1975*, p. 84.

61. Benn, *The Unseen Wall Street of 1964–1975*, p. 85.
62. Benn, *The Unseen Wall Street of 1964–1975*, pp. 86–87.
63. Benn, *The Unseen Wall Street of 1964–1975*, pp. 86–87.
64. Benn, *The Unseen Wall Street of 1964–1975*, pp. 86–87.
65. Benn, *The Unseen Wall Street of 1964–1975*, pp. 87–88.
66. Terry Robards, "Amex Fines 2 Members for Spreading a Rumor," *New York Times*, November 28, 1970.
67. Benn, *The Unseen Wall Street of 1969–1975*, pp. 88–89.
68. "F.I. duPont Will Receive $15-Million from Perot," *New York Times*, November 26, 1970.
69. Benn, *The Unseen Wall Street of 1969–1975*, pp. 89–90..
70. Terry Robards, "F.I. duPont Rescue Seems to End Wall Street Crisis," *New York Times*, December 17, 1970.
71. "House Approves Plan to Insure Brokers' Clients," *New York Times*, December 2, 1970.
72. "House Approves Plan to Insure Brokers' Clients."
73. "Investor Protection Act, Westlaw 5920 (Legislative History)."
74. "Merrill Lynch Sets Goodbody as a Unit," *New York Times*, December 11, 1970.
75. Conference Report No. 91–1788, Security Investor Protection Act of 1970.
76. Conference Report No. 91–1788, Security Investor Protection Act of 1970.
77. Eileen Shanahan, "Senate-House Unit Clears Investor Protection Plan," *New York Times*, December 19, 1970.
78. "New Regulations Pledged by S.E.C.," *New York Times*, December 23, 1970.
79. Terry Robards, "F.I. duPont Two Top Officers Replaced," *New York Times*, December 30, 1970.
80. "Bill Is Signed for Investor Protection," *New York Times*, December 11, 1970.

ACKNOWLEDGMENTS

I want to thank Kathy Huck, my editor, for separating the wheat from the chaff. I also want to thank Judith Regan for her patient guidance and support in telling this story. Jessica Moran must be thanked as well for assistance in the editing and rewriting.

Many of the stories told herein were told to me when I was a young lawyer by a wonderful old lawyer named Justin D'Atri, late at night at a financial printer waiting for pages of prospectuses to come out. Justin is gone, as are late nights at the printer for young lawyers. Old age and technology have taken those from us, and much fun has been lost by both.

Last (and in no particular order), I want to thank my wife, who tolerated my taking time away from the family writing this book.

IMAGE CREDITS

Photo of JFK: Bentley Archive/ Popperfoto/Getty Images

Photo of Bill Cary: Byron Rollins/AP Photo

Photo of Keith Funston: Philippe Halsman/ © Philippe Halsman Estate 2022

Photo of Tino DeAngelis: Carroll/AP/ Shutterstock

Photo of N.Y.S.E.: Bettmann Archive/ Getty Images

Photo of John A. Coleman: Bettmann Archive/Getty Images

Photo of LBJ with Larry O'Brien: Francis Miller/The LIFE Picture Collection/Shutterstock

Photo of Abbie Hoffman: Arty Pomerantz/ NYPost/The Mega Agency

Photo of Manny Cohen with David Rockefeller: Jack Harris/AP

Photo of Robert Haack: Bob Peterson/ Getty Images

Photo of Gus Levy with Robert Haack: Anthony Camerano/AP/ Shutterstock

Photo of Roy Cohn: Arthur Schatz/Getty Images

Photo of Michael Bloomberg: Edward Hausner/The New York Times

Photo of Murray McDonnell: Morgan Collection/Getty

Photo of RFK: Bride Lane Library/ Popperfoto via Getty Images

Photo of Gene Rotberg: Michele Iannacci/ World Bank Group. License: CC BY NC-SA 4.0 and https:// archivesphotos.worldbank.org/en /about/archives/photo-gallery /terms-of-use

Photo of Donald Weeden: AP Photo/David Bookstaver

Photo of Francine Gottfried: Richard Corkery/NY Daily News Archive via Getty Images

Photo of Sean McDonnell with Michael J. Meehan III: Morgan Collection/ Getty

Photo of Edmund Muskie: Trinity Mirror/ Mirrorpix/ Alamy Stock Photo

Photo of John Moss: AP/Shutterstock

Photo of Richard Nixon with John Mitchell: Wally McNamee/Corbis via Getty Images

Photo of Peter Flanigan: Magite Historic/ Alamy

Photo of Larry O'Brien: Corbis via Getty Images

Photo of John Connally: Stan Wayman/ The LIFE Picture Collection/ Shutterstock

Photo of John Mitchell: Alfred Eisenstaedt/The LIFE Picture Collection/Shutterstock

INDEX